Pro SharePoint 2010 Governance

Steve Wright
Corey Erkes

Apress®

Pro SharePoint 2010 Governance

ISBN-13 (pbk): 978-1-4302-4077-8

ISBN-13 (electronic): 978-1-4302-4078-5

President and Publisher: Paul Manning
Lead Editor: Jonathan Hassell
Technical Reviewers: Aaron Korb
Editorial Board: Steve Anglin, Mark Beckner, Ewan Buckingham, Gary Cornell, Morgan Ertel,
     Jonathan Gennick, Jonathan Hassell, Robert Hutchinson, Michelle Lowman, James Markham,
     Matthew Moodie, Jeff Olson, Jeffrey Pepper, Douglas Pundick, Ben Renow-Clarke, Dominic
     Shakeshaft, Gwenan Spearing, Matt Wade, Tom Welsh
Coordinating Editors: Annie Beck and Tracy Brown
Copy Editor: Elizabeth Berry
Compositor: Mary Sudul
Indexer: SPi Global
Cover Designer: Anna Ishchenko

Distributed to the book trade worldwide by Springer Science+Business Media New York, 233 Spring Street, 6th Floor, New York, NY 10013. Phone 1-800-SPRINGER, fax (201) 348-4505, e-mail orders-ny@springer-sbm.com, or visit www.springeronline.com.

For information on translations, please e-mail rights@apress.com, or visit www.apress.com.

Apress and friends of ED books may be purchased in bulk for academic, corporate, or promotional use. eBook versions and licenses are also available for most titles. For more information, reference our Special Bulk Sales–eBook Licensing web page at www.apress.com/bulk-sales.

Any source code or other supplementary materials referenced by the author in this text is available to readers at www.apress.com. For detailed information about how to locate your book's source code, go to http://www.apress.com/source-code/.

This book is dedicated to Thomas Jefferson, Abraham Lincoln, and Gouverneur Morris, the authors of good governance.

—Steve Wright

Contents at a Glance

Contents

About the Authors

 Steve Wright is a Senior Manager in Business Intelligence Management (BIM) for Sogeti USA in Omaha, Nebraska. Over the last 20-plus years, Steve has worked on air traffic control, financial, insurance, and a multitude of other types of systems. He enjoys speaking at user group meetings and MSDN events and holds 43 different Microsoft certifications. Steve has authored and performed technical reviews for many previous titles covering Microsoft products including Windows, SharePoint, SQL Server, and BizTalk. For the last several years, he has focused on building highly-customized SharePoint-based Business Intelligence solutions.

 Corey Erkes is a manager consultant for Sogeti USA in Omaha, Nebraska. Corey has worked with a wide range of companies at different points in the lifecycles of their SharePoint implementations. He is passionate about SharePoint and loves working with companies to utilize the many features it provides to bring an immediate return on investment to an organization. In addition to his work as a consultant, Corey is also one of the founding members of the Omaha SharePoint Users Group.

About the Technical Reviewer

 Aaron Korb is a senior consultant for Sogeti USA in Omaha, Nebraska. Aaron has worked with a variety of industries implementing and maintaining SharePoint solutions. His work with SharePoint dates back nearly ten years to the beta "Tahoe" product. His favorite areas are bringing immediate value to customers by implementing powerful SharePoint features that map to the requirements of business. He has done extensive work with business groups to better understand how to leverage SharePoint for long-term solutions that align with each customer's unique needs.

Acknowledgments

As I finish my third book in a year, I would like to thank my wife, Janet, and our children, Jon, Evan, and Troy, for putting up with it all. I would also like to thank my coauthor, Corey Erkes, and our technical editor, Aaron Korb. Finally, thanks to everyone at Apress for giving us this opportunity.

—Steve Wright

First, I would like to thank Steve Wright for providing me the opportunity to help author parts of this book. Thank you, Steve, for keeping me on track during the writing process. Thanks also to Aaron Korb for sacrificing his time to make sense out of our thoughts and provide valuable feedback. Lastly, I would like to thank my wife, Laura, for allowing me the time away to write this book. I would not be where I am today without your constant love and support. And to Aidan, I hope you look at this book one day and realize that you can accomplish anything you want if you put your mind to it and work hard.

—Corey Erkes

Introduction

Governance is the process of creating policies and rules and assigning roles and responsibilities to make a system work properly. Even if your attitude is "Good Government is Less Government," very few of us would want to have no government. In short, governance is the difference between order and chaos.

In this book, we will explore the concept of governance as it applies to a business's use of the SharePoint family of products. It is assumed that the reader is familiar with the concepts of web sites, collaboration, and portals as they are used in SharePoint. SharePoint provides a platform for creating, storing, and retrieving information. This information is generically referred to as *content* and it can take many forms, such as documents, calendars, lists, and web sites. The features of SharePoint allow users within an organization to collectively or individually create content and publish it for others to use. By making this information quick and easy to find, categorize, and organize, SharePoint can provide a lot of business value. SharePoint is also a very extensive product that contains many features that can cause problems if not used correctly.

Who This Book Is For

This book is intended for anyone who will be involved in the governance of a SharePoint-based site. This should include both IT and non-IT business owners, developers, administrators and, perhaps most-importantly, those who will represent the system's users.

The early chapters are non-technical in nature. They cover the best ways to structure and manage the governance process. We would encourage everyone on the governance team to become familiar with this information. Later, there is technical information about the features and options available on the SharePoint platform. Not everyone will need to be familiar with these details.

CHAPTER 1

A SharePoint Manifesto

We the users, in order to form a more perfect collaboration, establish function, insure business utility, provide for the common security, promote the general usability, and secure the value of information for ourselves and our coworkers, do ordain and establish this governance plan for the portal of our organization.

First, an apology to the memory of Gouverneur Morris, the author of the Preamble to the US Constitution. The paraphrasing above is a modest attempt to make a point about *governance*. The purpose of the original Preamble was to describe the reason for the rest of the constitution and for the government of the United States as a whole. Governance is the process of creating policies and rules and assigning roles and responsibilities to make a system work properly. Even if your attitude is "Good Government is Less Government," very few of us would want to have no government. In short, governance is the difference between order and chaos.

To paraphrase another great American statesman, Abraham Lincoln, effective governance should be "of the users, by the users and for the users." The key to any SharePoint implementation is adoption. If users don't want to use the site, they won't use it any more than is absolutely necessary. To get the full value out of SharePoint, it must be a place that users go to make their lives easier. Good governance can help achieve that goal.

Governance OF the Users

In this book, we will explore the concept of governance as it applies to a business's use of the SharePoint family of products. We assume the reader is familiar to some degree with the concepts of web sites, collaboration, and portals as they apply to SharePoint. SharePoint provides a platform for creating, storing, and retrieving information. This information is generically referred to as *content* and it can take many forms such as documents, calendars, lists, and web sites. The features of SharePoint allow users within an organization to collectively or individually create content and publish it for others to use. By making this information quick and easy to find, categorize, and organize, SharePoint can provide a lot of business value. SharePoint is also a very extensive product that contains many features that can cause problems if not used correctly.

Establishing a SharePoint Server 2010 environment is reasonably simple, but maintaining it and controlling it in a way that maximizes its benefits to the users and the business is not. SharePoint consists of many interrelated subsystems and services such as Search, Content Management, Record Management, PerformancePoint Services, and so on. SharePoint also serves as a platform for integrating and delivering other Microsoft products such as Dynamics, Project Server, and SQL Server Reporting Services. Additionally, there are numerous third-party vendors that provide SharePoint-based products to provide solutions for backup and recovery, data archiving, image management, and many other things. With all of these potential features available, it is reasonable to assume that not all of them will be appropriate for your environment.

One of the most important decisions to be made when delivering a SharePoint-based solution is to determine which of the supported features should be made available to the end users and which should not. The most common mistake made by organizations when they adopt SharePoint is to install the product and tell their users to "go ahead and use it." This approach can cause many problems, but the two most common are the following:

1. No one uses the system because they don't really know what it can do for them.

2. Users begin dumping huge amounts of data into SharePoint with no organization or categorization.

By governing the features available to users, the goal is not to prevent the use of certain features, but to encourage the use of those features that are of most value to the organization.

Governance BY the Users

If we are honest with ourselves, most of us have to admit that we do not like people telling us what we can and cannot do. On the other hand, we like to be in control. An effective governance team must include the people who will be using the system if they are to feel that they have any say in the running of the system. It must also include the IT professionals responsible for installing, configuring, and maintaining the infrastructure that supports it. Finally, the executives and managers responsible for funding the system and insuring that it is returning value to the business must also have a seat at the table.

Building an effective governance team is the first step in building a truly collaborative environment for end users.

Governance FOR the Users

A SharePoint solution will only be successful if people use it. This seemingly trivial statement is the key to understanding why governance is critical. If your users consider the SharePoint services provided to be a hindrance to their everyday tasks, they will quickly abandon the system and it will fall into disuse. Effective governance should include plans to drive adoption and training of users as well as ensuring that the system is meeting their needs and making their jobs easier. In organizations that successfully adopt SharePoint, it quickly becomes an invaluable tool that grows to support every aspect of the business.

In this book we will examine how to create just such an environment. Everything you do in governing the SharePoint environment should drive a productive, stress-free user experience.

Finding What You Need in This Book

SharePoint governance covers a lot of ground because SharePoint is such an extensive product line. Fortunately, not everyone involved in the governance of a SharePoint solution needs to be intimately familiar with the technical details of the platform. This book is divided into different parts that are targeted to different audiences.

Part I: Establishing Governance

The first part of this book will introduce the concepts and processes involved in creating and implementing a governance strategy for your organization. Anyone involved in the governance of the system should be familiar with these concepts. These are general business concepts that do not include a great deal of technical detail.

Chapter 2: SharePoint Governance Overview

This chapter introduces the conceptual framework used throughout the rest of the book. It will define key terms and divide the process of governance into manageable pieces. We will start by defining a set of terms and establishing what our goals are in creating a governance plan. SharePoint implementations often encounter similar challenges. We will look at these and consider ways to overcome them. Finally, we will discuss the need to match the policies used in your situation to the purpose of the site and the culture of your organization.

Chapter 3: The Planning Process

This chapter covers the steps required to set the scope of the governance effort and develop a high-level governance plan. This includes identifying the roles and responsibilities of everyone involved and establishing a team to ensure that the plan is implemented effectively. This team will need to include management, IT, and end-user personnel to ensure that all plans are realistic, supported, and targeted to the needs of the users.

Chapter 4: Implementing and Maintaining Controls

This chapter covers the process of implementing a good governance plan. This involves mapping the services to be provided to the features of the SharePoint platform. Creating a robust system requires taking the end user's goals and feedback into account before, during, and after deployment of the solution. Implementing a sustainable, flexible, long-term solution requires planning for security, upgrades, enhancements, and any other changes that may affect the organization's use of the system.

Chapter 5: User Training and Adoption

SharePoint sites are designed to be very intuitive out of the box, but to fully leverage the power of SharePoint, some end-user training is required. Users can be classified into three distinct groups: casual users, power users, and site owners. Each of these groups requires a different level and type of training. One of the most common reasons for failed SharePoint deployments is a lack of understanding on the part of the end users. People will not use features they do not understand or are not aware of.

Part II: Information Technology Governance

This section covers governance from the point of view of the IT organization responsible for implementing and maintaining the system. IT Governance is centered on controlling the installation and maintenance of the servers and software that make up the solution. This includes configuring and securing all of the services to be provided to end users. Effective IT governance prevents the proliferation of unmanaged sites and services and provides for a stable user experience.

Chapter 6: Types of SharePoint Sites

The level of governance required for a site depends on the purpose of the site and the nature of the information to be created and managed. This chapter examines the common types of sites deployed in a SharePoint environment and discusses the policies and controls that are appropriate to each.

Chapter 7: Services and Deployment

This chapter discusses the techniques used to deploy and manage services in a SharePoint environment. Services such as Search and Content Management are discussed in some detail. We also discuss the use of asset classification taxonomies, security, and quotas to protect the system from chaos and outside intrusion.

Chapter 8: Managing Operations

Once a system is deployed it is critical that it be monitored and managed effectively. This chapter discusses the different types of SharePoint farm configurations along with the types of monitoring that need to be performed. Planning for security and capacity requirements is also covered.

Part III: Information Management

This section examines information management (also known as *information architecture*) as it applies to SharePoint. Information management is concerned with organizing the information stored within the SharePoint sites so that it can be used to generate the greatest value. Concepts covered include taxonomies, audiences, legal and compliance issues, search, site navigation, and the user interface. The purpose of information management is to classify, protect, and deliver business data in a way consistent with the goals of the business.

Chapter 9: Information Architecture Overview

Information architecture refers to organizing and categorizing the information stored in the SharePoint content databases. This chapter provides a primer on the concepts associated with designing and managing the information within a set of SharePoint sites. Topics covered will include site hierarchies, metadata, and taxonomies.

Chapter 10: Delivering Information

Once data has been created, classified, and stored in the site, the users need the ability to find and access that information. This chapter discusses the features in SharePoint that support the creation of metadata used for audience targeting and finding information with Search. There is also a discussion of the social media features in SharePoint and a detailed conversation of security as it relates to information discovery and security trimming.

Chapter 11: The User Interface

This chapter deals with the presentation of information within SharePoint sites. SharePoint content is organized into hierarchies of sites, each consisting of several pages and other types of content items.

Navigation controls (also known as Menus) are used to traverse this hierarchy. Designing rich navigation and a pleasing overall site appearance often drives the user's perception of the site. This chapter covers the design aspects of branding sites including themes, master pages, and page layouts.

Part IV: Application Management

While SharePoint comes with many sophisticated features, any major SharePoint implementation will require some customization or enhancement. This can include anything from minor changes such as creating custom lists or color themes to extensive rebranding or code development. Application management allows the organization to control the way potentially harmful functionality is tested and deployed without threatening the stability of the system. Applications to be managed can include SharePoint itself, other Microsoft Server products, non-Microsoft SharePoint enhancements, and custom developed functionality.

Chapter 12: Customizations and Tools

Customizing SharePoint sites consists of many facets that all need to be managed. From the branding of the site to the introduction of new content and functionality, these updates must be created and deployed in a way that maintains the look and stability of the system. This chapter discusses several of these tools and when they are appropriate. Establishing policies and controls around customizations is a key to proper governance.

Chapter 13: Packaging Solutions and Sandboxing

When developing new functionality for deployment on the SharePoint platform, there are different means for packaging the artifacts involved. This chapter discusses the best practices around deploying custom features to SharePoint and managing the updates to these packages. One of the most important features involved in the deployment of custom functionality in SharePoint 2010 is the sandbox service that runs such code in a protected environment. We discuss when use of the sandbox is and is not appropriate.

Chapter 14: Application Lifecycle Management

This chapter discusses Application Lifecycle Management (ALM) as it applies to custom SharePoint solutions. We discuss source and configuration control as well as the environments used to develop, test, and deploy these solutions. Topics covered include best practices for source control, test environments, issue tracking, and upgrades.

Part V: Appendixes

The final section contains a set of resources you can use to jumpstart your organization's SharePoint governance effort. This includes online resources, document templates, and checklists.

Appendix A: Online Resources

This appendix contains numerous links to business, technical, and product information on the Internet. Links to valuable sites and blogs devoted to IT, Information, and Application architecture on the SharePoint platform are also provided.

Appendix B: The Governance Plan

This appendix contains an outline for a comprehensive governance plan that includes all of the concepts covered throughout the book. You are encouraged to use this outline as a starting point for your own governance plan document. This template can be customized to your organization's needs by adding or removing sections as appropriate to your situation.

Appendix C: Governance Checklists

This appendix contains a set of checklists that IT and business professionals can use to ensure that each of the concepts discussed is addressed in the final implementation plan. These checklists are split up using the same conceptual framework used to structure the rest of the book:

- Governance Planning Checklist

- IT Management Checklist

- Information Management Checklist

- Application Management Checklist

Summary

As you explore the concepts of SharePoint Governance, you need to keep in mind the goals the organization has for adopting SharePoint in the first place. These usually include ease of use, business efficiency, new capabilities, security, and legal and compliance issues. You should strive to balance the need for control against the need for flexibility.

In the end, the success or failure of a SharePoint system is determined by its users. If the system makes their lives easier, everybody wins. This is why effective SharePoint governance is governance OF the users, BY the users and FOR the users!

CHAPTER 2

SharePoint Governance Overview

In this chapter, we will introduce the conceptual framework used throughout the book and define the terminology used to describe and govern SharePoint solutions. By the end of this chapter, you will understand the purpose and process of governance and, hopefully, where you fit in.

What Will You Learn in This Chapter?

- Why you need governance and how it should be structured

- How the services provided by the portal are identified

- How to define the roles and responsibilities associated with controlling a SharePoint solution

- How the segments of IT, information, and application management relate to one another

- The purpose and general structure of a governance plan

- The common issues experienced in a SharePoint environment when governance breaks down

The Purpose of Governance

Why establish governance over any human activity? Why not just let everyone do their own thing? Isn't freedom supposed to be a good thing? For an answer, take a look at any country in the world where the government has failed and a new one has not replaced it right away. It is not a pretty picture.

Of course, failing to assign storage quotas on your corporate intranet isn't likely to result in hordes of crazed co-workers fighting to the death over the last of the copier toner. More likely, the system will just crash or be left in an unusable state. Developing policies and standards and assigning responsibilities to the appropriate departments creates a system that can support business needs without becoming an impediment. Or maybe users shouting angry slogans while waving burning torches are a normal part of your corporate culture?

The most important consideration in developing your governance strategy is determining the needs of the users and adapting the governance plan to meet those needs as effectively and unobtrusively as possible. This requires an understanding of the users' business processes, preferences, and working culture. SharePoint is a widely varied product with many features that can be productive, useful, confusing, or annoying depending on the needs of the system's users and how those features are leveraged.

The two most common mistakes when establishing governance are to implement too much governance or too little.

There is no such thing as a SharePoint installation with no governance. Anarchy is not a default; it is a choice. Even if an organization has intentionally avoided putting any restrictions on users, that is a governance choice. SharePoint sites where users have absolutely free reign are all too common. The result is most often a site clogged with massive amounts of data, but very little useful information. Users can't find anything except the most recent content they added themselves. Older data or content contributed by others may as well be on a floppy disk in someone's desk for all the good it will do them. Eventually, the site becomes slow and unreliable and falls into disuse.

Too much governance, on the other hand, robs users of the opportunity to innovate and use their creativity to find new ways to do business. If you have an inherently collaborative corporate culture, unnecessarily restricting access to SharePoint's collaborative features such as team sites, document workspaces, wikis, and social networking may cause that collaboration to shut down. Alternately, team members may abandon the portal to collaborate effectively. Overly aggressive security restrictions can also prevent users from finding valuable information they need to make important business decisions. Too much governance, like too little, is likely to result in a system that users don't choose to use.

No one wants to live in total anarchy or a police state. That's why effective governance must take a "Goldilocks" approach. Not too little, not too much. Not chaos, not prison. You want users to be comfortable using SharePoint. It should be as natural a part of their work day as opening their e-mail. Otherwise, they will seek easier ways to perform their tasks outside of the portal. After all, Goldilocks didn't stay in the bed that was too hard or too soft, but in the one that was just right.

Services

The first concept we will introduce is that of a *service*. In this context, a service is a set of features that the portal provides to the community of end users. In SharePoint, these services might include discrete subsystems like Excel Services or PerformancePoint Services, but they also include more general services like authentication and secure (SSL) site access. A service is the basic unit of functionality to consider when planning the governance of your portal.

A service has a lifecycle that starts with installation and configuration of the service, also known as *provisioning* the service. Once the service is provisioned, it must be monitored and evaluated to see how well it is meeting user needs. When improvements are needed, the service may need to be reconfigured or upgraded to meet new or refined requirements. At some point, it may be decided to remove a service because it is no longer needed. When a service is decommissioned, it is often necessary to migrate its associated data to another service or system.

As shown in Figure 2-1, governing the lifecycle of a service is a continuous process that doesn't end as long as the service is in production. This ensures that the service continues to meet the requirements of the organization in a sustainable way. This cycle of continuous monitoring and re-evaluation will be a recurring theme as you examine all of the processes used to govern a SharePoint portal.

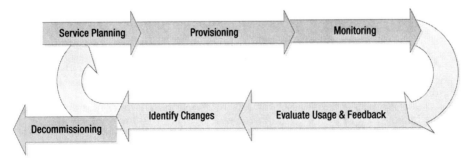

Figure 2-1. The lifecycle of a service

The first step for any SharePoint team is to identify the services to be provided. These services can be broken down into two general categories: mandatory and optional.

Mandatory Services

Some services provided by SharePoint are mandatory in the sense that, just by deploying SharePoint, those services are made at least partially available; they cannot be turned off completely. These services provide the infrastructure on which the rest of the SharePoint site is built. These services must be planned before any SharePoint solution can be successfully deployed. Some of the more important of these services are

- *Authentication*: The ability to identify users on the site. Even public-facing sites that allow "anonymous" access must have the ability to identify certain users in order to support updating site content. By default, SharePoint users are identified using an Active Directory domain. Alternately, users can also be authenticated using claims-based services that use other types of credentials.

- *Authorization*: The ability to control access to resources within the site. Share-Point uses an internal set of permissions, similar to file Access Control Lists (ACLs), to control access to all of its resources.

- *Data Storage*: SharePoint stores configuration, content, and other critical data in a series of MS SQL Server databases hosted on database servers within the organization.

- *Farm Administration*: SharePoint's Central Administration (CA) web site is the primary tool for configuring the services within the farm. There are also command-line tools and scripting languages that can be used for administration. The end users of these tools are generally limited to the IT professionals tasked with maintaining the portal.

Each of these services must be installed, configured, and monitored to keep SharePoint running well. The key decisions to be made to govern these services are listed in the checklists in Appendix C.

Optional Services

SharePoint contains a large number of subsystems that can be turned on and off by farm administrators or other privileged users. These are the optional services. Depending on the edition of the SharePoint product your organization is using, you will have different optional services to choose from. Here are some examples:

- SharePoint 2010 Foundation Services
  - Business Connectivity Services
  - Client Object Model
  - SharePoint Designer Support
  - Security Sandboxed Solutions
- SharePoint 2010 Server Standard Edition
  - Audience Targeting
  - Search

- • Content Organizer
- • Document Sets
- • My Sites
- • SharePoint 2010 Server Enterprise Edition
    - • InfoPath Forms Services
    - • Visio Services
    - • Chart Web Parts
    - • PerformancePoint Services
    - • Excel Services
    - • Context-Sensitive Search

Additional services may be made available by adding other Microsoft or third-party products designed to extend SharePoint's functionality. Some Microsoft extensions include Project Server, SQL Server Reporting Services (SSRS), Dynamics, CRM, and Team Foundation Server. Other third-party products and extensions provide additional collaboration, document management, data management, and reporting capabilities within SharePoint. SharePoint is also a powerful development platform on which organizations can build their own custom applications.

All of these services have different configuration options and security considerations. Planning for the provisioning, monitoring, and user training around these services is a critical first step. Once comprehensive service planning is complete, the next step, provisioning (shown in Figure 2-2), should be fairly straightforward.

One of the unfortunate truths to note about SharePoint, or any complex platform, is that it is often more difficult to upgrade or reconfigure a service than it is to initially deploy it. This reprovisioning requires at least as much planning as the original installation. We will revisit this situation several times later in this book.

Service Monitoring

Monitoring a service involves collecting data about how the service is being used and how well it is serving its intended function. Monitoring can take several forms, depending on the service. The NT Performance Monitor (PerfMon.exe) can be used to collect a variety of metrics about the use of each server such as CPU, memory, network, and hard drive usage. System event logs and SharePoint log files can be used to diagnose problems as they arise. Finally, SharePoint's built-in usage tracking features can be used to produce reports detailing how different services are being used in production.

Note: Don't forget to collect data from the most valuable resource you have: the users! Help desk tickets, complaints, compliments, and any other form of feedback you can get are invaluable service planning information.

Monitoring the services provided would be pointless without some way of using the data collected. The governance team needs to periodically evaluate the data collected to identify services that are not meeting the organization's needs for some reason. These may include services that are not being used effectively due to technical problems, user unfamiliarity, or changes in the needs of the users. Services may also need to be reconfigured to provide better functionality. Also, services that have not been deployed may need to be considered for addition to the catalog of services provided.

Service Decommissioning

The final stage of any service is decommissioning. In this stage, for whatever reason, it has been decided that the service will no longer be offered to users. Decommissioning a service is often difficult because there may be one or two users or groups of users that want to continue using the service. In these cases, the organization must make the trade-off between continuing to maintain the service and transitioning these users to an alternative way of performing these tasks. In most cases, this will involve moving, or *migrating*, the data already present in the service to a new location or, at a minimum, archiving that data so that it can be referenced later as needed. Decommissioning a service should not be viewed as a failure, but as a strategic decision made for the benefit of all users and the organization as a whole.

Once the necessary service changes have been identified, planning must begin for provisioning, reconfiguring, or decommissioning services to meet the needs of the user community. This closes the loop on the service lifecycle and allows the system to grow and change as needed.

Governance Segments

The next major concept to understand relates to segments. Governance segments can be thought of as the three dimensions of system management. Each segment covers a set of activities that must be performed to effectively govern the site. These segments provide a useful means of categorizing these activities and understanding how they are related to one another.

As shown in Figure 2-2, the three segments are Information Management, IT Management, and Application Management. Each service deployed in a SharePoint solution needs to be evaluated from the point of view of each of these segments.

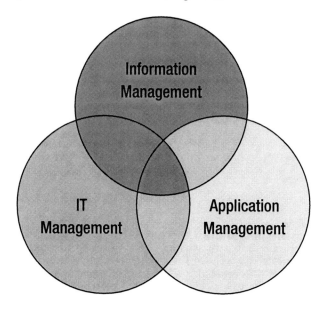

Figure 2-2. SharePoint governance segments

IT Governance

Governing a SharePoint solution from an Information Technology perspective is probably the most obvious segment. SharePoint is a family of extensive, complex software products, after all. The first interactions most organizations have with SharePoint are within the realm of the IT department.

IT governance refers to all the activities associated with installing, configuring, and managing the SharePoint servers and product features. In other words, this is how you keep the lights on. A major failing of many governance efforts is that IT governance is only considered a concern of the IT department. This is a very dangerous assumption, since the IT department is composed of a set of people with very specialized skill sets that probably don't represent the needs of the end users very well. This is why IT governance must be managed by the entire governance team, not just the IT department.

Another way of thinking about IT management is in terms of a *service catalog*. As discussed earlier, a service is a set of features that provide certain functionalities to the users. IT management is concerned with implementing and tracking those services once they are deployed. Together, these services form a service catalog that must be managed.

IT management is also concerned with

- Enforcing policies for access and usage
- Managing the lifecycle of content in the system
- Classifying and delivering content assets
- Backup and disaster recovery
- Implementing and maintaining security controls
- Preventing rogue installations of SharePoint
- Updating SharePoint with patches and service packs
- Controlling custom component deployment
- Mapping proposed services to the features of the SharePoint platform
- Monitoring usage and providing data to the governance team

A good way of establishing and measuring IT management is through the use of a service level agreement (SLA). An SLA is an agreement between the provider of a service and the consumer of that service. In this case, the SLA is between the governance team (<u>not</u> the IT department) and the end users of the portal. This agreement should cover issues such as performance and reliability targets, customization policies, storage quotas, problem reporting and resolution, and chargebacks to user organizations, if applicable.

Tracking system performance against an SLA and the other policies established by the governance team will allow the organization to focus its resources where they can do the most good. IT Governance will be the subject of Part II later in this book.

Information Management

The Information Management segment, also known as Information Architecture, is concerned with defining how the data stored in the portal will be turned into usable information. Data must be structured and relationships documented before valuable insights can be derived. These structures and relationships must be mapped into features within SharePoint to be leveraged by users in an effective, easy-to-use way. Good information management is the difference between a valuable business resource and a pile of useless data.

When defining the structure of information in SharePoint, it is important to understand the distinction between *content* and *metadata*.

Content is a fairly simple concept for most people to grasp because they can directly see it. Content items are the web pages, documents, announcements, and other pieces of information that are uploaded to or created on the portal site.

Metadata is a more difficult, and correspondingly more important, concept to master. *Metadata* is usually defined as data about data. When a user contributes a piece of content, SharePoint automatically captures certain information about that content. This includes information like who created the content and when, what name it was given, where in the site hierarchy it was placed, and so on. This data is vital for SharePoint to store and deliver the content. Information architecture extends this information to include additional fields that give more context about the item. This might include information such as the department the item is associated with, compliance requirements for the item, or the roles of users to whom the information is likely to be of interest.

A good example of familiar metadata is found in Microsoft Word or any of the Microsoft Office products. Word provides a large number of predefined metadata fields that can be set on the backstage page as shown in Figure 2-3. SharePoint has the ability to use these metadata fields, as well as others, to automatically categorize and deliver information to users based on their interests and context within the site. The key is to define these fields and ensure that they are populated consistently. This establishes the organizational context or taxonomy of information in the site.

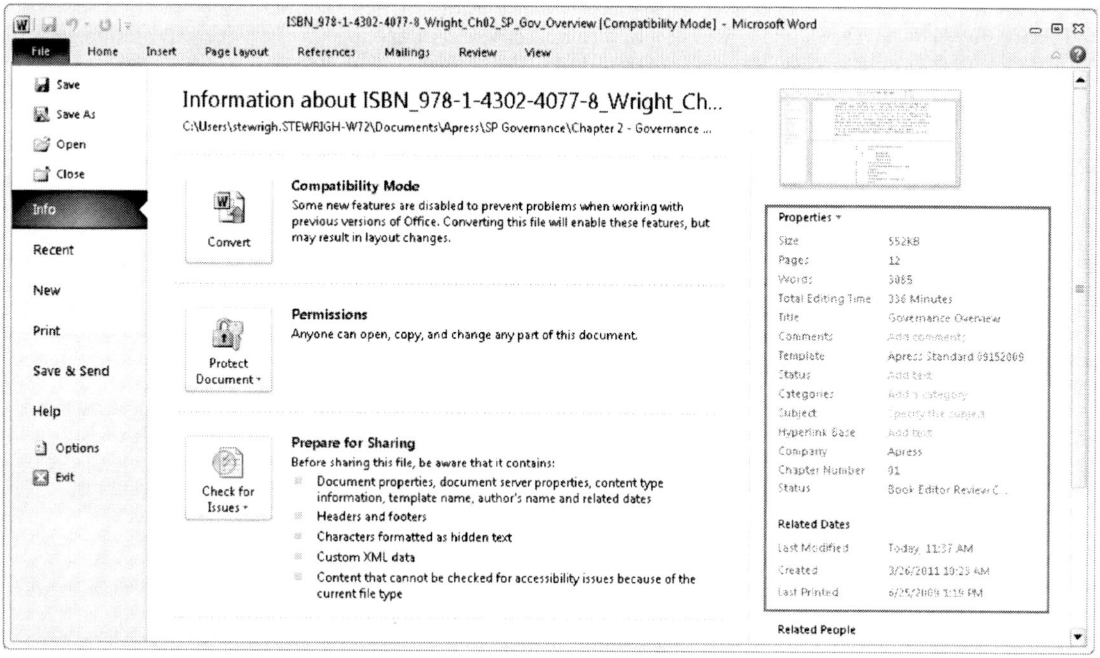

Figure 2-3. Microsoft Word metadata

Information management is also concerned with structuring the user interface for the sites and designing the site hierarchy. This generally involves creating a series of high-level wireframes that define the regions of each type of page and the site navigation that will be used to traverse the various sites.

Some of the more mechanical aspects of the site also fall under the heading of information management. These include versioning of content, determining appropriate levels of access and control for various types of information, and handling other user interface issues related to the presentation of data such as branding and sites that use multiple languages. These are often some of the most complex issues to be managed because of the large amount of redundant information that can be created.

Part III of this book will cover information management in much greater detail. We will also examine managing complex information sets in SharePoint including search catalogs, social media features, and document and records management.

Application Management

The third and final segment of effective governance is application management. An application in this case refers to any programmable components added to the SharePoint platform. These components may come from Microsoft, other vendors, or software developers within your own organization.

Governing the deployment, use, and maintenance of these components is important because these types of components are the most likely to contain bugs or incompatibilities that can undermine the stability of the system. This doesn't mean that deploying such components is a bad thing or even particularly risky. It just means that extra care should be taken to ensure that changes are tested and deployed in a managed environment.

SharePoint is designed as an extensible platform for deploying highly-scalable intranet and Internet portals. When developing new functionality to be deployed in a SharePoint environment, it is necessary to understand where the application components fit within the SharePoint stack. Figure 2-4 shows the design layers within a SharePoint solution. Each layer is built using the features exposed by the levels beneath it.

Without getting into too much technical detail at this point, the bottom layers are composed of the same components used by any web-based application on the Windows platform: the .NET Framework and ASP.NET. MS SharePoint 2010 Foundation is an ASP.NET application that is installed on top of this set of components. The MS SharePoint 2010 Server products contain additional features that are built on the SharePoint Foundation. Additional application components are then deployed at the top layer of the stack.

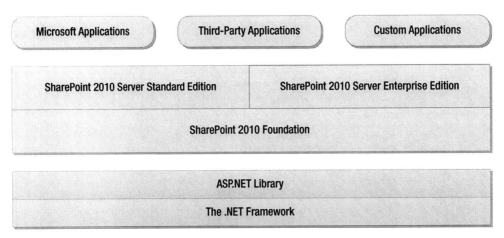

Figure 2-4. Application layers in SharePoint

It is not necessary to understand the deep technical issues associated with each layer in order to effectively participate in governing a SharePoint site. However, it may be helpful to understand where a proposed application or enhancement fits into this stack. The issues that the governance team must address involve the policies that will be used to determine which components are appropriate for inclusion as services in a particular portal. This includes limiting the tools that are allowed and the testing that is required.

There are several tools that are commonly used to develop SharePoint solutions. These include

- *SharePoint Designer 2010*: This application is used to create content and data structures within SharePoint. It can also be used to customize business process workflows and the user interface.

- *InfoPath Designer 2010*: This tool is used to create intelligent forms that can be used on the site to collect and present business information.

- *Visual Studio 2010*: This is Microsoft's primary software development tool. With Visual Studio, professional developers can create enhancements to SharePoint that can be as sophisticated as needed to provide whatever functionality is required.

- *Microsoft Office 2010*: In addition to creating documents and content for SharePoint, some office applications, such as Excel, Access, and Visio, have their own macro languages. SharePoint also contains server-based services designed to host applications written using these programs.

Part IV of this book is devoted to Application Management. This section will cover many of the technical considerations that go into protecting a SharePoint environment from unwanted instability from poorly-developed applications. Standardizing procedures for developing, testing, and maintaining custom applications, as well as packaged solutions, is an important part of a complete governance strategy.

The Governance Team

In the preceding sections, we used the phrase *governance team* several times. What exactly do we mean by this? In a larger sense, this could refer to anyone in the organization with an interest in making the portal successful. Specifically, however, we are referring to the group of people responsible for making this success happen.

Note　The governance team is also sometimes called a *governance committee*. Unfortunately, the word *committee* has such a negative connotation in most organizations that the term *team* better reflects the cooperative nature of what you are trying to accomplish.

The purpose of the governance team is to establish and maintain the policies, standards, and resources needed to make the solution successful for the business over its entire lifetime. It is the governance team that will identify requirements and services, evaluate feedback, and see that needed changes are implemented.

An effective governance team needs to have the following:

- Representatives from each group of stakeholders with the authority to speak for those they represent.

- Enough members to adequately represent all of the stakeholders of the system, but no more.

- A stable membership. Members may come and go but not so quickly that there is no focus or long-term commitment to the effort.

- A wide variety of perspectives on the business requirements and value of the system.

Figure 2-5 illustrates the major categories of members that should be represented on the governance team. Each of these groups brings a different perspective and insights to the management of the system. Leaving out one or more of these groups is a common and often fatal flaw in many governance plans.

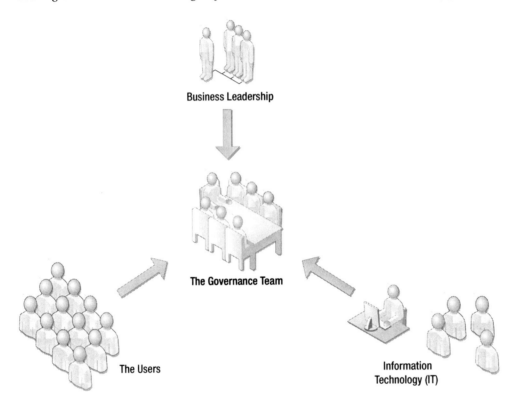

Figure 2-5. The governance team

Business Leadership

The governance team needs to include leaders from the various business areas to ensure that the system is generating real business value. This may mean having your CIO or CTO on the team or it may mean having a member of their staff that has been designated with the authority to speak for them. Other business leadership positions that need to be represented include many of the common functional areas found in most companies. These will include Human Resources, Legal and Compliance departments,

Finance, and Marketing and Sales. All of these groups need to be heard if the system is going to remain viable and be successful.

Authority is the key here. If the members of the governance team do not have the authority to make decisions, the team cannot accomplish anything. This doesn't mean that the team makes decisions in a vacuum. It simply means that once the governance team has collected the necessary information and considered its options, it is capable of making a decision that will be supported by all stakeholders.

Business leaders help the governance team determine the best ways to make the portal pay dividends to the organization in the most efficient ways. They also bring the resources necessary to invest in the hardware, software, and services necessary to deploy and upgrade the system over time.

It is very common to get commitment from business leaders early in the planning process, given the need they see for a solution and the expense of creating that solution. Once the system is in place, it is common for executives and other managers to lose focus on the ongoing maintenance of a SharePoint solution. The governance team needs to find ways to keep them engaged without requiring too much of everyone's time. Losing the input of these team members may lead to a loss of support from management as the system fails to meet their expectations.

IT Staff

The second major set of stakeholders is the IT department staff responsible for the day-to-day operation of the portal. The two general categories of technical staff associated with most SharePoint installations are administrators and developers.

Administrators are responsible for installing and configuring the SharePoint product on the servers. They monitor the system and fix problems as they occur. They are usually the first line of support for end users when they experience problems. As a result, administrators value stability and predictability above all else. The person sleeping next to the pager has a vested interest in seeing to it that the pager does not go off.

Developers are responsible for implementing new services and maintaining existing services. Depending on the organization and the nature of the services provided, this may include writing code, creating business process workflows, creating InfoPath forms for data entry, or creating other types of components that provide functionality to the users. Applications coded to run under SharePoint are generally deployed using "solution packages" and are activated as features. Developers create these artifacts and provide support and maintenance for them once they are in production.

There are additional roles that IT staffers may play in governance for the portal. IT Project Managers are well suited to leading and coordinating the processes of the governance team. Even if a project manager isn't leading the governance team, they will need to be involved in any non-trivial implementation or development efforts.

Infrastructure administrators are also important to maintaining a SharePoint environment. These IT professionals maintain the systems that interact with SharePoint including the network configuration, database servers, and the Active Directory domain. Because of SharePoint's broad scope, there is often a need to integrate it with other IT systems such as e-mail servers, customer relationship management (CRM) and enterprise resource planning (ERP) systems. The infrastructure support for these interactions must be planned for extensively.

One of the difficulties that SharePoint can bring to the IT department is that it tends to blur the lines between administration, development, and users. This is largely a result of SharePoint's tendency to store logic as content. We generally think of end users creating content and developers creating logic (that is, programs). In SharePoint, there are situations where logic and content get blended together.

For example, is an InfoPath form content or code? InfoPath form templates and completed forms are stored in SharePoint libraries, just like documents, so they would seem to be content items. On the other hand, they may contain complex business rules and even .NET framework code. The need to test and version form templates is also critical. This would seem to suggest that they are code elements to be maintained by developers. We will discuss these issues in later sections of this book, but for now, just be aware that these types of issues will need to be addressed. The only strategy that is sure to fail when governing these types of situations is not to address the issues.

Knowledge Workers (Users)

The final set of governance team members is easily the most important to success. These are the users. End users are the reason the portal exists, after all. Ironically, users are the group that is most often excluded from governance because they are often seen as "an IT thing."

When selecting users for the governance team, remember that they will need to represent the interests of all of the system's users. Ideal candidates will be middle -to senior-level subject matter experts (SMEs) in the various business areas the system will serve. They should be willing and able to act as user advocates within the team and mentors for users within their own part of the organization. These team members will be on the front lines driving adoption of the solution and collecting feedback for the governance group to evaluate.

When describing users, it is helpful to categorize them by their level of familiarity with the product and the features they routinely use.

The first group of users consists of *casual users*. Casual users see the portal as nothing more than a web site. They open a web page, navigate through the site to find information and then shut their browser window down. They are strictly information consumers. They don't generally have or need a detailed understanding of how information on the site is structured or maintained.

The next group comprises the *contributors*. These users contribute new information to the existing portal site structures. This may include uploading Office documents, creating events and announcements, maintaining calendars, or publishing information through blogs or wikis. In a well-run, highly-collaborative portal you want most of your users to be regular contributors. This is the type of user that adds value to the portal year in and year out.

The final group of users is indispensible for a successful portal. These are the *power users*. A power user has a solid understanding of how to create and maintain content within the portal. In SharePoint, power users create and customize sites, lists, and libraries. They post helpful information for others and act as mentors.

When looking for users to put on the governance team look for users with the skills and desire to become power users. Contributors can also give useful insights when usability issues arise since their more limited understanding of the system may better reflect the average user.

The Governance Plan

As we have discussed governance, we have frequently mentioned the need for planning. All of the various decisions made by the team should be documented in a central location. This document, or set of documents, is called the Governance Plan. The plan should be created early, revised continuously and referenced frequently. To paraphrase an old aphorism, plan the governance and govern by the plan.

In Chapter 3 we will go into some detail about the ways that organizations have found to plan the governance of SharePoint. For now, we will consider the general outline of the planning process and accompanying documentation.

Figure 2-6 depicts the process to follow when developing and implementing your governance plan. You may notice that this diagram looks very similar to Figure 2-1, which described the lifecycle of a service. This is no accident. A service is one of several types of items that you will apply the planning process to. As a result, its lifecycle will mirror the processes used to govern it.

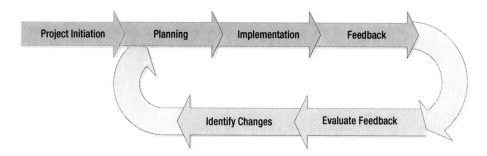

Figure 2-6. *Planning process flow*

Before you can deploy any hardware or software for your portal, you have to establish why you are building it and what you hope to get out of this process. You will gather requirements and resources for the project. You need to identify and involve the stakeholders. This is the project initiation phase where you begin building your governance team and strategies.

Once the team is assembled and you have a good idea what you are building and why, it is time to begin detailed planning for the initial implementation of the portal. The planning phase is generally the longest initial phase of a successful SharePoint rollout. In this phase, you establish the roles, responsibilities, rules, and standards that will guide the implementation of the system. You identify and prioritize the services that the portal must provide and begin mapping those services to the features of the Share-Point product line or other related components.

The plan you have created should be detailed enough to allow you to produce a set of procedures and checklists that will make the initial implementation of the system, if not exactly simple, then at least smooth and predictable. A difficult initial implementation is a sure sign that not enough effort was put into planning. As a result, the governance plan will tend to be incomplete. Always take the time to update the governance documentation with as-built information collected during the actual deployment of the system.

Just as you saw with service planning, it is important to plan for change. Any portal that is being regularly used will naturally need to be updated, enhanced, or changed in some way. This is a constructive process that should continue for the life of the system. Begin by collecting feedback from the system and the users. You will use this data to find areas where the system is not meeting the needs of the users and try to improve it. You may find new services that are needed or old ones that should be eliminated. This effort is best viewed as a lessons-learned or continuous-improvement cycle rather than a series of crises to be managed. Always remember that changes must be planned just as vigorously as the initial implementation was or the system will quickly become unmanageable. The governance plan is a living document that must be regularly updated in order to remain relevant.

Chapter 3 will dive into the details of planning and creating the governance plan document. Here we will discuss a high-level outline for the types of information that should be included.

Vision and Goals

The first decisions to be made will involve the purpose and goals of the system to be governed. These are the framing decisions that will guide the rest of the governance effort. Normally, these are stated as a vision and a set of goals.

The vision statement is a general statement of purpose or intent for the system. The content of these vary widely from one organization to another even for very similar implementations. The vision should convey the value that the portal will bring to the users and the organization.

The goals of the portal are a set of intended results to be achieved. These are more specific than the vision but are broad enough to be applied to the system as a whole. In Chapter 3, we will discuss goal-setting using the S.M.A.R.T. methodology. SMART goals are designed to be stated, measured, and evaluated in a concrete way.

Together, the vision and goals established early in the project will provide the guiding principles on which the governance team can base its future decisions. They establish a pattern of preferences that will support accomplishing the goals laid out and achieving the stated vision.

Roles and Responsibilities

One of the most important items on the team's agenda will be to establish the roles and responsibilities of the team members.

Each member brings a unique perspective and skill set that should be leveraged. Each role should be laid out in detail along with the responsibilities that accompany it. In later chapters, we will describe some of the common roles and responsibilities that need to be considered in a SharePoint governance environment.

Policies and Standards

Another of the governance team's main functions is to establish policies and standards. These words are sometime used interchangeably but not in this context. There is an important distinction between them that must be understood and maintained.

A *policy* is a rule that must be enforced by the system, the business, or the users. It is not optional. In fact, policies are not generally created by the governance team but rather identified by them. For example, protecting a list of customer credit card numbers from unauthorized access is not just a good idea, it is required under the law. The Healthcare Insurance Portability and Accountability Act of 1996 (HIPAA) requires that private health information be stored and protected in certain ways. The Security and Exchange Commission (SEC) requires certain documents to be retained for a given period of time. SharePoint has facilities to help implement many of these controls. Setting appropriate policies within your governance plan will help to protect the users and the organization from civil, criminal, or other severe penalties.

A *standard*, on the other hand, is more flexible. Standards are best practices or preferred ways of doing things. While the system should encourage compliance with standards, it is recognized that there may be cases where they do not apply. User interface design is an area that is often handled using standards. By creating page and site templates, you can encourage users to adopt a common style and structure within the portal.

Ongoing Maintenance and Planning

As mentioned previously, the governance plan should be a living, changing document just as the portal is a living, changing system. In this section of the plan, you establish strategies for handling that change.

The procedures detailed in this section are generally concerned with communicating with and eliciting feedback from the users. Here are some of the items to consider including:

- *Problem Resolution Process*: No matter how well planned and implemented the system is there will always be issues that come up. A low-stress means of reporting, fixing, and communicating these issues will help the users feel that their concerns are being addressed.

- *Content and Functionality Requests*: Users need a way to request new sites, access existing sites, or enable new functionality. This process often goes hand in hand with problem resolution, but it may take other forms as well.

- *Communication and Adoption Plan*: This plan sets out how users will be educated and trained in the use of the portal. Without an appropriate adoption plan, most portals will fail to become an integral part of the business.

- *Governance Plan Updates*: This plan describes the process that will be used to change the plan. This includes new services, standards, policies, and anything else covered by the plan.

- *Upgrades and Enhancements*: This section details the strategies to be used in updating the system hardware and software including custom and third-party components.

Common Pitfalls in Governance

We have discussed a number of good governance practices and we will discuss many more throughout this book. Let's take a moment to understand the types of problems to avoid through good governance.

The Goldilocks Approach

At the beginning of this chapter, we described the Goldilocks approach to governance: not too little, not too much. As you move forward you need to remember that the users of the system are real people who value their freedom and their contributions to the organization.

Each organization has its own culture and sometimes multiple cultures. Seek to understand the culture of your organization and fit your governance practices to the culture. Do not expect users to do things your way just because you control the system they use to do their jobs. Their attitudes and habits have been formed over long periods of time and will not change overnight.

When trying to determine the level of governance to use, remember that productivity and business value are the goals, not centralized control. Give users as much freedom as is consistent with the needs of the organization, but not more.

Engaging Users

SharePoint is a user-friendly product in most situations, but it can seem complicated to new users. In our experience, a new SharePoint portal that is deployed without a sufficient user adoption plan results in one of two situations: users either love the system to death or they hate it.

For example, early reports out of Microsoft indicated that when SharePoint was first deployed internally, most employees loved the ability to create their own content and sites. This is not surprising, since Microsoft employs so many engineers and IT professionals. Within a few weeks there were tens of thousands of sites and no way of finding anything. As a result, the system probably became unstable and difficult to use. The users loved it to death.

Other implementations have gone the other way. Giving a portal application to a large group of non-technical users and giving them the order to "use it!" is not effective in most cases. Users can sometimes "use" SharePoint for months but have no clue as to the full power at their disposal. This is both good and bad. It is good because the system was easy enough to use that they didn't need in-depth knowledge. It is bad because there is no way for the business to fully leverage the investment that has been made. Frustration is often the outcome of this situation. Users feel that the system should be easy to use but it is not because they don't understand the basics.

As mentioned several times before, users are the reason the portal exists. The governance team must find ways to engage the users. There are many ways to do this and we will discuss some of them in later chapters. The most important strategy is to create a user adoption plan that lays out how the system will be promoted and the types of training that will be provided for end users.

Roles and Responsibilities

One of the key goals of the governance process is to establish roles and responsibilities for everyone involved in the solution. Failure to clearly define these can cause the system to rapidly degrade.

Unclear lines of responsibility can result in political fights and finger pointing within the organization. SharePoint has features for delegating authority and responsibility for different parts of the site to different groups of users. Failing to use these correctly can cause a lot of confusion.

Another common problem comes down from management. A SharePoint portal is never a "fire and forget" project. Management must buy in to the idea that this is a product that will be maintained and upgraded continuously throughout its lifetime.

Implementation

The last category of common pitfalls that befall many SharePoint installations are problems of implementation. This refers to all of the processes that go into creating and delivering a solution to the users.

Insufficient hardware infrastructure is a very common cause of problems. SharePoint is designed to be highly scalable. The product can run on a single server up to a farm containing dozens of servers. Capacity planning is vital to getting in front of the demand users are placing on the system. The lead time generally needed to provision new servers and storage assets can be lengthy, so predicting hardware requirements ahead of time will help to keep users happy with the portal's performance.

Redundancy is also of critical importance. The ability to keep running after hardware failures, recover lost data, and perform disaster recovery are the difference between a reliable system and an approaching catastrophe.

Insufficient IT staffing is also all too common when running SharePoint. As the users become more comfortable with the portal, they will place greater demands on the IT staff to support and upgrade the servers and deploy new services.

SharePoint is an extensive family of products that provide a vast array of functionalities. Often, SharePoint is deployed with all of the bells and whistles turned on for users. This leads to unsupportable areas of functionality and frustrated users. This is why service planning is so important. By planning and deploying only those services we are prepared to support we can eliminate the need to fix problems caused by overenthusiastic users who have "discovered" services on their own.

When looking to add services that aren't directly supported by the SharePoint platform, avoid reinventing the wheel. There are many good third-party products that enhance SharePoint's standard features. Before performing large-scale customizations, check out Microsoft partners for workflow, image management, data archiving, backup/recovery, disaster recovery, and other features. There are also many good web sites (such as SourceForge, CodePlex, and the like) where prebuilt customization can be downloaded, often for free. Last, if development is not your organization's core competency, outsource it.

Summary

In this chapter, we have

- Introduced the concepts of SharePoint governance including segments and services
- Learned to identify services in a SharePoint environment
- Discussed the importance of establishing roles and responsibilities within the governance team.
- Described the segments of IT and information and application management
- Introduced the ideas for creating the governance plan and governance team
- Examined a set of common pitfalls experienced in SharePoint installations where governance is not handled appropriately

Governance Planning

One of the hardest parts of performing effective governance is getting started. This chapter will describe the steps that need to occur to go from "We want a SharePoint Site" to "We have a Plan." While the steps outlined are intended to be in chronological order, there are plenty of valid reasons to choose a different sequence for certain items. Specifically, consider the steps that happen before and after you establish the governance team. Do you establish your vision, goals, and scope before building the team or as part of forming the team? Questions like these can best be answered by considering the culture of your organization. Don't assume that the process outlined in this chapter is the only process that can work.

What Will You Learn in This Chapter?

- How to get started with SharePoint Governance
- How to establish the portal's vision and scope
- How to build an effective governance committee
- When to begin the process of communicating with the rest of the organization
- How to structure the governance team's outputs into policies, standards, and procedures
- How to document these procedures so that they can benefit the users going forward
- How to create feedback mechanisms that will enable the end-user community to provide ideas for improving the site and its governance

Getting Started

So your organization has decided to deploy a SharePoint-based solution. You are looking at hardware, software licenses, networking, and all of the other technical details that go into deploying SharePoint. At this moment, there are many non-technical issues that you should be considering, but they are probably not at the forefront of your mind, perhaps because they seem obvious or they appear to be someone else's concern. These include

- Who is the executive sponsor for this project? This is another way of saying "Who is paying for this?"
- What are you trying to accomplish?

- How will you maintain the system once it is in place?

- How will you make sure the system provides the services the business needs? How will you be able to tell if it is not providing value?

These questions all lead to the need for governance. Unfortunately, answering them won't get the system up and running any faster, and failing to answer them won't prevent the system from going into production. This is why so many sites are deployed without an established governance plan and, consequently, why so many fail. In a way, SharePoint's relatively inexpensive startup costs and easy setup are major contributors to this problem. No business would consider implementing a multimillion-dollar data center without a very clear idea of what it will be used for and how it will be managed.

Ideally, the executive sponsor should be the person initiating the governance of the system. This is the person who is providing the funding for the project and has the authority to control the requirements to be met. The sponsor therefore has a vested interest in seeing that the system is well-managed and returns value to the company. Often it is an IT manager who is tasked with creating the SharePoint environment by someone else in the business. In that case, they should immediately identify the executive sponsor and engage them in the governance effort. Without the sponsor's involvement, effective governance will not be possible since there will be no authority behind it.

The next task is to establish the site's vision. This is a statement that describes why the site is being created and what value it is expected to return to the organization. There are many references available for writing good vision statements and many ways to write them. Here are a few suggestions to keep in mind:

- The statement should be written as though the system already exists and has achieved all the goals set for it.

- The statement should be one or, at most, two sentences.

- The vision should be general enough to cover the entire purpose of the system but specific enough to guide later decisions regarding its implementation.

- The statement should describe the portal's role within the organization and the value it is intended to provide.

The vision statement will be different for an intranet, an extranet, or an Internet site. It will vary depending on the reach of the portal across departments, divisions, or the entire company. The vision should reflect the most important features that will provide value to the company without dwelling on the obvious. A vision statement describes what the site aspires to achieve on behalf of the business.

In addition to the vision statement, this may be good time to consider creating a mission statement. The mission statement is similar to the vision statement in that it helps guide future decision-making. The difference is that a mission statement describes what the system is going *to do*, whereas a vision statement is about what the system is going *to be*. It may also be more appropriate to consider the mission statement right after the governance team is established.

Once the vision and the mission are defined, you need to understand the scope of the governance effort. This goes hand in hand with the scope of the system to be governed. For example, if the site will serve as the intranet for one division within the company, the governance effort will focus on the needs of that division. The scope allows you to say what is and is not relevant to the project, allowing you to focus on what is most important.

Start Communicating

Communication between the governance team and the rest of the organization is the key to a successful portal. At this point in the formation process it is a good idea to begin opening the lines of communication. Formal communication and education plans will come later but, for now, just get the word out.

- Ask for volunteers for the governance team.

- Ask for proposed content and functional requirements.

- Ask for any and all ideas that might add value to the portal being developed or the governance effort around it.

Establishing a Governance Committee

Now that you understand what you are, and are not, trying to accomplish, you need to bring together a group to lead the governance effort. This group will be the *governance committee*. Do not let the word *committee* get in the way. If your organization's culture views committees as bad things, call it something else. Some common alternatives are *steering committee, leadership team, center of excellence* and so on. Whatever its name, this group will set the policies and standards that make the system work.

Identify Stakeholders

In Chapter 2, we considered the types of people that should make up the governance team. These include IT, business, and management leaders. Specifically, you need to determine who the system's stakeholders are. These are the people and departments with a vested interest in seeing the project succeed.

In searching for the system's stakeholders, consider these questions:

- Who is paying for the system?

- Who is accountable for the success or failure of the system?

- Who will be using the system?

- Who will be impacted if the system does not meet the business's needs?

- Who will spend time implementing or maintaining the system?

- Who will be responsible for defining the information architecture of the system?

- Who will provide and consume the content of the system?

It is unlikely that all of the stakeholders will be able to commit the time necessary to actively participate in the governance effort. Instead, each area should appoint one or more representatives to participate. These representatives should have the experience and authority to make binding decisions for their respective groups.

These team members will become mentors for users and advocates for the system within their part of the organization. Be sure that anyone to be included in the governance team is committed, both in time and interest, to the effort.

They should also be rewarded and recognized for their contributions. Participating in this type of activity can be very time consuming when it is done well. It is important that this time be factored into their overall workload and career plan. Asking anyone to perform this type of work over and above their normal 40-hour-a-week job will inevitably turn this into a low priority task for them.

Set the Objectives for Governance

Like any project, the governance of a SharePoint portal needs to have a set of well-defined goals or objectives. Just as with vision statements, there are many ideas about how to set goals. One of the most common approaches is to use the S.M.A.R.T. approach:

- *Specific*: Objectives should specify exactly what is to be accomplished.

- *Measurable*: Objectives should be quantifiable and concrete so that progress, success, and failure can be judged objectively.

- *Attainable*: Objectives should never be set in such a way that they cannot be fully achieved. Setting a goal that is hard to reach is good. Setting a goal that is out of reach is pointless.

- *Relevant*: Objectives should always contribute to the achievement of the mission and vision of the project.

- *Time-bound*: Objectives should come with an expiration date. An open-ended objective is of little use since it never actually has to be met.

When setting goals for a SharePoint portal project try to remember why the project is being undertaken. The objectives should move the organization closer to the achievement of the vision while providing a measuring stick for gauging that progress.

Objectives for the governance of a portal often map to the value to be provided to the business. These may include things like reducing the total cost of ownership (TCO) for the system and establishing standards and policies for the organization. As we discuss in Chapter 4, these objectives are met by defining and implementing services within the portal for business users.

Another consideration when establishing goals for governance is creating a balance between flexibility and control. As emphasized in Chapter 2, good governance requires a balanced approach. Too little control can cause a lack of focus and a waste of time and resources. Too much control can stifle innovation and cause the system to fall into disuse. One of the objectives of the governance effort should be to strike this balance effectively.

Assign Roles and Responsibilities

One of the primary purposes of governance is to ensure that everyone involved understands what is expected of each member of the team. This process begins by establishing the roles of each person or department and then assigning responsibilities to those roles. Table 3-1 describes some common roles associated with SharePoint governance.

Table 3-1. Common Governance Roles

Role	Description
Executive Sponsor	This project "champion" is usually associated with the part of the business providing the resources for the project.
Project Manager	This person drives the project forward and is often in charge of facilitating meetings, ensuring deadlines are met and communicating with the organization on behalf of the team.
Business Owner	This is usually a manager or senior staff member from one of the business units that make use of the system. Business owners help to establish the requirements for the system and provide a channel for user feedback.
User Mentor (Coach)	The mentor or coach is committed to helping users get the most out of the system and may perform formal or informal training, write blog posts, answer questions, or do other forms of mentoring as needed.

Role	Description
Power User	This person is proficient with the design and implementation of new content within the portal and may or may not be technical, depending on the type of content they help to author.
IT Manager	IT Managers provide direction to the administrators and developers associated with the system.
Application Developer	Application developers create new customized functionality for the portal. This may include new Web Parts, workflows, InfoPath forms, etc. Developers perform highly technical customizations beyond the scope of power users.
System Administrator	System Administrators install, monitor, and update the servers associated with the portal.
Support	Support resources are available to answer questions and solve problems when they are reported by end users.
Information Architect	This person helps the business owners define the metadata, workflows, site structures and other components that control the organization of information in the portal.
Web Designer	This person helps to establish the look and feel of the site in conjunction with the Information Architect and also assists the developers and power users to implement the web site design.
Site Owner	Each SharePoint site has one or more owners who control access to the site.
Site Designer	The site designer controls the creation of lists, libraries, and other content within the site. Often, the site owner and site designer are the same person.
Site Contributor	A site contributor adds new or updated content to the site.

Defining responsibilities for the preceding roles may be as simple as creating the list and assigning the responsibilities for each role. It is often the case that while one role may be responsible for a task, other roles are also involved. A convenient way to record these interdependencies is to use a RACI chart. RACI defines the contribution of each role to a task as either:

- *Responsible*: This is the role primarily responsible for accomplishing the task.

- *Accountable*: This is the person to whom the responsible person is accountable. This is also sometimes called *Approver* or *Authority*.

- *Contributor*: This is one or more additional roles that are involved in the completion of the task, sometimes called *Consulted*.

- *Informed*: These are the roles that have an interest in the task and must be kept informed as to its status. They do not have any authority over or make any contribution to completing the task.

There are numerous variations on the definitions of these terms, but the general idea is the same. A common way to document these tasks and responsibilities is to use a table (Table 3-2) that has tasks listed down the left column and roles listed across the top row. Each cell in the table reflects the responsibility of that role with respect to the task.

Table 3-2. Sample RACI Chart

Task	Executive Sponsor	Project Manager	IT Manager	App Manager	System Developer	Admin
New Feature Development						
Identify Feature	A	R	C	I	I	
Define Requirements	A	R	R	C	I	
Design Solution	-	I	A	R	C	
Implementation	-	I	A	R	I	
Deployment	I	I	A	C	R	

As your governance effort begins, the list of tasks will be fairly short. As your system grows and issues arise, the list can be expanded as needed to ensure that everyone is comfortable with the roles of all involved.

Develop Governance Planning Documents

The governance team's purpose is to set standards and policies and communicate them to the rest of the organization. To do this, some documentation will be necessary. In this section, we will describe common features and layouts for this documentation. Of course, the needs of your organization will require variations to the document set described here. This discussion should be viewed only as a starting point.

Common Document Features

Before getting into the details of the documents, let's look at some best practices.

- *Revisions*: Each document should include a revision history that allows readers to know what parts of the document have been updated from one version to the next. This alleviates the need to reread the entire document each time a version is released.

- *Publishing*: Each document should be posted in a known location on a regular basis. This allows the documents to be found quickly and easily when needed.

- *Feedback*: Each document should explicitly request feedback and explain how to provide feedback to the author. This can be an online form, e-mail address, and so forth. These are living documents designed to help readers, not encumber them.

- *Sign-offs*: Documents should be published only after they are officially approved by the governance team. This is not to say that drafts should not be circulated. They definitely should! But users must be able to find the official documents when needed.

The purpose of these documents is not to get in the way of productivity. They are meant to be read and understood to help everyone in the organization get the most out of the governance process and the portal. Never fill these documents with boilerplate text that adds no value for the reader. Try to make these documents long on detail and short on description. Lists, tables, and figures can often be used to provide the same, or better, understanding of a topic than large amounts of text. These documents should be as long as they need to be, but no longer.

The Governance Plan

The most important document created by the governance team will be the governance plan. This plan will document the decisions made by the governance team in a way that allows them to be easily referenced and used by the team and others affected by those decisions.

Here is one possible outline for a governance plan:

- Governance Overview
    - Vision & Mission
    - Scope
    - Key Objectives
    - Guiding Principles
- Roles and Responsibilities
    - Role Definitions
    - Role Assignments
    - Responsibility (RACI) Matrices
- Content Policies and Standards
    - Site Structure
    - Security Policies
    - User Interface Standards
    - Metadata Management
    - Content Management
- Technical Policies and Standards
    - Monitoring Requirements
    - Uptime and Performance Goals
    - Outage Planning Procedures
    - Support Requirements and Schedules

- Customization Policies and Standards
  - Site Provisioning
  - Themes
  - Content Management
  - Information Management Policies
  - Sandboxed solutions
- General Procedures
  - How to …
  - How to …
  - How to …

The *governance overview* will contain many of the items we have already discussed, including the portal's vision, mission, scope, and objectives. In addition to these are a set of *guiding principles*. These are also known as *framing decisions*. The idea is to document the high-level strategic direction for the portal and governance effort. For example, these decisions may include items such as the following:

- Publishing will be preferred in sites at the department level and above.
- The use of My Sites, personalization, and social media will be supported and encouraged throughout the portal.
- Copyrighted material will be stored only in specially designated sites.
- No customer personal information will be stored within the portal.
- Versioning will be used whenever practical.
- Large media files will be stored outside of the portal but accessible within the portal using Remote BLOB Storage (RBS).

The preceding decisions may be technical in nature when necessary, but more often they will be related to business requirements such as compliance and security considerations. These will be among the first decisions made by the governance team. They will shape all of the decisions made later. These principles should be chosen to help drive the group toward fulfilling the group's vision and mission.

Roles and Responsibilities will document the roles as described earlier in this chapter. Additionally, this section will grow to contain additional tasks and the responsible roles for those tasks. The assignment of individuals to roles can be included in this document or referenced in another location (such as a SharePoint list!).

Content Policies and Standards cover the creation and management of content within the SharePoint sites in the portal. The items in this section are described in detail in Part 2 of this book.

Technical Policies and Standards cover the management of the servers that support the portal. These are the IT Management questions covered in Part 3 of this book.

Customization Policies and Standards provide guidance on the creation of content or logic that is not native to SharePoint. This may include user interface elements such as page layouts and themes or user-defined logic such as workflows, InfoPath forms, or solution packages. These techniques are described in Part 4.

General Procedures are those processes that allow users to get things done. This is typically a list of "How-To" articles. Each article describes how to access help and resources provided by the portal and the governance team. This is basically a high-level frequently asked questions (FAQ) list for the users. These procedures may also be posted directly on the portal to make them easier to find. Some examples of these procedures include

- How to get support
- How to find training materials
- How to provide feedback to governance committee
- How to request a new site or site/content access
- How to report a problem or request a new feature
- How to request new site collections

Your organization will determine its own needs for the contents of the governance plan. More ideas for the governance plan can be found in Appendix B of this book. Appendix C contains a set of helpful checklists that can be used to establish and organize your governance plan.

Additional Planning Documents

When creating the governance plan it is often useful to create a set of subordinate plans to support it, similar to Table 3-3. Each plan is still part of the governance process but is often maintained by one department or set of individuals because of their limited audience.

Table 3-3. Additional Common Governance Roles

Plan	Description
User Communication and Training Plan	This plan will describe the techniques to be used to communicate with the end-user community. This will include maintenance and support schedules and procedures. It will also include resources for user training to help users get the most out of the system. See Chapter 5 for more details.
Operations Plan	This plan will describe how the system will be monitored, updated, and protected. This should include backup and restoration plans, disaster recovery, usage and performance monitoring, bug and issue tracking, etc. The operations plan is described in more detail in Chapter 8.
Application Lifecycle Management Plan	This plan will describe the processes to be used to create customized solutions for the portal. It will detail items such as source code control, sandbox solution policies, release scheduling, etc. These processes will apply only to customizations that are centrally created and deployed. Policies for end-user customization should remain in the main governance plan document. Application Lifecycle Management (ALM) and application management in general are described in Part 4 of this book.

Closing the Loop

With the governance team assembled and the initial documents and processes established, it is time to move into action. As the project moves forward you will want to perform regular reviews, collect user feedback, monitor feature usage data, and track bugs and issues. As a team, the governance committee should look at all of this information and plan future services and upgrades.

In Chapter 4, we discuss the process of designing and managing services in the portal. Keep in mind the service lifecycle described in Chapter 2 and shown in Figure 3-1.

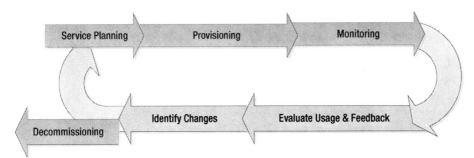

Figure 3-1. *The lifecycle of a service*

Summary

In this chapter, we have

- Described the process of getting started with SharePoint Governance
- Discussed how to establish the vision and scope for your SharePoint site and the governance effort that supports it
- Looked at the process of establishing a governance committee
- Considered the need for early and effective communication with the rest of the organization
- Described the governance policies and standards documents that need to be created
- Explored the types of feedback mechanisms that can be used to enable the site's users to provide ideas for improving the site and its governance

CHAPTER 4

Implementing Services

In this chapter, we will discuss how to establish the controls needed to govern the portal. Controls include the automated and manual processes used to manage the portal. The strategy we will use is to divide the functionality of the portal into manageable components, called services, as described in Chapter 2. We will identify the services to be implemented and walk through the planning for the service's lifecycle.

What Will You Learn in This Chapter?

- Why portal functionality should be divided into manageable services
- How to identify and categorize services for governance
- How to prioritize the services for implementation in the portal
- How to plan the implementation of a service
- How to plan for the monitoring of a service after deployment
- How to plan for the maintenance and upgrades associated with a service
- How to plan for the eventual decommissioning of a service
- How to divide and conquer services

Let's take a moment to review the concept of services introduced in Chapter 2. A *service* is a discrete set of features that the portal provides to the community of end users. By aggregating the features of the system into services, you divide the governance of the system into manageable pieces.

▓ **Note** Remember that in a governance context a service is a conceptual collection of features. SharePoint contains many subsystems that are also called services, such as Excel Services or PerformancePoint Services. SharePoint services may or may not map directly to governance services. A governance service may contain one or more SharePoint services, or none, along with other features that are not part of any SharePoint service. The services described in this chapter are governance services unless explicitly noted otherwise.

Recall that a service always has a lifecycle (Figure 4-1). Start by identifying and planning for governance of the service. Then the service is implemented and released to the user community. The governance plan will include monitoring the usage and performance of the service. You then collect feedback from the users to plan future upgrades and changes to the service.

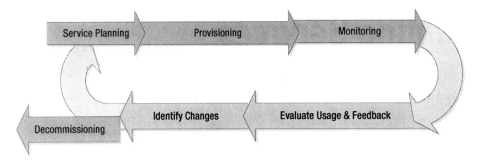

Figure 4-1. The lifecycle of a service

Try not to think of service planning as a one-time effort. The governance team will be involved in monitoring and reevaluating each service continually over time. This allows the system to grow and evolve as needed without becoming clogged with unused or unusable services that no longer provide the value they should.

Identifying Services

The services to be implemented in a SharePoint portal will fall into one of three categories. The first and most common type of service is inherent in the SharePoint product line, such as Publishing or PerformancePoint Services. (We will discuss some of these later in this chapter.)

A service can also be built around a third-party product that provides features on top of SharePoint. Common examples of this are data archiving, workflow, and image/document management systems. These products require separate licensing and configuration beyond that of the SharePoint server itself. When implementing this type of service, be sure to evaluate the vendor's upgrade practices. If the vendor publishes patches and interim versions (point releases) between major releases, these release schedules will need to be integrated with the portal's maintenance schedule. Some commercial add-ons also require special hardware such as storage or networking infrastructure.

A third source of services may be your own Information Technology (IT) department. Custom-built applications built on SharePoint can provide an excellent return on investment because they can provide value to the business that cannot be achieved in other ways. A custom solution might be as simple as automating a business process using a set of InfoPath forms and workflows. It could also involve significant .NET Framework programming to implement new Web Parts, event handlers, workflow activities, or background processes (timer jobs).

Other sources of solutions for SharePoint are open- or shared-source sites such as CodePlex.com. CodePlex is sponsored by Microsoft and, as of November 2011, contains almost 1,700 open source projects for SharePoint. These projects include Web Parts, best practices, site templates, management and administration tools, and so on. These projects are provided on an "as is" basis and are not supported by any vendor. Therefore, from a governance point of view, these should be treated in the same way as internally created custom solutions. The advantage to using open source solutions is that much of the work is already done.

The other way to categorize services in SharePoint is as mandatory or optional. *Mandatory* services are those that must be present at all times in order for the system to function. We will describe some of these later in this chapter. Note that the mandatory services described are required for technical reasons. Your organization may have regulatory or compliance needs that will require some otherwise optional services to be made mandatory. For example, a portal that is hosting corporate records subject to Sarbanes-Oxley regulations may require SharePoint's records management features to be available.

Optional services are those that are deployed because they provide value to the organization. Some services will depend on other services in order to function properly. For example, to use SharePoint's automated content deployment mechanism, you must also be using the Publishing features. While it may be tempting to lump a group of interdependent features into a single service, remember that the goal is to simplify governance of each service. Combining features with different audiences, requirements, and monitoring capabilities into a single service will make that service more difficult to manage.

Establish Mandatory Services

In this section, we will describe the most important mandatory services that the governance team needs to be aware of. These services should be evaluated and planned before any servers are installed.

Infrastructural Services

The infrastructural services form the foundation for the rest of the system.

Hardware Infrastructure

When planning the hardware for a SharePoint environment, the governance team in conjunction with IT will need to perform capacity planning. *Capacity planning* involves creating a profile of how the system will be used and the level of performance to be expected. Much of this information may be laid out in a Service Level Agreement (SLA) between the governance team and the user community.

When developing the hardware plan for a portal, consider the following:

- *User load*: How many users will be using the system at one time? Which services will be most heavily used?

- *Storage volume*: How much data will be stored in the portal, including old versions and all types of documents?

- *Storage type*: Will all content be stored on a single SQL Server, Network Attached Storage (NAS), or a Storage Area Network (SAN)? Will any data be accessed using SQL Server's Remote BLOB Service (RBS)?

- *Network bandwidth*: How much data will be sent and received by the portal?

- *Network routing*: Will a network load balancing appliance be needed? What about new firewall settings?

- *Server tiers*: All SharePoint portals require one or more web servers and one or more database servers. Does your portal need separate search query and indexing servers? What about other application tier services such as Excel Services, Access Services, or PerformancePoint Services? These services can be hosted on the front-end web servers, but this can cause performance to degrade for end users.

Even the best capacity plan is never perfect. As time passes, content tends to become larger. If your portal is successful, the addition of new services and more active users will increase load on the servers.

When the farm is initially deployed, collect a set of performance and usage metrics. These will form a baseline that can be used for comparison later. As the system's load and storage size increase, these measurements will allow the governance team to proactively predict when additional hardware resources will be needed. This will prevent end users from noticing a slow-down in the system that can cause them to abandon their use of the portal.

Authentication

Authentication is the means used to identify users when they connect to the portal. This usually involves providing a user name and password, but where those credentials are stored and how they are validated can vary greatly. SharePoint supports two modes of authentication: classic and claims-based.

- *Classic mode* authentication is the same mechanism used by most web sites and the previous versions of SharePoint. Credentials are checked against a Windows identity provider, either Active Directory (NTLM) or Kerberos. The information obtained includes basic attributes about the user including the security groups to which they belong.

- *Claims-based* authentication is new in SharePoint 2010. A claim is a set of information about a subject that is provided by a trusted claim provider. This information is delivered in an encrypted security token issued by the provider. The user presents the claim as evidence of their identity in order to use the system.

Active Directory and Kerberos, and many other providers, can also be used as claims-based authentication providers. When performing forms-based authentication (where the user logs on with credentials stored in a database, for example) components known as membership and role providers act as the providers of the claims. Another common technique is to use a centralized identity store such as Windows Live ID to provide claims using the Security Assertion Markup Language (SAML).

Considerations for authentication include:

- Where will the user's name and password be stored?

- How will the user change their password?

- Who will create and deactivate users?

- What configuration is necessary to bring those credentials into SharePoint?

- How will the portal establish a trust relationship with its claims providers?

It is not uncommon to use multiple forms of authentication within a single SharePoint farm. For internal users on an intranet, the most common form of authentication is Active Directory. Kerberos is becoming more popular as more administrators become familiar with it.

For external users on an extranet or a public web site, it is often impractical to use Active Directory. More often, forms-based authentication or an Internet-based identity service such as Windows Live is used.

The decision to use claims or classic mode authentication will depend on the type of authentication to be performed. In general, if there is no need to use classic mode authentication, new SharePoint installations should use claims-based mode.

Authorization

Authorization refers to the process of determining which users are allowed to perform which actions. If authentication answers the question "Who are you?", then authorization is concerned with "What can you do?" To understand authorization in SharePoint, you will need to master the four concepts shown in Figure 4-2.

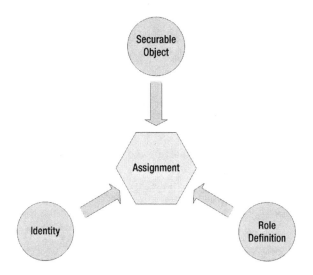

Figure 4-2. *Authorization process*

We have already touched on the first concept, *identity*. A user's identity includes their user name and any security groups to which they belong. There are two types of identities within SharePoint: domain and SharePoint groups.

- *Domain identities* are the user and group names defined by the claims provider or classic mode provider used to log in to the system. Domain user and group names are used identically once the user is logged in to SharePoint. The members of a domain group cannot be altered from within SharePoint.

- *SharePoint groups* allow domain users and groups to be grouped together to simplify managing permissions. SharePoint groups can be edited through the web interface. They can also be configured to allow members to add themselves or to request membership from the group owner. A disadvantage of SharePoint groups is that they are specific to the site collection in which they are created. They cannot be referenced across multiple collections.

A *securable object* is any object within SharePoint that can have permissions assigned to it. This includes items such as sites, site collections, lists, libraries, and list or library items. These are the objects to which access is to be authorized.

A *role definition* defines a permission or an action to be taken. Examples would include view a site, edit a list item, and delete a page. Additionally, SharePoint allows the creation of permission levels. A *permission level* is a group of permissions that have been declared as a unit. Assigning a user a permission level for an object grants them all of the rights associated with that permission level. Some common permission levels include Full Control, Contribute, Read, and Design. Permission levels can be created and edited within SharePoint's web interface. Like SharePoint groups, permission levels are defined within a single site collection.

The last concept to be understood is that of an assignment. An *assignment* is created when a user (identity) is given a certain set of permissions (role definition) to a piece of content (securable object). An assignment establishes a three-way connection between the identity, role definition, and object described above to define the rights of any user that might attempt to access the object.

▓ **Note**   SharePoint permissions are additive. If a user is assigned rights based on membership in more than one group, for example, their resulting rights are the sum total of all of the rights possessed by those groups.

When a user attempts to access an object, SharePoint searches for any assignments for the identities associated with that user. These include the user's domain user ID, all domain groups, and any Share-Point groups to which the user belongs. The resulting list of assignments is used to determine the rights the user has to the object.

The two items that will be most important to plan are the permission levels and SharePoint groups to be created. Here are some things to keep in mind:

- Will group memberships be managed in SharePoint Groups or domain groups? SharePoint groups are defined only within each site collection but they can be easily managed through the web interface. Domain groups are global, but they must be maintained outside of SharePoint.

- How will users request and be granted access to each group?

- Are the standard permission levels provided by SharePoint appropriate for your needs? If not, they can be altered, or new levels can be created to suit your situation.

- Site owners typically assign permissions within their sites. Who will own each site and how will ownership be transferred when users leave the organization?

- Who will be responsible for removing access from users that leave the organization?

A last concept to understand with regard to authorization is *inheritance*. Each object within a SharePoint site collection has a parent object from which it can inherit its permission assignments. Sites inherit from their parent site, lists inherit from the site that contains them and list items inherit from their parent list.

By default, a new item will inherit the permission of its parent object. This inheritance can be broken by an authorized user. Breaking inheritance causes the assignments from the parent object to be copied to the child object. As a result, the child will still have the same permissions as the parent, but any changes made to the child's permissions later will not affect the parent. Any objects which inherit permissions from the child will continue to do so, but now they will get the permissions directly from the child, not from its parent.

E-Mail Integration

While e-mail integration is not strictly mandatory for SharePoint to function, it is important enough in most cases to be considered mandatory. Many features within SharePoint will not function without the ability to send out e-mails. Two examples of these are workflow, which must be able to notify users of their tasks, and alerts, which cannot be sent except through e-mail.

SharePoint has two separate e-mail configurations: incoming and outgoing. Outgoing e-mail is used to provide alerts and notifications for workflows and certain administrative events. Incoming e-mail is used to allow users to participate in e-mail discussion lists, send documents into a document library, or submit other types of data into SharePoint.

When designing e-mail integration for your portal, consider these questions:

- Outgoing e-mail is needed in most intranet portals. Is incoming e-mail really needed or desirable?

- Will the local SMTP service be used on the web servers or will an e-mail server outside the farm be accessed?

- What security configurations are required to forward e-mail into and out of the SharePoint farm?

- How will the e-mail servers and firewall be configured to prevent the SharePoint site from being used as a relay point for SPAM e-mail traffic?

- How will incoming SPAM be filtered from the SharePoint mailbox?

SharePoint uses the SMTP protocol to send and receive e-mail from an e-mail server. A common scenario is to configure the Windows SMTP Service on one or more of the SharePoint servers in the farm, but any SMTP-enabled server application can be used. When using the local SMTP service it is usually necessary to configure it to relay messages to another server for final delivery. This can create a security hole if it is not configured carefully. Be sure to involve network engineers before deploying any new SMTP servers within your network.

Administration and Monitoring

Administration and monitoring services provide administrators with the ability to configure and monitor the SharePoint server farm.

Central Administration

SharePoint's primary administration interface is the Central Administration (CA) web site. This web site contains tools for almost all administrative functions within SharePoint. This web site must exist on exactly one SharePoint server within the farm. Using this site, farm administrators can create new web sites and site collections, configure farm services, and allocate resources and quota limits, and a multitude of other tasks using a simple web interface.

Some best practices and tips regarding Central Administration include

- Ensure that web traffic to the CA site cannot originate on the Internet. Use firewall settings or network routing to prevent access to hackers.

- Consider hosting the CA web site on an application tier server that does not communicate with the Internet.

- Limit the number of farm administrators. Only highly-trained personnel should be allowed to access CA.

- Keep a log of all changes made through CA.

- The CA web site can be moved from one server to another using the SharePoint Products and Technologies Configuration Wizard.

- The randomly assigned port number assigned to the CA web site at installation can be changed using the Windows PowerShell Set-SPCentralAdministration commandlet.

While most administrative actions can be performed using the CA interface, some will require the use of SharePoint's command-line tools. The Windows PowerShell interface allows administrators to write sophisticated, object-oriented administration scripts. This is the preferred scripting tool for SharePoint 2010. The STSADM tool used in previous versions of SharePoint is still available in 2010 but is considered deprecated and is included only to support backward compatibility.

Logging and Tracing

SharePoint uses a Universal Logging System (ULS) to consolidate trace information from all of the various components that make up the product. These logs can become very large. Adequate space must be allocated to store them or the system may be unable to record critical data. Also, if the default location on the system's C-drive is used, the logs can fill up the system drive and cause the system to fail.

These logs should always be moved to another drive specifically allocated for log files. Note that the log files on each server in the farm are stored in the same location. Therefore, the log file location must exist on every server in the farm. This may require provisioning additional disks.

For more detail on the configuration options associated with SharePoint's log files, see Chapter 7.

Usage and Health Data Collection

SharePoint can be configured to collect extensive information about the usage of the system. This information provides valuable feedback about how users are using the system. Which sites are visited most often? Which features are used most often? SharePoint can also automatically evaluate the state of the server farm and provide proactive alerts when problems are detected.

For more detail on usage and health data collection, see Chapter 7.

Identify Optional Services

Now that the mandatory services have been identified and planned out, we will discuss the optional services provided by SharePoint out of the box. Your organization may choose to package these services differently according to your own governance needs. This discussion will focus on the governance considerations associated with each feature.

Microsoft categorizes the features of SharePoint 2010 using the SharePoint wheel diagram shown in Figure 4-3. We will use the same categorization to explore the potential services provided by SharePoint.

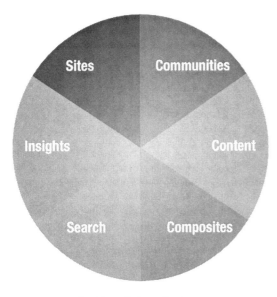

Figure 4-3. The SharePoint wheel

Sites

Services in the Sites category allow users to create and manage web sites within the portal (see Table 4-1).

Table 4-1. Site Services

Service Name	Description	Considerations
Site and Site Collection Provisioning	This service defines how users request new sites to be created. SharePoint contains features for allowing users to manage their own sites including	SSSC can be customized to use workflows for approval and to collect additional information about the site collections created.
	• *Self-Service Site Creation (SSSC)*: Allows a user to request or automatically create site collections within the portal.	Be sure to limit the users allowed to create site collections and subsites. Creating large numbers of sites can degrade system performance and make information hard to find.
	• *Self-Service Subsite Creation*: Users with appropriate rights within the current site can use site templates to create a subsite that they can manage as the new site's owner.	Automatic site deletion sends warnings to the site's owner before deletion occurs but it does not require that permission be granted before the site collection is destroyed.
	• *Automatic Site Deletion*: Allows the farm administrator to configure the farm to automatically delete unused site collections after sending warning messages to the site's owner.	Perform regular backups to enable recovery of data from deleted site collections if it is needed.
Accessibility	SharePoint 2010 is designed to conform to most modern web coding standards, including	• Determine and document any accessibility requirements that apply to the portal.
	• Web Content Accessibility Guidelines (WCAG) 2.0 (Level AA)	• Ensure that custom solutions adhere to these standards and do not compromise SharePoint's ability to conform.
	• HIPAA Section 508 accessibility standard	
	• Accessible Rich Internet Applications (ARIA) markup	• Silverlight Web Parts and controls may produce non-compliant interfaces.
	• HTML 4.01	• HTML 5 support is not yet available in SharePoint 2010.
	• XHTML 1.0/1.1	
	• Levels: Transitional, Strict, Frameset, and Quirks mode	

Service Name	Description	Considerations
Multilanguage Site Support	SharePoint has built-in features for supporting sites that need to be presented in multiple languages: *Multi-Language User Interface (MUI)*: This feature allows Language Packs to be added to a SharePoint farm. These components provide translations of all of the content provided by SharePoint including menus, columns, forms, navigation controls and so on. The user can select the language they wish to use in the web interface from a list of available languages. *Site Variations*: This feature allows for the management of user-created content in multiple languages. A main site is created and then variation sites are created for each language. SharePoint contains workflow definitions designed to manage the translation process for updating variation sites. When a user accesses the main site, they are redirected to the correct variation site based on configurable criteria that can be based on properties such as the language being used in their web browser.	Which languages will be supported on each site? Additional language packs are loaded and updated separately from the rest of the SharePoint product. Site variations are part of the SharePoint publishing feature. Non-publishing sites cannot have variations. Who will be responsible for completing the translation workflows for each site? The content for each site variation is versioned and promoted separately. This can cause multi-language content to consume correspondingly more storage space.

Content

These services provide users with the ability to create and manage content within their sites (see Table 4-2). All of these topics are covered in more detail in Chapter 6.

Table 4-2. Content Services

Service Name	Description	Considerations
Publishing	SharePoint's publishing features provide a full-featured Web Content Management (WCM) solution for content stored in SharePoint content databases. This includes approval workflows, rich metadata, release scheduling, content deployment and page layouts.	• Determine the users with Contributor and Approver permissions in each published site. These are configured through site permissions. • Publishing must be enabled at both the site collection and site level in order to be functional. Some sites within the collection can be excluded from publishing by deactivating the site-level publishing feature.

Service Name	Description	Considerations
		• Publishing is most appropriate on public-facing, divisional and departmental sites. Team collaboration sites do not benefit from publishing features.
Records Management	This feature is designed for managing official corporate records. Records are managed for auditing and discovery purposes. This feature is targeted toward supplying the tools for complying with regulations such as Sarbanes-Oxley.	• Define a small number of policies that can be applied to a large segment of documents. Do not attempt to give each document its own policy. This rapidly becomes unmanageable. • Enable the auditing of read accesses only when absolutely necessary. This can generate very large amounts of audit data. • Use expiration policies to help trim unneeded content from large portal sites. Custom workflows can be used to automate approvals, archival and deletion of content items.
Information Management Policies	This feature allows the creation of policies that can be applied consistently to manage content. These policies control auditing the accessing and updating of documents and expiration policies for automating review and deletion workflows. These policies can also be used to automatically add standard labels and barcodes to documents retrieved from SharePoint based on the metadata for the document.	• Define a small number of policies that can be applied to a large segment of documents. Do not attempt to give each document its own policy. This rapidly becomes unmanageable. • Enable the auditing of read accesses only when absolutely necessary. This can generate very large amounts of audit data. • Use expiration policies to help trim unneeded content from large portal sites. Custom workflows can be used to automate approvals, archival and deletion of content items.

Communities

The SharePoint community services encourage collaboration and productivity by centralizing the sharing of information in the portal (see Table 4-3).

Table 4-3. Community Services

Service Name	Description	Considerations
My Sites	The My Sites feature provides a private workspace for each user. This area can be customized extensively to make the individual more productive. My Sites provide an excellent alternative to storing sensitive data on the user's desktop. The user's My Site can also be used to publish information such as Blogs and documents to the rest of the organization.	• My Sites are most often enabled on intranet sites. • The governance team should publish appropriate use rules for My Sites. For example, no pornography, business use only, limited personal data (photos, etc.), and quotas. • My Sites can be integrated with audience targeting and Outlook Web Parts to act as the user's primary desktop. This makes for a good user experience when using thin-client browsers instead of personal desktops. • My Sites are created automatically the first time a user clicks their "My Site" link. Site templates can be created and deployed using a set of role-specific rules if desired. For example, users in Finance might be given a different default My Site design than users in IT. • The My Sites feature can be disabled entirely if it does not fit the organization's culture or security requirements.
Online Presence	The Online Presence feature allows a user to determine if another user is online and to connect with them via e-mail or Instant Messaging (IM). For example, if a user has a document checked out, another user would see an indicator next to that user's name in SharePoint. That indicator shows whether the user is online at the moment. If so, the user needing the checked-out document could initiate an IM session directly from the SharePoint site to request that the document be checked in. If not, the user could send the request via e-mail.	• Online presence requires that SharePoint be integrated with an enterprise communication application such as Live Communication Server, Office Communication Server, or Microsoft's new Lync Server product. • The user must have one of Microsoft's IM clients installed. These are Office Communicator, MSN Messenger, Windows Live Messenger, or Windows Messenger. • Online presence can only be enabled at the web application level. Individual sites or site collections inherit this setting from the web application they reside in.

Service Name	Description	Considerations
		• Online presence can be complicated in an extranet scenario since some users may not be part of the organization's IM infrastructure.
Social Media	Social networking is supported by several features within SharePoint. These can be enabled or disabled as needed.	• Determine which features will be supported and disable any that will not.
	• *Ratings*: Allows users to rate the content on the site using a point scale such as "5 stars!"	• Training users on the use of these features is vital to getting the most value from them.
	• *Tags*: Allows users to associate keywords with content items. This is a type of free form metadata that users can use to bookmark, search for, and share information.	
	• *Colleagues*: Allows a user to identify other users with similar interests or responsibilities within the organization. A user can track their colleagues' portal contributions and receive alerts for events that affect them. They can share their colleague list to enhance the social network within the organization.	
	• *Blogs and Wikis*: Allow users to create self-published news feeds and informational sites.	

Composites

These services provide users with the ability to create composite applications. These are solutions that draw from multiple technologies and data sources. (See Table 4-4.)

Table 4-4. Composites Services

Service Name	Description	Considerations
Sandboxed Applications	The sandbox service (or User Code Service) allows user-generated executable code to run safely within the SharePoint environment. This feature is used to allow non-IT departments to develop custom solutions for their needs and deploy them safely to the portal. This feature is also used in multi-tenant environments to isolate code associated with different tenants.	• See Chapter 13 for details on managing sandboxed solutions within the farm. • Sandboxed solutions can be enabled or disabled at the site collection level. • Sandboxed solutions can be allocated limited computing resources to prevent them from impacting the farm as a whole. • Sandboxed solutions can only access data within the site collection to which they are deployed. • Sandboxed solutions that are deemed safe can be redeployed at the farm level for use throughout the farm. • The resources consumed by sandboxed solutions can be monitored in detail allowing for chargebacks to other departments.
Custom Business Process Automation	SharePoint provides the ability to automate custom business processes using workflows and custom data entry forms. A workflow might be triggered by an event such as editing a document or a document passing its expiration date. A typical workflow consists of a series of tasks to be performed by various users. Data can be collected in custom data entry forms and many types of actions can be executed as a result. • *Windows Workflow (WF)*: Workflows are implemented using the .NET workflow engine (WF). SharePoint acts as the host application for the workflow engine. • *InfoPath Forms Services*: This service application renders InfoPath forms using HTML and manages the user's interactions with the form.	• Workflow and InfoPath forms can be enabled and disabled using features in SharePoint. • Web-based InfoPath forms require the InfoPath Forms Services application to be configured. Otherwise, the user must have InfoPath loaded on their desktop in order to use the form. • The security restrictions imposed on web-based forms may make them unsuitable for certain situations. • SharePoint Designer access must be enabled in order to use SPD to create workflow definitions. Definitions created in a development environment can be published to a production environment that does not permit Designer access using a solution package as described in Chapter 13.

Service Name	Description	Considerations
	• *Workflow Design*: Workflows can be designed directly within SharePoint using SharePoint Designer (SPD) 2010 or in Visual Studio. Visual Studio workflows can be more complex than workflows created in SPD and are often deployed using solution packages. See Chapter 13. • *InfoPath Designer*: InfoPath Designer allows users to create custom data entry forms that include logic and access to other data sources. See Chapter 12.	• More complex state-machine workflows can be created only in Visual Studio. These are best created by professional developers. • SharePoint's built-in workflows for approval and collaboration can be used as a starting point for custom workflows. They can be copied and edited as needed.
External Data Integration	SharePoint 2010 implements an enhanced set of tools for integrating external data, such as relational tables, into the SharePoint environment. • *Business Connectivity Services (BCS)*: This service application allows outside data to be mapped into the SharePoint environment. This data can be read and written through the browser interface or the SharePoint API. All access permissions in the data source are enforced in SharePoint as well. • *External Content Types*: This is a specialized SharePoint content type that contains the information needed to interface with the external data. • *External List*: This is a new SharePoint list template that supports external content types and provides the user interface for accessing external data.	• SharePoint 2010 contains far better tools for working with external data than did SharePoint 2007. Specifically, no external tools or XML coding are required to build BDC data models for SharePoint 2010. • The external data accessed is never stored in SharePoint's content databases. BCS provides a seamless pass-through to the external data source. • SharePoint 2007's Business Data Catalog (BDC) is now a layer under the Business Connectivity Services (BCS) application in SharePoint 2010. • Write access to external data may cause problems in the external data source. These actions should be carefully evaluated before implementation. • An external list hosting BCS data is like any other list in SharePoint in most respects. It can be accessed through any of the office applications, through web services, and from other locations within SharePoint. • The items in an external list appear as content within SharePoint. As a result, they can be included in search indexes and results. • BCS can access data from virtually any data source including most relational database systems, web services and data accessed through custom coded .NET assemblies that act as connectors.

Insights

These services enable enterprise data to be visualized and analyzed using advanced interactive tools (see Table 4-5).

Table 4-5. Insights Services

Service Name	Description	Considerations
Business Intelligence Dashboards	Dashboards provide a quick, intuitive means for users to access enterprise data and make decisions. A typical dashboard (Figure 4-4) contains one or more pages of charts, graphs, Key Performance Indicators, images, and custom components to present business data that can be interactively filtered and explored. This allows the user to perform ad-hoc analysis on the data using a simple web-based interface. SharePoint Server 2010 contains three primary subsystems for creating this type of dashboard: • *Excel Services*: Allows users to publish Microsoft Excel spreadsheets to SharePoint libraries that can be imbedded in web pages within SharePoint sites. SharePoint can render the entire spreadsheet or only certain items such as charts or graphs. Spreadsheet calculations occur within the Excel Calculation Service hosted within SharePoint. • *Visio Services*: Allows users to create Microsoft Visio diagrams that can be published to SharePoint libraries. These diagrams can be embedded in site pages. Visio supports binding these diagrams to enterprise data to modify shape colors, labels, and other *Data Graphics* objects. This is a powerful way to present complex data. • *PerformancePoint Services (PPS)*: PPS was previously a separate Microsoft server product, but it has now been folded into SharePoint 2010. PerformancePoint is used to build BI dashboards as described above.	• While creating and publishing Excel and Visio documents can be accomplished by users with minimal training, creating PerformancePoint dashboards requires more technical development skills: • For advanced business users, the organization's IT department may be able to create a library of reusable dashboard components that users can assemble into fully functional dashboards. • The data sources used to connect dashboards to backend data, such as relational databases, require security credentials. These should be designed to promote ease of use and reuse while maintaining the security of the data. • The data connection library template is the preferred location to store secure data connection information. • Not all Excel and Visio documents can be published. There are restrictions on the features that can be rendered on a web page. Documents that use those features can still be stored in SharePoint but they cannot be embedded in a page.

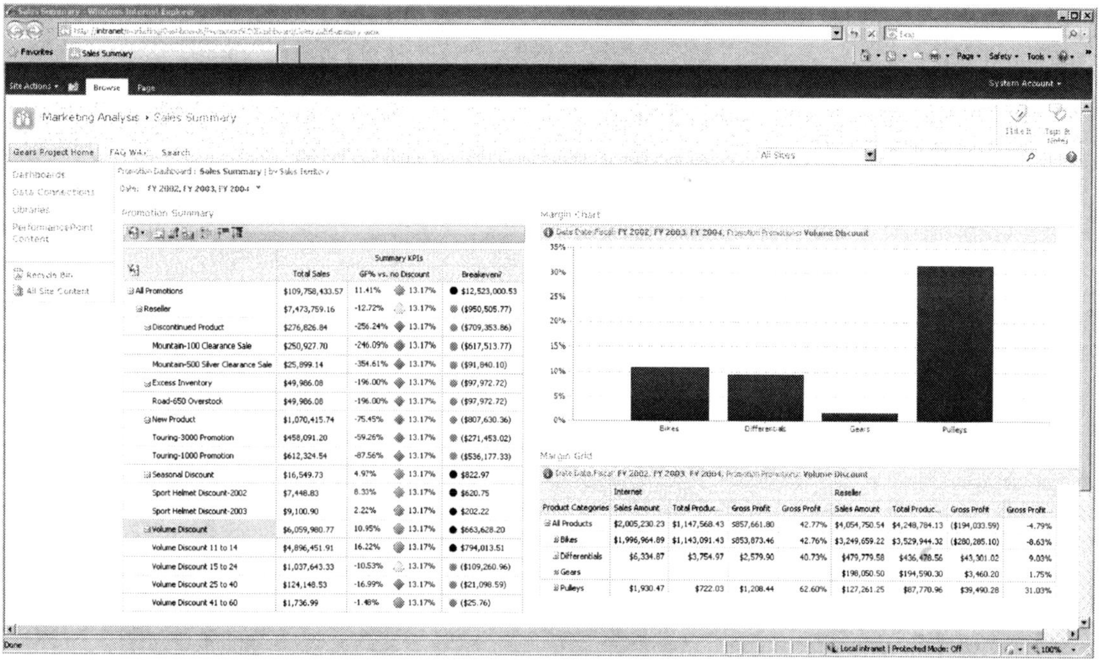

Figure 4-4. A dashboard for business intelligence

Search

SharePoint's search capabilities extend well beyond the portal itself. SharePoint search can include content from other web sites, network file shares, Exchange folders, and more (see Table 4-6).

Table 4-6. Search Services

Service Name	Description	Considerations
Farm-Level Search Functionality	The SharePoint 2010 product family has three separate implementations of search. These are available in various product SKUs. The important thing is to identify which search engine is appropriate for your situation. • *SharePoint 2010 Foundation Search*: This is a very basic search engine that is part of the SharePoint Foundation product. This search engine only indexes data within the local SharePoint server farm's content databases. It is intended for small departmental SharePoint deployments.	• SharePoint SKUs that include the FAST search option are significantly more expensive than standard licenses. • The type of search engine to deploy depends on the type and location of the content being indexed and the total volume of that data. • SharePoint server with the enterprise search engine will be appropriate for most company intranets and extranets. • Very large company intranets or public-facing Internet sites may find the features of FAST search attractive.

Service Name	Description	Considerations
	• *SharePoint 2010 Enterprise Search*: This search engine is designed for enterprise-wide deployments. This is the search engine included with the SharePoint Server 2010 product SKUs. Enterprise search can index content within SharePoint or elsewhere in the organization. It is intended for small to medium scale intranets. • *SharePoint 2010 FAST Search*: The FAST search engine is a recent addition to the SharePoint product line. This search engine is designed for massive scale and high performance. FAST also supports search provider federation which can be used to integrate results from other search services into SharePoint.	• The basic SharePoint Foundation search engine will not be appropriate for any but the most basic SharePoint installation.
Managed Metadata	SharePoint's managed metadata service provides a central location to define terms for the organization. These terms can be used to identify, organize, and navigate the content of the farm. These properties also become valuable keys for locating data through search.	• Establish standards for creating metadata term sets. These can form the basis of a shared language across the enterprise. • Term sets can be associated with site column and content type definitions that can also be centrally managed. • Metadata can be used to automatically generate navigation menus within the SharePoint interface. This allows users to navigate to content based on its meaning rather than its location within the portal.
Audience Targeting	A badly underused feature of SharePoint is the audience targeting of content. This allows the system to deliver the most relevant content to each user automatically. An audience is a set of users in the system. The members of an audience can be specified directly, much like a SharePoint group's members, or through the use of rules based on the user's profile properties.	• *Audience targeting is not a security feature.* No content is protected or exposed based on its audience targeting properties. Content that is not targeted to a user can still be accessed using normal site navigation. Only setting permissions on an item will prevent it from being accessed. • Create a standard list of audiences and the criteria for membership. Publish this list and encourage users to specify audiences when publishing new content.

Service Name	Description	Considerations
	For example, all users in the IT department could be part of the "IT" audience. Users that have listed an interest in playing in the company softball league could be in the "Softball" audience. Audiences are periodically evaluated to update their membership based on the rules for the audience. SharePoint has a set of Web Parts that are specifically designed to scan the portal for items of interest to the audiences to which the current user belongs. All SharePoint Web Parts have the ability to appear or disappear from a web page based on whether the current user is in a specified audience.	• Audiences are updated based on a timer job that can be scheduled to run whenever needed. Running this job is resource intensive so it is best done when the system is not being heavily used. • The default home page for each portal site can be designed to bring out the most relevant content to the user. Use SharePoint's built-in targeting web parts to create a user-relevant dashboard for each portal site on its home page. Other site pages can be used to present specific data when the user explicitly requests it. • Lists and libraries need to have audience targeting enabled before users will be able to target content items to audiences.

Prioritize Services

Now it is time to plan the deployment of the features to be supported on the portal. Your governance team has compiled a list of mandatory services and a list of optional services. The next step is to determine which services will be supported immediately after the launch of the site.

At first, the impulse to say "I want it all!" may be overwhelming. However, there are several reasons why it may be a good idea to roll out services over time instead of all at once. Consider these items when planning the order and release schedule for your services:

- Mandatory services have to be deployed when the portal is initially deployed.

- Training IT staff and users on all of the features being deployed may be unrealistic. Rolling out features that aren't ready to be supported or used is a recipe for failure.

- There is a trade-off between time to market and functionality. Implementing more functionality in the initial rollout will necessarily delay that rollout.

- Governance-related tasks such as collecting requirements, establishing policies and standards, negotiating SLAs, and deploying monitoring tools need to be factored into the timeline of the deployment of each service.

- It is often a good idea to target the features in the first release toward a specific set of highly-motivated users. These are the users that are most eager to use the system and will reap the biggest "quick win" for the organization.

- The initial deployment will create a multitude of lessons learned. By rolling out services over time you allow the IT staff, users, and governance team members to learn from their challenges (a.k.a. mistakes, problems, errors, and boo-boos).

- Some services require the presence of other services in order to function. If a feature is included in a release, all services upon which it depends must be included in that release or an earlier one.

Once the order of deployment is determined and a rough timeline is projected for each, it should be possible to spot a good cutoff point for the initial deployment. For example, if adding a group of services will delay the launch of the portal by a month or two, it may make sense to release without them and add them into the portal down the road.

The governance team will need to consult with users, business owners, and technical staff to determine the best way to achieve value quickly and sustainably. The goal is to deliver functionality at the moment the business is ready to leverage it. Deploying features too early can result in poor adoption and wasted resources. Deploying services after they are needed can result in angry users, lost opportunities and the unwanted substitution of another solution for the problem. This last result can also cause poor adoption and a waste of resources.

Planning for Implementation

When implementing a new service you must determine what components will be needed and how they will be deployed. This includes acquiring these components and planning the installation procedures to ensure the deployment goes smoothly.

If custom components are to be created, lead time will be required for developing and testing those components. A project manager or project management office can be very helpful in these cases. See Chapters 12, 13, and 14 for details about managing the development of custom solutions for SharePoint.

Many services require the integration of third-party products. These need to be purchased prior to setting up the stage environment for functional testing. The stage environment is a good place to practice installing these products. While a third-party product will always come with installation instructions, those instructions are not designed to account for the unique requirements of your portal.

A new service may introduce new security or regulatory requirements. These need to be documented and understood before deployment. Any new business processes that must be established to ensure compliance must be implemented as part of the service rollout even if they exist outside of SharePoint.

When rolling out new services, the portal's capacity plan should be updated as well. The service may generate large loads on the servers or large amounts of content that will need to be stored. If new hardware will be required to support the new service, in addition to the existing site, that hardware should be deployed before or in conjunction with the new service. Always try to take a proactive approach to farm performance.

Last, you need to consider how long the service will take to implement. There are two parts to this question. The first comes before deployment. This involves all of the planning and development we have discussed up to now plus the planning we will discuss in the following sections. All of this must be done before touching the production configuration. Also, a release date should be scheduled that includes time for communication, training, and any downtime that is required. Some types of services may require significant downtime while others may not require any.

Planning for Monitoring

To effectively govern a SharePoint portal, it is necessary to understand how it is being used. Chapter 7 discusses the monitoring tools that are available within SharePoint. When planning a new service in your farm, think about the following:

- What needs to be monitored? These may include performance counters, event logs, SharePoint logs, disk files, database sizes, and so on.

- Monitor usage and capacity continuously. Establish a baseline and monitor the growth of usage, computing resources, and storage volume consumed by the service.

- What level of usage is expected? If the service is more or less successful than expected, how will the governance team know?

- Create user feedback mechanisms as part of the initial deployment of the service. Do not try to collect feedback only after a problem has been noticed. Leverage SharePoint's built-in tools like content ratings, social media, and surveys.

- Instruct the help desk on how to relay important user problems to the appropriate personnel quickly.

Planning for Maintenance

Maintaining a portal service is similar in many respects to maintaining any IT system.

The first and most important consideration is protecting the organization's data. This means creating a backup schedule and testing restoration procedures frequently. Most of SharePoint's built-in services store their data within SharePoint's content databases. The principal exception is the search feature. SharePoint Search uses additional databases and index files that are not part of the content databases in SharePoint. While it is usually possible to re-create this information by recrawling the content source, restoring the file from a backup is often more time and cost effective.

Microsoft releases upgrades and patches on a more or less regular basis. The governance plan should assign the responsibility to monitor these releases regularly as they are posted on Microsoft's sites. Testing published updates in a stage environment is always preferable to deploying them in production first. The same is true for updates to any third-party products deployed in the farm.

Custom-built solution packages will also need to be upgraded from time to time. Chapter 13 contains a discussion on the technical aspects of creating upgradable solutions. Once the updated components are created, they should be tested and deployed like any other updates to the farm.

Just like service deployments, updates may require downtime for proper installation. Establishing and communicating maintenance schedules and outage windows to the portal's users will prevent many issues over time.

Planning for Decommissioning

When a service is no longer needed, a plan should be created for decommissioning the service. Normally, this detailed planning isn't done until the service has been identified for removal. During the initial implementation of the service, there are a few items that need to be considered and documented to support the possible need to decommission the service later:

- Where is all of the data for the service stored? Is it only in SharePoint's content databases or are there other databases and files involved?

- How can the service's data be archived or dumped into another form for later use? For example, does it make sense to dump the data to a series of Excel spreadsheets or some other type of file?

- What data migration tools exist to move the data from the old service into a new location or service? What APIs are available to support the creation of such tools if needed in the future?

- Once the service is decommissioned, what storage space or other resources can be reclaimed? How would those resources be reclaimed?

Summary

In this chapter, you have

- Learned how identifying services allows you to divide and conquer the tasks associated with governing the portal.

- Explored the different types of services that may be required and how to identify their requirements.

- Discussed how to prioritize services for implementation.

- Examined the considerations associated with the implementation of a new service in SharePoint.

- Discussed the process of planning for the monitoring of a service.

- Explored the options for upgrading and maintaining a service within a production environment.

- Looked at the considerations surrounding the decommissioning of a service.

CHAPTER 5

User Training and Adoption

This chapter will examine how to get users actively involved in the portal, both as consumers of information (visitors) and as producers of content (contributors). Having a well-managed portal is only half the battle. The more important task is getting people to use it.

Telling users that this new portal is great and will make their lives better is a good way to get their attention, but it will not hold it long enough for them to log in the first time. Telling users that "this is the way we do things now, so use it" might work briefly in some organizations, but experience has shown that users have a greater capacity to resist unwelcome change than management has to impose it.

What you need to do, and what we will seek to do in this chapter, is to create real motivation and enthusiasm for the potential of the portal for the business and individual users.

What Will You Learn in This Chapter?

- Why users sometimes resist using a new resource like SharePoint

- How to create a plan for driving adoption of the portal within the organization

- How to set goals for user adoption of a new portal

- Which high-level strategies have been shown to work well when introducing a new or dramatically upgraded portal experience to users

- How to create a formal communication plan for managing the interactions between the governance team, end users, and the staff that support the portal

- What types of communication strategies lend themselves to a SharePoint portal deployment

- How to create a training plan for creating the necessary skill sets within the organization

- How to identify training methods and content appropriate to different sets of users

- How to effectively deliver training to end users

- How to plan for supporting users in a production environment and collecting feedback for the governance team

Driving Adoption

In this chapter we are going to examine how to create a comprehensive plan for driving users to adopt the new SharePoint solution. As with so many other aspects of governance, you will see that adoption planning is a continuous process that feeds back upon itself, as shown in Figure 5-1.

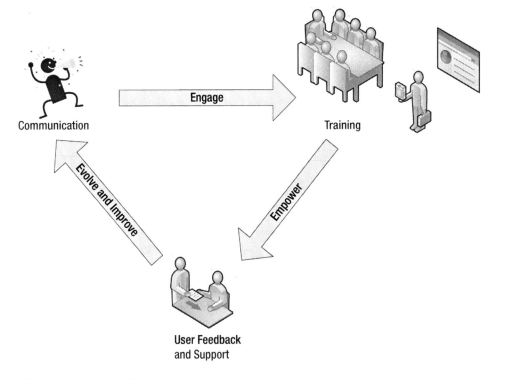

Figure 5-1. Driving adoption

To persuade anyone to do anything the first step is to communicate. In this case, you need to communicate the value of the new system to the prospective users. This includes creating awareness of the solution and its features and the benefits it will bring to individuals and the business as a whole. To some extent this is a simple statement of facts but it also has to include elements of salesmanship or cheer leading. It is not enough that users simply know the system exists; they have to *want* to use it.

This communication creates engagement within the user community. The next step is to turn that engagement into a desire to build skills around the solution. SharePoint is a web-based solution and is, therefore, quite simple to use if all the user is doing is reading information. However, if the user is going to truly leverage the system and create value, they will need a somewhat deeper understanding of how the system can benefit them.

These skills empower the user to contribute content and grow the solution. As the portal and its content expand and become a more integral part of the company's fabric, it will need to evolve and respond to the needs of the users as they change. This is the point at which collecting and respecting user feedback becomes critical. The governance team will use this information to update the services offered by the portal and the policies and standards that go into governing it.

To achieve this type of positive feedback loop, the governance team needs to establish plans for communicating with, providing timely and effective training to, and supporting end users as they adopt the solution provided. We will examine some possible strategies and tactics for making this happen. We will also show you how to create a formal communication plan and design a training program that will support the adoption effort.

Why Users Stay Away

One of the most common problems when deploying a new SharePoint portal is a lack of adoption. *Adoption* refers to the rate at which users begin actively using the solution and, therefore, realizing the value it returns to the organization. A lack of adoption occurs when users refuse to try the features of the new portal, or else try or even use them for a time, and then abandon the portal in favor of another solution. After the time and expense put into deploying a full-featured portal solution, this type of problem can cause the entire project to be deemed a failure. Why would users choose to ignore the tools that have been provided to them?

There are several possible causes for this resistance but most can be described as *organizational inertia*. This is the dark side of having a strong corporate culture. Every organization has a culture. These are the traditions, practices, and preferences that have been developed over time for handling the processes and issues faced by the group. These prejudices must be addressed before widespread adoption can be expected. Ideally, you want to mold the solution to the existing culture to make the transition as painless as possible. Remember, change is hard.

Even if the new portal is not replacing an older solution, the processes and content to be hosted on the site probably already exist elsewhere in the organization. The new solution has to compete with the known solution before it can even be evaluated on its own merit. Even when the existing solution is deemed poor, or nonexistent, getting users to eagerly embrace change can be difficult.

Often, collaboration tools like SharePoint are regarded as just another management fad. Experienced employees will perceive a similarity between the new solution and something the organization tried last year . . . and the year before . . . and the year before . . . and so on. Why bother learning this tool when it will just be gone in a few weeks or months like all the others? The governance team has to get out the message that this solution has the backing of top management and failure is not an option.

Another common issue affecting adoption is a lack of awareness among prospective users as to the advantages and benefits accruing to the new tool. SharePoint is a complex tool with many features and options. New users do not usually know what those features are or how they can be leveraged to improve their day-to-day work processes. It is easy to become overwhelmed when first encountering SharePoint because of the myriad of menus, pages, and options available to different types of users. Getting good information into the hands of the right users is critical to creating a natural migration of users and content into the portal. We will discuss strategies for delivering this information and packaging it so that it can be easily consumed by busy users.

The lack of timely follow-through from training to usage can also become an obstacle to adoption. That is, when users acquire the newly required skills, they need to apply those skills within a limited period of time or they will be lost. How many times have you attended a week-long training class only to realize a month later that you haven't used anything you learned and you don't even remember what you were taught? We will discuss the timing of user training to ensure that skills are acquired just in time to be useful. This will help to ensure that they are also permanent.

In short, adoption is all about motivation. You need to make the new solution more attractive than any previous solution or process that existed. This means not only building a better set of tools, but creating the perception that these tools really are better and worth the time to learn. In this chapter we are going to look at a structured way to plan for adoption as well as a number of specific techniques that have proven successful in the past.

Goals for Adoption

To begin developing your adoption strategy, you need to lay out some goals. As discussed before, when creating goals it is important to be S.M.A.R.T. about it. The adoption goals set by the governance team need to be *specific, measurable, achievable, relevant,* and *timely.* While these goals will necessarily be unique to each situation, there are some common themes to keep in mind:

- You need to win the hearts and minds of users. Your ultimate goal is to make the portal the place where users naturally to go to find and share information.

- You want to engage users early to begin using and contributing to the portal. Getting a continuous flow of fresh content into the portal will go a long way toward engaging users' interest.

- The portal's content should continue to grow and evolve as the users find new and innovative ways to use it. Be sure that this progress is measured and communicated back to the user community.

- Do not forget why the portal was implemented in the first place. The organization identified a problem to be solved and implemented this solution in the hopes of delivering a return on its investment (ROI).

The portal needs to show a return on investment, but there are two parts to the ROI of a portal. The *quantitative ROI* comes from the time and money saved by the use of the system. This may be an increase in productivity or the ability to complete some process that was not possible in the past. This type of ROI can be difficult to measure but there are many tools and known techniques for doing so.

To drive user adoption there needs to be a *qualitative ROI* as well. This comes from making life better and easier for the users. This is a return on the investment the users make in learning and adapting to a new way of doing business.

It isn't always true that "if you build it, they will come." You stand a much better chance of getting people in the door on a hot day if you have good air conditioning. The goal of your adoption plan will be to ensure that everyone knows that you now have air conditioning!

Adoption Strategies

In this section we will explore some high-level strategies that can be used to promote adoption of the system. These are general techniques for structuring the overall approach for driving adoption. In the sections that follow we will describe some more tactical techniques for driving adoption in the communication and training plans for the site.

Start Small

A major hindrance to adoption is overwhelming the users with features they do not understand or that the organization is not prepared to support. SharePoint is a large (okay, huge!) product. Dumping the entire toolset on a group of unprepared users is like turning a bunch of children loose in a room full of dangerous power tools. The best that you can hope for is that no one touches anything.

Go back to the beginning when the new portal was first proposed. What was the thought process behind it? What problem was the organization trying to solve? Was there some type of content to be created or presented? Was there a regulation to be complied with? Was there a business process to be improved or automated? Once this set of problems has been identified, look for those that are causing the most pain for the organization or the users. These can become the "killer apps" for your portal. Solving these problems can produce the quick wins necessary to get adoption started.

Instead of trying to deploy every feature supported by the SharePoint platform, consider limiting the initial rollout. Find a few well-chosen features and a set of motivated end users to target the first release to. You may call this a "pilot project" or just "version 1." The important thing is to start small enough that success can be achieved and measured but big enough for success to be important to the users.

Below is an example of a plan for rolling out a typical portal environment for a large organization. In this case, publishing information to the entire organization is the primary goal. Collaboration features and business intelligence come into play later in the portal's lifecycle.

Phase 1: Publishing Focus

- *Branding and Navigation*: Establish the user interface.

- *Metadata Definition*: Create an information architecture.

- *Search*: Provide a convenient means of finding information throughout the organization.

- *Publishing*: Create workflows for approving and publishing content.

- *Audience Targeting*: Drive relevant data directly to the users that need it.

- *Enterprise and Divisional Portals*: Create content valuable to the entire organization.

- *Support for Departmental Portals*: Empower new parts of the organization to contribute on their own terms.

Phase 2: Collaboration Focus

- *Team Sites*: Allow users to contribute and collaborate on content.

- *Site Provisioning*: Provide users the ability to create their own collaboration areas without going through IT.

- *My Sites*: Give users a personal workspace to create and share information.

- *Online Presence*: Help users connect with one another more proactively. Make the portal a normal part of their daily routine.

- Social Media Features: Provide users with familiar tools for providing feedback and organizing content.

Phase 3: Business Process Improvement Focus

- Sandboxed Applications: Allow non-IT departments to create custom solutions for the portal.

- *Business Process Automation*: Leverage forms and workflows to automate custom business processes.

- *Records Management*: Manage documents for compliance and e-Discovery.

- *Business Intelligence Dashboards*: Allow users to perform interactive analysis using data from throughout the enterprise.

Rolling out manageable functionality incrementally will help users become comfortable with the solution at their own pace. Go for the quick win by identifying and targeting your organization's killer app.

Leverage Existing Data

As we can attest, nothing is scarier than a blank page. When a SharePoint portal is initially installed it is just an empty vessel waiting to be filled with content. At that moment, it provides very little, if any, value to the organization. Consider ways to maximize the value of the portal by loading up the content your company already has.

Any organization consisting of more than one person has collaborative data. It may be in e-mails, file shares, web sites, or some other type of information sharing system like Lotus Notes or a previous version of SharePoint. Loading this data into your new environment brings immediate value and relevance to both the portal and the data. The goal is to begin diverting the flow of information through the portal instead of less productive systems.

For example, e-mails tend to proliferate inconsistent copies of documents across the organization and conversations carried out via e-mail tend to vanish as soon as the conversation is over. By storing documents in SharePoint and sending links via e-mail, a central repository is created that helps manage versions and create consistency. Collaborative conversation spaces such as document and meeting workspaces, wikis, blogs, and discussion groups enable users to carry on these conversations in a more functional and durable manner.

When considering the migration of existing data, you need to consider how users find, create, and update that data. SharePoint's search functionality is a natural fit for finding data, but which data should be loaded? How should it be updated?

Here are some tips for using data migration to drive your adoption strategy:

- Evaluate each source system separately. The data migration tools available will vary as will the organization's need to find and update the data.

- Clean source data before loading it into SharePoint. This involves reorganizing data, removing duplicate data, creating metadata, and assessing relevance and size. There will never be a better time to *not* load data.

- SharePoint Enterprise Search has the ability to index information from many sources in many formats. These documents can be made available in search results without being physically moved into SharePoint.

- Consider migrating only the most recently updated content into SharePoint. Older data can still be accessed through the search feature until it is no longer needed.

- Once data is migrated into SharePoint, the old system should either be decommissioned or set into a read-only mode. Ensure that all new content is created in SharePoint, not the old system. Otherwise, the old system will never be able to go away.

By helping users find all of their data and making new and updated content easy to access, SharePoint can become the focus of the users' routine. Find ways to encourage new content to be created only in SharePoint.

Provide Incentives and Recognition

A good way to create engagement is by providing positive incentives for using the system. The details depend on the corporate culture of your business. Do your users respond to tangible or intangible benefits? Is public recognition highly valued? Do people respond more to prizes or a pat on the back?

There are many ways to provide incentives through SharePoint. The possibilities are limited only by your creativity. To target many different types of users, consider mixing and matching these types of initiatives. This should be a continuous project to help re-engage users on a continual basis.

The following sections look at some suggestions or programs to try. You can also look on open source sites such as CodePlex and SourceForge for pre-built components for these and other programs.

The Scavenger Hunt

Create a scavenger hunt where users are challenged to answer a series of questions based on the information available in the portal. These questions should make the user explore the site and try out features such as navigation, search, My Sites, and social computing. Give a prize for the individual or team that submits the most correct answers in a given time period or the first to answer all questions. These types of programs are often coordinated by Human Resources or a social committee within the organization. Try to leverage these existing groups whenever possible.

Most Popular Content (by Rating)

Use SharePoint 2010's content rating features to have users rate the content throughout the portal. On the portal's home page, create a web part that displays the highest rated content on the site. Be sure to prominently include the name of the contributor for each piece of content. This provides a listing of the site's most valuable content and recognition for the contents creators.

Most Popular Content (by Usage)

Create a listing similar to the one described above based on the usage data collected by SharePoint. This will show users where other users are frequently going to find information even if they have not explicitly rated it.

Most Active Team Sites

Again, use usage data to create a listing of the most active team sites in the portal. This will give those teams recognition for leveraging the power of SharePoint's collaboration tools.

Most Active Contributor

Create a listing of the users that have made the greatest number of new or updated content submissions. These are your true power users and they are your most valuable resource. Be sure to recognize them and cultivate their enthusiasm.

Most Active Social Tagger

SharePoint's social tagging feature allows users to add freeform metadata to content items. This information can be leveraged by other users as well. Recognize those users that contribute this type of content enhancement.

Weekly "Kudos" Recognition

Give users an easy way to nominate their coworkers for a kudos award or a pat on the back. List these prominently on the site's home page so that everyone knows what a star they are. These kudos are not necessarily for anything having to do with the portal. It is just for anything someone does to help some-one else get their job done.

Best Practices Recognition

Recognize innovative end users for coming up with new ways to use the portal. The governance team can collect these ideas from IT, end users, or anywhere else feedback is collected. Those ideas that can be of use to everyone should be promoted and encouraged.

Success Stories or "Wins"

Similar to best practices, success stories describe how users are benefiting from the use of the portal. Communicating these stories provides encouragement and recognition across the organization.

Rolling Display of Incentive Programs

All of the above ideas can be used together without overloading the portal's home page by creating a Web Part that displays one or two of these results at a time. Each time the home page is hit, or perhaps on a timer, a different recognition program's results can be presented.

Communication Plan

Any complex project needs to have a plan for communicating important information to its stakeholders. The governance team will establish a communication plan for the purpose of ensuring that the right information is delivered to the right individuals at the right time. For a SharePoint portal, the communi-cation plan can also help drive adoption by keeping the governance team and user community engaged with one another.

As an integral, ever-changing part of the organization, it is important that communication about the portal be timely and ongoing.

Before the site is launched, the communication plan can help build awareness of and excitement for the coming solution. This message will create the momentum needed to ensure a smooth and produc-tive launch for the site.

At launch time, the communication plan can help drive the initial training of contributors. The mes-saging delivered at this time should also aim to bring new users to the site to become acquainted with its value. The goal is to turn excitement into engagement so that users will actively explore the site.

Once the site is in place, the communication plan should help maintain and grow the value, both real and perceived, being delivered to the organization. By continuously drawing users' attention to new features and content, these communications can help users expand their use of the system. Promoting new or existing features will create more opportunities for users to create content and find new ways to collaborate with their coworkers.

The types of messages to be delivered by the governance team through the communication plan will vary greatly depending on the nature of the site and the culture of the organization. Common topics will include new features and content, upgrade and maintenance plans, requests for user feedback, best practices, training opportunities, and general information regarding the policies and standards pub-lished by the governance team.

The communication plan for a SharePoint site is really no different than that of any other project or corporate initiative. To help drive adoption, it should include elements that promote the portal and its value to the individual users. It should also obey the basic requirements of any large-scale communi-cation strategy; it should be tailored to its audience and cover the who, what, when, why, and how of each topic.

Communication Strategies

As part of the overall adoption plan, the communication plan implements some of the tactical details associated with the adoption strategies discussed earlier in this chapter. In this section, we will show you some of the ways the communication plan can be leveraged to support the portal's adoption strategy.

Most medium-to-large organizations already have one or more departments that specialize in communicating with stakeholders in the organization. These may include Human Resources, Marketing, and others. Leverage these skills and communication channels to effectively deliver the governance team's message. Look for opportunities to piggyback on existing corporate communications such as weekly or monthly newsletters, distribution lists, and so on.

Engage management to help deliver the message that the portal provides value to users and the organization. The portal's executive sponsor should already be engaged in the governance effort. Use this resource to engage other executives to include messaging in their presentations and corporate communications.

Tailor the message to the audience receiving it. Do not overwhelm users with large numbers of communications or lengthy e-mails. Users are busy and will only read a communication as long as its value to them outweighs the inconvenience of reading it. Target communications to users for whom they are most relevant. SharePoint's audience targeting features are an excellent way to prevent your most important messages from getting lost in the noise of the users' everyday work.

Use fun and interesting activities to engage the hearts and minds of users. Creating incentives that encourage users to engage with the portal will make the adoption process much more effective. The goal is to make the system a positive force in their environment.

Be sure to trumpet your successes. When an initiative or upgrade is successful make sure everyone knows it. When someone comes up with a new way to use the portal, promote it, and be sure to give them credit.

Lead adoption by example. Encourage users to naturally reroute their collaborations through the portal by making it the default choice for your own communications. Publish news and announcements to the portal instead of sending e-mail or posting a notice in the break room. When an e-mail is necessary, include a link back to the portal instead of including the details in the e-mail. Never send documents in e-mails. Instead, post them to the portal and provide a link. Have the executive sponsor and all members of the governance team do the same.

Document Template

There are many sample communication plans available online. The outline below represents one possible template for such a plan.

- **Vision and Scope**

- **Goals**

  - To monitor the communication events completed

  - To gain feedback on communication events

  - To improve communications processes

- **Guiding Principles**

  - The high-level framing decisions that describe the communication strategy to be used

- **Communication Strategies and Methods**

  - Details the general responsibilities for carrying out the communication plan

- Describes the role of the governance team in crafting the messages to be delivered
- Describes the preferred communication channels to be used for delivering the message
- **Communication Stakeholders**
    - Identifies each stakeholder by name, department, and role
    - Describes the information needs of each stakeholder
    - Identifies each stakeholder's preferred method of communication
- **Implementation Plan**
    - Includes a high-level schedule of milestones to be achieved in implementing the plan
    - Details the budget, material, and personnel resources available for carrying out the communication plan
    - Describes the various tools used to create and deliver the messages to be conveyed
- **Communication Events (Action Plan)**
    - Identifies each type of communication that needs to occur
    - Details a specific set of goals and techniques to be used
    - See "Communication Events" below
- **Evaluation Criteria**
    - Describe measurable criteria to determine the progress and effectiveness of the plan after implementation

Communication Events

The communication plan will lead to the implementation of many different types of communication events. These events will be designed to deliver a single message to a single audience to achieve a certain set of goals. This part of the plan is often a list of events formatted similar to the examples in Table 5-1.

Table 5-1. Communication Events

Event	• System Maintenance Announcement (temporary site outage expected).
Timing	• Outages to be scheduled on the third Saturday of each month, as needed. • Sent three days prior to the outage. • Resent on the day of the outage.
Goals	• To ensure that users are aware of a pending outage. • To allow users to voice concerns prior to the outage. • To allow users to make any accommodations that needs to be made in response to the outage.
Target Audience	• All users
Message(s) to Convey	• This outage is routine, necessary, and well-planned. • No data will be lost. • The system will be restored as rapidly as possible.
Method(s)	• Post a notice on the portal's home page. • Send notice in an e-mail.
Responsible Resource(s)	• IT–System Administration

Event	• Initial Notice of Proposed New Feature.
Timing	• Sent when new feature has been identified by the steering committee.
Goals	• To gauge the level of user interest in the proposed feature. • To solicit feedback on requirements. • To identify pilot users.
Target Audience	• All users (or primary feature audience)
Message(s) to Convey	• The new feature is expected to create significant value for the company and individual users. • User feedback is needed and respected. • Users needed to help set requirements.
Method(s)	• Post a notice on the portal's home page. • Send an e-mail to relevant user management requesting involvement and feedback.
Responsible Resource(s)	• Steering Committee–Project Manager

These communication events will cover the gamut from routine outage notices to disaster recovery notifications. They will include topics such as upgrades, training, and incentive programs. Some events will occur regularly, such as planned outages and backups, while others will occur only as needed. Planning these communications ahead of time will allow them to occur in a predictable pattern that users can rely on to provide them with the information they need in a timely manner.

Training Plan

The next step in driving adoption of the portal is to ensure that all users have access to the information needed to make use of it. While SharePoint is designed to be easy to use for everyday information access, providing users with additional training is necessary to encourage active collaboration and content distribution.

In this section, we will discuss developing a strategy for providing training to users. This will include different levels of training for different roles that users may need to perform within the portal. We will also discuss different delivery channels and the best timing for delivering training.

Depending on how your organization is structured, the training plan may be a part of the communication plan or a separate document. It might also fall directly under the main governance plan. In any of these cases, the same decisions need to be made and documented. These decisions are the focus of this section.

Training Strategies

In developing the training strategy for the portal, consider that there will be many different users with the need to learn different things at different times. It is tempting to put together a week-long user training course that presents everything in one giant download of knowledge. Unfortunately, this is a very ineffective way to promote knowledge retention and therefore user adoption of the portal.

Experience suggests that users retain knowledge best when it is relevant to their immediate or near-term needs. Think of this as just-in-time training.

When users are first introduced to a new portal, the most important thing is for them to be able to find data. This implies that they need to see how to navigate the site, search for data, and understand the information resources that are available to them.

As they get more comfortable with the site they will need skills that enable them to contribute and structure information and collaborate with other users. These users may need to understand documents, metadata, wikis, and blogs. If they will be participating in SharePoint's publishing workflows they will need to understand their role in the approval process.

Some users will progress to the point of becoming power users, site owners, or content organizers. These users will need more specialized training. When scheduling the training for users, keep in mind what the nature of their interactions with the portal are and will soon become. Do not attempt to attempt to teach a novice user how to attach metadata to a new document. This information is of no use to someone who does not know where, how, or why to contribute such a document or even what *metadata* refers to.

The training resources provided need to match each user's learning style as well. Some users are quite comfortable sitting down with a technical manual and reading cover to cover. These users will be happy with any type of training offered. Unfortunately, they are the exception, not the rule.

Most users will have very limited time to invest and that investment needs to pay off quickly. This means you need to provide multiple channels that match their preferred style of learning. Some users will prefer a hands-on approach that uses a tutorial format to lead them step by step through a certain process. Others will want a task-based approach that offers the help they need at the moment they need it without leading them on unneeded tangents.

Users will have different roles within the organization and different levels of interest. Top executives are notorious for refusing to learn new IT tools. Find ways to engage these users without requiring them to learn skills beyond those normally associated with using a web browser. This leads to classifying users with different roles in the portal such as casual users, power users, and content organizers. We will discuss the training appropriate to these different audiences in the next section.

When designing training, remember that the goal is to help users leverage the tool to its fullest extent and value. Ensure that this training includes not only technical details of how to use the product in general but also the standards and practices that your organization has adopted through the governance plan. Engage the curiosity and desire to learn that most users naturally bring to this process even if they are not aware of it.

Audiences

The community of users of the portal can be broken down into many audiences. Each of these audiences will have a shared set of interests and needs with regard to the system. By identifying these audiences and creating training with their needs in mind, we can create a program that is optimized to minimize the time investment of users while maximizing the value they and the organization receive from it.

While the "audiences" we are referring to here are not the same as those used with SharePoint's audience targeting feature, there may well be some overlap in their definitions. Audience targeting can be very useful in delivering just-in-time information to end users while the go about their work.

The audiences we will define will be broken down into two dimensions: portal user roles and site user roles. These categories are somewhat arbitrary and your organization will very likely need to define more roles that correspond to the users in your environment. These listing are presented as a starting point for developing your customized training plan.

Portal User Roles

Portal user roles define the relationship between a user and the portal as a whole (see Table 5-2). These roles are generally aligned with the skill sets that the user has and how they use them to create, maintain, or manage content in the portal.

Table 5-2. Portal User Roles

Role	Description	Common Tasks	Skills Needed
Casual Users	Primarily use the portal to find and consume information only.	• Visit site pages. • Perform content searches. • Use social media features. • Contribute content. • Perform collaboration.	• Limited to using a web browser. • Should understand how to search and navigate the site.
Content Organizers (a.k.a. Content Stewards)	Contribute and assist in organizing content within the portal. Responsible for making information easy to find.	• Create new content areas including sites, lists and libraries. • Contribute content and assist users in updating metadata. • Consolidate repetitive or duplicated data. • Move content to the proper locations.	• All skills of casual users. • Understand and actively implement the information architecture used in the portal. • SharePoint Designer.

Role	Description	Common Tasks	Skills Needed
Power Users	Understand the deep functionality of the platform.	• Develop new ways to leverage the platform to create business value. • Mentor less sophisticated users. • Advocate for users when new features are needed.	• All skills of content organizers. • Create custom workflows and forms. • Package sandboxed solutions (usually without code). • SharePoint Designer. • InfoPath Designer.
Help Desk Resources	Responsible for answering questions from users.	• Answer calls and help desk tickets. • Ensure that the system is meeting users' needs. • Provide feedback to governance team about the performance of the system.	• Level 1: Same skills as a Content Organizer. • Level 2: Same skills as a Power User.
Farm Administrators	Responsible for the reliability and security of the portal.	• Install, configure, and monitor the SharePoint infrastructure. • Manage the security of the resources in the system. • Resolve level-3 help desk tickets related to site administration.	• SharePoint Central Administration web site. • Windows PowerShell. • Hardware and network infrastructure. • Monitoring tools. • Governance and Operational Plans.
Solution Developers	Responsible for custom functionality in the portal.	• Implement custom functionality. • Create solution packages for farm deployment. • Fix bugs and prepare upgrades to custom packages. • Resolve level 3 help desk tickets related to custom functionality.	• SharePoint application architecture and design. • SharePoint Designer. • InfoPath Designer. • Visual Studio. • Solution packaging and upgrades. • Governance and Application Lifecycle Management plans.

Site User Roles

Site user roles define the relationship between a user and a particular site or site collection (see Table 5-3). These roles are aligned with the user's need to contribute or manage data within a content container such as a site, list, or library.

Table 5-3. *Site User Roles*

Role	Description	Common Tasks
Visitors	Visit the site only to consume the information presented.	• View the content of the site using a web browser
Contributors	Contribute new or updated content to the site.	• Upload new content. • Update existing content. • Manage metadata on content. • Initiate content approval workflows to request publication of content (publishing sites only).
Designers	Design the look, feel, and content structure of the site (publishing sites only).	• Create lists and libraries. • Update page layouts. • Update local site navigation.
Approvers	Approve new content to be made available to visitors (publishing sites only).	• Participate in approval workflows to publish content.
Site Owners	Manage the security roles for all users within the site.	• Grant and revoke user permissions (roles) on the site. • Create subsites.
Site Collection Owners	Manage the security roles for all users within the site collection and for all sites within the collection.	• Grant and revoke user permissions (roles) on the sites in the collection. • Manage sandboxed solutions within the collection.

Levels of Training

As noted before, not all users need to understand every feature of SharePoint or the portal in order to use it effectively. Design training materials around the skills that need to be learned. Keep in mind the existing skills of the user and the roles the user will be playing in the portal.

The following sections describe some common levels of training that organizations often create.

Basic Portal Usage

This level of training is for users that have never used the portal before. Topics should include

- How to access the portal
- How to navigate from one content area to another
- How to search for information
- How to request help
- How to report a problem

Collaborating and Contributing Content

Once users are ready to move from consuming to producing content, this level of training should include

- How to upload new or updated documents
- How to use document versioning
- How to create new team sites and pages
- How to assign metadata to content
- How to use discussion boards

Using Social Media

If SharePoint's personalization and social media features are enabled in your environment, this level of training should include

- How to add and use content tags
- How to rate content
- How to access and use your personal site (My Site)
- How to use the colleagues feature to create a social network
- How to update wikis and blogs
- How to use online presence to connect with other users

Publishing Content to the Portal

This level of training only applies to users that will be contributors, designers, or approvers on sites that use SharePoint's publishing features. Topics should include

- How to create and update a publishing page
- How to submit content changes for approval
- How to design and use page layouts
- How to approve and schedule content for publication

Managing Security

Farm level security will be managed by farm administrators, but managing security on sites and site collections is often delegated to site owners within individual business units.

- Understanding site and site collection permissions
- How to create a SharePoint security group
- How to assign permissions and permission levels to users and groups
- How to assign appropriate permissions to different user roles
- How to manage sandboxed solutions within the site collection

Feature-Specific Training

Beyond these levels of training will be many sets of skills that apply only to users of certain features. For example, only users who need to create custom business processes will need to understand workflows and forms. Only users who will be using or creating business intelligence dashboards will need to understand how dashboards are constructed.

The sets of training required will vary based on the services deployed in your environment. When a new service is deployed (see Chapter 4), the training plan should be reviewed to ensure that any required training materials have been accounted for.

Delivery Strategies

Delivering training in a portal environment can often be difficult because users tend to be very busy. The intent of most portals is to make users more productive, so asking those users to cease being productive to learn about it can create an inherent conflict.

In the following sections, we will examine some strategies that can help optimize the delivery of training around your portal.

Remember the Basics

Training is a continuous, ongoing and recurring endeavor.

- As long as the portal exists, some form of training will be needed.
- New users will always need to be brought up to speed.
- Existing users' skills will always need to be updated and reinforced.

The timing of training is just as important as the content.

- Provide only the skills that are needed (no more, no less).
- Provide training at just the time the individual user needs it (no sooner, no later).
- Make training and review materials available to users for continuous self-study.

Use Multiple Channels

Because of the different roles, time-constraints, and learning styles of your users, it is unlikely that a single method of delivering training will be effective. Provide your users with a smorgasbord of training options to choose from. At a minimum, these should include

- *Personal Assistance*: This may include help desk support, lunch-and-learn presentations and user mentoring.
- *Formal Classroom Training*: While formal training is not appropriate for all cases, it still has its place.
- *Books and Documentation*: Many users, especially those with a technical bent, may prefer an impersonal approach for developing certain skills. These should be made available electronically at a minimum. Hard copies of some materials may also be appropriate. Some materials, such as your organization's governance plans, should be published and easy to find as well.

- *Online Resources*: We have described various options for delivering training information online including Tips of the Day, FAQs, user communities, and online tutorials. These are most effective when linked to relevant pages on the portal.

Providing users with ubiquitous training opportunities will improve their ability to acquire the skills they need to be successful. Using a variety of methods and formats for that training allows users to select the approach that is most valuable to them.

Focus on Convenience

Because most users can invest only limited time in developing the skills needed to leverage the portal, focus on making training as convenient as possible for them. This reduces the time needed to acquire skills thus increasing the individual return on that investment.

- *Lunch-and-Learn Sessions*: Schedule a half-hour session to present basic skills in an informal presentation. Note: Providing a free lunch is an excellent way to encourage participation.

- *Online Tutorials*: Buy or produce a set of 10 to 20 videos that teach an individual skill. These videos can be presented as links throughout the portal. These should be fun and helpful to the users.

- *Frequently Asked Questions (FAQs)*: FAQs are one of the oldest and most common forms of user training. That is because they work! By placing FAQs in SharePoint they can be automatically included in search results. A wiki is a good way to develop an FAQ since it allows users to contribute comments and new questions.

- *Cheat Sheets*: A simple one- or two-sided laminated sheet with simple instructions for common tasks.

- *Links from Content*: Within the portal's content, add links to training anywhere that users might need it. It is usually a good idea to deemphasize the links in some way, such as with a smaller font or less bold color. These links should be helpful, not annoying.

- *Create Custom Help Pages*: The SharePoint help system is designed to accept custom content. Consider using this feature to create help specific to the governance and information architecture of your portal.

- *Subject Matter Experts and Mentors*: Identify users that have the skills and attitude to become power users and mentors. These people can be identified by monitoring their contributions and use of social media. Treat them well. They are a valuable resource.

- *Social Media*: Create user communities, wikis, blogs, and any other technique already discussed to drive users to find their own answers or another user who can provide them.

It is sometimes frustrating that users often seem unwilling to commit the time and effort necessary to learn new skills. Remember to see training from the user's perspective. Training becomes attractive only when the *perceived value* of the skills outweighs the *perceived investment* in time and effort to be made. These skills will help them in the long term but they must be paid for in the short term. If people were easily motivated to sacrifice in the short term in support of their long-term interests, no one would smoke or be overweight.

User Feedback and Support

For a portal to evolve and grow there must be a way for users to feed requests, issues, random thoughts, and likes and dislikes back into the system. This is how you close the loop on driving adoption.

As part of the overall user support plan, the user's needs and wants must be assessed. The following sections offer some strategies for implementing user support and feedback processes that are usually successful in accomplishing this.

Establish and Train a Portal Help Desk

Most organizations have some type of IT help desk. If this help desk will be used to field calls from the users of the portal, the personnel working the phones will need to receive additional training.

First-line support personnel will need to know how to use the portal at least as well as most power users. This knowledge should include the functions of a visitor, contributor, or owner of a site. They will also need to be familiar with the site structure of the portal and the information architecture employed. This will allow them to resolve most routine issues immediately when users call.

When a problem cannot be solved by the first-line help desk, additional resources need to be available. These are usually the farm administrators and developers responsible for creating and maintaining the system. When issues reach this level, they need to be recorded in detail and resolved so that they do not occur again.

Be sure that the help desk records the nature of the questions being asked in all help desk calls. Frequently asked questions provide a good gauge as to what training is lacking. The governance team can use this information to update the training and communication plans.

Many organizations choose to use online forms to track help desk tickets. This is a good way to record information, and workflow can be used to manage the process of resolution. These forms provide a record of the issues being addressed for the users and are a valuable source of information for the governance team.

Do not let these forms and workflows get in the way of providing personal attention to users. It is easy for a busy help desk to let incoming calls go to voice mail or to require all requests be submitted through an online form. While this may improve the help desk's productivity, it will degrade the end user's productivity and cause adoption to suffer.

A user who has a simple question about the proper way to submit a piece of content will not use an online form to get the answer. They will submit the data incorrectly or simply not use the portal for that data at all. This is the opposite of what you are trying to promote. The best help desks are always answered by a person, not a computer, and provide the user with answers, not paperwork.

Provide Contact Information for Content

When a user visits a piece of content in SharePoint, give them the ability to provide feedback to or start a conversation with the user(s) responsible for that content. This can be the user who created, last updated, or is the owner of the content. This type of direct user-to-user feedback helps connect users in a very personal way.

Each site in SharePoint has a site owner or group of owners. Each team site has a list of team members or contributors. Consider adding lists of these users to the home page of each site.

SharePoint's Publishing feature records a contact user for each page in a publishing site. The Contact Details Web Part can be included in your page layouts to add contact info to each portal page.

The online presence feature can be used to provide a direct conduit between a site visitor and the user responsible for that content. Avoid making any one person the contact for large amounts of content. This can lead to that person being overwhelmed and the content being left unsupported.

Create Online Self-Help Communities for Users

One of the most valuable resources the governance team has is that set of users that have invested the time to become power users. Consider establishing a community site where these users can work with one another and other users to answer questions and collaborate on new ideas.

Microsoft publishes a site template for this type of site called The Productivity Hub. This site can be loaded with packaged content for SharePoint, Windows, and other products. Your power users, help desk personnel, administrators, developers, and content organizers can augment this content with discussion groups, FAQs, wikis, and blogs. This community site can become a valuable resource for both new and experienced users.

Provide Help Proactively

Look for ways to provide helpful information to users before they start looking for it. These resources can be made available throughout the site to help users quickly find answers on their own.

- *Cheat Sheets*: Create a one- or two-sided laminated sheet of easy-to-use frequently asked questions. Provide these to users for posting in their office or in public areas.

- *Tip of the Day*: Add an announcement Web Part to the portal's home page that displays useful tips on getting the most out of the portal. Make these postings small and quickly consumed by a user as they open the home page first thing in the morning.

- *Customize Help*: SharePoint's help system can be customized to show the most relevant help topics in your environment. You can suppress help for features that are not deployed and you can add additional help content to SharePoint's help system.

- *Leverage Ratings and Social Tagging*: Monitor the rating and tagging occurring in the portal to determine the information needs of users. Are users confused by certain features? Are they using metadata appropriately? These and similar questions can be answered to provide help to users where it is needed most.

Actively Solicit User Feedback

The feedback that users explicitly offer is some of the most valuable. These include suggestions for new or improved features, changes to the information architecture to make content more relevant or any number of other topics. The catch is that users usually only provide this type of feedback when they are asked for it and when they are sure someone is listening.

The most direct way to get this kind of feedback is to go to the user and ask for it. Consider sending out periodic surveys asking for opinions on the features and changes that are available on the portal. These could be in the form of e-mails to a select audience of users or a link on the portal.

Be specific. Don't ask "Do you like the portal?" The question itself is annoying and pointless since the answer is not actionable. Instead, ask questions like "Have you ever learned something you didn't already know from the 'Tip of the Day' box?" Then follow up with questions like "What did you learn?", "Did you use the tip in your work?", "Is there something you wish had been included in the 'Tip of the Day' box?"

Do not overwhelm users with this type of survey. It should be short, focused, and infrequent. If the user feels their time and opinion are being respected, they will be far more inclined to give real answers. If they feel they are being bombarded with requests for information that will ultimately be ignored, the request will be ignored as well.

Never require or coerce feedback from users. Reward them for it. Send thank-you notes in response to a survey. Have a real person send follow up questions and engage the user in a conversation when valuable insights can be gained.

Other techniques for collecting explicit user feedback include posting a suggestion box, in the form of an e-mail address or an online form. Encourage users to rate and provide comments on content.

Of course, the most important part of collecting user feedback is using it. The governance group needs to get this information continuously and act on it. As part of the communication plan, those actions need to be promoted among the users so that they know their feedback is important.

Training and Adoption Resources

In this book's appendixes, you will find a listing of resources for all aspects of SharePoint governance. In this section, we will describe a few of the most valuable of these where training and adoption are concerned.

- *The SharePoint Adoption Kit* (http://sharepoint.microsoft.com/iusesharepoint/Pages/get-the-kit.aspx): This site contains many resources to jump start your adoption effort. These include end-user videos, cheat sheets, tips and tricks, poster and e-mail templates, and best practices documentation. Best of all, it's all *free*!

- *The Productivity Hub 2010* (http://www.microsoft.com/download/en/details.aspx?displaylang=en&id=7122): The Productivity Hub is a package of training materials for end users. It is provided as a backup of a community site for end users. This site can be loaded with packaged content for SharePoint, Windows, and other products.

- *The SharePoint Shepherd's Guide by Robert Bogue* (http://www.sharepointshepherd.com): Robert Bogue seems to have made educating SharePoint end users into a personal mission. He takes a task-oriented approach to training users. This approach creates small lessons ideally suited to providing answers without requiring a large investment of time on the users' part. He has self published books and videos for SharePoint 2007 and 2010. His content is also available for corporate licensing on intranets.

- *Microsoft Learning Center for SharePoint* (http://www.microsoft.com/learning/en/us/training/sharepoint.aspx): This site provides links to training materials published by Microsoft. Some of these resources are free and others are available at a cost. Your organization's licensing agreement with Microsoft may entitle you to use some of these resources without paying additional fees. These resources include complete training plans and classroom and online classes and books.

- *Channel 9 SharePoint Videos* (http://channel9.msdn.com/Tags/sharepoint): Channel 9 is an online TV station owned by Microsoft that hosts video segments covering Microsoft's products. It includes forums for discussing these topics as well. This is a technical site targeting IT developers and administrators.

Summary

In this chapter, we have

- Explored the factors that can cause users to reject a SharePoint portal, preventing it from delivering value to the company.

- Discussed strategies for driving adoption for new and existing portals within the enterprise.

- Described the communication, training, and user feedback cycle for promoting adoption.

- Detailed the contents of a formal communication plan that is appropriate for a SharePoint portal governance effort.

- Examined the types of communication strategies that are known to work well for driving adoption.

- Explored the types of training that need to be made available to users within the organization and how they can best be delivered.

- Described how to plan for supporting users in a production environment and collecting feedback for the governance team.

CHAPTER 6

Managing Content

This chapter will explore the roles and responsibilities usually assigned to the Information Technology (IT) department when governing a SharePoint environment and look at how an IT department can help users manage their content. This involves creating, organizing, and updating content. But just as important as creating content in SharePoint is managing the removal of old, obsolete data. Data that is no longer needed can cause resource and performance problems as well as exposing the organization to data consistency and compliance issues. This chapter will focus on the tools provided by SharePoint to manage the entire content lifecycle.

What Will You Learn in This Chapter?

- Which processes are relevant to managing a SharePoint environment from an Information Technology perspective.

- The level of governance that is appropriate for different types of sites that may be hosted within SharePoint.

- How SharePoint organizes content, both physically and logically, within its databases.

- How an IT organization can control the lifecycle of content that is created in SharePoint.

- The features provided by SharePoint for controlling the creation and management of content.

Introduction to IT Management

Managing a SharePoint farm involves using the many tools available to manage the technology platform made up of the SharePoint server farm and the site content contained within the farm.

Managing a SharePoint server farm is similar to managing any other IT-related system. Requirements for performance, reliability, maintenance, and functionality must be established to implement the systems to support the needed functionality. These systems must be deployed, configured, monitored, backed up, and upgraded regularly. Service Level Agreements (SLA) often define these requirements and how they will be met. Chapter 7 will focus on the tools available on the SharePoint platform and how they can be used to manage the infrastructure provided by the SharePoint family of products. Chapter 8 will look at the creation of an Operations Plan for the SharePoint farm that defines which tools will be used and for what purposes.

In this chapter, we will focus on the content stored within a SharePoint server farm. We use the term *content* generically to refer to any new information that is introduced into the sites hosted on SharePoint by the end users. This may include calendars, announcements, documents, forms, and many other predefined or custom types of data objects. Interestingly, the most common types of content within SharePoint are often web sites and the web pages that make up those sites. From a more IT-centric point-of-view, SharePoint content is anything stored within SharePoint's content databases, which are relational data stores used to house all content in SharePoint. Of course, SharePoint does a great deal more than simply store content. (If storing content were the only requirement, a set of shared network folders would be just as useful as a SharePoint farm.) For example, SharePoint also has features that allow users to define metadata that describes the information and even actively route users to the information they need. These features will be examined in Chapters 9, 10, and 11 on information management.

The IT department is concerned with establishing the policies and standards that allow the users to leverage information management features without jeopardizing the integrity of the organization's data. The most important step is to define the structure of the content to be deployed and how it will be maintained. This includes managing how sites and other content are created, updated, and deleted by users of the system. SharePoint stores information at a variety of levels including site collections, sites, and list and library items, each of which has its own set of controls that can be applied as needed. This discussion will take a top-down approach by starting with the governance of the entire server farm and working our way down to describing some of the more important features available for managing the content lifecycle.

Types of SharePoint Content Containers

A SharePoint server farm may contain many thousands of sites and millions of individual pieces of content. This content is logically organized from the user's perspective into sites, lists, and libraries. However, to effectively manage content, it is necessary to understand the physical layout as well.

The highest-level container within a SharePoint farm is the web application. A web application maps directly to an Internet Information Services (IIS) web site and indirectly to one or more Uniform Resource Locators (URLs). Web applications expose content through their URLs and control features such as the authentication of users to the site.

Each web application is associated with one or more content database. These are physical SQL Server databases that exist on a database server somewhere on the network. Depending on the importance of the content, these servers may exist in clustered or otherwise redundant configurations to ensure that they are always available. The content databases for a SharePoint farm can grow quite large. They contain all of the sites, pages, and documents that exist within the SharePoint environment. A web application can use more than one content database to allow for greater performance and scalability, but each content database can be associated with only a single web application. (See Figure 6-1.)

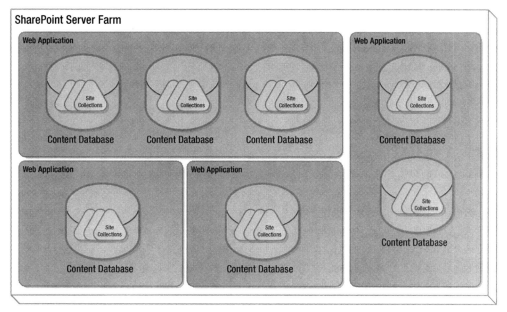

Figure 6-1. SharePoint content containers (farm-level view)

Each content database contains one or more site collections. Site collections are the logical boundary of a site in SharePoint. For example, the security configurations for sites cannot be inherited across a site collection boundary. The navigation controls that appear on SharePoint pages are designed, by default, to take their information only from a single site collection. This tends to isolate the content in one site collection from content in another unless an explicit accommodation is made to link them.

Site collections are also important in that they are used for two of SharePoint's most important management features: quotas and sandboxing. These are described in more detail in Chapter 13. These features allow farm administrators to control the resources and storage space that sites can be allocated.

Each site collection contains a single hierarchy of web sites. Each of these sites (sometimes called *Webs*) can contain a set of pages, lists, and libraries (see Figure 6-2). The lists and libraries contain the content elements that make up the site. Each site can be based on a different template, use different branding, and have separate security permissions.

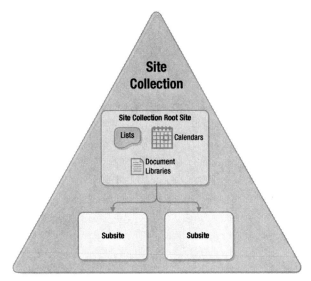

Figure 6-2. *SharePoint content containers (site collection view)*

The containers illustrated in Figure 6-2 cover all of the content items normally found in a Share-Point server farm. There is one type of content that can be stored outside of SharePoint's content databases. Because SharePoint's content is stored in relational databases, SharePoint is very good at storing and using metadata describing the information it contains. It is not as efficient when storing large amounts of unstructured data such as audio and video files. These objects are called Binary Large Objects, or *BLOBs*. SharePoint 2010 has introduced the ability to leverage SQL Server's Remote BLOB Storage (RBS) mechanism to store this data.

When RBS is used to store large files, the metadata for the files remains in the content database for use by SharePoint; only the content of the file itself is moved elsewhere. The definition of a BLOB can vary depending on the needs of the system, but typically BLOBs

- Are larger than average MS Office document files

- Contain no data that is useful without accessing the entire file

- Cannot be updated, only replaced or deleted

When a SharePoint farm contains many BLOBs and they are stored in the content databases, the farm's performance can be compromised. In this case, it is best to move the BLOBs out of the content databases using RBS. Often BLOBs can be stored using less expensive disk storage. They can also be backed up separately from the content databases that reference them so that they can be managed using tools and procedures that are more appropriate for large binary files. More information about Remote BLOB Storage in SharePoint 2010 can be found on the Microsoft Developer Network (MSDN) at `http://technet.microsoft.com/en-us/library/ee748649.aspx`.

Managing Different Types of Sites

When you build a SharePoint environment, you typically intend it for use either inside or outside of the organization. It is also very common to deploy systems that serve multiple purposes with both inward- and outward-facing components. As a result, most SharePoint server farms can be classified as intranets, extranets, or Internet (public-facing) sites.

Intranets

An intranet site is intended for users within the organization. A company may use its intranet to publish business information, reports, and other documents internally on its network or to communicate recent events and happenings across the organization. Historically, intranets have been the most common type of sites created using the SharePoint family of products. The collaboration features of SharePoint allow users to create, share, and find information quickly with very little training.

While an intranet can be organized in many different ways, the structure shown in Figure 6-3 is a common layout for an enterprise-wide intranet.

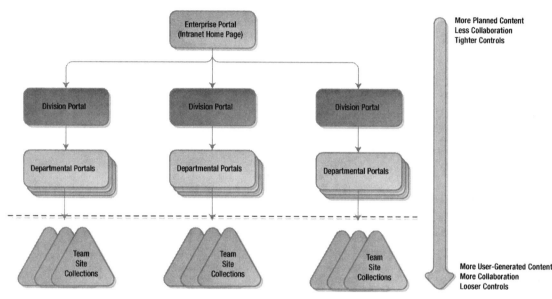

Figure 6-3. *Typical intranet structure*

At the top level is the intranet's home page. This page is often set as the default employee home page to encourage everyone in the organization to visit it regularly. This site usually contains information of general interest such as announcements and press releases. For user-specific content, a good approach is to use SharePoint's audience targeting features, described in Chapters 9 and 10. For example, a new HR policy published in France could be targeted to appear only on the home page of employees in that country.

The intranet root site does not usually contain a great deal of content. Its primary purpose is to provide a landing page for anyone accessing the site for the first time. The next two layers, shown in Figure 6-3, represent the organization of the enterprise. Each division, functional department, or area of specialization may have its own portal site where it can publish its own specific information for consumption throughout the organization. For example, the IT department's portal might contain items such as a calendar of planned outages, service request forms that can be filled out and submitted through the site, and reference documents on IT policies and practices.

These types of intranet sites are all referred to as *portal* sites, a generic term that describes a site used to publish information from one part of the organization to other parts of the organization. The enterprise, divisional, and departmental portals can be made up of any number of layers of sites and may have any structure that makes sense to the users; for the most part, they usually mirror the company's organization chart. There are some common approaches to managing portal sites within an intranet.

- Portal sites typically use SharePoint's publishing features. This allows content to undergo a review process before being made visible outside of the department.

- Portal sites are initially created by the IT department to ensure they are properly configured and secured. The content is then added to the site by the department that owns it.

- Each portal site allows anyone in the organization to access, but not update, most information. SharePoint's detailed security settings can be used to restrict access to sensitive information without creating an entirely new set of sites to protect it, as needed.

- A small set of users within the portal-owning department is given the responsibility to update the content in the portal. These users are called *contributors*.

- An even smaller set of *approvers* is designated to review and give final approval before information is published and made visible on the portal.

- When a department's information is needed on another site, SharePoint has Web Parts that can expose it on other sites, either by directly referencing the content or by routing it through audience targeting. This prevents duplicate copies of these documents from being created.

- Only finished content should appear in a portal site. Collaboration is not generally the focus of a portal site. Content should be created in team sites and only published to the portal once it is complete.

Below the dotted line in Figure 6-3 is a set of team site collections. These are the sites where content is created and collaboration thrives; they may represent projects, meeting or document workspaces, or any other set of information. These sites are frequently created, updated, and removed without the involvement of IT. Here are some common policies around team sites:

- Team sites do not typically use SharePoint's publishing features. These sites are collaborative in nature, making content approval an unnecessary burden. However, versioning can, and usually should, still be applied to this content.

- Team sites are usually created by the team using them. IT will often create a site collection for the team and then assign one or two site collection administrators to manage it going forward.

- Team sites are typically private to the team using them. This may be more about avoiding the confusion that results from releasing unfinished content than about security, depending on the type of information being created. If a non-team member needs to access the site, special permissions can always be added to permit access.

- Team sites are ideal for creating content collaboratively before publishing it to the rest of the organization. For example, the finance department might use a team site to prepare the company's annual report. Only after it is finished would the content be published outside the department.

- Content stored within team sites is still available throughout the organization to users that have permissions to access it. SharePoint's Search and audience targeting features perform security *trimming* to prevent unwanted exposure of information within the farm.

Extranets

The term *extranet* is one of those words that seems to mean something different to everyone who uses it. In this book, an extranet refers to a set of SharePoint content that is to be made available both internally and externally; it can be thought of as an intranet that allows certain outsiders to have access. The key feature that distinguishes an extranet from a public Internet site is that only authenticated users are given access to the site.

A very common scenario where an extranet is used is when a company needs to exchange information with its customers, suppliers, or partners. As shown in Figure 6-4, an extranet site straddles the edge between the inside and outside of the organization's network. The outside traffic is routed through the corporate firewall and into the SharePoint server farm.

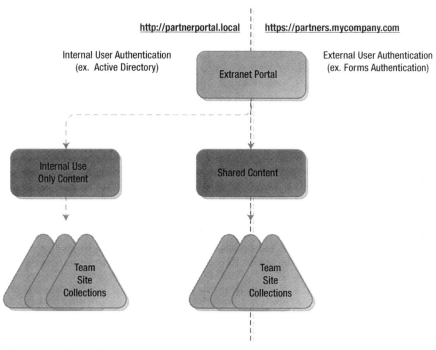

Figure 6-4. Typical extranet structure

When dealing with an extranet, the first question to be answered is "How will we authenticate outside users?" In an intranet, the most common authentication method is to integrate with the company's Active Directory or other LDAP directory. The problem is that these directories do not typically include accounts for non-employees, nor should they in most cases. To handle this problem, SharePoint allows a web site to use multiple *authentication providers* containing different sets of credentials. External credentials are often stored in a relational database or other non-LDAP store.

SharePoint 2010 introduces the concept of *claims-based* authentication. This is a new authentication mode that allows SharePoint to receive authentication tokens from a wider variety of providers. When using Windows account integration (NTLM or Kerberos), either mode—*claims-based* or *classic*—is acceptable. When implementing custom authentication such as forms-based authentication systems, claims-based tokens are required. A library of documents and walk-throughs relevant to claims-based authentication can be found on MSDN at http://msdn.microsoft.com/en-us/library/gg430136.aspx.

As shown in Figure 6-4, SharePoint has the ability to expose the same content on two different URLs, one internal and one external. When accessing the site using the internal URL, the user provides internal credentials to access the site. When accessing the site using the outside URL, generally using an encrypted (SSL) connection, the user provides external credentials. The result is that in either case the user has access to the same site content, using different URLs but a common set of security policies.

Internet Sites

An organization that wishes to publish information to the Internet will want to establish extensive reviews prior to the public release of information. Tight controls should be maintained to protect the organization from embarrassment and liability.

SharePoint's publishing features, known as Web Content Management (WCM) features, are ideally suited to creating this type of web site. Publishing sites implement several features that help to control the information shown to anonymous (public) users:

- Content versioning

- Page layout templates

- Approval workflow management

- Content scheduling

- Content deployment

SharePoint's *approval workflows* provide a process template for reviewing proposed changes in the context of the site without exposing them publicly. Once the approval is given, the content can be made accessible to all. Approval workflows use the Windows Workflow engine that is hosted within SharePoint. This allows users to create custom approval processes using SharePoint Designer or Visual Studio.

Content scheduling provides a mechanism where content that has been approved can be held back until a certain time. When the scheduled date and time are reached, the content will automatically appear on the web site with no further attention from the content's creator, approver, or administrators.

Content can be scheduled to disappear automatically as well. For example, a page promoting a holiday special could be scheduled to appear on the site on December 1 and automatically vanish on December 26.

Content deployment refers to the process of moving published content from one site collection to another. The most common use of content deployment is to allow designers and content contributors to work in a non-production environment. Only after content is approved for publication does it move into the production server farm. This ensures that content is developed in an environment where it cannot accidentally be publicly exposed.

In software development, it has long been standard operating procedure to develop in one environment, test in another, and operate production on yet another set of servers. Content development in SharePoint can benefit from a similar approach. The advantages of this approach revolve around allowing only certain types of operations in each environment. There are also different numbers of users and network infrastructures to consider, as shown in Table 6-1.

Table 6-1. *SharePoint Content Development Environments*

Environment	Users and Infrastructures
Authoring Environment	Small number of users and servers, SharePoint Designer access enabled Content authoring allowed
Stage Environment	Small number of users and servers No authoring or designer access Receives deployed content from the authoring environment Used for performing final reviews of new content
Production Environment	Full complement of servers No authoring or designer access Receives deployed content from the stage environment Used to serve web pages to the Internet

By using SharePoint's content deployment feature, these environments can be separate site collections within the same or different server farms. As a best practice, the production environment at least should be a separate SharePoint farm. Three common designs for content deployment are one-, two-, and three-farm topologies.

In a *single-farm topology*, shown in Figure 6-5, authoring is performed in one site collection, and content is deployed to production in a second site collection. There could also be a third site collection for staging if desired. The weakness of this approach is that many of SharePoint's security controls are applied at the farm level and therefore cannot protect against accidental changes in this configuration.

Figure 6-5. *A single-farm topology*

In a *two-farm topology*, shown in Figure 6-6, authoring is performed in one SharePoint farm, and content is deployed to production in a second farm. The authoring farm need not contain as many servers as the production farm, because it will presumably have far fewer users.

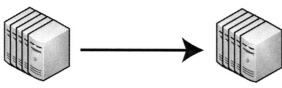

Figure 6-6. *A two-farm topology*

A *three-farm topology*, shown in Figure 6-7 adds an intermediate staging environment that can be used for a detailed review of the completed content before final deployment to production. In this topology, content can be deployed to production either from the stage farm or directly from the authoring farm.

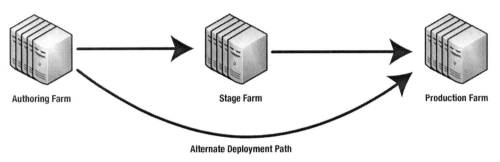

Authoring Farm   Stage Farm   Production Farm

Alternate Deployment Path

Figure 6-7. A three-farm topology

Planning the Content Lifecycle

SharePoint is a powerful content creation platform. Creating sites, documents and other content items is as simple as using a web browser. As a result, many SharePoint installations become clogged with massive amounts of obsolete, unused and contradictory information. To avoid this situation, a good SharePoint governance plan should include processes for managing the entire content lifecycle (see Figure 6-8).

Figure 6-8. The content lifecycle

Content in the farm will generally go through a series of lifecycle phases. The content is initially created and published to a site on the farm. Over time, it is read and updated several times. At some point, the item may fall into disuse. This could be because it is superseded, obsolete, or no longer needed. The simplest case is where an end user realizes that the data is no longer needed and removes the content manually. The far more common case is one in which content is left inactive (static and unused) for a long period of time. This type of content requires disk storage space, indexing by the search service and, perhaps, audience processing. All of these require the use of resources that return no value to the organization.

In the next section, we will examine some of the features the SharePoint platform support the creation, management, and removal of content as part of a planned content lifecycle.

Self-Service Site Creation

As you saw in Figure 6-2, all content in SharePoint is stored in site collections. The creation of these site collections is a key component in managing the storage allocated to content in the farm. Site collections can always be created by farm administrators, but in some environments, it may be useful to allow end users to request and create their own site collections, requiring little or no involvement by the farm administrators. This feature is known as *Self-Service Site Creation (SSSC)*.

■ **Note**   The terminology is a little confusing here. *Self-Service Site Creation* refers to creating site *collections*, not subsites within a site collection. We will discuss controlling subsite creation in the next section.

SSSC can be enabled by a web application and any user with read permission can use it. If you wish to restrict access, SSSC can be reconfigured through the SharePoint Administration (STSADM) command-line tool or the Central Administration web site. (For more on STSADM, see Chapter 7.)

The options on this page allow the farm administrator to enable or disable SSSC and, if enabled, to require that a secondary contact be provided (see Figure 6-9). The primary contact for the site collection will be the user who created it. Both the primary and secondary contacts are configured as site collection administrators for the site collection. Enabling this option is a good idea since it helps administrators in the event that the primary contact is on vacation or has left the organization.

Because end users are allowed to create their own sites using SSSC, it is more important than ever to control the effect these sites have on the farm.

- Solutions deployed into these site collections are automatically run within the SharePoint Sandbox Service. The sandbox service should be configured to manage the resources and load balancing that affects the running of these solutions. See Chapter 13 for details.

- Quotas should be established for sites created through SSSC.

- Site auto-deletion, described later in this chapter, should be applied to prevent the proliferation of unused site collections.

- These site collections reside in the content databases associated with the web application. There are rules for which database is used when a new site collection is created. These rules should be configured to produce the desired distribution of sites.

When a user creates a new site collection, they use a page located at /_layouts/scsignup.aspx relative to the site collection's root URL. Unlike most pages in SharePoint's LAYOUTS directory, this page is commonly customized by organizations that wish to use the SSSC feature. The default SSSC page (see Figure 6-10) allows the user to supply a limited set of metadata for the site collection. Common customizations to this page include the creation of additional metadata, such as the department to be charged for its storage and resource use, and creating a custom request workflow to be performed before the site collection is actually created. These workflows and customizations need to be extensively tested since they affect the entire farm.

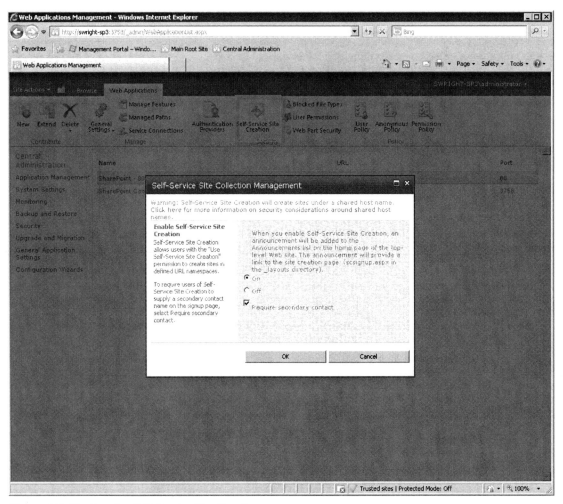

Figure 6-9. Configuring Self-Service Site Creation

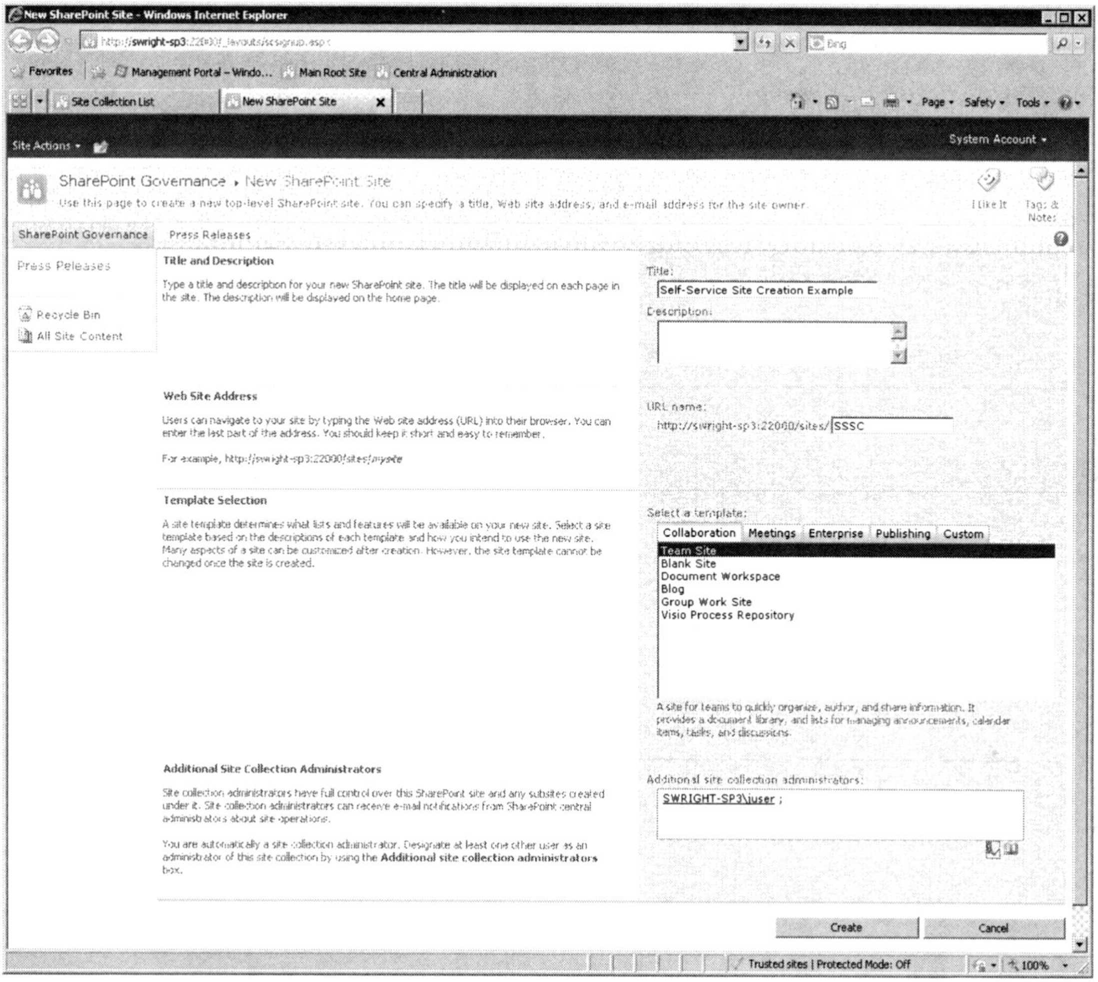

Figure 6-10. Using Self-Service Site Creation

Self-Service Subsite Creation

Within each site collection is a hierarchy of subsites. The creation of these sites is managed by assigning permissions to users.

There are two built-in permission levels that allow a user to create subsites: Full Control and Manage Hierarchy. Assigning these permission levels to a user or group of users will enable them to create subsites under the current site. Unassigning these permission levels will prevent users from doing so.

In some situations, it may be preferable to not allow users the right to create subsites even on sites that they own. The easiest way to accomplish this is to remove the Create Subsites permission from the Full Control and Manage Hierarchy permission levels. This will ensure that only site collection administrators can create subsites within the site collection.

While subsites create a logical separation of content in one area from another, it is important to remember that the site collection controls the storage and resources available within a site. You cannot set quotas at the individual site level. Also, any sandboxed solution within the collection can access content within any of the collection's sites.

Site Collection Auto-Deletion

SharePoint Server allows farm administrators to manage the automatic removal of unused site collections. This prevents unneeded information from consuming valuable storage and other resources.

To configure this feature, the farm administrator uses the Central Administration web site as shown in Figure 6-11.

Figure 6-11. Configure automatic site collection deletion

When enabled, this feature will check for unused site collections and send e-mail notifications to the site collection's administrators. The purpose of the e-mail is to let the responsible users know that they have content that is not being used. If they do not confirm that the content is still needed, it may eventually be deleted from the system.

The configuration of automatic site collection deletion is set at the web application level. Typically, this feature should be turned off in any web application that contains officially published information such as that found on intranet portal sites. Of course these sites are unlikely to go unused for long periods as well. The more common use of auto-deletion is to manage site collections created using Self-Service Site Creation. These are often created, used briefly and then forgotten. Another good use for auto-deletion is to clean up personal sites (a.k.a. My Sites) for users that no longer use the SharePoint farm.

The problem with configuring automatic site deletion is the possibility of losing important information. When a site collection is deleted using this feature, it is permanently destroyed. It is not archived or backed up and there is no Recycle Bin from which to restore it. Before enabling this feature, the organization should ensure that none of the sites to be deleted contain critical information. Regular backups can help with this problem. There are also third party products that perform archiving and deletion of content as part of a comprehensive content management strategy.

Controlling Content with SharePoint Features

The SharePoint family of products contains many features that help manage the processes around creating and delivering content within sites. In this section, we will take a high-level look at some of those features and how they can be used to govern content in a SharePoint environment. This will not be an in-depth technical discussion. The goal is to become familiar with the types of controls that are available and how they can contribute to a comprehensive governance plan.

Site Templates

A *Site Template* in SharePoint is a preconfigured site that can be used as a model for a new site when it is first created. SharePoint comes with several built-in site templates for team sites, workspaces, blogs, wikis, and so on. Each template contains a set of lists and libraries along with metadata and default content for the site.

When creating a new site, one of the options the creator selects is the template to be used. The available templates are categorized as collaboration, meeting, enterprise, publishing, or custom sites, as shown in Figure 6-12.

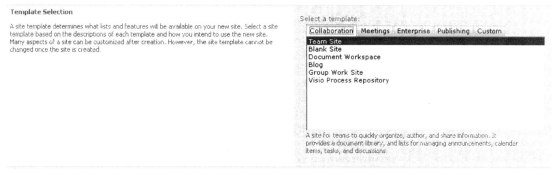

Figure 6-12. Template selection during site creation

Site templates allow farm administrators to promote a standard look and feel along with the structure of sites. The built-in site templates can be removed from SharePoint and replaced with customized site templates built specifically for the organization. Creating new site templates is remarkably easy because SharePoint has the ability to save an existing site as a site template.

Publishing

SharePoint supports two major categories of sites: collaboration sites and publishing sites:

- *Collaboration sites* (also called *team sites*) are used to create and share content. Content that is added to a collaboration site is generally available to all users of the site immediately. Collaboration sites usually contain document libraries, calendars, discussion boards, blogs, and the like.

- *Publishing sites* support a much more formalized means of creating and sharing content. The content created in a publishing site is not immediately available to all users. Content must go through a configurable approval process before it is exposed to non-privileged or anonymous users. SharePoint also has the ability to schedule the publishing and retraction of content at given times and dates. These features are collectively referred to as *Web Content Management* (WCM).

Publishing is supported by a separate set of site templates that are available when creating a new site. Publishing can also be added to an existing collaboration site by turning on SharePoint's Publishing features for the site. Doing so adds the libraries and metadata necessary to support the publishing process.

Quotas

Quotas allow farm administrators to control the resources used by a site collection. This permits storage space and processing resources (CPU, memory, etc.) to be allocated and automatically monitored.

The farm administrators create a set of quota templates and associate a template with each site collection. Each template defines the maximum amount of storage space that can be consumed by the site collection. Because site collections can contain their own sandboxed solution code, a quota template also allocates a number of *resource points* to the site collection. (See Chapter 13 for a discussion of the resource point system.)

When a site collection reaches a threshold for storage or resource points, an e-mail can be sent to the site collection's administrators. If the problem is not addressed and the site collection attempts to exceed their quota limit, the site collection will be automatically frozen (storage) or locked out (resources). For example, a site collection could generate a warning when it reaches 80 MB or 200 points. The site could then be locked automatically when the content reaches 100 MB or 100 points.

▓ **Note** Resource points are calculated on a daily basis. If a site collection is disabled for exceeding its resource point quota, the total will be cleared and the collection re-enabled the next time the relevant timer job runs. This usually occurs once per day, during the night.

A good practice is to identify the types of sites that will be hosted and create a quota template for each. These templates can then be used whenever a site is created ensuring that consistent quotas are enforced. The farm should be monitored regularly to ensure that the farm has sufficient capacity for all of the allocations that have been made. Frequent quota violations may indicate that the server farm should be expanded, content should be restructured using more site collections, or the quotas should be adjusted to better reflect the sites being managed.

Locks

When a site is locked in SharePoint it can mean that either the site has been placed into a read-only mode or it has been made temporarily inaccessible. This can happen as the result of a quota violation or a manual action by a farm administrator.

Access Requests

SharePoint sites are secured using a set of site permissions that control what each user is allowed to do within that site. For example, one user might have read-only access to the site while another has the right to add content but not to delete anything. SharePoint enforces these restrictions through the web interface.

Managing all of these permissions can become an overwhelming process if all security rights are managed by a single group of people. All SharePoint sites have one or more owners that have the ability to grant access rights to other users. To simplify this process even more, SharePoint supports a feature called *Access Requests*.

Access requests can be enabled at the site, list, or library level. When a user attempts to perform some action for which they do not have rights, they will see an access denied message like the one shown in Figure 6-13.

Figure 6-13. Access Denied

After clicking the "request access" link, the user can fill out a request form that will be e-mailed to the user designated to handle the access requests for that site, list, or library. The e-mail will contain the details of the request and a link to the page on which the permissions can be granted.

Auditing

Content auditing in SharePoint creates an audit trail of content updates, accesses, and removals. This can be critical when dealing with compliance and other legal issues.

The overhead associated with creating and storing this log is substantial but often justified. Share-Point contains tools for reporting on this data and managing the size of the logs retained. Enabling auditing in certain critical site collections can make the process of finding electronic documents for lawsuits and compliance audits (also called *e-Discovery*) far less expensive and time consuming for the organization.

For more information on managing e-Discovery with SharePoint, see the article on TechNet at http://technet.microsoft.com/en-us/library/ff453933.aspx.

Workflows

Workflows in SharePoint allow end users to define their own business process templates and have those processes automated by SharePoint. The best example of a workflow in SharePoint is the content approval workflow used with the Publishing feature. This workflow manages the process of requesting approvals, reassigning approvers, requesting revisions, and obtaining final approval of the content.

Workflow definitions can be created and modified using either SharePoint Designer or Visual Studio. (End users typically use SharePoint Designer, whereas professional developers tend to prefer Visual Studio.) Workflow definitions are stored and configured within a site collection; they can be copied to other site collections and customized as needed.

SharePoint Designer

SharePoint Designer 2010 is a Windows client application published by Microsoft specifically for creating content in SharePoint. It contains powerful tools for creating workflows, content types, sites, and pages in SharePoint. The use of SharePoint Designer can be enabled, disabled, or restricted at the web application or site collection level.

Most large production SharePoint installations restrict the use of SharePoint Designer because of the ability for end users to create problems for themselves. Generally, SharePoint Designer should not be used directly in a production site that contains extensive branding or critical public information. To create content for these sites, it is best to set up a non-production environment and use content deployment as described earlier in this chapter. SharePoint Designer can then be enabled in the authoring environment and disabled in production.

Digital Asset library

Digital assets such as images, audio files, and video files, require special metadata and management processes. SharePoint has a built-in asset library template specifically for use with this type of content. Because these files can become very large, you should also consider using Remote BLOB Storage (RBS).

Information Management Policies

Many of the features discussed in this chapter should be applied to large categories of content. It can be difficult to maintain a consistent approach to configuring all of these tools, however. Information management policies in SharePoint allow users to create sets of rules that govern how content is managed. These policies act as functional templates that can be applied to content throughout the farm; this ensures that the rules are applied uniformly and can be managed in a single location.

An information management policy can include controls such as the following:

- *Expiration Policy*: This defines how long content should be retained and what happens when that time expires. Common options are to automatically delete the content or to start a custom workflow that allows an end user to determine the content item's fate. This policy works at a far more granular and configurable level that the automated site deletion feature described earlier in this chapter.

- *Auditing Policy*: This controls the level of auditing that is required for the content. Some documents may only require an audit trail for changes, while others may need to have a record created each time they are accessed.

- *Labeling and Barcode Policies*: These policies are used to automatically generate standardized document labels or barcodes for each document. These can be printed and affixed separately or included in the image of the document that is provided by SharePoint. These labels and barcodes are generated using the document's metadata stored within SharePoint.

- *Policy Statement*: Each information management policy template can include a statement regarding the purpose and function of the policy. This statement will appear whenever the document is viewed using a compatible document viewer such as one of the Office 2010 client applications.

Information management policies generate reports that can be used to track the audit information and usage of the documents controlled. This is useful for e-Discovery and compliance audits. For more information on planning information management policies, see the TechNet article at http://technet.microsoft.com/en-us/library/cc262490.aspx.

Summary

In this chapter, we have

- Described the processes that are relevant to the IT organization when managing a SharePoint environment.

- Compared the levels of governance that are appropriate for intranet, extranet, and Internet sites in SharePoint.

- Examined the physical and logical layout of content stored within SharePoint.

- Described the mechanisms an IT organization can use to control the lifecycle of SharePoint content.

- Examined the features provided by SharePoint for controlling the creation and management of content.

CHAPTER 7

Managing the Server Farm

In Chapter 6 you saw how the IT organization can help users manage their content. Setting standards and policies for managing the server farm's configuration is just as important as it is for managing content, so in this chapter you will look behind the scenes at how the server farm itself is managed. We will show you the tools in SharePoint that allow you to control the configuration of the farm and all of its components. We will then show how a SharePoint farm can be monitored and maintained. This will lead us into Chapter 8 where we will discuss creating an operational plan for your SharePoint environment.

What Will You Learn in This Chapter?

- The concepts of farm management and the reasons for creating an operational plan

- The more important types of configuration tools available in SharePoint for creating a stable, robust environment

- How SharePoint web applications can be configured to produce secure, reliable results

- The logging mechanisms that can be used to monitor and diagnose issues in a production SharePoint farm

- How to monitor the usage and health of the farm

- Best practices around performing server maintenance and software upgrades in a production server farm

- The options available for making backups of the content and configurations in the farm

Introduction to Farm Management

Managing a SharePoint environment has many things in common with managing most other enterprise-grade applications. The goal is to create a system that is reliable, maintainable, and performant. To do this, the system needs to be installed and upgraded in a consistent, documented way. The data and configurations for the system should be backed up regularly with plans in place for restoring those backups locally or in a remote disaster recovery facility. The system should be proactively monitored to ensure that problems are addressed before they impact users. The capacity of the system, for both processing

97

and storage, should be compared to the current usage and tracked over time to allow advanced planning for needed upgrades.

In a SharePoint environment, several additional challenges need to be considered when designing a plan for managing a large installation:

- A SharePoint Server farm consists of many different types of servers that may perform different types of functions. There may be web servers, application servers, indexers, crawlers, search query processors, and multiple database servers.

- Not all executable logic on the system is deployed and controlled by the central farm administrators. Think workflows, sandboxed solutions, InfoPath forms, etc.

- In a multi-tenancy or hosted environment, several organizations may be accessing the same hardware platform.

- Security rules can vary from one part of the farm to another.

- The various subsystems that run within SharePoint each have their own configuration options. Some may even have more than one set of configured services.

- Each component in SharePoint may consume storage and processing resources and log diagnostic events in very different ways.

We will break down the tools for managing a SharePoint farm into three categories: configuring, monitoring, and maintaining. There is often a fine or virtually nonexistent line between these categories, but we will use them for explanation purposes. As in Chapter 6, we will not attempt to present all of the technical details concerning these tools, but, rather, we'll present an overview of the toolset available.

Additional information can be found on the Microsoft Developer Network (MSDN) or TechNet web sites or in any number of specialized technical publications. Also consider downloading the SharePoint 2010 Administration Toolkit available from Microsoft on TechNet at http://technet.microsoft.com/en-us/library/cc508851.aspx.

Configuring SharePoint

Configuring a SharePoint farm involves setting many individual controls; we will examine some of the most important settings and discuss the options available. We will break these settings into two groups: those configured at the farm level and those that apply to a specific web application. Most of the options that are configured at the site and site collection level were covered in Chapter 6, since these are more relevant to managing content than to managing the farm as a whole.

Farm-Level Configurations

In this section we will touch on some of the more important features provided by the SharePoint platform for managing the configuration of the farm at the farm level.

Farm Administration Interfaces

One of the more confusing aspects of configuring a SharePoint farm is that there is usually more than one way to accomplish the same task. This is because SharePoint has three separate administration interfaces.

The simplest interface available to farm administrators is the Central Administration (CA) web site. The CA web site is automatically created by the SharePoint installation program when a SharePoint farm is initially created. Most administration tasks can be performed using CA and a series of simple-to-use web pages. This interface is ideal for administrators who are not comfortable writing code or for performing tasks that do not need to be automated.

The next interface, available from the Windows command line, is the SharePoint Administration (STSADM) tool. The *STS* in the name of this tool dates back to the days when SharePoint was known as SharePoint Team Services. This tool accepts any of a very large number of commands that are executed against the farm's configuration. These commands include listing, adding, and removing site collections. At last count, there were 177 separate STSADM commands. The tool also includes an interface that allows the development of additional commands that can be installed to perform custom actions. This tool is ideal for administrators who need to automate repetitive tasks and prefer to use Windows command language files.

■ **Note**　Microsoft considers the STSADM tool deprecated and may not include it in future versions of the product. New scripts should be written using the SharePoint 2010 Management Shell interface described below.

The last interface is based on the Windows PowerShell environment. This interface is called the SharePoint 2010 Management Shell. This is a command line–style environment that allows more flexible object-oriented scripts to be created. Like the STSADM tool, the management shell provides a large number of commands (known as *command-lets* in PowerShell) that provide access to the configuration actions in SharePoint. One advantage of the management shell interface is that it allows for easier processing of repetitive tasks using built-in looping and command connections. Because it is object-oriented instead of command-oriented, the management shell is most appropriate for use by administrators or developers who are comfortable writing code in more sophisticated programming languages.

The differences between the three administration interfaces are mostly a matter of convenience and familiarity for the administrators using them. With only a few exceptions, anything that can be done in one tool can be done in any of them. For automating tasks, the Central Administration web site is a poor choice; STSADM is a simpler but less flexible interface because of the limitations of the Windows command language. Also, Microsoft's strategy is to move away from the batch environment and promote Windows PowerShell as the alternative moving forward. If you are interested in learning one of the command-line interfaces, the management shell is the preferred choice.

SharePoint Managed Accounts

Service accounts have always been a challenge when configuring enterprise applications. These are the accounts used by the application to load and execute on the system. In general, some of the best practices around service accounts are as follows:

- Always use an Active Directory domain account, not a local system account.

- Change the account's password regularly.

- Avoid using the same service account for everything.

- Use different accounts for different purposes, even within the same server farm.

- Assign only the privileges required for that service account to perform the actions required, and no more.

Unfortunately, many of these practices also make managing service accounts so difficult that few organizations adhere to them properly. SharePoint 2010 has introduced the use of managed accounts to simplify the process of maintaining good security around service accounts.

A *managed account* is a service account that has been registered with SharePoint. This is an Active Directory domain account that has been granted a set of permissions for a specific role in the server farm. The user name and password are given to SharePoint once and can be reused as necessary when configuring the farm. These service accounts are typically configured during the initial installation of the server farm, but they can be reconfigured later as necessary.

The most difficult part of dealing with service accounts has always been the need to change the password regularly. Once the password was changed in Active Directory, the services that depend on it would begin failing until the password was manually updated in each and every place the account was used, which could be hundreds of individual configurations. Obviously, this was time consuming and error prone. As a result, it was also very rarely done. Using managed accounts, the credentials for the account are stored securely within SharePoint. As illustrated in Figure 7-1, SharePoint even has the ability to automatically generate new passwords on a regular basis. SharePoint changes the password in Active Directory and stores the strong password it generated in its own configuration. This allows the accounts to be kept secure without requiring manual password setting by the administrators.

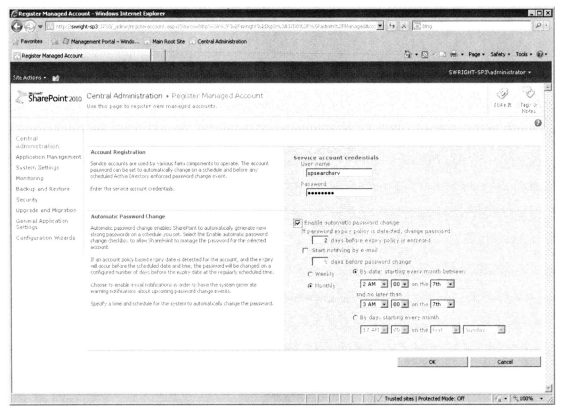

Figure 7-1. Creating a managed account in Central Administration

SharePoint Features

In SharePoint, a *feature* is a piece of functionality that can be turned on or off as needed. Features are extensions to the SharePoint platform that may or may not be needed in a particular situation. Most of the functionality in the SharePoint platform can be turned on or off using features. Turning a feature on can radically change the behavior of a SharePoint site. SharePoint's Publishing feature is an excellent example; when this feature is activated, new libraries, workflows, and page publishing mechanisms suddenly appear in a site that previously held simple content.

When considering the design and activation of features, it is important to remember that each feature has a declared scope. This defines the breadth of effect the feature can have within the SharePoint Farm. (See Table 7-1.)

Table 7-1. Feature Scopes

Feature Scope	Description	Common Types of Components
Web	Affects the contents of one SharePoint site	Document libraries Lists and list templates Files Custom menu items (Actions)
Site	Affects all of the sites within one site collection	Site columns Content types Web Parts Stapled features Site templates Workflows
Web Application	Affects all of the site collections within a web application	Web Parts Document converters Custom menu items Stapled features
Farm	Affects the entire server farm	Web Parts Custom menu items Stapled features

The details for creating and deploying features are discussed in Chapter 13.

Sandboxing

A new feature introduced in SharePoint 2010 is the *sandbox service*, also known as the User Code Service. The purpose of the sandbox service is to allow non-trusted executable code to be introduced into the SharePoint environment without compromising the security, performance, or reliability of the server farm. Code deployed to the sandbox service is said to be "running in the sandbox."

Code running in the sandbox is isolated from the rest of the server farm's executing code. This isolation includes running this code in an entirely different set of Windows processes, which allows these applications to be started, monitored, configured, and stopped without impacting any other part of the system. Here are some of the most important points to remember about sandboxed code:

- Sandboxed code is deployed to a site collection's Site Solution Gallery and always runs within the context of that single site collection.

- Sandboxed code can access resources only within the site collection to which it is deployed.

- The actions available to sandboxed code are severely limited using a set of Share-Point API proxy libraries and Code Access Security (CAS) policies.

- Site collection administrators are ultimately responsible for deploying and removing sandboxed code.

- Farm administrators are responsible for configuring the sandbox service, monitoring its use, and setting quotas that can be used to automatically disable non-compliant code in the sandbox.

- InfoPath forms can contain .NET managed code that will run in the sandbox when they are run as browser-based forms.

For custom code to run *outside* the sandbox, it must be deployed to the server farm's solution gallery by a farm administrator. Only then will it be allowed to run in a full-trust execution environment. As such, this code must be thoroughly tested and trusted prior to deployment.

Security experts insist that code should always run under a *least privileges* set of permissions. This means that code should never be able to do anything that it does not truly need to do. In the context of custom SharePoint solutions, this implies that all custom code should run in the sandbox unless there is an overwhelming reason to move it to the farm level. As a practical matter, code that is trusted and intended for use across all of the farm's site collections will generally be deployed as a farm solution, whereas custom code developed for a specific purpose for a small set of users will typically reside in the sandbox.

The details for creating and deploying solutions containing sandboxed code are discussed in Chapter 13.

User Profiles and My Sites

A user profile in SharePoint contains all of the metadata about a particular user. This may include items such as name, phone number, office location, and specialties and skills. Custom metadata can be added to the profiles managed by SharePoint as well. The data for these profiles is either provided by the users themselves or an external system such as a Human Resources database or Active Directory.

Profiles are stored and managed by SharePoint's User Profile Service. This service application provides a common set of data for users throughout the farm. Farm administrators can configure the service to provide custom behaviors such as the following:

- Policies can be set to control the visibility of user profile properties to other users.

- User profile information can be used to create target audiences that can control the delivery of information to end users.

- Users can have the ability to update certain of their own profile properties while others remain read-only.

The user profile feature is also used to support social media features in SharePoint. These include adding ratings and tags to content within the farm; there can also be references and notes on external resources. These social features can be controlled using the Use Social Features permission.

The *My Sites* feature allows each authenticated user to create a web site that is used as a personal workspace. This site can be used to share information for others or to create new content in a private area for later publication. My Sites often contain personal, sensitive information, so great care should be taken when planning for this feature. The volume of data stored in My Sites can be limited to prevent the system from being overwhelmed with private data. The My Site feature can be disabled at the farm level or given to a limited set of users using the Use Personal Features permission.

Search

Configuring search is a wide-ranging and complex topic, so we will just touch on the main concepts that relate to managing search in a farm. Search is composed of two major processes: crawling and querying.

Crawling refers to accessing content items and creating an index of their contents. Crawling is a network and disk-intensive process that produces large amounts of index data. One or more servers are often designated just for crawling content in a large search environment. The data collected is written to an index file on the server's hard drive.

- Index files should be stored on a separate set of disks from other data before the high I/O requirements of the crawling and indexing process.

- Sufficient disk space should always be available to prevent the indexing process from crashing.

- A good rule of thumb is to allocate space for your index files equal to at least 30 percent of the total volume of the content being indexed.

- Each source of content will have one or more scheduled times for indexing to occur. Manage these jobs to limit the impact of the crawling process.

- Crawl content only as often as necessary to keep the index up to date.

- Configure more important or frequently updated content sources to be crawled with High priority instead of Normal (default). This will cause them to be indexed first when multiple sources are scheduled for processing.

When a user accesses the search page on a SharePoint site, a search query is executed against the index files. The search queries do not have to run on the same servers in the farm as the indexing process. Separate servers can be used if needed for performance reasons. In this case, the search service will manage the copying of index files from the index servers to the search servers.

- Consider configuring different servers to process crawls and queries if both may occur at the same time.

- The servers running queries will contain a copy of the index files. These should be on disks that can be read quickly.

Configuring search is described in more detail in Chapter 10.

Web Application Management

In this section, we will look at some of the controls that can be used to manage web applications. Remember that a web application can contain many site collections that are referenced through a common set of URLs.

Content Databases

As described in Chapter 6, each web application is configured with one or more content databases. The content databases contain the site collections that are visible through the web application.

As shown in Figure 7-2, each content database has a set of properties that control its use within the web application.

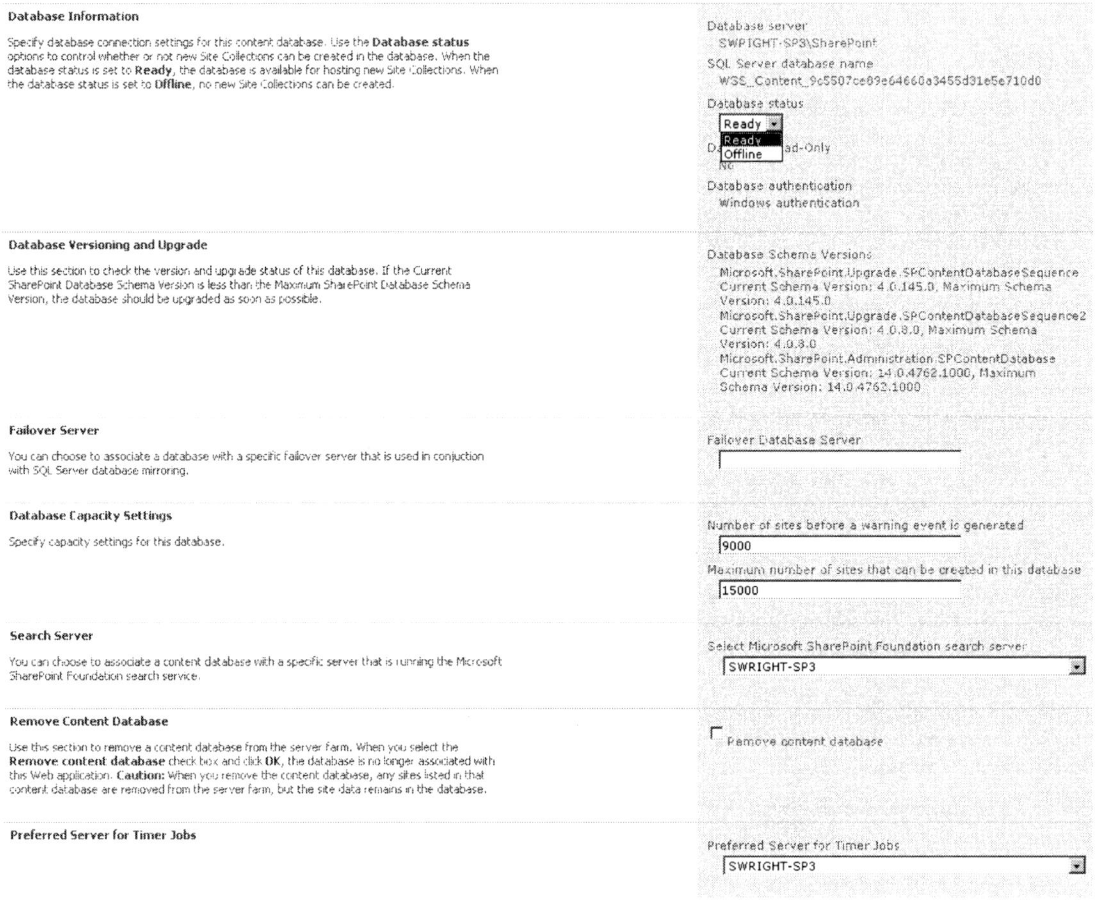

Figure 7-2. Content database properties

- *Database Information:* Includes the following important options:
    - *Status*: A content database can be set to *offline* to prevent new site collections from being created.
    - *Read-Only*: If a database is set to read-only mode in SQL Server, SharePoint will still access content but no updates will be allowed.
- *Database Version*: As new releases and patches are released for SharePoint, changes to the objects within a content database are sometimes required. The version information helps you diagnose problems and plan for upgrades.
- *Failover Server*: Defining a failover server allows a content database to be automatically recovered after a failure using SQL Server database mirroring.

- *Site Collection Capacity:* These settings provide warning and quota levels for the number of site collections that can be created within a content database. Note that this is not related to the amount of data in the site collections, only their number.

■ **Tip**   When a new site collection is to be created in a web application, one of the content databases is selected to contain the new content. The database selected is the one that has the greatest number of site collections available before reaching its limit. For example, if one database currently contains 100 sites and has a limit of 1,000, but another has 200 sites with a limit of 2,000, the second database will be selected because it has 1,800 site allocations left. This fact can be used to create a round-robin allocation scheme by setting all content databases to have the same number of available site collections.

- *Search Server:* This setting only affects the SharePoint Foundation search service. The enterprise search service in SharePoint Server 2010 is not affected.
- *Timer Job Server:* This setting is used to assign a server to process timer jobs associated with the content database.

For performance and reliability reasons, it may be preferable not to have all of a farm's content databases running on the same SQL Server or cluster. Placing a small number of heavily used content databases on a high-end SQL Server system may improve performance considerably. Placing infrequently used content on slower database servers and disk subsystems can save a great deal of money on hardware.

When a SQL Server fails, only the content databases on that server become unavailable. Using database mirroring, it is possible to create redundancy for important content databases without implementing expensive clustering solutions on the database server tier of the farm. Only the SharePoint configuration database is absolutely necessary for the farm to remain operational. This database should always be deployed on a redundant SQL Server environment such as a cluster.

It goes without saying that all of SharePoint's databases should be backed up regularly. These backups can then be used for disaster recovery, populating test systems, and restoring data that has been accidentally removed from the farm. The options available for backing up and restoring content will be discussed later in this chapter.

Security Policies

Each SharePoint web application has a set of security policies that can be configured and enforced throughout all site collections in the web application. To configure these policies, the farm administrator can use Web Applications Management in Central Administration as shown in Figure 7-3.

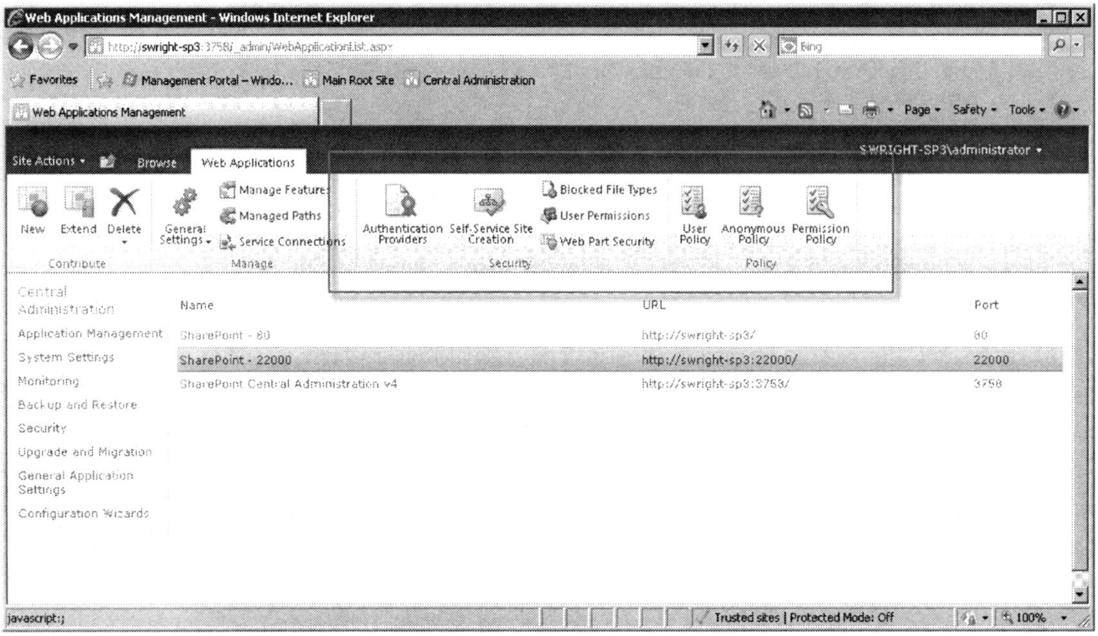

Figure 7-3. *Web application security policies*

Each of these policies will be discussed in the following sections.

Authentication Providers

An *authentication provider* is a component that defines the means SharePoint uses to authenticate users. Each web application can support multiple authentication providers in different zones which are accessed using different URLs. For more information on such scenarios, see the discussion on extranets in Chapter 6.

Self-Service Site Creation

This policy controls the ability of users to create their own site collections. This feature is discussed in detail in Chapter 6.

Blocked File Types

A web application can be configured to exclude specific types of files. The most common example is to exclude executable files since they may contain viruses and other malicious code. When a user attempts to upload a blocked type of file they will be informed that their upload could not be completed.

As you can see in Figure 7-4, the configuration is a simple list of file name extensions. To block new file types just add the extensions to the list. To allow them, remove the extensions.

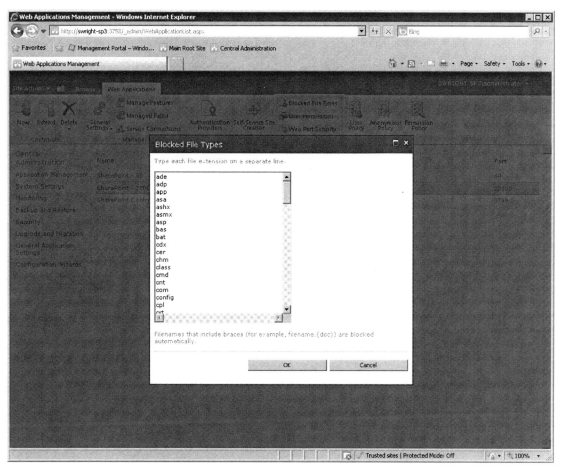

Figure 7-4. Blocked File Types dialog

User Permissions

Permissions are defined by SharePoint to allow granular assignment of access rights within the platform. The User Permissions dialog can be used to disable certain SharePoint permissions within a web application. Disabling a permission at the web application level will make it unavailable throughout the site collections associated with it. No user will have the disabled permission within the web application.

This feature should be used with great care because it can cause unexpected consequences. For example, disabling the "Create Subsites" permission has the effect that no one can create a subsite within the web application. This includes site collection and farm administrators as well.

It is usually more appropriate to remove permissions from the default permission levels within the site collections. That allows the permission to be granted to individual users as needed without having them automatically assigned through permission levels. Disabling of permission levels at the web application level is most often used for locking down public-facing web sites that must be tightly controlled.

Web Part Security

Web Parts allow users to create pages using pre-compiled components. These components can be configured and connected to produce highly functional web sites without writing any source code. In some cases, the functionality of Web Parts may need to be reined in as shown in Figure 7-5.

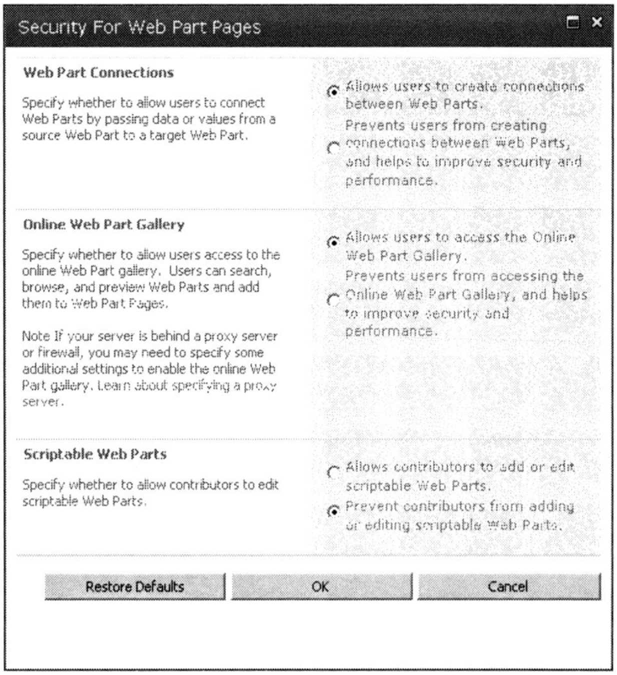

Figure 7-5. Web Part security policy

Using this dialog, a farm administrator can

- Prevent users from creating connected Web Parts. Web Part connections allow data from one Web Part to be used to populate another. You can experience performance issues with this feature, but disabling it is not usually necessary. Well-written Web Parts should not cause these problems and this feature is too valuable to forgo in most cases.

- Prevent users from using the Online Web Part Gallery. This gallery contains Web Parts from Microsoft or other vendors that can be downloaded and used within the local SharePoint farm. If your organization wants to ensure that only approved Web Parts are used, disabling this gallery would be appropriate.

- Prevent editing of scriptable Web Parts. Certain Web Parts allow users to enter HTML or other types of markup that may contain program code such as JavaScript. A malicious user could add script to these controls that could cause serious problems for the web site. Users with Contribute rights on a site can edit Web Parts, but this option allows scriptable Web Parts to be excluded from this rule. By default, this option is set to prevent contributors, but not site collection administrators, from editing these Web Parts.

User Policy

The User Policy dialog is used to assign web application permission policies to users. These permissions apply to the given user for all site collections in the application. As Figure 7-6 illustrates, each user is assigned one or more permission policies.

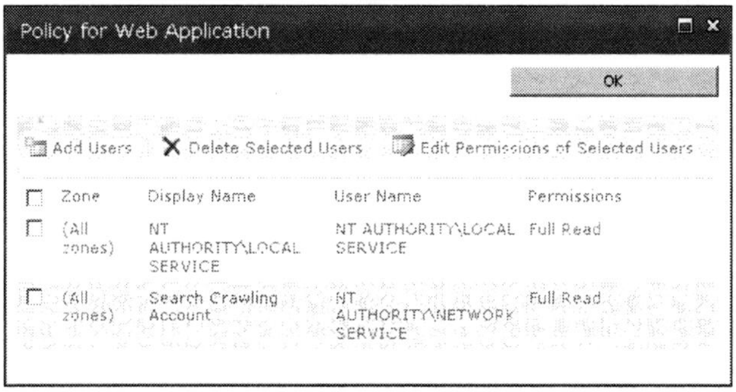

Figure 7-6. User Policy configuration

A common use for web application–level user policies is to grant universal read access to the service account used to crawl content in the SharePoint farm. Another good use case is to delegate administration responsibilities for the web application by giving a user full control access. This allows the user to act with complete autonomy within the confines of the web application without being made a farm administrator.

Separate policies can be used for specific zones. When a user accesses a web application from a given zone, the set of permissions associated with that zone are applied. For example, a user may have full control of a web application when accessing it via the intranet zone, but only read access when the access is received from the Internet. A policy could even be used to deny all users write access from the Internet zone, assuming there are no blogs or other social media features on the site that require write access. This is one more way to lock down access coming from the Internet without disabling needed functionality from inside the organization.

Anonymous Policy

A web application's anonymous policy applies only to those site visitors that have not been authenticated. While each authentication provider, site collection, and site can have their own configurations regarding anonymous users, the web application's policy takes precedence.

This policy is applied to a single zone or all zones in the same way as the user policy described in the previous section. In this case, the policy applied can only prohibit, not grant, access to a site, as shown in Figure 7-7.

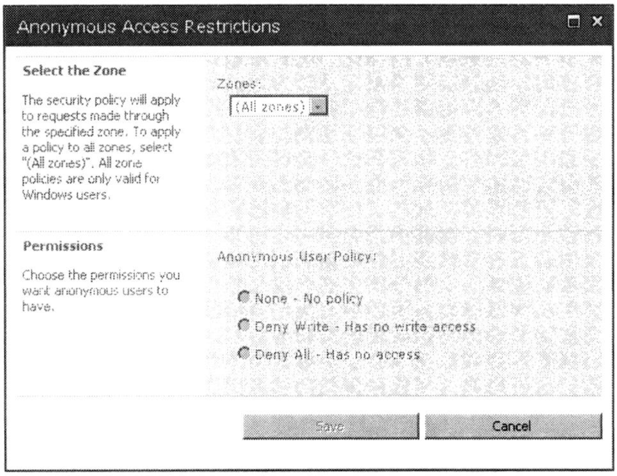

Figure 7-7. Anonymous policy configuration

The usual reason for this type of policy is to prevent users from the Internet defacing a company's web site. No matter how the individual site permissions are configured, write access can be denied to all users in a particular zone. Setting the policy to Deny All has the effect of making the site completely unusable from a given zone.

Permission Policy

Permission policies at the web application level are similar to permission levels within a site collection. They define a named set of permissions that can be assigned to users at the web application level. The list of available permissions available for web applications is different, but the concept is the same.

One important difference between permission policies and permission levels is the ability to *deny* permissions. At the web application level, permissions can be denied as well as granted. A permission that is denied cannot be granted by any other means. If a permission is granted through one policy and denied through another, the result is that the permission is not granted.

Permission policies can also be used to grant specific site collection rights to users as shown in Figure 7-8.

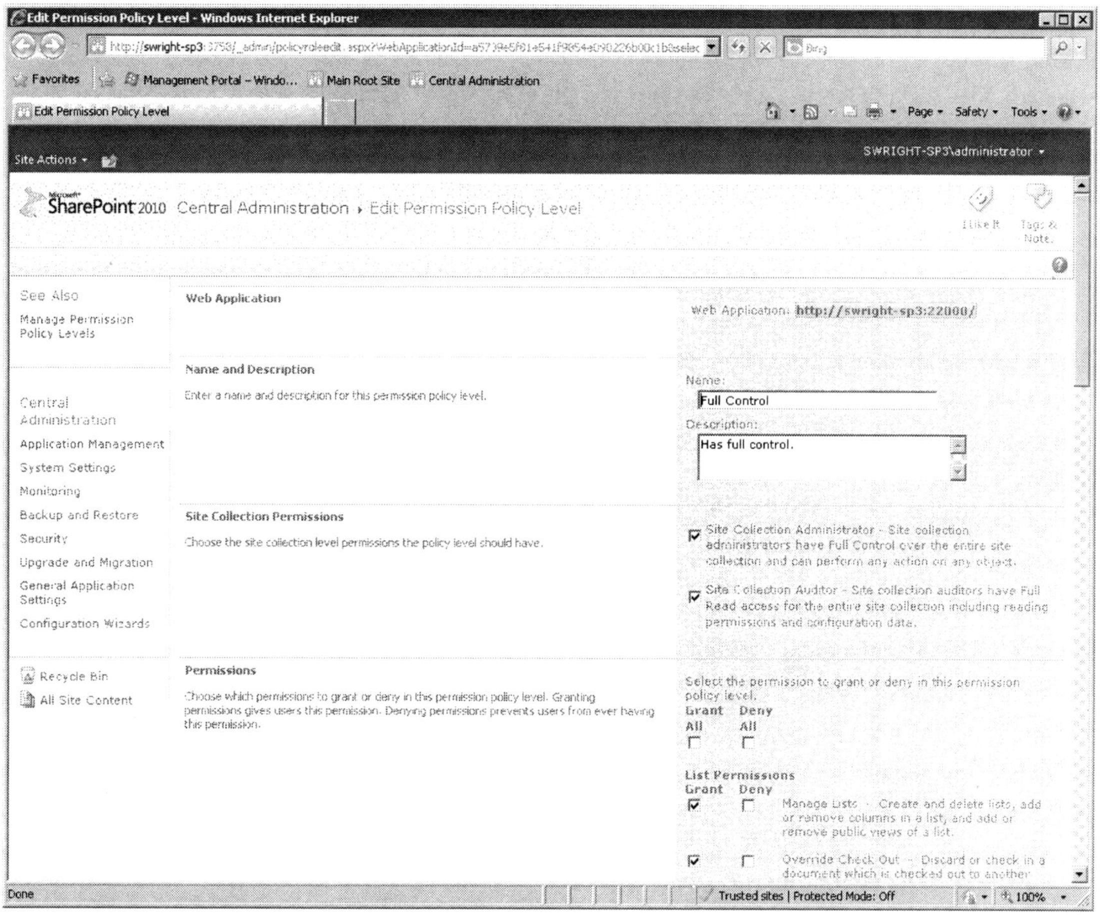

Figure 7-8. *Permission policy configuration*

Handling Large Lists and Queries

All of the documents and content items in SharePoint are stored in lists. An ordinary list might include a few to a few hundred items. As lists become larger, performance issues can occur. To be clear, the size of the list itself is not the problem. SharePoint can easily handle lists with millions of items. Performance begins to suffer when a list is used in certain ways.

Whenever a list or library is displayed on a web page, the user is presented with one of several possible *views*. A list's views define the fields, sorting, and filtering for a listing to be displayed. When SharePoint attempts to display a view, a *query* is run against the SharePoint content database. This query and the results from it can cause the server farm's performance to degrade if the results are not limited properly.

■ **Note** Queries are not only used by SharePoint's default list viewing pages. Custom code using the SharePoint API also has the ability to execute queries against lists and views. These queries are subject to the same performance considerations and configuration settings described here.

As a general rule of thumb, a query should not return more than 5,000 items. There are several strategies for making this happen. A common practice is to separate list items into separate lists, or folders within a list, such that each view can only contain 5,000 items or fewer. Filtering views to display only certain types of items can also produce the desired results in some situations.

To ensure users do not query large views that may degrade performance, SharePoint contains controls that can limit this risk:

- The farm administrator can limit the number of list items that a single query can return. This may prevent large views from being fully populated. The view or query will need to be redefined to allow all of the data to be returned.

- Certain types of fields in a view can cause extra performance load on the system. These fields include references to other lists (lookups), person or group fields, and workflow-related fields. The farm administrator can limit the number of fields of these types in a query to place a boundary on their impact.

- Because of the need to perform security trimming, list items with long lists of unique permission assignments can cause queries to run slowly. The farm administrator can limit the length of these permission lists to ensure that queries are processed efficiently.

- Separate override options and size limits can be set for privileged users. These options should be used carefully because the queries submitted by these users will still degrade performance.

- If it is necessary to process large queries from nightly timer jobs or other processes, a time window can be configured that will allow these queries to run only at those times.

To configure these options, the farm administrator can use PowerShell or Central Administration. These settings are found under Web Applications Management ➤ Resource Throttling (Figure 7-9). Of course, each of these configuration options limits the end user in some way, but setting them to reasonable values should prevent undue frustration for the users without jeopardizing performance.

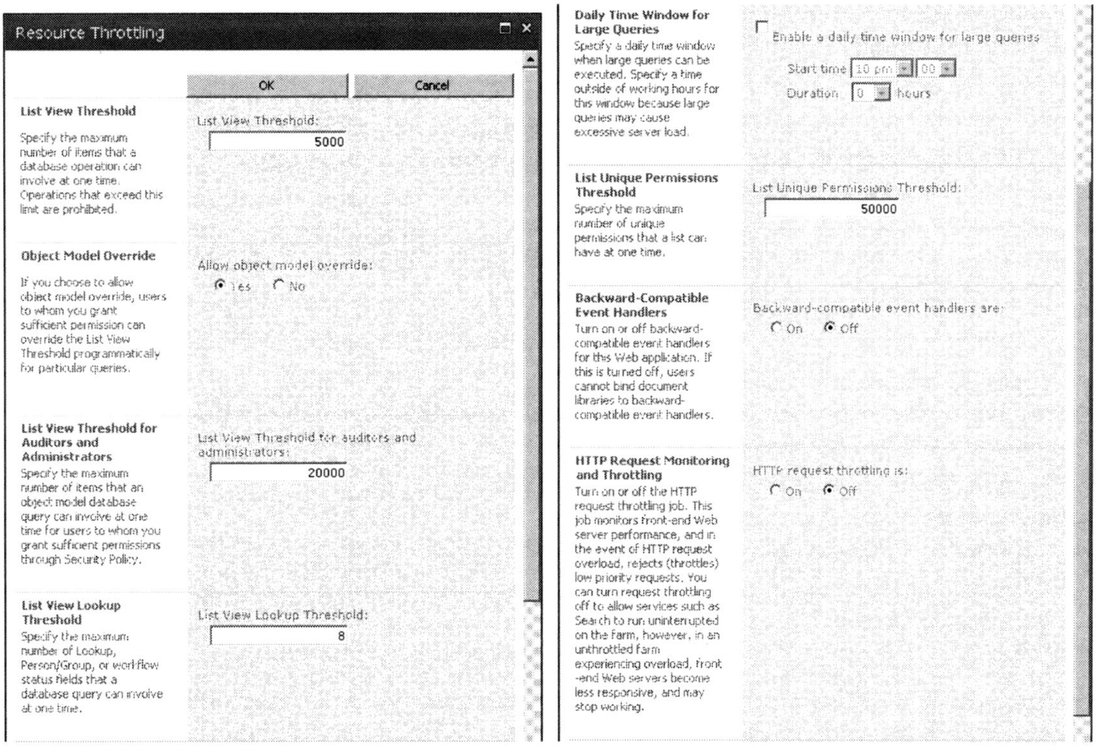

Figure 7-9. Controlling large list access

Request Throttling

As the load on a server increases, the time required for the server to complete each request increases. Eventually, the server becomes unusable for everyone until the server has a chance to catch up. Internet Informration Services (IIS) uses a system of request queues to hold the outstanding requests that have been received but not yet processed. In a high-load situation, these queues can become saturated to the point where the requests waiting to be processed are so old that the user is probably no longer waiting for the response. These requests will eventually be processed but their results will just be discarded. Obviously, this is a significant waste of resources.

SharePoint 2010 has introduced a new feature called *HTTP Request Monitoring and Throttling.* This section describes the default configuration for a web application, which should prove effective in most cases.

Every five seconds SharePoint records a set of Windows performance counter values. If these counters indicate that the server is too heavily loaded, SharePoint will make a note of this. If the server remains at high load for three consecutive checks of these counters, it will enter a *throttled* state. The server will remain in this state until it detects that the server's load has returned to a normal level.

When a server is in a throttled state, incoming requests are managed in a way designed to shed load from the server and allow it to return to normal functioning. SharePoint monitors incoming requests at the point where they move from the IIS request queue into the SharePoint application. The way that SharePoint handles requests in this state depends on the nature of the request.

113

- A user who attempts to retrieve an ordinary page (HTTP GET) will receive a 503 – Server is Busy message from the server. No further processing of the request will occur. This allows SharePoint to effectively discard this type of request. The user will have to retry their request in order to load the page.

- A user who attempts to send a completed data entry form (HTTP PUT/POST) will receive higher priority for processing because discarding such a request can be very inconvenient for the user.

- Search requests, which are notoriously resource intensive, will not fail outright, but they will be processed with a lower priority to ensure that other requests are not delayed.

- Timer jobs that are already running will be allowed to continue processing normally. New timer jobs will not be started while the server is throttled.

Request throttling can be enabled or disabled using the Resource Throttling dialog in CA (see Figure 7-9) or a PowerShell script, or through the SharePoint API. The farm administrator can configure the monitoring interval, performance counters, and counter limits using only PowerShell or the SharePoint API. There are also configuration options for controlling how SharePoint identifies different types of incoming requests for special handling in a throttled state. All of these settings are configured at the web application level.

Request throttling is primarily intended for dealing with temporary spikes in server load. The users should notice very little impact due to servers entering the throttled state because they should not remain there long. The only visible impact might be an occasional 503 – Server is Busy message.

If the load remains high for an extended period of time, this may indicate a Distributed Denial of Service (DDoS) attack is in progress. In this type of attack a large number of computers are compromised by a hacker. These systems (sometimes called *zombies*) are then used to send large numbers of meaningless requests to a web site with the intent of overwhelming its web servers and making it unavailable to legitimate users. The chance of a DDoS attack affecting a company's intranet is slight if it is not accessible from the Internet. For an Internet site that receives a DDoS attack, request throttling can help to mitigate the effects of the attack but it cannot prevent the attack or terminate one that is in progress. Other tools, outside of SharePoint, are required to accomplish that.

Application Pools

SharePoint sites are hosted on Microsoft's Internet Information Server (IIS) web server. One of the features of IIS is the use of application pools to isolate web-based applications from one another. If the code associated with one IIS web site crashes, it can cause only its own application pool to fail. Sites hosted in other application pools will remain unaffected.

SharePoint uses this feature to implement web application isolation. Each SharePoint web application is implemented as an IIS web site. As such it can be hosted in a separate application pool. Each application pool creates a certain amount of overhead on the system, so planning is called for.

- Web applications that contain custom farm-level code should be run in a separate application pool. Note that this does not affect sandboxed code, which always runs in the sandbox service, not in IIS.

- Web applications that need to run using different service accounts will need to run in separate application pools since the service account identity is associated with the application pool.

- Each application pool has memory requirements to be met. Be sure to plan for the memory requirements of all of the application pools that will run on the servers.

- In-place Service Level Agreements (SLAs) may require that certain processes run in isolated environments.

- Application pools can be configured to recover automatically from failures or to remain offline if they become unstable.

Monitoring SharePoint

Monitoring is one of the most often overlooked aspects of SharePoint farm administration. Ironically, the reason for this is because most SharePoint server farms will run well for quite a while without regular monitoring. Unfortunately, the definition of *well* is far too broad to risk an organization's most valuable data. To most users, the system is either up or down. Monitoring allows you to answer questions such as "How well is it running?" and "Will it still be running tomorrow?"

Diagnostic Logging

An important part of managing any IT system is collecting diagnostic information that can be used to solve problems or understand how the system is behaving. Like any Windows application, SharePoint writes important events to the Windows Event Logs. These messages include information on processes that are starting and stopping, errors that are occurring, or any other events that might need to be correlated with non-SharePoint events that may be logged.

SharePoint also implements other means for recording diagnostic information. These will be discussed in this section.

SharePoint Trace Files (ULS)

SharePoint uses a system for recording trace information known as the Unified Logging System (ULS). The ULS is a collection of files that contain information recorded by SharePoint and the service applications that run within it. These logs can also be used by custom-built components to record operational and error information in a way that automatically correlates it with other events occurring in the farm.

SharePoint automatically creates a new ULS log file every 30 minutes to limit the size of each file. Files can still become quite large, however. The files are stored in the LOGS directory under the 14-hive by default. Using a default installation path, this folder is at C:\Program Files\Common Files\Microsoft Shared\Web Server Extensions\14\LOGS. One of the first configurations to be made in a new production server-farm is to move these files to another hard drive on each server in the farm. The C-drive is critical to the running of the operating system. Despite being compressed, the ULS files can quickly fill up the drive and crash the system.

The ULS can and should be configured to prevent unnecessary data from filling up disk space. These settings can be accessed using Central Administration under Monitoring ➤ Configure Diagnostic Logging.

- The farm administrator can set how many days of log files should be kept on each server. The default is 14 days. ULS files older than that number of days will be automatically removed from the system. If there is a need to log large amounts of data or to maintain an indefinite history of log files, it may be preferable to back up and remove these files every 30 minutes when each file is closed and the next file is created.

- A maximum amount of disk space to be consumed may be optionally configured as well. When this limit is reached, the oldest log files are automatically removed to free up space.

ULS logs are written as ordinary text files, so it is possible to read them using a text editor such as NotePad. However, they can be difficult to read directly because they are not formatted conveniently and they can be very large. To simplify working with these files, Microsoft provides a ULSViewer application which can be downloaded from MSDN at `http://archive.msdn.microsoft.com/ULSViewer`. Figure 7-10 illustrates a screenshot from this tool. Microsoft does not support the ULSViewer, but it should serve the needs of small to medium SharePoint farms. Organizations with very large SharePoint installations may wish to invest in Microsoft System Center (`http://www.microsoft.com/en-us/server-cloud/system-center/default.aspx`) or third-party system management tools.

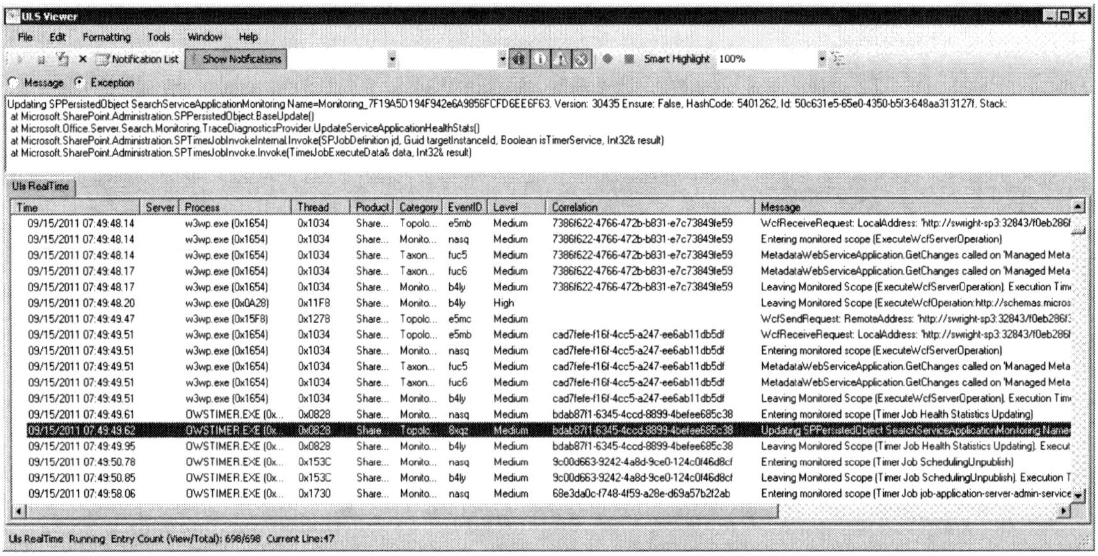

Figure 7-10. *ULSViewer application*

Event Throttling

SharePoint is a large and complex piece of software. This implies that it can produce a vast quantity of trace data. To limit the impact of logging this information, SharePoint can be configured to restrict the logging of events based on the category of the event, the severity of the event, and whether the event will be logged in the Window Event Logs or the ULS trace file.

The category of the event describes where the event came from and what it pertains to. For example, an event might be logged by the Excel Services Application and pertain to accessing *External Data*. Each category can be configured separately or together with other types of events, as shown in Figure 7-11.

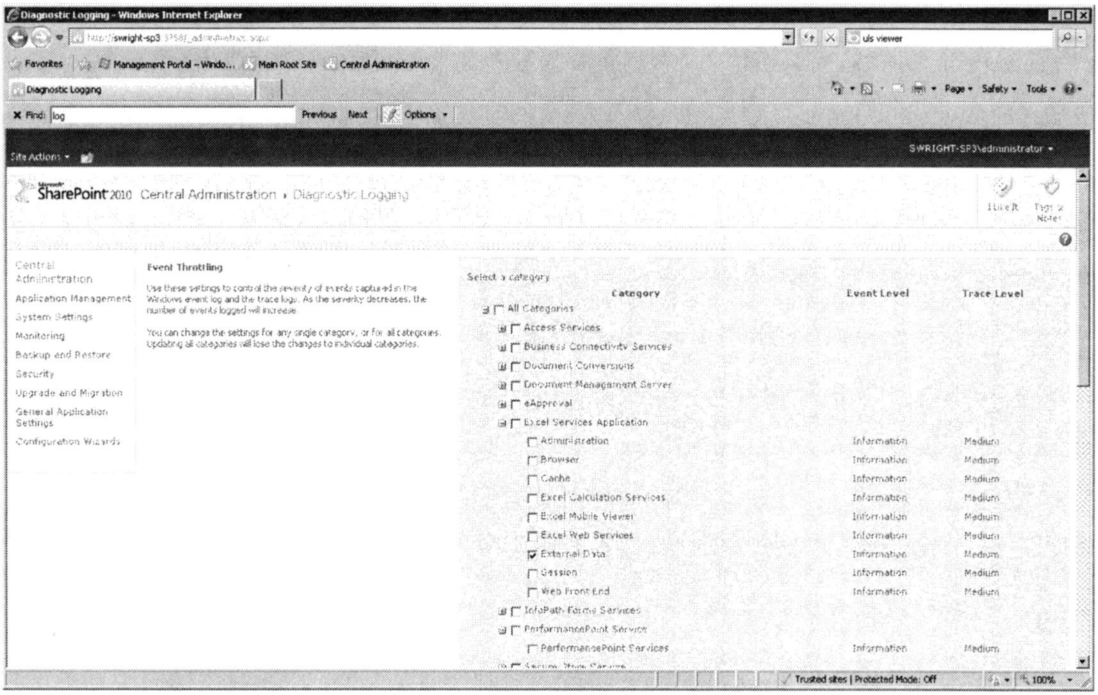

Figure 7-11. *Configure diagnostic logging*

The severity of an event refers to its likely impact on the rest of the system. Events destined for the Windows event logs are assigned a severity, in increasing order according to severity, including Verbose, Information, Warning, Error, or Critical. The ULS logs use the severity levels of Verbose, Medium, High, Monitorable, and Unexpected. When logging is configured for an event, one of these levels is designated as the minimum level to be recorded. For example, if an event is configured to be logged at the Information level, all events will be logged except for those at the Verbose level.

A separate severity level is configured for each category of event and destination of the event record. This allows the farm administrator to limit the generation of trace information while capturing the most important information.

By default, all events with a severity of Information or higher are logged to the Windows event logs and events at or above the Medium level are recorded in the ULS trace files. These settings produce significant trace logging but minimal event log traffic. This is appropriate for most farms.

Event Log Flood Protection

A new feature in SharePoint 2010 is the ability to prevent event floods from overwhelming your log files. An *event flood* occurs when a component detects a problem, reports it, and then continues to experience the same problem over and over again. This can quickly fill up the server's event logs. It can be almost comical when you lose the original cause of an error because the event log was overwritten by errors resulting from a side effect of the actual problem.

To prevent this situation, SharePoint 2010 will monitor the frequency with which each event is being recorded. If it sees the same message recorded more than five times in two minutes, it will record the fact in the log and cease recording each occurrence of that event. A summary event will be written every two minutes with counts of the suppressed events until the flood subsides. Then it will return to logging each event.

Event log flooding applies only to the Windows Event logs and not the ULS trace log files. This feature is turned on by default and can be turned off on the same page where event throttling is configured in CA. The threshold count and quiet period for event flood detection can be set using Windows PowerShell, but not CA.

Correlation IDs

Because of the amount of event and trace data that can be generated by the various components of SharePoint, it can be difficult to tell which events are related to one another. The logs are stored sequentially as items are written to them. Requests being processed simultaneously may generate events that are mixed together in the sequence of the logs. SharePoint addresses this problem using Correlation IDs.

A *correlation ID* is a Globally Unique Identifier (GUID) that is assigned to each request processed by SharePoint. An event that is recorded by SharePoint as a result of a request will be associated with that request correlation ID.

■ **Note** Correlation IDs are also included in some error messages, event log entries, and other interfaces such as the Developer Dashboard. The Developer Dashboard is a diagnostic panel that can be turned on by a developer to debug problems on a SharePoint page.

Looking back at Figure 7-10, notice the Correlation column. This column lists the correlation ID associated with each entry in the ULS log shown. By filtering this list by correlation ID, you can eliminate the unrelated events and see only those events that correspond to the request in question.

SharePoint Logging Database

SharePoint 2010 introduced a new form of proactive logging called the SharePoint Logging Database. This database collects a variety of data from all of the servers in the farm. This gives the administrator a single source for this information without the need to explicitly enable logging or combine log files.

The logging database is stored on the back-end SQL Server in a database called WSS_Logging. The tables in this database are numerous and difficult to query directly. Fortunately, Microsoft has provided a series of views (Figure 7-12) to simplify retrieving information from these tables.

Figure 7-12. *WSS_Logging views*

■ **Note**   Unlike every other SharePoint database, Microsoft fully supports querying and writing reports against the WSS_Logging database. All of the other databases in SharePoint are still off limits.

Much of the data that goes into this database is collected by a set of timer jobs. To prevent runaway data collection in a new farm, these jobs are disabled by default. To collect the information provided by these *Diagnostic Data Providers* simply enable the timer jobs using Central Administration.

- Diagnostic Data Provider: Event Log

- Diagnostic Data Provider: Performance Counters - Database Servers

- Diagnostic Data Provider: Performance Counters - Web Front Ends

- Diagnostic Data Provider: SQL Blocking Queries

- Diagnostic Data Provider: SQL DMV

- Diagnostic Data Provider: SQL Memory DMV

- Diagnostic Data Provider: Trace Log

The following list itemizes some of the types of information that can be reported from the logging database. Remember that, unlike ULS or Event Logs, these views contain information from all of the servers in the farm. This data covers the entire contents of the farm including diagnostic, health, and feature usage information.

- Unified Logging Service (ULS) logs

- Windows event logs

- Performance counters for memory, I/O, and CPU utilization

- SQL Server Dynamic Management Views (DMVs)

- Usage information for various features

- Search service crawling and querying

- Timer jobs

Do not assume that the only data available in this database is reflected in the views that are currently present. When a new type of information is configured for collection, new tables and views will appear in WSS_Logging to hold that information. These database objects are created on demand as needed. For example, in Figure 7-12, the ULSTraceLog view was created only after the Diagnostic Data Provider: Trace Log timer job was run for the first time in this farm.

It is important to remember that the logging database is populated in addition to the ULS and event logs, not in place of them. Turning on large amounts of logging in either mechanism can generate unmanageable amounts of log data. Consider which tools will be used for which purposes in your organization and configure them accordingly. Be sure to plan for the storage space required for log and database files when they are being fully used. Running out of space for these logs can result in the loss of critical information at the worst possible time.

The information in these tables is useful for both diagnosing problems and planning future upgrades and features. This database collects data over time that can be used for trending performance, usage, and search performance.

Usage Data Collection

In addition to collecting data about the general health of the server farm, SharePoint can also collect information about usage patterns for the system. This includes information like the number of times each page is hit, how many unique visitors have been seen, and what browsers have been used. This information is very useful for planning.

Usage data is collected by two timer jobs. The first job copies the usage data from each server in the farm and stores it in the usage tables within SharePoint. This job runs every 30 minutes by default. The second timer job processes all of the collected information to produce a series of reports that can be accessed from CA. The processing job runs once a day by default. The timer jobs for usage data collection are named as follows:

- Microsoft SharePoint Foundation Usage Data Import

- Microsoft SharePoint Foundation Usage Data Processing

Health Analyzer

The SharePoint Health Analyzer is a process that evaluates the configuration and performance of the server farm on a continual basis. The analyzer runs as a series of timer jobs that fire on various schedules. Each job executes a series of checks based on the rules configured in the farm. Figure 7-13 illustrates the default list of rules provided by SharePoint. These rules can be rescheduled, reconfigured, or disabled as desired.

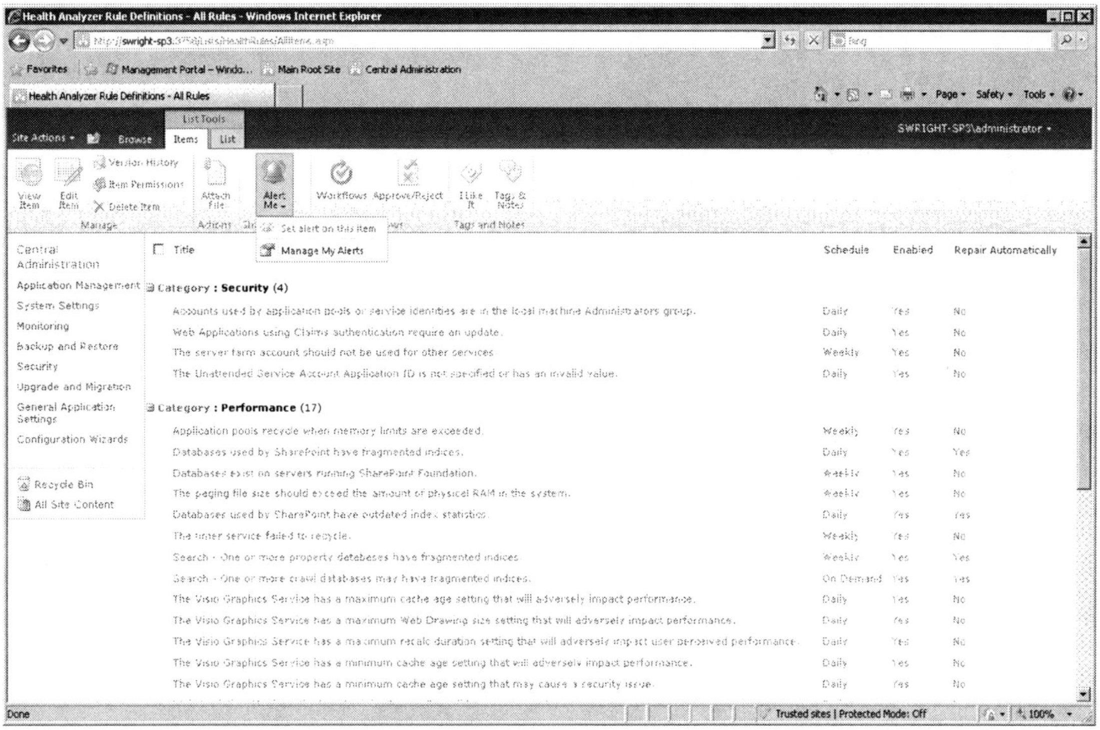

Figure 7-13. Health Analyzer rules

Each rule is actually a piece of executable code installed within SharePoint. New rules can be created by a developer using the SharePoint API. These rules can then be added to the farm and configured like any of the built-in rules provided by SharePoint.

When a rule is executed by the analyzer, it can produce exception reports against the server farm. In some cases, the rule can even automatically correct the problem if it is configured to do so. Otherwise, the report is simply logged for later analysis by a farm administrator. As shown in Figure 7-13, SharePoint's alert mechanism can be used to proactively send notifications of problems to certain users.

When a problem is detected, it is added to a list and can be viewed in CA as shown in Figure 7-14.

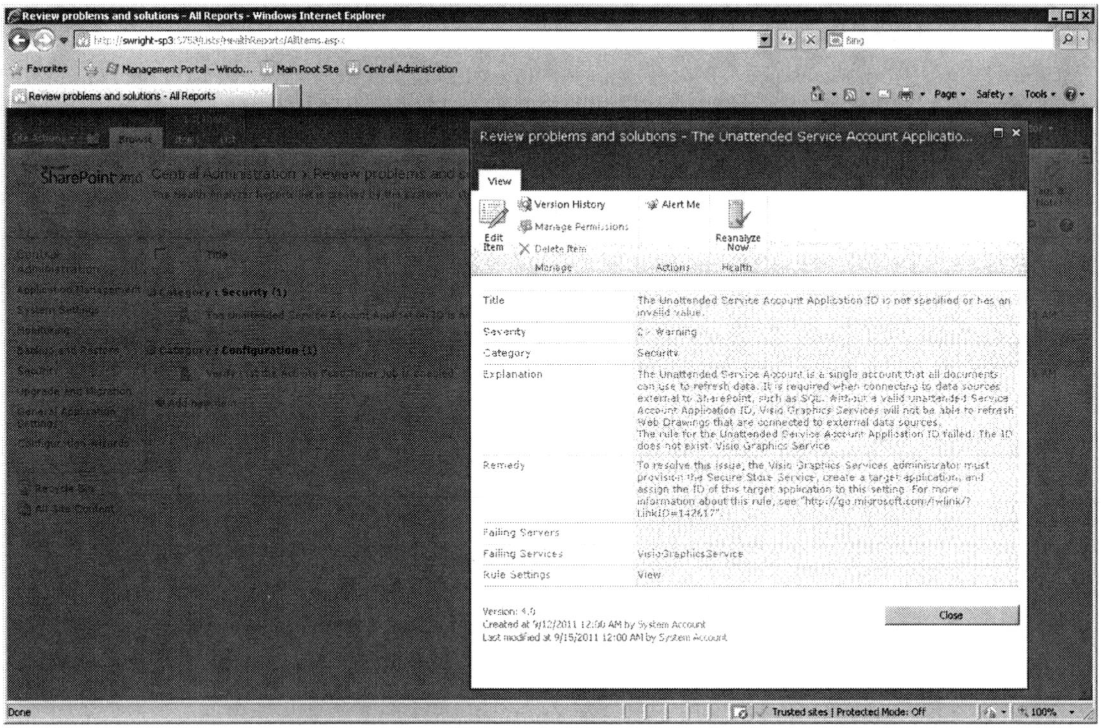

Figure 7-14. Health Analyzer alerts

By setting analyzer alerts and creating your own custom rules, the Health Analyzer provides a means of actively monitoring SharePoint's infrastructure without the need to constantly review settings and log information.

Maintaining SharePoint

In this section, we will discuss the routine activities that need to be performed in a SharePoint farm to keep it running properly. This includes installing new SharePoint releases and upgrades and performing regular backups. These are some of the least glamorous, and correspondingly most important, processes that IT professionals do every day. If all goes according to plan, the end users will never know that they are happening.

Backup and Restore Configurations and Content

Backing up data in SharePoint is just as important as backing up your e-mail or network file system. In this section, we will look at the tools and techniques supported by SharePoint to make backups of all the data within a SharePoint environment. Remember, too, that anything that is backed up may have to be restored. The planning for both scenarios goes hand in hand.

The term *backup*, as used in this section, refers only to data redundancy—that is, moving a copy of your critical data out of the farm so that the farm can be recovered to a known state within a known period of time if data is lost due to a failure.

Other forms of redundancy should also be considered when planning for the long-term use of any IT system. *Hardware redundancy* refers to having multiple servers performing the same function or having extra servers available to quick replacement in the event of hardware failures. Terms like Disaster Recovery (DR) and Business Continuity Planning (BCP) are often used inconsistently to refer to *facility redundancy*. A redundant facility allows the business to move operations to a different location in the event of a catastrophic failure such as a fire, earthquake, or flooding.

Hardware redundancy and facility redundancy are not directly addressed in this chapter, but a comprehensive data redundancy plan is a necessary component in any disaster recovery plan.

Recovery Requirements

When planning for backup, the requirements for recovery of lost data will drive the strategies and techniques to be used. The more aggressive the requirements are, the more the solution will cost to implement them. The requirements associated with backup can be categorized into three primary categories:

- *Recovery point objective*: Refers to how much data can be permanently lost in the event of a catastrophic failure. This goal is usually stated as a period of time such as one hour's, one day's, or one week's worth of data that may be lost. While it is tempting to say "We can't afford to lose ANY data!", remember that such a requirement is all but unobtainable without massive costs. Setting a realistic objective for each type of data allows valid trade-offs to be made.

- *Recovery time objective*: Indicates how long the farm may be partially or completely unavailable while the recovery process is going on. Again, bringing the system back up instantly after a failure is not realistic. Restoring databases from tape or disk, reinstalling software, and rebooting and reconfiguring servers all take time no matter how well planned they are.

- *Recovery granularity objective*: Guides the type of restoration that may be called for. SharePoint contains many layers of data including farms, web applications, site collections, sites, lists, and list items. Using the correct tools, it is possible to restore data at any of these levels.

These recovery objectives form the most important parts of an organization's Service Level Agreement (SLA) with its users.

What Is Backed Up?

SharePoint is a more complex platform than the average e-mail or database server. It contains information in files, databases, the registry, and in proprietary stores.

Configuration information is stored at various levels and places throughout the farm. The central source of configuration data is the SharePoint configuration database in SQL Server. Each web application has its own web.config file that configures the IIS web site hosting the web application. Solution packages deployed at the farm level are also treated as configuration data as are the settings associated with the various Windows services running on the servers.

Service applications, such as Excel Services or PerformancePoint Services, are usually composed of an application configuration, a proxy configuration, and one or more databases. Depending on the service, restoring the proxy is often the most difficult because it is the item that connects the service to the rest of the farm. Be careful to plan service restorations thoroughly.

The search service is even more complex than the average service because of its distributed nature and the plethora of data repositories involved. In addition to the service assignments to servers, the search service depends on an administration databases, crawl databases, property databases, and multiple index files deployed on various servers.

SharePoint content is stored in content databases as described earlier in this chapter. In addition to sites and lists, content databases contain elements including InfoPath forms, workflows, sandboxed solutions, and certain site customizations.

While many customizations are stored in the content databases, others are not. Special care should be taken to ensure that these customizations are not left out of the recovery plan. Some of these are

- Farm solution files

- Site definitions

- XML configuration file changes

- Files deployed manually to the Global Assembly Cache (GAC), a web application's bin directory or the 14-hive directories

- Binary Large Objects (BLOBs) stored outside the content database using the Remote BLOB Storage (RBS) feature

New Features in SharePoint 2010

The 2010 release of the SharePoint platform introduced some new features that were sorely needed by administrators in previous versions. These features allow for more granular and flexible backup and restoration strategies to be implemented without the use of third-party tools.

Granular Backup and Restore

The Granular Backup feature allows an administrator to create a package that contains only a small subset of the content in a content database. This package can then be imported into another location within a SharePoint farm. This eliminates the need to back up and restore an entire content database just to retrieve one document or list item.

Unattached Content DB Export

SharePoint content databases are ordinary SQL Server databases. They are used to serve farm data only once they are *attached* to a web application. To recover older or misplaced content from a previously recorded backup, it is necessary to restore that backup to a SQL Server. In the past, the administrator would then be required to attach the content database to a SharePoint farm so that its content could be accessed. SharePoint 2010 now allows for data to be backed up (or exported) to a granular backup package without being in an attached content database. This prevents the other data in the content database from ever being made part of the SharePoint farm.

Backup Using a SQL Database Snapshot

Because it is possible to back up data from a detached content database, it is also possible to use a SQL Database Snapshot to better control the data being backed up. In a very busy system, it is sometimes difficult to make a consistent backup of a content database that is in constant use. Using SQL Server to create a database snapshot essentially creates a point-in-time image of the content in the database. The snapshot is a read-only representation of the database as it existed at the moment the snapshot was taken. The original database is still fully available to end users. Once the backup is completed, the snapshot can be discarded if desired.

Tools

Because of the variety of data making up a SharePoint farm, a variety of tools can be used to back up and restore some or all of this data. In this section, we will quickly describe the most commonly used tools and their pros and cons.

The Windows operating system contains its own file-based backup utility named Windows Backup. Because this tool is file-based, it should not be used for backing up SQL Server databases while SQL is running. It can be used for backing up the files that make up the SharePoint product and some of the configuration of the farm. Unfortunately, there are too many items that cannot be backed up safely, or at all, for Windows Backup to be a useful tool in a SharePoint context.

Most of SharePoint's data is housed in SQL Server databases. As such, it is tempting to use SQL Server's excellent backup tools. In many cases, such as individual content databases, this is a perfectly valid choice. However, there are configurations and files stored outside of SQL Server that are critical to restoring a complete farm configuration. While SQL Server backup is a component in a complete solution, it can never be the whole answer.

SharePoint 2010 includes its own internal backup and recovery system. When a SharePoint backup is initiated with this tool, the administrator selects how much of the farm to back up and what type of backup to perform (full, differential, or transactional). The backup is performed within SharePoint, which collects all of the configuration settings for the backed up components, along with backups of the relevant databases and files, and writes them to a directory structure in a file system on the network. These files can then be backed up to disk or tape as ordinary files. All of the control information needed to successfully restore the backup is included in the backup files.

The SharePoint backup system can be initiated using either CA or Windows PowerShell scripting. Oddly, one feature that is not a part of SharePoint's backup system is automation. There is no way to configure SharePoint to automatically back up some or all of a farm on a schedule. The recommended approach is to create PowerShell scripts for each backup action. These scripts are then scheduled to execute on a regular basis. This can be done using Windows Task Scheduler or some other task automation tool.

Finally, several vendors offer third-party SharePoint management tools. These tools can help simplify planning, automation, and recovery from failures. Microsoft's product in this category is Microsoft System Center. When dealing with backup and restoration in SharePoint, Microsoft offers the Data Protection Manager (DPM) add-on for System Center.

Software Updates and Patches

Like any piece of software, SharePoint 2010 requires the installation of regular patches and upgrades. Because a SharePoint farm consists of many services running on multiple servers and accessing various databases, installing software updates without corrupting the system or causing excessive downtime can be a challenge.

■ **Note** In this section, we are discussing *software updates* not *release upgrades*. While the processes used to upgrade from one version of SharePoint to another are similar in some ways, the processes in this section refer specifically to installing hotfixes and service packs to an operational server farm.

General Update Flow

Each update package received from Microsoft includes its own set of fixes and installation instructions. Always carefully review these prior to any update to a production farm. The overall process for deploying patches to a SharePoint farm is outlined in Figure 7-15.

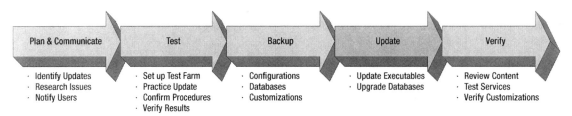

Figure 7-15. Update process overview

The first step is to identify the updates to be deployed. Microsoft releases hotfixes and service packs with interdependencies and prerequisites. These need to be researched and understood before a deployment plan can be created. Once the outline of the steps to be followed is complete, the release should be scheduled and that schedule communicated to the end-user community.

Testing product updates is just as important as testing custom code releases. Specifically, you need to be sure to test the exact sequence of steps to ensure that any conditions unique to your environment are accounted for. The best approach is to create a test server farm that matches the production environment as closely as possible. Be sure to have at least one of each type of server (database, application, web front-end, etc.) that exists in the production farm. Place a copy of the production content databases and services on the test farm, and be sure to include any customizations that exist in production. Performing a successful upgrade on the test farm gives much greater confidence that the update will succeed in production.

Before beginning any major configuration change in a production server farm, always make sure that a complete, current set of backups is available. This will ensure that, should a problem be encountered during the update, a rollback to the previous configuration will be possible. Do not forget to practice recovering from backups from time to time. A backup that cannot be successfully restored is not a real backup.

Once the backups are in place and the update has been tested, you just need to wait for the scheduled maintenance window to actually perform the update. Bear in mind that even if you plan the update to create little or no downtime, updates should still be scheduled for a time window when unexpected problems will cause minimal disruption. We will discuss the details and strategies for managing updates in the following sections.

After the update is complete there should be a plan for verifying that the system is back up and running properly and that all services are available to the users. This plan should include verifying the patch levels in CA, ensuring that all services are running and all customizations are working as expected.

What Is Updated?

The exact updates performed when deploying a package depend on the nature of the changes being released. Service packs typically contain large numbers of updates and may require significant downtime to deploy. Hotfixes, on the other hand, generally contain one or two specific changes and can often be deployed very quickly with little or no downtime. The components updated fall into two major categories: product files and databases.

Product files can be executable files like EXEs and DLLs or support files like ASPX or XML files. These files need to be installed on each server in the farm. SharePoint 2010 updates implement the concept of *backward compatibility.* This means that the product files can be loaded before the final upgrading of the farm because newer files always support farms that include servers using older configurations. There are limitations to the support offered by backward compatibility, depending on the changes being made, but the concept helps to make deploying updates much simpler than in previous versions of SharePoint. As each server and component is patched, the farm administrator can verify the versions deployed using CA (Figure 7-16).

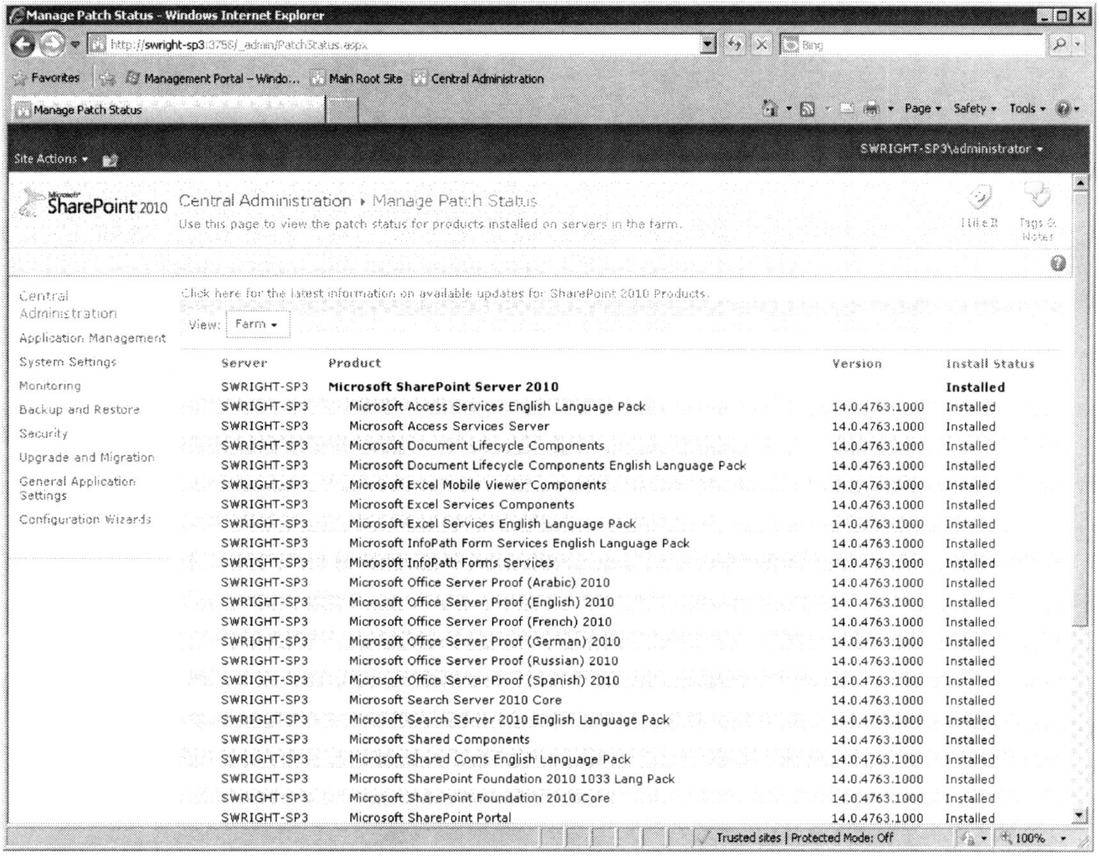

Figure 7-16. *Manage Patch Status (Central Administration)*

SharePoint relies on a number of SQL Server databases. Each of these databases contains tables, views, and other objects that support the storage and retrieval of information for the SharePoint farm. Each of these databases may be updated by a software update. For example, a table may need to be created or altered in one of these databases. CA can also be used to monitor upgrade processing in SharePoint's databases (Figure 7-17).

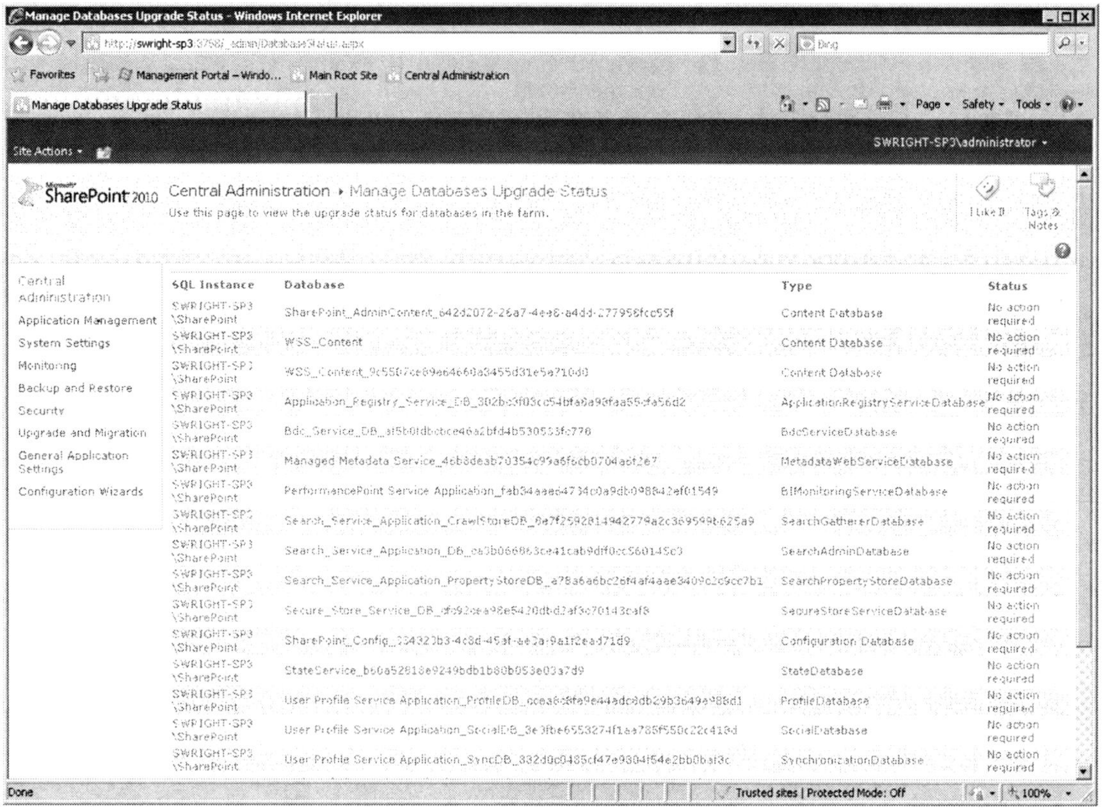

Figure 7-17. Manage Databases Upgrade Status (Central Administration)

Update Phases

Any release package will come with some instructions for installation, but the general steps involved are similar, as shown in Figure 7-18.

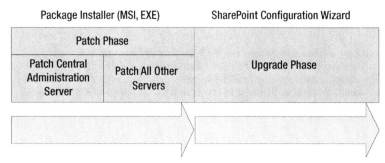

Figure 7-18. Software update phases

Installing software updates in a large farm happens in two phases: patching and upgrading. These phases map to the deployment of product files and the updating of database objects, respectively.

In the *patch* phase, the package installer is run on the servers in the farm, starting with the server hosting the CA web site. This ensures that the processes associated with CA are never running on an older version of SharePoint's executables than other servers in the farm. After CA is patched, the other servers are patched as well.

In the *upgrade* phase, the SharePoint 2010 Products Configuration Wizard application is run on each server to perform any remaining actions required to complete the upgrade of the farm. The most common tasks performed involve modifying one or more of SharePoint's databases, but other actions may be taken as well. The upgrade phase usually takes much longer to complete than the patch phase because of the need to update large amounts of data in some cases.

Again, always be sure to read the instructions supplied with the update package because there may be special considerations that will change the order of operations for the update process.

Strategies

The discussion up to now has given a general outline for how updates are applied. What if your environment has special needs? How much downtime can you afford? Can you commit hardware and personnel resources to reducing downtime?

SharePoint 2010 supports three main strategies for managing a software update deployment. Table 7-2 compares the pros and cons of each.

Table 7-2. Update Strategies

Description	Pros	Cons
Perform update with an immediate upgrade.	Simple to plan and perform	Causes significant downtime
Perform update but postpone the upgrade.	Permits a shorter service window	Does not eliminate downtime altogether More complex planning involved
Perform update on a standby server farm.	No downtime	Requires duplicate production hardware and farm configuration

The three strategies listed trade simplicity for downtime. In the first case, a simple server-by-server installation and upgrade are performed. This requires the farm to be taken offline while the update is performed. The second scenario uses the backward compatibility concept to update the servers' software in one phase and then upgrade the farm's databases individually or in groups to limit downtime.

The final option involves creating a completely separate standby server farm that is fully operational. The production content is migrated into the standby farm, where it is upgraded, while the active farm continues serving users. The content databases in the active farm should be locked to prevent updates during the upgrade because those changes would be lost. When the update is complete, the standby farm is switched into the active position and the previous active farm becomes the standby. Obviously, this process requires a great deal of planning and hardware investments, but it has the potential to completely eliminate downtime in many situations.

Summary

In this chapter, we have

- Described farm management and the operational plan
- Explored the ways in which the configuration controls available in SharePoint can be used
- Described the configuration options available for web applications in SharePoint
- Explored SharePoint's logging system and how it can be used to monitor the farm and resolve issues
- Described the collection and reporting of usage data in SharePoint
- Explained the mechanisms to monitor and analyze the health of the server farm
- Described the processes for performing software installations and upgrades to a running server farm
- Looked at the options available for making backups of the content and configurations stored in SharePoint

CHAPTER 8

Managing Operations

Depending on the size and complexity of the farm, managing the daily operations of a SharePoint farm can be a full time job. SharePoint 2010 introduced many new services and features that make monitoring operations of the farm and its users much easier than in previous versions. Monitoring the overall SharePoint farm health as well as how the users are interacting with SharePoint is critical to the overall success of the environment.

What Will You Learn in This Chapter?

- Different levels of farm taxonomies and configurations
- What to monitor within the SharePoint farm
- How to monitor the SharePoint farm and what tools to use
- Important considerations for security planning
- Important considerations for capacity planning

SharePoint Farm Configurations

SharePoint Server provides a ton of features and capabilities that are used by many organizations in many different ways. The SharePoint farm should be configured to meet the needs of the business, whether that is a small, medium, or large farm deployment. Regardless of the size of the farm and depending on the needs of the business, configuring the farm following best practices can eliminate a lot of headaches down the road. Because SharePoint 2010 has a services-based architecture, adapting to change and changing configurations has never been easier.

While hardware and software requirements are outside the scope of this book, all the configuration information is based on recommendations from Microsoft at the following link: http://technet.microsoft.com/en-us/library/cc262485.aspx. Determining the configuration of the farm greatly depends on its intended use. If the farm is going to focus on collaboration and content management, more resources should be focused in the web tier, such as having a Network Load Balancer (NLB) to route traffic appropriately and provide redundancy. If the farm is going to be used primarily for business intelligence (BI) purposes, it's important to have additional servers in the application tier as this is where the BI services live. Understanding the business needs and configuring a farm to map to these needs is the key. However, SharePoint is flexible and additional servers can be added and configured without rework.

Limited Deployments

Microsoft defines a limited deployment as an evaluation environment or an environment that is meant to support fewer than 100 users. A limited deployment could include a single server (standalone installation), where all the roles, including SQL Server, reside on the one machine. A potential challenge when using the standalone installation is the use of SQL Server Express 2008 and the limitation of a 4-GB database. SQL Server Express also does not provide a GUI-based management tool, such as SQL Server Management Studio. This is a separate download that is not installed and configured as part of the standalone configuration. This approach also limits the ability to add an additional server down the road if more resources are needed to meet user demand. However, installing SharePoint 2010 on a server that contains a full version of SQL or SQL Server 2005 SP2 or higher, from a SQL perspective, mitigates a lot of the risk encountered when using the standalone configuration. Keep in mind that even if a full SQL Server instance is available, installing SharePoint in the standalone mode will still utilize SQL Server Express. (See Figure 8-1.)

A limited deployment could also include a two-tier farm. A two-server farm is normally considered the minimum when implementing a production environment. This approach would split SQL Server out onto its own server, with the Web and application roles on the other. This approach can support up to 10,000 non-concurrent users, and has the ability to expand if needed to better support future growth. However, keep in mind that all SharePoint web requests and services utilize a single server. Continuous monitoring of the farm and its ability to meet user demand should be performed. If SharePoint becomes a business-critical application within the organization, the farm should be scaled out to support a high availability solution. This farm configuration would include a redundant front end as well as a redundant back end.

 Standalone or single server install

Figure 8-1. Limited deployment

It's not uncommon for a successful SharePoint Proof of Concept (POC) to end up as a production SharePoint farm. This is strongly discouraged, because the POC most likely didn't follow best practices during installation and configuration, and doesn't contain the hardware or redundancy to support a production environment. We recommend that a new SharePoint farm be rolled out and the POC farm be either decommissioned or used as a demo or development environment.

Small Farm Topologies

A small farm is a good entry point as it can serve a large number of users and scale out based on utilization of the SharePoint services. This type of topology generally has three to five servers in the farm. This topology typically includes two web servers, which can support 10,000–20,000 non-concurrent users as well as provide redundancy if a Network Load Balancer is routing traffic appropriately. The application layer typically has one to two servers, depending on which SharePoint services are being utilized.

Determining up front how SharePoint is going to be used will help define the farm topology needed. How heavily are the services going to be used? How heavily is search going to be used? How many concurrent users are expected? If the SharePoint farm is going to utilize many of the services, a dedicated application server to host these services is recommended. A SharePoint farm that is utilized heavily for search would include a dedicated server hosting the search databases. This approach would be recommended for those environments with up to 10 million items in the index.

As you can see in Figure 8-2, the key is to understand the needs of the business and build the farm appropriately. The small farm topology provides a great base to build on as the needs of your SharePoint farm increase. The beauty of SharePoint from an architecture perspective—especially in SharePoint 2010 with the introduction of the services vs. the Shared Service Provider—is that it's easy to scale as the use of SharePoint increases.

Web/Query Server

Application Server

All SharePoint databases

Figure 8-2. Example small farm

Medium Farm Topologies

A medium farm topology typically has five or more servers, with defined web, application, and data tiers. (See Figure 8-3.) A general rule is that each web server can handle 10,000 non-concurrent users, or 100 concurrent users. However, this will depend greatly upon the client services utilized on these machines. The application tier typically has a dedicated search server, running the Search Query and Site Settings service. Another server, or possibly two, may be present in this layer to run different SharePoint services.

If the business intelligence–related services are going to be utilized, we recommend they be broken out onto a separate server as well. These services would include Excel Calculation Services, PerformancePoint Service, and Visio Graphics Service. The data tier might also include two servers, one for the search databases and the other for all the other SharePoint databases. This approach would be typical in an environment with heavy search utilization.

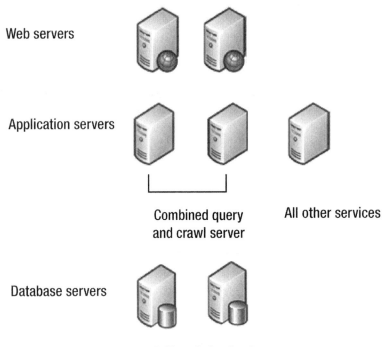

Web servers

Application servers

Combined query
and crawl server   All other services

Database servers

All SharePoint databases

Figure 8-3. Example medium farm

Much as with the small farm topology, it is important to understand the business needs and configure the farm to exceed those needs. Having already defined web, application, and data tiers, the farm can be upgraded within the appropriate tier based on the needs of the business. Table 8-1 shows all the Share-Point 2010 services that are available and the Microsoft recommendation for which tier in the farm the service should run.

Table 8-1. Microsoft-Recommended Tiers for SharePoint 2010 Services

Service	Server Recommendation
Access Database Services	Application Server
Application Registry Service	Application Server
Business Data Connectivity	Application Server
Central Administration	Application Server
Document Conversions Launcher Service	Application Server
Document Conversions Load Balancer Service	Application Server

Service	Server Recommendation
Excel Calculation Services	Application Server
Lotus Notes Connector	Application Server – start on index server
Managed Metadata Web Service	Application Server
Microsoft SharePoint Foundation Incoming E-Mail	Application Server or Web Server
Microsoft SharePoint Foundation Subscription Settings Service	Application Server or Web Server
Microsoft SharePoint Foundation User Code Service	Application Server
Microsoft SharePoint Foundation Web Application	Web Server
Microsoft SharePoint Foundation Workflow Timer Service	Web Server
PerformancePoint Service	Application Server
Search Query and Site Settings Service	Application Server
Secure Store Service	Application Server
SharePoint Foundation Search	Application Server
SharePoint Server Search	Automatically configured on correct servers
User Profile Service	Application Server
User Profile Synchronization Service	Application Server
Visio Graphics Service	Application Server
Web Analytics Data Processing Service	Application Server
Web Analytics Web Service	Application Server
Word Automation Services	Application Server

Large Farm Topologies

A large server farm is normally implemented to handle a large amount of web requests, heavy utilization of many of the SharePoint services, with numerous databases in the data tier to support everything in the web and application tier. High availability is also a concern in each tier in these types of configurations. An NLB is used to route traffic between the web servers not only for load balancing, but also in case one web server goes offline, so that the other web server can pick up the requests. Redundancy is also normally present in the application tier. Those services that are heavily utilized or business critical are often load balanced as well. It's also possible that a single server in the farm will host a single service based on user demand.

The data tier will include numerous databases to support the many services being used in the application tier. These databases are normally grouped together based on their purpose and then the groups are broken out onto different SQL Servers. (See Figure 8-4.)

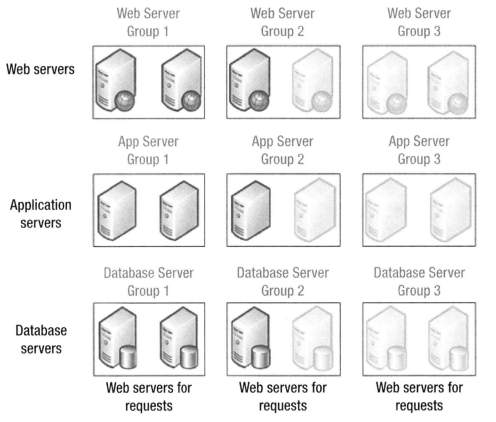

Figure 8-4. Example large farm

Monitoring

To ensure the availably and reliability of your SharePoint 2010 farm, daily monitoring of the physical servers, operating system, and important SharePoint 2010 services should be performed. Performing preventative maintenance and checking nightly backups will prevent larger issues from happening later down the road. This will also allow for maximum uptime and ensure that Service Level Agreements (SLAs) are being met. A daily checklist should be established so that key components within the SharePoint farm are not overlooked. This process will also establish an initial baseline of the farm so that it will be more apparent when and if problems arise. The checklist should utilize the following items and review the information:

- SharePoint 2010 Health Analyzer
- SharePoint 2010 Unified Logging Service
- SharePoint 2010 Timer Jobs
- Windows Server Event Logs
- SharePoint 2010 Usage Data and Health Data Collection
- SharePoint 2010 Web Analytics

This section will describe the monitoring tasks performed in each of the items found in the preceding list. For those more serious SharePoint installations, Microsoft System Centers Operations Manager may be used to monitor these same items.

Database maintenance is an important piece of the overall health of the SharePoint farm. This function is typically performed by a database administrator (DBA) and therefore falls outside the scope of a typical SharePoint farm administrator. For more information about database maintenance for SharePoint 2010, the following white paper available in TechNet is a great resource: http://technet.microsoft.com/en-us/library/cc262731.aspx.

SharePoint Health Analyzer

SharePoint has many features that log and monitor the health of the farm, the details of which are summarized and analyzed for potential issues within the farm. If issues are identified, the Health Analyzer will proactively look for a solution or recommend a potential fix for the issue. The Health Analyzer can be found in Central Administration, within the Monitoring section, and then in the Health Analyzer section. However, if the Health Analyzer finds an issue, a notification will be present at the top of the Central Administration home page. In many of the solutions you will find a "Repair Now" option, which, when selected, will resolve the problem. Those issues that do not have this option will have a hyperlink that leads to more information about the issue and recommends a solution.

The Health Analyzer is preconfigured to look at a set of predefined rules to monitor SharePoint. The predefined rules are broken down into four categories: security, performance, configuration, and availability, as shown in Figure 8-5. However, these rules can be extended and custom rules can be created to better support your environment. More information about the configuration of the Health Analyzer can be found at http://technet.microsoft.com/en-us/library/ee663484.aspx.

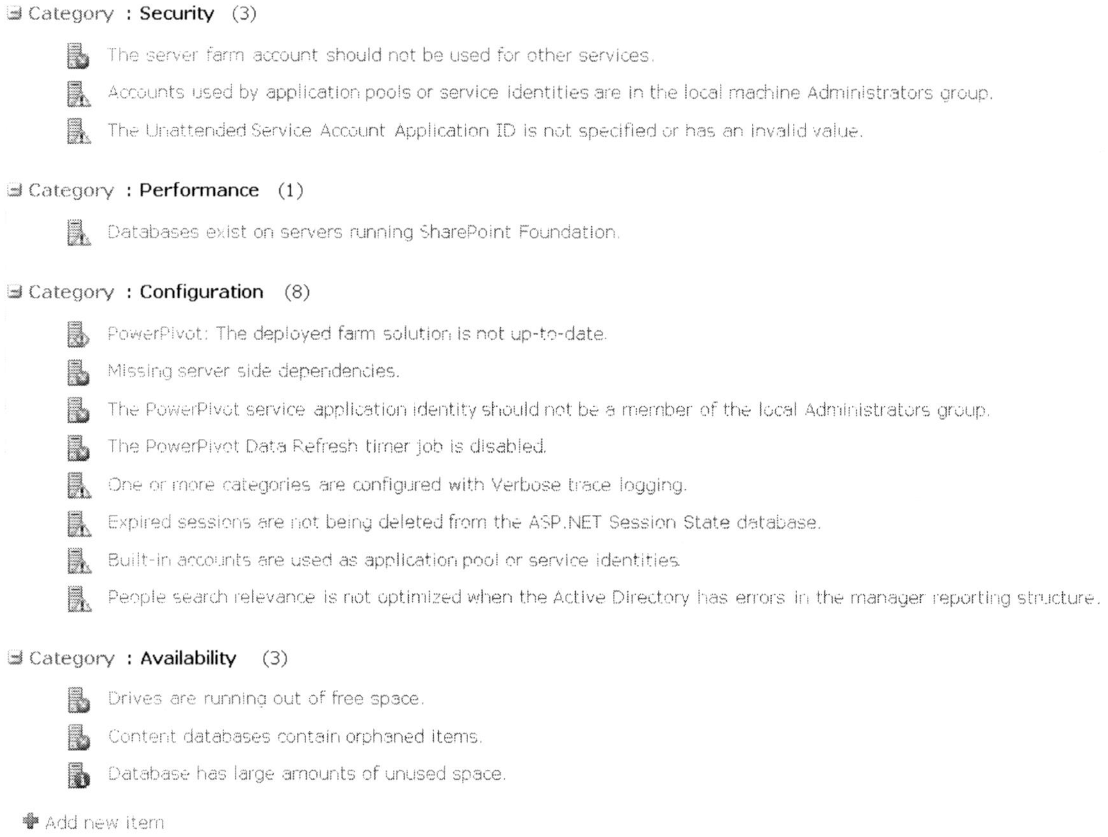

☐ Category : **Security** (3)

    📋 The server farm account should not be used for other services.

    📋 Accounts used by application pools or service identities are in the local machine Administrators group.

    📋 The Unattended Service Account Application ID is not specified or has an invalid value.

☐ Category : **Performance** (1)

    📋 Databases exist on servers running SharePoint Foundation.

☐ Category : **Configuration** (8)

    📋 PowerPivot: The deployed farm solution is not up-to-date.

    📋 Missing server side dependencies.

    📋 The PowerPivot service application identity should not be a member of the local Administrators group.

    📋 The PowerPivot Data Refresh timer job is disabled.

    📋 One or more categories are configured with Verbose trace logging.

    📋 Expired sessions are not being deleted from the ASP.NET Session State database.

    📋 Built-in accounts are used as application pool or service identities.

    📋 People search relevance is not optimized when the Active Directory has errors in the manager reporting structure.

☐ Category : **Availability** (3)

    📋 Drives are running out of free space.

    📋 Content databases contain orphaned items.

    📋 Database has large amounts of unused space.

    ✚ Add new item

Figure 8-5. SharePoint Health Analyzer

SharePoint 2010 Unified Logging Service

The SharePoint Unified Logging Service (ULS) provides a centralized location for all error and information logging messages related to SharePoint and its services. Even though these logs can sometimes be difficult to review, they provide the best overall insight into issues within the farm. The default location for the logs is C:\Program Files\Common Files\Microsoft Shared\Web Server Extensions\14\LOGS, even though it is best practice to put these on another drive so it doesn't fill up the drive and crash the server. Because these logs are so difficult to read, a number of tools have been created to better interrogate these logs. One of the more popular ULS log viewer tools is available on CodePlex at http://ulsviewer.codeplex.com/. If you find this tool doesn't fit your needs, a quick Bing search will show results of many more similar tools that are available to make viewing the ULS logs much easier.

    Trace logs can quickly consume a large amount of disk space, especially when configured with settings other than the default. To manage this growth, administrators can change the default settings to better serve their environment. For example, by default, log files are kept for 14 days. However, an administrator has the option (disabled by default) of placing a maximum on the overall disk space that the log files can consume.

SharePoint 2010 also introduced a logging database, WSS_Logging by default, which can provide further information and is accessible via the SharePoint object model. A good overview of this feature can be found at http://sharepoint.microsoft.com/blogs/fromthefield/Lists/Posts/Post.aspx?ID=124.

Usage Data and Health Data Collection

In addition to Diagnostic Logging, SharePoint Server 2010 also logs information related to the overall health of the farm, using web analytics and health data collection. This new SharePoint 2010 feature can be found within Central Administration, under Monitoring, and under the Reporting section. As an administrator you have the ability to monitor individual events, such as feature use or page requests. As with Diagnostic Logging, these operations add additional overhead and need to be managed appropriately. However, the collection of the data can be scheduled to minimize the performance impact. Figure 8-6 shows the Configuration usage and health data collection options, which can be found within Central Administration ➤ Monitoring ➤ Configure web analytics and health data collection link.

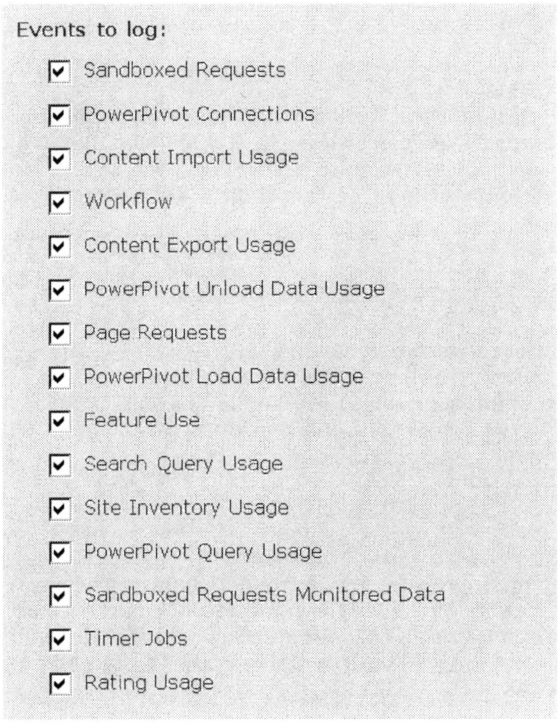

Events to log:

- ☑ Sandboxed Requests
- ☑ PowerPivot Connections
- ☑ Content Import Usage
- ☑ Workflow
- ☑ Content Export Usage
- ☑ PowerPivot Unload Data Usage
- ☑ Page Requests
- ☑ PowerPivot Load Data Usage
- ☑ Feature Use
- ☑ Search Query Usage
- ☑ Site Inventory Usage
- ☑ PowerPivot Query Usage
- ☑ Sandboxed Requests Monitored Data
- ☑ Timer Jobs
- ☑ Rating Usage

Figure 8-6. SharePoint web analytics and health data collection

Timer Jobs

Timer jobs are an important piece of SharePoint monitoring as these tools rely on timer jobs to perform monitoring tasks and collect monitoring data. Timer jobs run on a set schedule that can be configured out of the box. You may want to change the schedules that the timer jobs run on to collect data more frequently or less frequently. You may also want to disable jobs that collect data if you are not interested in the data they return. More information about configuring the SharePoint Health Analyzer timer jobs can be found here `http://technet.microsoft.com/en-us/library/ee748593.aspx`.

Event Throttling

Event throttling enables administrators to filter out events based on event type or severity. If the farm is experiencing an issue with a certain service or component, an easy way to gather more information about the issue is to change the event level and trace level within the issue category. The default settings for all categories are as follows:

- Event Level: Informational
- Trace Level: Medium Level

After completing troubleshooting in which event throttling was turned up, all categories within the Diagnostic Logging should be returned to their default state. This can be done by selecting the "Reset to default" option within the throttling dropdowns. The settings not currently set to default will appear in bold font. More information on event throttling can be found at `http://technet.microsoft.com/en-us/library/ee748656.aspx`.

Correlation IDs

Correlation IDs are GUIDs that are assigned to each user conversation within SharePoint. The GUID is provided within error messages, normally found displayed on a SharePoint page after an error has occurred. This GUID can then be used to quickly find any corresponding entries in the ULS logs. Correlation IDs also cross multiple servers, so if an issue arises that crosses multiple machines, the single Correlation ID can provide a complete overview of all requests.

Windows Server Event Logs

The Windows OS also provides an event log similar to the SharePoint logs. Even though this log will contain information that is not specific to SharePoint, it is a good practice to review these logs daily because issues within the OS can potentially lead to farm downtime as well. The logs to review should include the Application logs, Security logs, and the System logs. These logs can be accessed from the OS Start Menu within Programs ➤ Administrative Tools ➤ Event Viewer.

Web Analytics

SharePoint 2010 Web Analytics provide detailed reports on how your SharePoint environment is being used, and how well it is performing. Administrators should use the reports to become familiar with how the environment is being used and to plan for future capacity or farm growth. Web Analytics is broken down into three areas: traffic, search, and inventory. Then each of these three areas is broken down again by web application, site collection, site, and search service. For more information about SharePoint Web Analytics, visit `http://technet.microsoft.com/en-us/library/ee663487.aspx`.

Traffic

The traffic reports show statistics such as the following:

- Total number of page views
- Top browsers
- Top visitors

Search

The search reports help the administrators understand how search is being utilized. They provide statistics such as the following:

- Total number of queries (number of searches performed)
- Average number of searches per day

In addition, search reports also provide statistics on "Best Bets." These search terms can then be discussed as an enhancement to the "Best Bets" already being provided by the search feature.

Inventory

The inventory reports help the administrators with storage, providing statistics such as the following:

- Disk usage
- Total number of site collections
- What languages are in use

In addition to the items described above, SharePoint backups should be monitored to ensure that they are occurring and should be tested to guarantee that a valid restore can be performed from the backup. This includes farm- and site-level backups, as well as content database backups. Disk space must also be monitored on each server in the farm, including the SQL server. The SharePoint logs consume a large amount of disk space if not configured properly, and issues can occur if additional logs cannot be added.

Backup and Recovery

In smaller SharePoint environments, it's common to perform a full farm backup weekly with a backup of each site collection nightly. This is often scripted through the use of Windows PowerShell and scheduled via the Windows Task Scheduler. Because all business needs vary, and the SharePoint farms themselves vary, it's important to work with the business and understand any Service Level Agreements that are in place in regards to system uptime and the recovery level needed. Determining what to protect, how to recover, and what tools to use to satisfy both is a good start in planning your backup and recovery process. This is a large topic, much of which is defined in great detail in the Plan for Backup and Recovery article on TechNet at http://technet.microsoft.com/en-us/library/cc261687.aspx.

Security Planning

SharePoint security is an area that can become a larger issue as times goes on if a security plan is not developed up front and constantly governed. A breakdown in security can cause unwarranted access to configuration options within SharePoint or potential access to content that is meant for only certain individuals or groups. A security lapse can cause user resentment with the environment and user adoption can suffer. The best way to ensure this does not happen is to understand the SharePoint default groups available within SharePoint and the different permission levels, and determine whether a custom group or permission level is needed. The process and policy for creating new permission levels and SharePoint groups should be documented within a security plan available to all end users.

Default SharePoint Permission Levels

SharePoint permission levels are the building blocks on which the SharePoint groups are created. The permission level is assigned to a group and therefore assigned to all users within that group. It's important to understand each permission level and what the user has the ability to do if assigned that permission level. By default, the following permission levels are available, if the publishing template is not used:

- *Limited Access*: Allows users to view a particular list of the document library without giving them access to the entire site. Users aren't typically added to this group directly, but indirectly from permission changes to an individual item in the list or site.

- *Read*: Allows users to view items on a page.

- *Contribute*: Allows users the ability to add, edit, or delete items on site pages or in lists and document libraries.

- *Design*: Allows users to change the layout of site pages through the browser or Microsoft SharePoint Designer 2010.

- *Full Control*: Includes all permissions.

If the publishing template is used, the following permission levels are available:

- *Restricted Read*: Allows users to view pages and documents.

- *Approve*: Allows users to edit and approve pages, list items, and documents

- *Manage Hierarchy*: Allows users to create sites, edit pages, and list items and documents.

SharePoint 2010 includes 33 different permissions, which are utilized in five default permission levels. For example, it's important to understand that permission levels such as "Contribute" or "Full Control" are associated with even more fine-grained groups of permissions. The best way to review the permissions assigned to the permission level is to go to the Site Permissions, select a permission level, and act as if you are going to edit the permissions. This will display the fine-grained permissions of the permission level. (See Figure 8-7.)

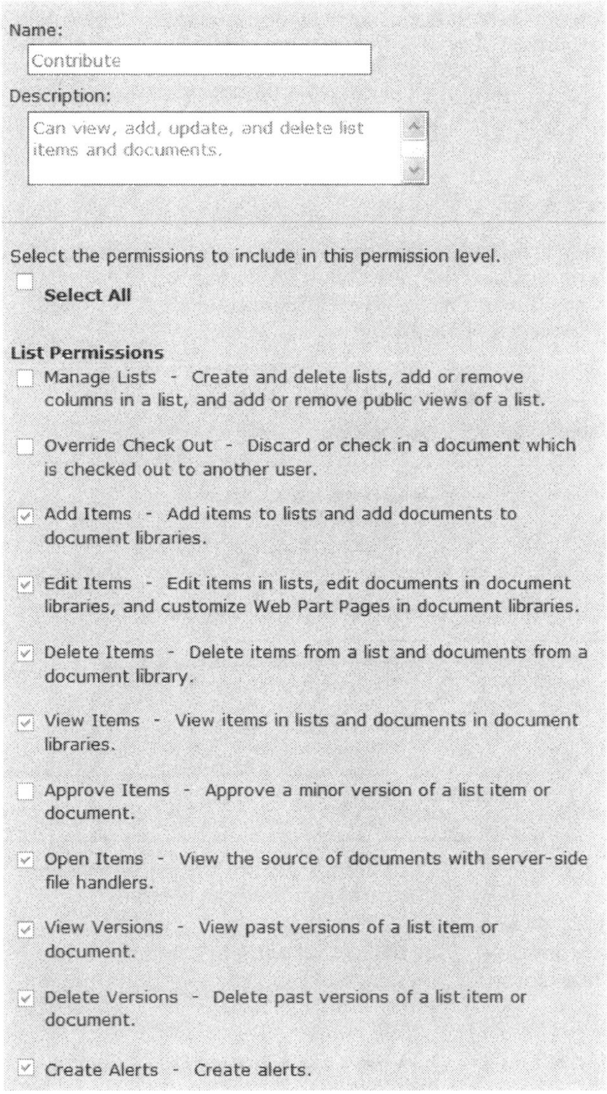

Figure 8-7. *Contribute list permissions*

Note While going through each of the permissions is outside the scope of this book, it is important to review the permissions associated with each permission level. This is especially true if a custom permission level is created. More information about when and why to create a new permission level will be discussed later in this chapter.

If different permissions are needed for a particular permission level we recommend that a new permission level be created with these unique permissions. This will help eliminate confusion for administrators who try to assign the correct permission levels to SharePoint groups. The most common reason for creation of a new permission level is to create a contribute-like permission level that removes the delete capability. This reason, among many others, will be further discussed later in this chapter.

Default SharePoint Groups

Before creating a security plan or a governance plan around SharePoint security, you must understand the default SharePoint groups. It's also critical to understand the permission level assigned to each group. The SharePoint groups can be different depending on which site template is selected. If a team site template is selected, the groups described in Table 8-2 are available.

Table 8-2. *Team Site Template Groups*

SharePoint Group	Default Permission Level	Description
Visitor	Read	Read permissions to site
Member	Contribute	Contribute permissions to site
Owner	Full Control	Full control permissions to site

If a publishing template is selected, the groups shown in Table 8-3 are available.

Table 8-3. *Publishing Template Groups*

SharePoint Group	Default Permission Level	Description
Restricted Readers	Restricted Read	Read permissions to site, cannot view historical data, such as versions.
Style Resource Readers	Read to Master Page gallery and Restricted Read to Style Library	By default, all authenticated users are members of this group for branding reasons.
Quick Deploy Users	Contribute permission to Quick Items list	Members can schedule Quick Deploy jobs.
Approvers	Approve, plus limited access	Can approve pages, list items, and documents.
Hierarchy Managers	Manage hierarchy, plus limited access	Can create sites, lists, and document libraries.

Note   Limited access is used to give access to an individual list or document library without giving access to the entire site.

A good practice is to make most users members of the Visitors or Members group. This will eliminate unwanted changes made to the structure, site settings, or appearance of the site. However, it is important to remember that a user that is in the Members group has delete privileges. SharePoint does not provide a default group that uses a permission level that provides the ability to create but removes the ability to delete. This type of functionality would require a custom permission level and a custom group. The reason to create a custom permission level and custom group will be discussed in the next section.

Besides the SharePoint groups described in the Tables 8-2 and 8-3, there are also SharePoint farm administrators and site collection administrators. The SharePoint farm administrators group allows for administration of SharePoint at the farm level, the highest level. This group should be very limited in users. The site collection administrators group allows for administration of SharePoint at the site collection level. Administrator at the site collection level allows for configuration of security groups, site structure, and appearance. This group should also be very limited in users.

Determine Need for Custom Permission Levels or Groups

The default groups and permission levels provide a framework that is solely used by some organizations or used as a foundation and built upon by other organizations. As described above, if these default permission levels or groups do not fit well with your organization, custom permission levels and groups can be created. While sticking with the permissions levels and groups provided out of the box, this cannot always be avoided.

Custom Permission Levels

If custom permissions are needed for a permission level, we recommend that a new permission level with the new permissions be created instead of changing the default permission level. Some common scenarios when a custom permission level is needed are as follows:

- Default permission level includes all permissions except one that is needed by a group of users
- Default permission level includes a permission that is not needed by a group of users

Be sure to give the new permission level a descriptive name and verbose description so that administrators and users understand what this permission level provides. However, these permission levels should be used with caution and precise permissions should be reviewed to ensure they satisfy exact needs before being assigned to a SharePoint group.

Custom SharePoint Groups

The need for custom SharePoint groups is more common, straightforward, and has less overall impact to the security of your site than custom permission levels. Some common reasons you might have for creating new SharePoint groups include the following:

- You need more or fewer roles within the organization than are available in the default groups.

- Your organization has well-known names for roles that perform different tasks.

- You want to create a direct mapping from a Windows security group or distribution list and the SharePoint group.

- You prefer different group names than the default names provided.

Custom SharePoint groups should be well documented and available to all administrators for use throughout the site. Microsoft provides a worksheet to document all custom permission levels and groups at `http://go.microsoft.com/fwlink/?LinkID=213969&clcid=0x409`.

Monitor SharePoint Security

SharePoint security can become very unwieldy very quickly, so it is important to monitor new permission levels and SharePoint groups that are created. The process of creating such items should go through a governing board to ensure these new items make sense within the environment. Check for sites that break inheritance of parent sites, as these too can become difficult to effectively govern. SharePoint 2010 provides visible notification if the site permissions break inheritance from the parent site. Limit the breaking of inheritance as much as possible; this is where security issues arise and things get out of hand. A good practice is to perform regular security audits of permission levels, SharePoint groups, and how they are being used in conjunction with Active Directory groups and distribution lists. Auditing security using the built-in tools or available third-party tools will make site administrators think twice before assigning a permission level to a group. This process should be fully documented in a Security Plan.

Capacity Planning

Many people think that capacity planning is performing up-front sizing for the farm during farm planning and rollout. While this is true, it is also equally important to continually monitor the farm and its use to extend the farm as needed to meet the demands of the business. Regardless of what point you are at in the SharePoint lifecycle, it is important to continually perform capacity planning. Capacity planning can be broken down into five subareas as shown in Figure 8-8: analysis, design, test/optimize, deploy, and monitor.

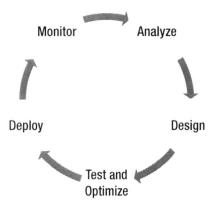

Figure 8-8. Capacity planning phases

Analysis

Understanding how the farm is going to be used, by how many users, and which services will be most utilized will help you better understand your capacity needs. To better understand the demand that the system will need to sustain, user base and usage characteristics will need to be determined. If you already have a SharePoint environment that you are looking to expand, or if you are looking to upgrade to a newer version, there are many tools available that will aid in this process. It's important to understand the current limitations of the hardware in the farm.

By understanding the current limitations, it will be easier to expand the farm in the correct manner. It's equally important to understand the workload of the current system. This will also help you determine whether the farm needs to be expanded. It's best to check with your organization to see if a tool has already been purchased to fulfill such a need. If you aren't set on a particular tool yet, following are a couple of free tools that provide get analysis at a great price.

Performance Analysis of Logs (PAL) Tool: Used throughout the IT industry to perform analysis on most of the major Microsoft products, such as SharePoint, SQL, BizTalk, IIS, etc. The PAL tool contains a threshold file that is specific to SharePoint that is used to evaluate the current farm based on best practices thresholds. The PAL provides a detailed report with an HTML-based graphical report. This tool is best used when focusing on the hardware of each server in the farm. The image in Figure 8-9 shows a graph of the memory available over a given time frame with an indication of what is considered a warning vs. a critical status. This tool can be found on CodePlex, at `http://pal.codeplex.com/`.

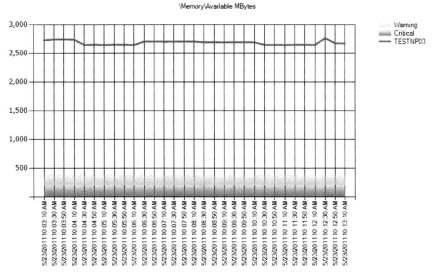

Figure 8-9. Available memory

Log Parser: The Log Parser is a tool provided by Microsoft that extracts data from the ULS and IIS logs. Some of the analysis it provides includes the following:

- Counting logged-in users
- User type distribution

- Request (RPS) distribution over time

- Distinct users over time

- Browser usage

- Slow pages

Utilizing both these tools (and perhaps others) to perform an in-depth analysis of your environment will provide a strong base as you start to design the farm architecture. Log Parser can be found at http://www.microsoft.com/download/en/details.aspx?displaylang=en&id=24659.

Design

Now that all the analysis has been performed, it's time to take that information and start designing a proposed architecture that will be able to sustain the expected demand. For a SharePoint farm that is actively utilized, this would mean reevaluating your current hardware or farm configuration based on the analysis performed. A common approach is to have either a small set of strong machines (scale up) or a larger set of smaller machines (scale out). Determining which approach works best for your environment may depend on many factors, such as capacity, redundancy, and cost, among others. The hardware of each server should be determined by what the role of that server is in the farm. An application server will contain more RAM than a web server, but could contain a larger data drive to compensate for the search query. Microsoft provides guidance on the minimum hardware and software requirements to run Share-Point 2010 based on farm topology. That guidance can be found at the following links:

- SharePoint Foundation 2010: http://technet.microsoft.com/en-us/library/cc288751.aspx

- SharePoint Server 2010: http://technet.microsoft.com/en-us/library/cc262485.aspx

While these articles provide a great baseline, keep in mind that these are the minimum requirements and that you need to utilize the information gathered during the analysis phase to build out and configure a farm to meet your specific needs. The design phase also should include the determination to use physical or virtual machines. While determining that approach is outside the scope of this book, it's important to understand the pros and cons of each approach, and to make sure that approach fits into the SLAs defined for the environment.

Designing a test environment should also be performed during this phase. This environment should mimic the production environment as closely as possible. While this approach may not always be possible, it's important to at least have the same server roles defined in the test environment that will be available in production. To reduce cost for this type of environment, redundancy can be removed because high availability is not often needed. In a test environment, you may be able to "virtualize" the physical servers in your production environment. However, keep in mind that deltas between the production architecture and the test architecture can prevent obtaining a 100 percent–accurate assessment.

Test and Optimize

A critical phase of capacity planning is testing the design that was laid out in the previous phase. It is in this phase that having a test environment that mimics production really pays off. Having the ability to perform load and acceptance testing in such an environment will provide greater confidence and proof that the design will meet the performance and capacity targets. Stress the system with a test load that represents the workload that was identified in the analysis phase. The tools identified in the analysis phase can be utilized again in this phase to determine if the hardware and configuration are meeting the demand.

A formal test plan and testing tools should be used to properly assess whether farm and configuration are going to meet performance targets. One or more testing tools should be identified and used during this phase. Two recommended testing tools are described here:

- *Visual Studio Team System*: A Microsoft product used by application development teams for software development. This tool contains a Team Test Load Agent, which has the capability to simulate a realistic workload.

- *Load Test Kit*: This tool is available as part of the Microsoft SharePoint 2010 Administration Toolkit v2.0. Generates a Visual Studio Team System 2008 load test based on SharePoint logs. More information on the product can be found here at http://www.microsoft.com/download/en/details.aspx?id=20022.

If you find during your testing that the environment does not meet the performance and capacity targets, you will need to scale out your farm further or consider revising the overall solution. For larger environments, this may constitute having dedicated farms based on roles, such as search or team collaboration.

Deploy

Once all the testing has been performed and the farm architecture has been proven to meet the performance and capacity requirements defined in the first phase, it's time to deploy the production environment. The deployment phase will differ greatly depending on the environment and situation. Capacity planning is normally performed for one of three reasons:

- Deploying a new SharePoint server farm

- Upgrading from a previous version of SharePoint to SharePoint 2010

- Improving performance capacity of current farm to meet demand

Regardless of the reason, it's important to perform each phase to ensure a successful deployment of the findings from the capacity planning exercise. This process is discussed further in Chapter 14.

Monitor

Even if the first four phases went well and a solid farm architecture was deployed and is meeting the performance and capacity requirements, that doesn't mean the farm doesn't need to be continually monitored. Monitoring the farm should occur daily, utilizing the information presented earlier in this chapter. As you monitor the farm and find the need to upgrade to again meet capacity and performance needs, these five phases should be revisited.

Summary

In this chapter you learned

- What to monitor within SharePoint

- How to monitor SharePoint and what tools to use

- How to plan for security

- Breakdown of SharePoint groups permission levels

CHAPTER 9

Information Architecture Overview

Information architecture is the science of how to organize and categorize content. When we talk about information architecture content in terms of SharePoint, we are referring to sites, lists, document libraries, and metadata. Creating a logical order and structure of this content is critical for the success of any SharePoint implementation. It is crucial to understand this content before we can govern it. This includes the different types of information, how it is created, who owns it, and how it will be disposed of or archived. SharePoint provides many features to aid in this process, but working with the business to understand these pieces it critical.

What Will You Learn in This Chapter?

- What site hierarchies are and how they relate to the business

- The importance of metadata and how to use it

- Why tagging content is so important

- The role of taxonomy and ways to approach it

Site Hierarchies

Determining the site hierarchy of your SharePoint implementation may seem like a straightforward task: break out the latest organizational chart and start creating sites to match this structure. While this isn't always a bad approach, it's important to understand the business, how it is broken down, and how each unit interacts with the others. Some common breakdowns of site hierarchies include:

- Line of Business

- Geography

- Product Line

- Organization Chart

To really know the business and its structure, it's important to get input from different people within different levels of the organization. What you will find is that these individuals or groups have slightly different hierarchies based on their level and needs within the business. A good approach to determining a logical hierarchy is to work with the different business units to get their take on a hierarchy. Once all the feedback from each group is captured, a hierarchy can be created based on the feedback.

Keep in mind this can be done at a high level, but also at a lower level within each business unit. The starting and ending point of the hierarchy is dependent upon the size of the business. Once a common hierarchy has been determined, be sure to share the results with the business, as this provides a great opportunity to get buy-in and show that feedback was taken into consideration.

SharePoint Hierarchy Considerations

Understanding the hierarchy provided by SharePoint is important to consider when determining the hierarchy of your SharePoint farm. SharePoint provides the hierarchy shown in Figure 9-1 for creating a SharePoint farm.

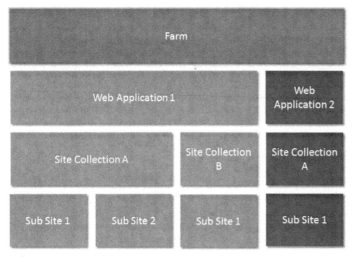

Figure 9-1. SharePoint Hierarchy

Most time is spent determining whether a new site should be created as a site or a site collection. It's important to understand the pros and cons of creating a site collection vs. a site and how that impacts your taxonomy. Some important items to consider when choosing a site vs. site collection include the following:

- *Storage Quotas*: Storage quotas provide a great way to keep data growth under control. SharePoint provides this capability at the site-collection level, but not at the site level. Defining a storage quota depends on the type of content being stored and the storage space available. 100 MB is a common storage quota for a My Site, and is sometimes used for collaboration sites as well.

- *Security*: SharePoint security is controlled at the site-collection level. By using multiple sites within the same site collection, it can become necessary to break inheritance. This can lead to numerous SharePoint groups being created which can lead to a security nightmare. Since SharePoint security is limited to the site collection, SharePoint groups defined in one site collection do not carry over to another site collection automatically.

- *Content Database*: A content database can store one to many site collections, but a site collection cannot span multiple content databases. A site collection can be moved into a separate content database, perhaps on a separate server, if needed. This could be for disaster recovery, capacity, security, or all of the above. A single site within a site collection is tied to the site collection, and therefore cannot be moved in its current structure.

- *Navigation*: Defining the navigation scheme is probably the biggest challenge when referring to site hierarchy. Sites within the same site collection appear automatically within the site navigation. Since site collections don't have a hierarchy, there is not automatic support for cross–site collection navigation. Most solutions that utilize cross-site collection rely on a custom navigation solution that reads an XML file to create the appropriate navigation.

Even with the information above, it is still difficult to create an effective site hierarchy. Microsoft provides a site planning data worksheet that can aid in this effort. This worksheet can be found at the following URL: `http://go.microsoft.com/fwlink/?LinkID=167837`.

Search vs. Click

There are two types of users within SharePoint: users who will click through the navigation and site hierarchy to find what they need and users who will go right to the search box and type in the key word of the content they are trying to find. With the advancement and emphasis placed on search in the world today, more and more users are utilizing search to find the content they need. However, it's important to satisfy both types of user, the searcher and the clicker. The clicker can be satisfied with a well-planned site for navigation and site hierarchy. If the site navigation and hierarchy follow the business and are intuitive to navigate, the chances of the end user finding what they are looking for is high. The searcher can be satisfied with a rich set of search results. This can be accomplished by having a strong information architecture utilizing content types and metadata across the enterprise. SharePoint 2010 has introduced metadata navigation, which aids both those using search and those who click through the hierarchy. As stated before, it's important to support both types of users. However, it's even more important to understand the users and how they interact with SharePoint. Ask the users how they find content in SharePoint. Through search? Through clicking through structure? This simple question will provide great insight into how users are interacting with the information and if there is a potential issue with the information architecture that needs to be addressed.

Metadata

Metadata is largely defined as data about data. If you were storing a Word document on a file share, typical metadata would include the file name, date modified, type, and size. While this data is definitely of value, SharePoint provides the ability to further describe the content through the use of custom metadata. These custom fields can be grouped together to define a content type, or a useable collection of data for a specific type of information. Content types can also be utilized to define information management policies, workflow, or standard templates. A collection of metadata grouped together to define a content type can inherit from another content type. The management of content types often begins with defining a core set of metadata that is needed in all content. This establishes a parent content type that can then be inherited from by other content types. Additional children content types can them be created and inherit from the base content types. It is crucial to define a complete set of parent content types as these will drive the information architecture in the environment. An example of the parent-child content type breakdown can be found in Table 9-1 and Table 9-2.

Table 9-1. Company XYZ Base Document Content Type

Name	Type	Source
Name	File	Document
Title	Single line of text	Item
Owner	Person or Group	Empty by default
Keywords	Managed Metadata	Empty by default

Table 9-2. Company XYZ Department Content Type, Inherited from Company XYZ Document Content Type

Name	Type	Source (Inherits from)
Name	File	Document
Title	Single line of text	Item
Owner	Person or Group	Company XYZ Document
Keywords	Managed Metadata	Company XYZ Document
Project Name	Single line of text	Empty by default
Project Type	Lookup	Empty by default
Assigned Resources	Person or Group	Empty by default

As shown in Table 9-2, the Company XYZ Department Content Type inherits the first four fields—Name, Title, Owner, and Keywords—from the Company XYZ Document Content Type while containing three custom fields that are specific to the Company XYZ Content Type. This approach maintains a base set of fields that must be inherited by all content types from it. This approach is an important part of determining the overall information architecture of the SharePoint portal.

When to create a content type vs. when to add the needed fields to the list typically depends on whether this content is going to be rolled up or the content in the new list reuses some or all of the fields defined in another list. Utilizing content types allows for rollup using the Content Query Web Part. This is a great way to roll up similar content, whether that is the same content type of children of a parent content type. When in doubt, we recommend that you create a content type since this provides more options as the environment changes. Remember to create content types at the highest possible level possible; content types created at a lower level cannot be rolled up to a higher level. For example, if a content type is created within a subsite of a site collection, it cannot be used at the site-collection level.

Automating Information Lifecycles

Without proper oversight, SharePoint content can become redundant or outdated. Many times Share-Point becomes a generic dumping ground that grows unmanageable with content of little to no value to its users. With the addition of content, finding the content you need becomes even more difficult. Using the appropriate metadata, SharePoint provides out-of-the-box information management policies that include

- *Retention*: Ability to ensure content is retained for a determined amount of time before disposal

- *Auditing*: Ability to track user behavior against defined policies and procedures by tracking viewing, downloading, and so on

- *Restrictions on Print*: Provides the ability to restrict printing on sensitive content

Retention policies can provide automated workflows to review content after a determined amount of time or perhaps delete content automatically if the content no longer needs to be retained. This approach will lead to a cleaner environment and provide less overall content for users to sift through to find needed content. Auditing provides the ability track user interaction with content that may be sensitive in nature. This information can provide great insight into content use throughout the portal. Microsoft provides a very detailed look into each policy available, as well as a policy worksheet to plan for information management. This content and worksheet can be found at the following Microsoft website: http://technet.microsoft.com/en-us/library/cc262490.aspx#section4.

Why Tagging Is Important

As described above, metadata is the driving factor behind strong information architecture. But what does tagging really gain you in the bigger picture? Creating metadata, especially those fields that utilize a lookup or choice field instead of a single line of text, provides a consistent form of terminology. This will help eliminate the use of terms that are similar but slightly different between departments or business lines. An example of this might be where one department might use a metadata field with the title "location" to describe the location of each office where another might use "office location." Having consistent metadata across sites will create continuity across your farm.

Correct tagging of content will also improve the overall search experience. Search utilizes metadata to refine the results provided back to the user through search. If content within the farm contains the term(s) used in the query, these results will filter to the top. Metadata can also be dynamic, so if you later decide that some of the terms need to change, these changes can be made at the top level and will filter through the content that use that term. SharePoint is even smart enough to supply you with the updated tag if you try to assign the old tag to the content. This feature comes out of the box, so you don't need to worry about how to update the metadata for this to happen.

While we see the benefits to tagging content, it's important to understand that there can be too much tagging, or metadata associated to content. Tagging content with too much metadata can almost be worse than no tagging at all as it will be difficult for the end user to sift through all the metadata and obtain relevant search results. While it's hard to put an exact number on how much is too much, content types that contain more than seven to ten metadata fields should be reviewed.

Governing Metadata

You might be asking yourself at this point why we are talking about metadata: this is a book on governance. Governance processes around management of content types need to be established and include policies and procedures for creation, modification, and deletion. The creation of metadata and content types cannot be an ad hoc activity. Some organizations may wish to include a procedure that includes a formal committee review of all metadata and content type creation requests. This committee reviews the request and validates that this metadata does not already exist and is something that will provide value to the business and its users. While it is nice to have such committees, it's important to stay nimble and not create too much process that it can hinder the business. The scope of use also needs to be taken into consideration when metadata and content types are defined. Some metadata may be limited to a specific department while other metadata may be used across geographic regions or lines of business. It's important during the creation of the parent content types and associated metadata to determine where this content is to live. If the content type and metadata are going to be used globally, these need to live in a specialized site collection known as the content type hub. This is a new feature in SharePoint 2010 that allows for the sharing of content types across site collections, something that wasn't possible in previous versions. We'll take a deeper look into the content type hub in the next chapter.

It is common to confuse metadata and taxonomy. Taxonomy utilizes metadata to create a classification and provide a hierarchal structure. You'll learn more about taxonomy as it relates to information architecture in the next section.

Taxonomy

SharePoint taxonomy can be defined as the practice of classification to provide a hierarchal structure. SharePoint utilizes metadata and content types to build this structure. Sharing this information across site collections was difficult using SharePoint 2007. This required the creation of custom solutions to deploy the metadata and content types to multiple site collections. SharePoint 2010 introduced the managed metadata service, sometimes referred to as the taxonomy service. This service provides the framework for the creation of a content type hub. The content type hub is configured once for each managed metadata service, and is responsible for managing content types that can be published to all site collections that are consuming the services provided in the managed metadata service. (See Figure 9-2.)

It's important to remember that a single site collection can consume multiple managed metadata services that are available in the farm. To understand how the managed metadata aids in SharePoint taxonomy, it's important to understand the key components of this service as defined by Microsoft:

- *Groups*: A collection of related attributes that contain one or more term sets

- *Term*: A word or a phrase that can be associated with an item in SharePoint Server 2010

- *Term Set*: A collection of related terms

- *Managed metadata*: A way of referring to the fact that terms and term sets can be created and managed independently from columns

- *Local Term Sets*; Created within the context of a site collection

- *Global Term Sets*: Created outside the context of a site collection

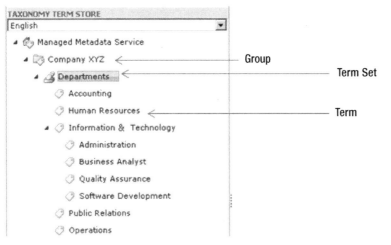

Figure 9-2. Taxonomy term store

Local term sets are scoped at the site collection and not available across the farm. Even though the impact of adding a term set at this level in the farm is of less impact than adding it above the site collection, it's still important to review all term sets before adding them to the site collection. Global term sets are managed outside the site collection and can be available in one to many site collections. The tasks allowed within the term store by role are defined in Table 9-3. Since global term sets are managed above the site collection level and access to SharePoint central administration should be limited, SharePoint provides the ability to delegate control of the creation of the global term sets. The SharePoint farm administrator should work with the business to establish owners of global term sets. Because of this delegation, it's important for users, especially farm and term store administrators, to understand the tasks each group is able to perform.

Table 9-3. Global Term Set Roles

Role	Allowable Tasks
Farm Administrator	Create new term store
	Connect to existing term store
	Add/remove term store administrators
Term Store Administrator	Add/remove term set groups
	Add/remove group managers
	Import term sets
	Create, rename, reuse, and delete term sets
	Modify term set's owner, submission policy, etc.
	Create, rename, reuse, and delete terms

Role	Allowable Tasks
Group Manager	Add/remove contributors
	Import term sets
	Create, rename, reuse, and delete term sets
	Modify term set's owner, submission policy, etc.
	Create, rename, reuse, and delete terms
Contributor	Create, rename, reuse, and delete term sets
	Modify term set's owner, submission policy, etc.
	Create, rename, reuse, and delete terms

While the addition of Term Sets is a welcome addition in SharePoint 2010, it is important to understand the governance needs around this subject. The following actions within the Term Store should be governed:

- Creation of new terms
- Renaming existing terms
- Merging terms
- Splitting terms
- Deleting a term
- Reusing a term
- Adding a new category
- Deleting a category

Because Managed Metadata is such an important piece of the SharePoint 2010 information architecture, Microsoft has provided great guidance and worksheets to aid in the creation of this taxonomy. That content can be found here at http://technet.microsoft.com/en-us/library/ee530389.aspx.

Folksonomy

SharePoint 2010 has introduced a new concept of allowing free tagging, which is referred to as folksonomy. While still falling under taxonomy, folksonomy is where a user may tag content with a predefined piece of metadata from a controlled structure. The submission policy within the Term Store Management Tool determines if the term set is open or closed, with *open* meaning that additional metadata can be added by the end user. While this may sound like a great option initially, it's important to understand the pros and cons of using a predefined taxonomy vs. a more user-driven taxonomy like folksonomy.

- *Pros of Folksonomy*:
    - *Flexible*: Not as rigid as the controlled structure and can better define the content

- • *Adaptability*: Can change more quickly as the business changes

  - • *Lower Cost*: Less time spent in creation of metadata for the business; now the business is creating it

- • *Cons of Folksonomy*:

  - • *Over-Tagging* : Tagging content with too much metadata to the point of irrelevance

  - • *Inconsistencies*: Tagging can lead to misspellings or incorrect terms for the business

  - • *Lack of Control*: Relying on business to tag content correctly and accurately, without the guidance that managed metadata provides

  - • *Skewed Perspective*: Two different users may use a different term for the same business term

As you can see, both approaches have their benefits and drawbacks. A good approach is to have a mixture of both, with a heavier emphasis on the controlled metadata. As you work through the creation of content types and metadata, it will become apparent when to utilize this new functionality. Performing regular audits of both taxonomy and folksonomy is a must to ensure an information architecture that is in line with the business. One common approach to reviewing this type of content is to form a committee of business users to perform regular audits as a group. In smaller environments this duty may be given to the site owner. Regardless of the size of the environment, regular audits are an important step for providing users with a strong information architecture.

Card Sorting

A great way to define the taxonomy is to use a process called card sorting. Card sorting is a technique where a group of subject matter experts, or users, generates a category tree. The process normally includes analyzing business content, typically documents, and working with the other subject matter experts to start grouping and categorizing the content. After the analysis is performed, these main groups are written on index cards or Post-it notes. The group then arranges the index cards, or Post-it notes into further categories and organizes them in a manner that makes sense in business terms. After these categories are defined, it is the task of the group to define the hierarchy and metadata around each category in the exercise. For larger environments, it may be more efficient to have multiple groups with different areas with different content to define. After the groups have finished, each group needs to present to the other groups and make a case for why the cards are sorted in that manner. This helps eliminate skewed perspectives and potentially allows views from different parts of the business with users of different skill sets.

Imagine you are responsible for creating the information architecture for a home furnishings store intranet. Your content consists of documents on sofas, tables, televisions, beds, and the like. For the card sorting exercise, each piece of information would be written on a notecard and organized in a logical manner. The group determines to sort and organize the content based on rooms within the home. Bed, nightstand, and dresser are organized under bedroom, while sofa, loveseat, and end table are organized under living room. The exercise continues and site navigation is determined based on the hierarchy defined in the card sorting exercise. You can quickly see how sorting content using this approach with other subject matter experts can define a thorough information architecture.

While this may seem like a very low-tech approach, it normally works extremely well; usually the content owners, or subject matter experts, are not very technical. For those who want to take a more technical approach to card sorting, there is software and online applications that can aid in this effort.

Determining Success

The success of the SharePoint environment is normally determined by how easily end users can find the content they need. Information architecture provides the foundation for findability by defining a common set of content types and metadata that is consistently applied to the organization. It's important to understand that defining the information architecture is not an IT practice, but a business practice. It is critical that the business be involved throughout the entire process. However, the governance of the information architecture cannot be imposed upon the business and create obstacles or barriers to productivity. Governance needs to be tied directly to organizational processes and should not be something that is rolled out during the initial deployment and then forgotten. All successful SharePoint implementations have a strong governance plan, but one that does not impede the processes of the business.

Summary

In this chapter you learned

- What site hierarchies are and how this relates to the business

- The importance of metadata and how to use it

- Why tagging of content is so important

- The role of taxonomy and ways to approach it

CHAPTER 10

Information Delivery

In the previous chapter we talked about information architecture and how best to use metadata, content types, and taxonomy to create an environment in which it is easy to navigate and find information. In this chapter, we are going to focus on how best to deliver that information through Web Parts and search. With all the content stored in the environment, and with different users interested in different content, how do you drive individual users to their desired content or drive the desired content to them? Luckily SharePoint has some cool features that make this possible and easy. in this chapter we'll investigate what those features are and how best to drive relevant information to the end user instead of having the end user navigate and search for content.

What Will You Learn in This Chapter?

- The types of information stored within SharePoint
- How content can get out of date and how to prevent it
- How to deliver information through audience targeting
- How the creation of wireframes for initial page layouts is beneficial
- How to deliver information using SharePoint Search and People Search

Types of Information Within SharePoint

Before we start looking at how best to deliver information within SharePoint, we should first look at what types of information are typically stored within a SharePoint environment. Lists and document libraries are probably the first to come to mind. These could include a Microsoft Word document outlining requirements for a recent project, a Microsoft Excel document with next month's sales forecast, or a contact list showing employees and their phone numbers used by a project team. This information could also include a custom Web Part displaying information from a backend system or some simple HTML that was created to display information to the end user. Many times this information is displayed through a Web Part direction on a SharePoint page. Depending on the backing content, the type of Web Part needed to display this information will vary. While the number of out-of-the-box Web Parts is too great to go through each one here, let's take a look at a few that are commonly used to display content within SharePoint (see Table 10-1).

Table 11-1. Common Web Parts

Web Part Name	Description
Document Library or List Web Part	Web Part available after a document library or list has been created that will display content from the container on a SharePoint page. Typically used to display needed information in a certain way (view) for easy access to information. These will appear in your available Web Parts as the name of the container.
Content Editor Web Part (CEWP)	Commonly used for quick markup of HTML to display information with a desired look and feel. The What-You-See-Is-What-You-Get (WYSIWIG) editor is very user friendly for even the non-technical user.
Content Query Web Part (CQWP)	Makes it possible to display content from across multiple sites by utilizing content types. Filtering of content types from within this Web Part is available as well as the option to customize the display through XSLT.
Summary Links	Web Part provides the ability to name hyperlinks and provide these links in an ordered manner. Commonly used for links external to the SharePoint environment.
Chart Web Part	New in SharePoint 2010, this Web Part provides the ability to visualize data through a chart utilizing data from a SharePoint list, Business Data Catalog, Excel Services, or even another Web Part.

While this is not an exhaustive list of the Web Parts available within SharePoint 2010, it does give you a brief look at some of the most commonly used Web Parts to display information. It's important to understand what type of content you are working with and which Web Part to utilize to best display this content. Often this is not a one-to-one mapping, so it may be necessary to try several and see what works best for the situation.

Customize Display of Information from Web Part

Choosing the correct Web Part to display the information is only half the battle. Often it will be necessary to display this information in a particular way. SharePoint document libraries and lists provide the capability to customize the view, or the way the content is displayed. This ability is not only available directly in the list or document library, but also in the list or document library Web Part. (See Figure 10-1.) Configuring the view will provide the ability to customize the view of the Web Part. This might include showing only certain metadata, sorting the content by metadata, or grouping by metadata. SharePoint provides the ability to create a custom view within the Web Part or reuse a view that has already been created.

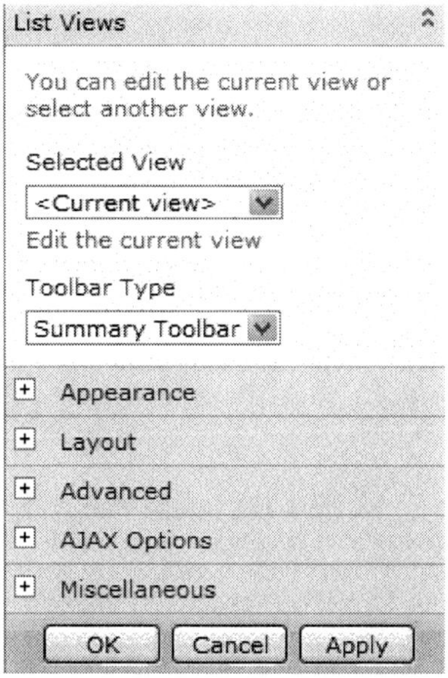

List Views ⌃

You can edit the current view or
select another view.

Selected View

| <Current view> ▾ |

Edit the current view

Toolbar Type

| Summary Toolbar ▾ |

[+] Appearance

[+] Layout

[+] Advanced

[+] AJAX Options

[+] Miscellaneous

| OK | Cancel | Apply |

Figure 10-1. View Settings within List Web Part

We recommend that you create a view outside of the Web Part. This will provide reuse as well as the ability to change the configuration of the view without having to edit the Web Part. If multiple views of the same content are needed, you can drive the audience to the list or document library instead. This will allow for multiple views and end users will be able to select their desired view. It's important to work with the content creators to determine how best to display the content; this group should know who is using the content and how they expect to see it.

Outdated Content

A business is an ever-evolving entity, and the content found within this entity is also evolving. SharePoint is a great repository to store a lot of this content as it provides many features for content management; versioning, approval, and auditing, to name just a few. One of the biggest challenges in any SharePoint environment is keeping the content within the portal fresh and relevant for the business. This might include the latest holiday PTO schedule or corporate news announcements. If the content is not up to date, end users lose confidence and may look elsewhere for the information they need. This is the most common way to lose end users.

Causes of Outdated Content

Outdated content within a SharePoint environment can be caused by many different factors. Understanding and planning for them while trying to govern the content will cut down the amount of outdated information. Let's look at a few potential reasons that content can become stagnant and possible steps to prevent it. Sometimes having no content is better than having content that is outdated.

Lack of Ownership

Typically, content within SharePoint is stored in the form of a Microsoft Office document in a document library, a SharePoint list, or a page within SharePoint. In each of these cases, a metadata field called Created By or Modified By is available to determine when the content was created or who modified it last. This field can provide great insight into how relevant the content might be. For example, depending on the business environment, it might be common for a content creator to have changed positions or left the company since the content was created. It's important for the business to transfer ownership of the content so, if changes need to be made, there is clear responsibility. In some cases, it might make sense for the new owner of the content to open the document just to record their name as the last to have modified the document. The key to this scenario is to have a plan when ownership of content changes. It's important to identify the content this person was responsible for and change ownership as soon as possible.

Change in Direction

In the world today there is constant change, and in the business world it is no different. Sometimes this change takes the shape of reorganization within a business, but change can also take place on a smaller scale, such as within a particular business rule or emphasis on a particular topic. For example, content that was originally created for a specific project or business focus may no longer be needed. It's important to identify this content and purge it as necessary. However, keep in mind that even though this content is no longer needed, there may be business or legal reasons for its retention. Removing this content will help eliminate the "noise" in the environment and provide less content for users to sift through when trying to find the content they desire.

Lack of Business Buy-In or Devotion to Role

It seems like every SharePoint implementation is going to change the business world and provide each business unit a site of their very own, where they can post content that is important to their team and the business units they support. This might include news related to the business unit in the form of announcements or a calendar with important events. While the individuals rolling out SharePoint know how to make this possible from a technical perspective, it's the business that often struggles with the ownership and resources needed to drive this content. On these types of deployments, it's often assumed by the business and IT that content creation will just start to "happen." However, content creation can be very time consuming and is yet another task for an individual or team that most likely already has a full workload. It's important to work with the business, define the role of content creator for the environment, and define expectations around this role. Content should not be created just for the sake of having new content out on the portal. The content that is being created should be relevant to the user base; this approach will gain user adoption and lead to a thriving environment. Keep in mind that this role may initially require training or oversight to be successful. Many companies utilize the publishing feature within SharePoint to aid in the approval and deployment process. This feature will be examined later in this chapter.

Lack of Archival or Disposal Process

Sometimes a business may already have a process in place to identify outdated content, but no process to purge it from the system. Depending on the content, it might be reasonable to consult a team or committee before deleting content from the system. While it may be straightforward to just delete the content that is no longer needed, it is more challenging to determine what content needs to be archived. Don't fall into the trap of keeping content around "just in case someone needs it later." The retention of content is normally defined by law or business rules; relying on defined retention policies driven by the business can help drive those tough conversations with end users who want to keep content forever.

Regardless of the reason, retention policies are typically defined at the content type and should be driven by the business. It's important to work with the business to understand content access and what the process is if the content needs to be retrieved and added back into the system. If that process does not exist, it needs to be created. While this may be uncommon, it is a situation that can come up and needs to be handled appropriately.

Possible Approaches to Limit Outdated Content

While it's extremely difficult to completely eliminate outdated content, there are numerous options for limiting it as much as possible. Having a dedicated content owner, as well as a backup content owner, is the best option for keeping outdated content at a minimum. If all the content within the portal is owned by an individual or team, this individual or team is responsible for keeping the content up to date or purging it as necessary. As described above, problems arise when this content does not have an owner. SharePoint also provides features that will help in limiting outdated content.

Content Lifecycle Management

Wouldn't it be nice if SharePoint just told you when content is outdated? Well, to a certain extent it can. SharePoint provides information management policies, which include a retention policy. The retention policy provides the capability to kick off a workflow after a predetermined amount of time has passed. The event of the retention policy can be triggered off a date/time metadata field within the content type associated to the list. A typical retention policy might include kicking off a Disposition Approval workflow after one year, which will allow participants in the workflow to decide whether to retain or delete expired documents. (See Figure 10-2.)

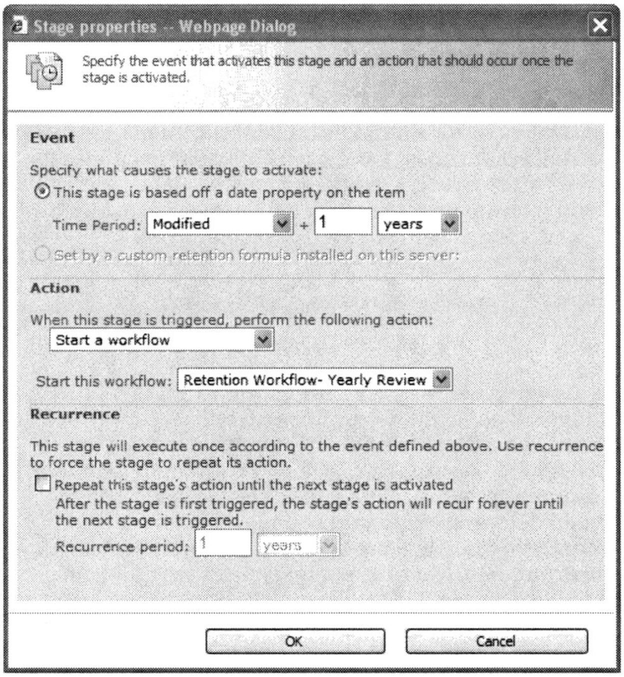

Figure 10-2. Retention stage

The following actions can be invoked when a retention policy has been triggered in SharePoint:

- Move to recycle bin
- Permanently delete
- Transfer to another location
- Start a workflow (out-of-the-box, SharePoint Designer, or custom)
- Skip to next stage
- Declare a record
- Delete previous drafts
- Delete all previous versions

The retention policy needs to be set at the content-type or folder level. Defining these policies for the needed content types should be performed during the information architecture planning phase which should be documented along with the content type and metadata. As always, it's important for the business team to drive these discussions as they know the content, and how the content should be retained.

Retention policies need to be established early on in the information architecture discussions. At the same time that you work with the content owners to discuss metadata and the grouping of these fields to define content types, work with the users to understand the benefits. Some of these retention policies may be driven by industry regulations, but a good majority of them will need to be defined internally. To ease concerns, remind users that a retention policy doesn't automatically mean that content is going to be removed from the environment—it might be archived to another system or dropped from SharePoint, with a link provided to the new location. These policies need to be well defined, along with the process to restore archived content, if needed.

Periodic Review by Content Owners

It may sound like common sense, but the content owners need to periodically review content and make sure it is still relevant to the business. As discussed earlier, business changes at a very fast pace, and the supporting content will need to be updated to reflect those changes. For larger environments, it might be easier to have defined content review meetings with many team members. This approach provides feedback from multiple sources, lessening the chance of decisions being made based on one person's view of the business and its needs. This approach can also be driven by the retention policy, as discussed above.

Archival Process

It may be the case within your environment that content continues to be stored within SharePoint because there is no alternative place to store the content. If content owners are not familiar with an available archival process, they may opt to continue to store outdated content in SharePoint rather than delete the content for fear they may need it someday. An archive process can take two different paths: an automated approach or a manual approach. An automated approach might utilize a retention policy that moves documents to another location after a predetermined amount of time has expired. This process works well in environments with rigid information management policies on how long content needs to be retained before removal. For those environments where retention policies are not defined, policies should be created or the site owner should have the capability to manually copy content from the site to an archive location.

Analytics Reports

A great way to find outdated content within SharePoint is to utilize the usage statistics to determine what content is being viewed. The usage statistics are available at the site collection and site web level, so determining what content is being consumed can be fairly easy to determine. While the analytics reports contain all kinds of useful knowledge, the information we are interested for this discussion is contained within the Top Pages section in the quick launch navigation. This report will show the top number of pages, as well as content, such as Word documents or lists, for the last 30 days. However, unlike previous versions of SharePoint, a date range outside of the last 30 days can be defined. Depending on your security model, it's possible that the site owner has access to this feature and can utilize it to better manage the site. Figure 10-3 provides an example of what statistics are shown at the site level and how the number of page views can be sorted to show the lowest amount first.

	Page URL (under http://cdwza7271:12345/sites/dataprogramsprints/cw)	Number of Page Views↑	Percentage of Overall
1	/_layouts/download.aspx	1	0.02 %
2	/_layouts/powerpointframe.aspx	1	0.02 %
3	/_layouts/settings.aspx	1	0.02 %
4	/_layouts/subedit.aspx	1	0.02 %
5	/_layouts/success.aspx	1	0.02 %
6	/_layouts/useredit.aspx	1	0.02 %
7	/_layouts/viewedit.aspx	1	0.02 %
8	/_layouts/viewnew.aspx	1	0.02 %
9	/_layouts/viewtype.aspx	1	0.02 %
10	/_layouts/wordeditor.aspx?...	1	0.02 %
11	/_layouts/wordeditorframe.aspx	1	0.02 %
12	/_layouts/wordviewer.aspx?...	1	0.02 %
13	/_layouts/wordviewerframe.aspx	1	0.02 %
14	/_layouts/xlviewer.aspx?...	1	0.02 %
15	/_vti_history/512/c w documents/c and w integrated table diagram.pdf	1	0.02 %
16	/c w documents/c and w semantic stickies.xls	1	0.02 %
17	/c w documents/choose a tool for business intelligence in sharepoint 2010.pdf	1	0.02 %
18	/c w documents/data program reporting and analytics relationship manager job description.doc	1	0.02 %
19	/c w documents/day 1 notes - wholesale sales.docx	1	0.02 %
20	/c w documents/forms/dispform.aspx?...	1	0.02 %
1-20	Total	20	0.48 %

1 2 3 4 5 6 7 8 9 10 ...

Figure 10-3. *Top Pages Analytics Report*

For more information about SharePoint 2010 Analytics Reports, visit the following Microsoft site: `http://technet.microsoft.com/en-us/library/ee663487.aspx`. If the SharePoint 2010 Analytics Reports are not able to be customized to fit your environment, custom Analytics Reports can be created extending the platform, and there are numerous third-party options out there to extend the custom analytics reports.

How to Deliver Information Within SharePoint

In the previous section, we looked at the types of content normally stored within SharePoint and some of the components used to display that information. While that provided a good foundation, you need to know how best to deliver that information in a way that is meaningful to the current user. There's been a shift in technology over the past several years: user characteristics and activities are now tracked and used to display relevant information to the user. This comes mainly in the form of advertising or marketing. However, because of this shift, end users typically expect relevant information will be pushed to them rather than having to search or dig for it. It's important to think in these terms as you determine how to deliver needed content to the users visiting your site.

Understand the Audience

To identify the best approach for delivering content, it's crucial to understand your audience and their needs. On a broader scale, it's important to understand the types of users that the portal will be supporting. What languages need to be supported? Do language packs need to be installed and does the Multilingual User Interface need to be configured? Will the portal have a strong collaboration component with users utilizing Office content, such as Word and Excel, to create needed content? Does it make sense to deploy Office Web Applications to provide the user the ability to browse and make minimal changes to this content directly in the browser without opening the client application? Do users need to share and edit content with other users within the organization? Asking these types of questions will help drive the best way to deliver content.

On a larger scale, it's important to understand that each user or group of users has a different perspective and priorities. While all users may be interested in broad topics such as company news or employee benefits, individual users are often more interested in items directly related to their projects and position within the company or team. Instead of having to navigate through the thousands of reports the business generates, for example, the specific report they're interested in is pushed to them or appears at the top of the list of these reports. The key here is to understand what each group or business unit interacts with often versus that content that might be referenced occasionally.

Another way to think about it might be to ask what content is needed to make business decisions vs. what content supports how you do business. This will require working with each team to identify what content is utilized most often and how best to structure it. This should include pushing needed content to users instead of requiring them to navigate or dig to find it. The next section will lay out a process to accomplish this task.

Tools to Define Information Delivery

The old adage, "A picture is worth a thousand words," is especially true when trying to define the layout and structure of a SharePoint page to support information delivery. This is especially true when working with users who aren't familiar with SharePoint and the general structure and layout the product supports. Mocking up a SharePoint site, including navigation, Web Parts, and branding, can help the end user to conceptualize their thoughts and visualize the layout.

A common approach to defining the layout and structure is to create a wireframe of each site or page within the portal. The wireframe should mimic the SharePoint page layout, including any navigation, search box controls, and available Web Part zones. Because this is such a common practice, Microsoft has provided Visio shapes to help in this process. These components can be found at the following link: http://www.microsoft.com/download/en/details.aspx?id=21480. If you do not have Microsoft Visio, you can use Microsoft PowerPoint to create wireframes for defining information delivery. This application provides a lot of the shapes and graphics that are needed to create a rich design. Otherwise, there are numerous third-party products that are designed specifically for creating wireframes.

Wireframes are an integral part of defining information delivery within any SharePoint environment. All the main sites within SharePoint should first have a wireframe created to define the content regions and how this content is displayed. This approach will allow you to work with the business and change the structure more easily instead of trying to mock the sites up directly in SharePoint. Regardless of the tools available, this is a process that should not be overlooked.

Audience-Targeted Content

As discussed earlier in this section, it's important to understand what content is important to which team or groups of users and how best to get that information to them in a logical manner. Most times this is done by creating a SharePoint site that has all related content in one place for that particular group to consume as necessary. While this is a perfectly good approach, sometimes it pays off to think about how you can drive this content to the user rather than drive the user to the content. SharePoint audience targeting provides the ability to target content based on characteristics of the current user. Remember that audience targeting should not be a substitute for security. Audience targeting utilizes memberships to limit what a user can see initially. SharePoint audiences can be based on the following information:

- Membership in Active Directory
    - Distribution List
    - Security Group
- Membership in SharePoint Group
- Location in Organizational Reporting Structure
- Public Properties in User Profile

Audience targeting using membership within Active Directory or a SharePoint Group does not require any configuration other than setting up a SharePoint Group if needed. We recommend that you utilize Active Directory distribution lists or security groups as much as possible since these are often controlled at a higher level within the organization and can reduce the burden of continually updating a SharePoint Group. It's important to understand the state of your distribution lists and security groups within your organization and whether they are being maintained effectively. This will determine whether you should utilize the groups provided within Active Directory or utilize SharePoint groups. You may also have to revert to using SharePoint Groups if your Active Directory is rigid and it is difficult to create additional groups.

Using the User Profile for Targeting

Audience targeting can also be performed using properties from the SharePoint 2010 User Profile. SharePoint provides 58 user profile properties, some of which are mapped directly from properties within Active Directory. These properties are located within the User Profile Service within Central Administration. To access these properties, navigate to SharePoint 2010 Central Administration, and select Manage service applications under the Application Management heading. From the Service Applications screen, select the User Profile Service Application. The profile properties can be found under the Manage User Properties link under the People heading. A screenshot of the available User Properties can be found in Figure 10-4.

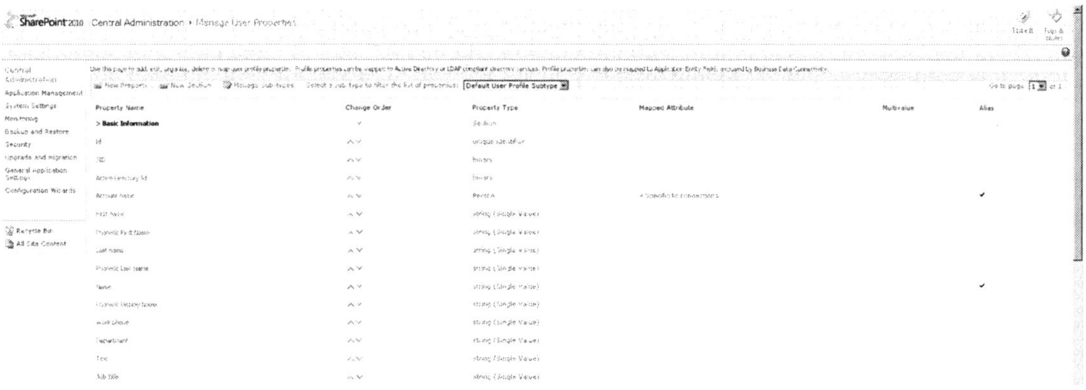

Figure 10-4. User Profile properties

The actual number of properties from Active Directory that can be mapped into User Profile properties depends on how populated and organized the properties are within Active Directory. To define an audience that uses User Profile properties, a rule needs to be created. Rules are made up of three components:

169

- *Operand*: User or Property
- *Operator*:
  - User Operand
    - Reports Under
    - Member Of
  - Property Operand
    - =, >, >=, <, <=, <>
    - Contains, Not Contains
- *Value*: string or user lookup

Let's walk through a few examples so you can better understand how creating an audience can benefit the delivery of information. In the first example, perhaps you want to show new hire information, such as forms and checklists, to only those employees new to the company. A rule such as the following could be created and applied to content to limit access to employees that started within that calendar year:

- *Operand* : Property: Hire date
- *Operator*: "<"
- *Value*: 01/01/2011

Another example might be to create a rule for content distribution to only employees that report to the Director of Human Resources:

- *Operand*: User
- *Operator*: Reports Under
- *Value*: Sally Gold (name of Director of Human Resources)

This same rule could be created in a slightly different manner:

- *Operand*: Property: Department
- *Operator*: "="
- *Value*: Human Resources

Finally, a very common need is to target specific information based on location, such as lunch menu or site news.

- *Operand*: Property: Location
- *Operator*: "="
- *Value*: Omaha

Audiences need to be compiled initially to create the list of users that meet the given rule, but they also need to be frequently compiled—as properties change within Active Directory, the audiences within SharePoint change as well. They can be compiled on a daily, weekly, or monthly basis; the compilation schedule will greatly depend on the amount of changes that take place within the organization.

Targeting Content to Audiences

We recommend that you first review the environment and determine where audience targeting is going to be used to deliver content before going through the process of creating audiences. It's not always necessary to jump into Central Administration and create an audience to target content. Keep in mind that you can also utilize Active Directory memberships directly in the content as well. These could include a distribution list for a department or an office location. Spend some time investigating Active Directory groups and what is available before diving in and creating your own. The following sections describe audience targeting methods used within SharePoint.

List Items Displayed in Content Query Web Part (CQWP)

The Content Query Web Part provides the ability to pull content from many different lists and roll them up into one container. Within the CQWP tool pane under Query, the Web Part provides the ability to apply audience filtering to lists that the Web Part is consuming, as displayed in Figure 10-5. This is independent of the option to audience target the entire Web Part, which can be found under the Advanced section within the tool pane.

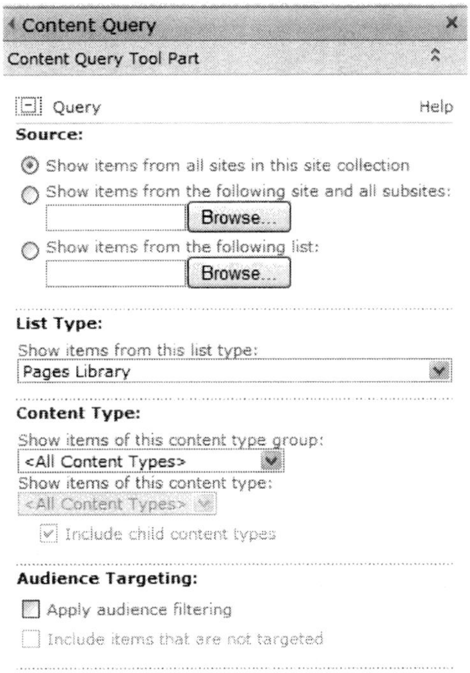

Figure 10-5. CQWP Audience Targeting

Web Parts

Any SharePoint Web Part can be targeted to an audience. This can be accomplished by selecting the appropriate audience, distribution list, or SharePoint group and entering that into the Target Audiences field within the Advanced section of the Web Part tool pane.

171

Web Part Pages

When the SharePoint publishing feature is activated, a library called Pages is created. This library contains all the supporting pages of the site. Like Web Parts, these pages can be targeted using audiences, distribution lists, or SharePoint groups. However, instead of entering the audience information within the Web Part tool pane, you'll need to edit the properties on the page item within the list and add the needed audience.

Navigational Links

Navigational links, in both the global navigation as well as the quick launch navigation, can be targeted to audiences. Links can be added to the navigational areas within SharePoint Server 2010 by clicking Site Actions ➤ Site Settings, and selecting Navigation under the Look and Feel section. (See Figure 10-6.) Some links may not be able to be audience targeted as they are part of the built-in site.

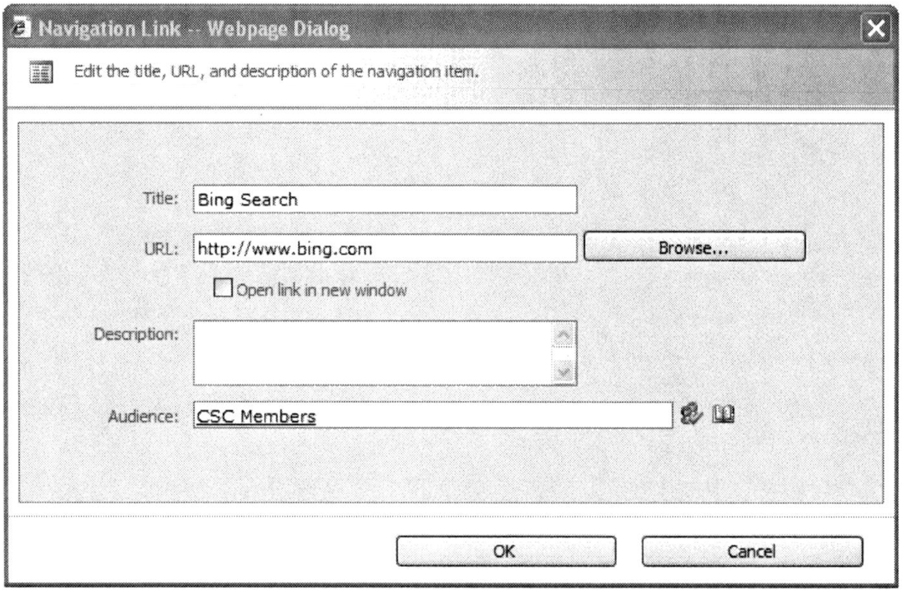

Figure 10-6. Targeted Navigational Links

This approach provides a very easy method of targeting navigation based on the audience. Using this capability could prove to be very useful in defining the overall site hierarchy.

Ratings

A new social component of SharePoint 2010 is ratings. You've probably seen this on popular retailer sites such as Amazon.com, which shows the popularity of an item based on user feedback in the form of a star rating of one through five. SharePoint 2010 has adopted this same approach; you can rate any list item or document library item with a star rating of one through five. While hovering over the stars, simply click the appropriate rating and your rating will be saved, as shown in Figure 10-7. While this doesn't target a single group or audience, this feature provides great insight into what other users feel is potentially good or bad content. These ratings also come into play during search, where content that has a higher rating is returned higher in the search results than content that has a lower star rating. Ratings are not enabled by default on a list or library. To enable this feature, navigate to the library settings tab of the list or document library, select Library Settings, and select Rating Settings under the General Settings section. This will need to be performed on any list or library, as Ratings are not turned on by default.

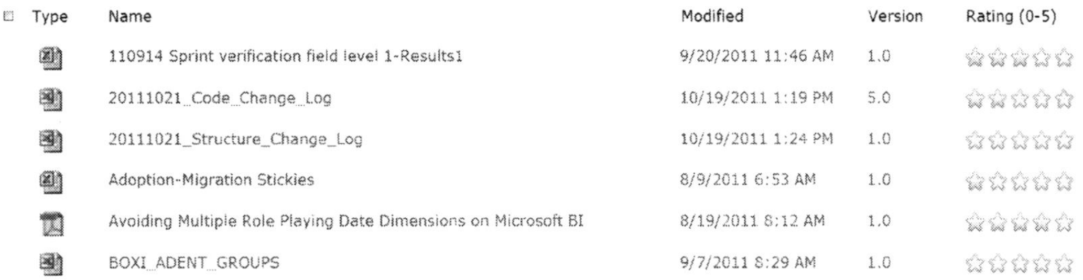

	Type	Name	Modified	Version	Rating (0-5)
		110914 Sprint verification field level 1-Results1	9/20/2011 11:46 AM	1.0	
		20111021_Code_Change_Log	10/19/2011 1:19 PM	5.0	
		20111021_Structure_Change_Log	10/19/2011 1:24 PM	1.0	
		Adoption-Migration Stickies	8/9/2011 6:53 AM	1.0	
		Avoiding Multiple Role Playing Date Dimensions on Microsoft BI	8/19/2011 8:12 AM	1.0	
		BOXI_ADENT_GROUPS	9/7/2011 8:29 AM	1.0	

Figure 10-7. SharePoint 2010 ratings

Targeting and Security

It is important to understand that audience targeting is not a substitute for security. Items that are not targeted to specific users are not inaccessible to those users. Depending on the targeting, users can potentially navigate directly to the item to avoid the audience targeting. SharePoint will automatically security trim the navigational elements based on the security settings of that site or element. Targeting navigational links is typically done with external resources outside of or to other SharePoint site collections.

Publishing

SharePoint Server 2010 Enterprise's publishing features provide a complete WCM solution for sites built on the SharePoint platform. When a change is made to a publishing site, it is not immediately visible to all users of the site, as is the case with nonpublishing SharePoint sites. Published pages must go through an approval process before they are visible to the site's general audience. They can also be scheduled for release at a later time.

Publishing Workflow Overview

Publishing is controlled through a SharePoint workflow that manages the state of each published item throughout its lifecycle. In this section, we will examine the flow of content items from creation through final publishing.

Workflow Sequence

Figure 10-8 depicts the typical publishing workflow for a published item.

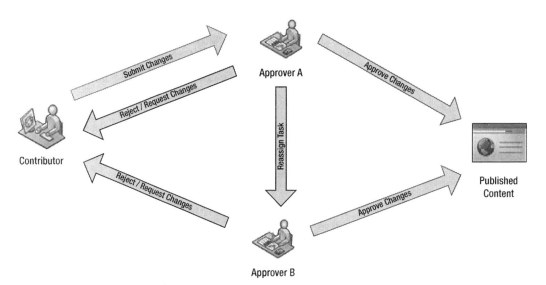

Figure 10-8. Page publishing workflow

The first step in the process is the submission of the changes by a site member or contributor. This initiates the publishing workflow and assigns a task to a set of designated approvers. By default, this task is assigned to the Approvers group for the site.

Approvers have several actions they can take with regard to the approval task:

- *Approve*: This action accepts the changes and publishes them to the site.

- *Reject*: This action rejects the changes and returns the draft to the contributor for possible resubmission at a later time.

- *Request change*: This action allows the approver to provide feedback to the contributor without terminating the publishing workflow. The contributor can make changes to the item and send the changes back to the approver for review.

- *Reassign task*: This action transfers the approval task to another user or group. This might be used, for example, when an organization wants to have all changes managed by a central group that is responsible for routing the changes to the correct department for approval.

Once an approver has approved or rejected the changes, the publishing workflow ends. SharePoint maintains a detailed log of all actions taken during a workflow. This log can be accessed through the Status item on the Publish menu tab for a page.

Versioning and Status

The most common type of item published in SharePoint is a web site page. Other items such as list items, images, and documents also follow the publishing process, but the examples in this chapter are pages. Just remember that a page is a type of document, and a document is a type of list item. SharePoint treats all items the same way when publishing is enabled and approval is required in the list or library.

Each page in the site has a version history associated with it. This is a record of each set of changes that the page has gone through over time. A *major version* is one that has been released to the general user community, or *published*. A *minor version* is one that has not been published. A page may go through several minor revisions before being published or republished. Each version has a number associated with it, such as 3.2. The whole number represents the published version, and the decimal represents the draft version. Whole-numbered versions, such as 3.0, are published versions of the page. Other versions are drafts based on the previously published version. A history of all versions of a page can be accessed by viewing the Version History for a page, shown in Figure 10-9.

Figure 10-9. Version History dialog box

As a page goes through the publishing process, it has a different *approval status* depending on the last action taken with respect to that page. The types of approval status are as follows:

- *Draft*: A draft version of this page has been created. A draft version can be viewed by users authorized to review drafts, depending on whether it is checked in or not.

  - A *checked-in draft* can be seen by all reviewers.

  - A *checked-out draft* can be seen only by the user to whom it is checked out. All other reviewers will see the previously checked-in version.

- *Pending*: When a page is submitted for publishing, its status becomes Pending.

- *Approved*: Once a draft version is approved, it becomes a major version and its status becomes Approved.

Scheduling Content

By default, when a draft is approved, it immediately becomes visible to site visitors. In some cases, this is not desirable. For example, when preparing the web site content for a new product release, the entire content-creation and approval cycle may need to have been completed weeks ahead of time. SharePoint's publishing features allow you to schedule content changes to appear, and disappear, automatically.

Content scheduling is available only in lists that require content approval and maintain major and minor versions of pages in their version history. These options can be set on the Versioning Settings page for the list or library. Scheduling can be enabled on the Manage Item Scheduling page for the list or library.

When creating content changes, the contributor can set a publishing schedule that includes conditions for starting and ending the publication of the version. Content can be scheduled to be published immediately upon approval (the default) or at a specific date and time in the future.

Content can also be scheduled for removal under a variety of conditions. The item may be configured not to be automatically removed; instead a reminder can be sent to the page's registered contact user for review on a periodic basis. Alternately, a specific date and time can be assigned for the version to be automatically removed. An optional notification can be sent to the page's contact user to warn them of the impending expiration of the page. By default, published changes remain in effect until they are superseded by a later version.

Simple Moderation

While the publishing workflow provides a robust review mechanism, in some cases a full review process is not necessary or desirable. If the group of content authors is the same as the group of content approvers, there would seem to be little point in a full approval workflow. In this case, SharePoint publishing supports a light publishing process called *simple moderation*. In simple moderation approval, a member of the Contributors group submits an item for approval, and a member of the Approvers group simply approves or rejects it. There are no workflows or tasks assigned to users in simple moderation.

Delivery of Information Through Search

SharePoint Search is a large topic unto itself, and there are many books devoted to this subject alone. Search offers a great way to quickly find information throughout a portal and is an important reason many organizations look to utilize SharePoint within their environment., However, understanding what users are searching for and how best to display the results can greatly affect the search experience. This section will focus on utilizing search and customizing some of the components to better deliver the information end users are looking for. But first, let's take a look at the three different versions of SharePoint Search that are available:

> *SharePoint Foundation Search:* SharePoint 2010 Foundation Search is the equivalent to WSS 3.0 Search that was available in the previous version. Foundation search is easily to deploy, configure, and administer. Foundation Search will index all your content and return and provide results with very little effort. There are no configuration options within the user interface (UI), other than setting up the index.

> *SharePoint Server Search*: SharePoint 2010 Server Search is the equivalent of MOSS 2007 search. The big different between Foundation Search and Server Search is that SharePoint Server Search can index Active Directory content as well as add additional content sources outside of SharePoint. SharePoint Server Search provides a rich UI to interrogate what is being searched and plan

accordingly with key features such as Best Bets. Search scopes are also a key feature that are heavily utilized in a search-focused implementation.

FAST Search: FAST Search was a product purchased by Microsoft and added to the SharePoint product in SharePoint 2010. While this product requires an additional license outside of the SharePoint Server Standard license or SharePoint Server Enterprise license, it does provide many neat features. While SharePoint Server Search can index approximately 100 million items, FAST Search can index around one billion items. Other features include scrolling preview, or the ability to preview PowerPoint slides or Word document pages directly in the browser through search results, or the ability to review similar results based off SharePoint comparing content with similar metadata.

Microsoft provides a great breakdown of the features in each product at the following URL: `http://sharepoint.microsoft.com/en-us/buy/Pages/Editions-Comparison.aspx?Capability=Search`.

What Content Can Be Crawled

For SharePoint to provide search results within the environment, SharePoint periodically crawls content, which builds an index of all the content that was crawled. This index is then used by the index engine and propagated to the query engine, which provides results when a search is executed. For example, if a user types a term into the SharePoint search box and hits search, the web server hands that off to the query server. The query server digs through the index and property database to determine a list of items to display in the search results. These results are security trimmed, or filtered, based on user permissions to content appearing in search, and finally rendered by the web server to the end user in the search core results Web Part.

While it's not necessary to understand the entire search process, knowing the basics will help troubleshoot or extend search when issues arise. For SharePoint Search to work, a crawl of the sites within the portal needs to be established. This can be done by viewing the available content sources in the Search Service Application: Search Administration, which is located in Central Administration, as shown in Figure 10-10. By default, the main web applications and site collections will already be an available content source under the Local SharePoint sites content source. It's important to understand that content outside of SharePoint can also be crawled and utilized through search. The following are available content sources that SharePoint can crawl:

- SharePoint Sites
- File Shares
- Exchange Public Folders
- Lotus Notes
- Line-of-Business Applications
- Web Sites

When configuring a file share as a content source, you'll need to determine the starting path, or folder, within the share to start to index. Work with the business to determine exactly what content needs to be indexed. It's not a best practice to crawl an entire file share, as these are typically very large in size and contain far more content then is needed. Permissions on the content within the file share will be utilized to trim content during search as needed. If a user doesn't have access to the content on the file share, this content will not show up in the search results.

When additional content sources are added, we recommend you create a new content source for each source. This allows for a separate crawl schedule to be used for content that is outside of the SharePoint environment. These sources can be crawled outside of the time of the main SharePoint crawl, and less frequently.

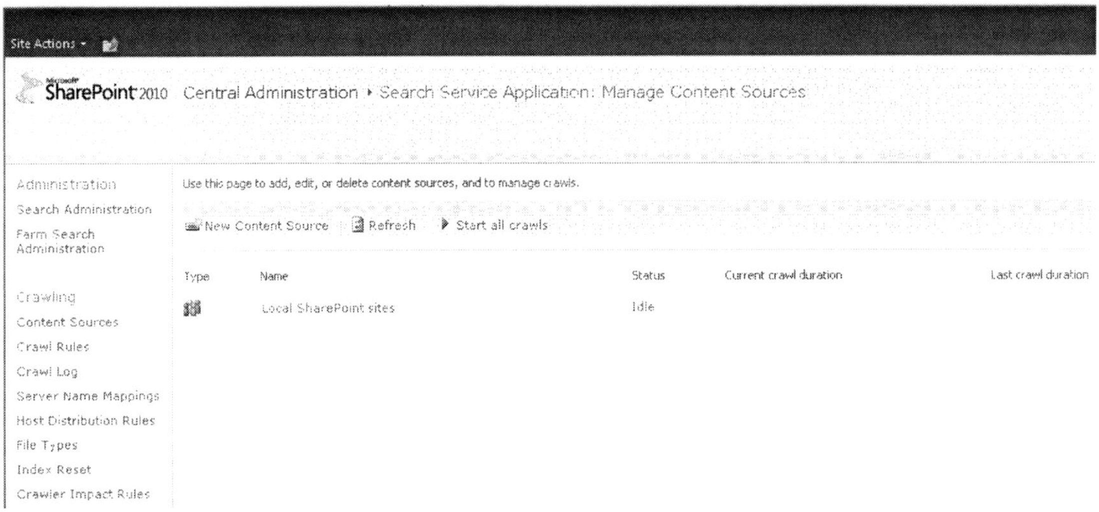

Figure 10-10. *Manage content sources*

How to Search for Content

SharePoint Search is very powerful when just typing in a term and hitting search. However, SharePoint provides a handful of additional ways to search that can make the search experience even better.

Wildcard Searches

New in SharePoint 2010, the wildcard feature broadens the search results by allowing symbols to be used to represent characters. For example, you could type Th* to search for all words that begin with the letters Th. Wildcard searches work only at the end of a word and greatly reduce the relevance of the returned results.

Boolean Searches

Boolean searches allow for terms such as AND, OR, and NOT. Using these terms will either increase or decrease the returned results based on how they are used. It's also worth mentioning that quotation marks can be used around phrases as well. For example, you could do a search such as ("Employee Rules" OR "Employee Regulations") AND "Termination". This would return all results that contain Employee Rules and Termination or Employee Regulations and Termination.

Property Searches

SharePoint allows properties to be used directly in the search box without creating a custom scope. You type in the search box title, "PTO Policy," or author, "Erkes," and do a search on specific properties. Any of the Managed Metadata properties can be used in this fashion.

You may already know about them, but there is a good chance that many users are unaware of these simple search enhancements. The features listed above provide a great opportunity to further educate the business team about how to improve the way they use SharePoint. You'll find that users desire an enhanced search function, but may not know that it's possible or don't want to ask. If the business plans on heavily utilizing search, creating properties is a must.

Search Relevancy Improvements

Just as it's important to understand a little bit about how search works, it's also important to understand a little bit about how the results are ordered the way they are. While the engine and internal formulas used to generate and rank results are tightly guarded, there are a few items that have been updated in SharePoint 2010 that Microsoft has shared.

Clickthroughs are probably the single biggest update in SharePoint 2010. A clickthrough is the method in which SharePoint Search captures your activity after search results have been rendered. After performing a search and results are rendered, Search monitors what links are clicked. For example, if you search for PTO form, and select the third result in the list, SharePoint tracks this selection. Over time, if users performing the same search continually select the third result, SharePoint will adjust the content and next time return it higher in the search results. This is a very powerful feature as it simply works on returning better results based on searches from your users.

Phrase matching has been added in the latest release as well. For example, if you perform a search for global organization, results with *global* and *organization* together will be ranked higher than those with *global* and *organization* but not together. This may seem like a small change, but it greatly improves the search experience. SharePoint Search also utilizes many of the new social features found in the latest version. If the document or list item has a social tag, SharePoint will return this item higher in the result set, especially if the same tag is used repeatedly.

While it's not a direct relevancy improvement but rather an improvement to the overall search experience, SharePoint 2010 contains refiners. These can be found on the left-hand side of the screen after a search has been performed, as shown in Figure 10-11.

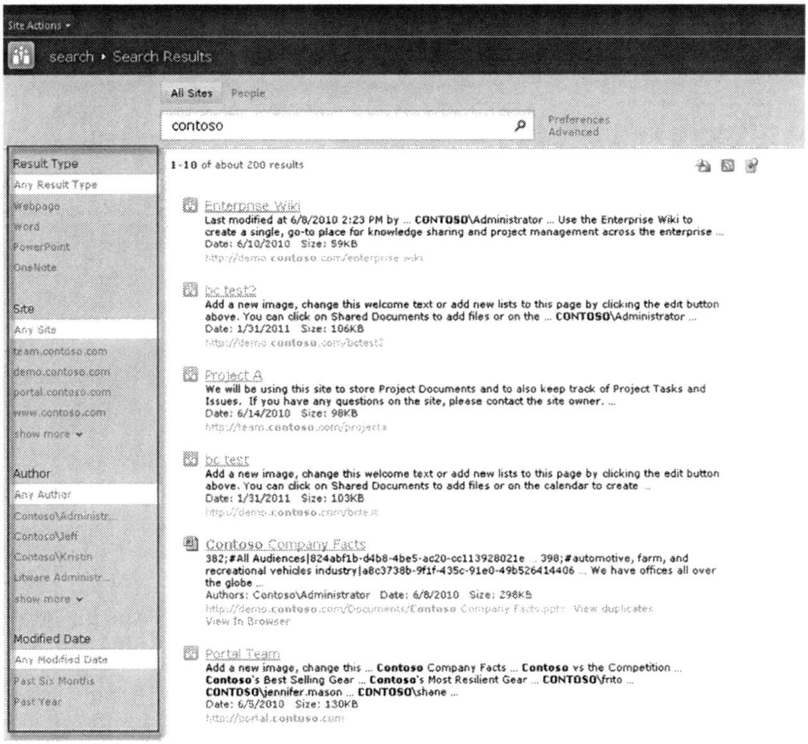

Figure 10-11. Search Refiners

Refiners allow for further refinement of the search results. For example, you search for *contoso*, but you know you are looking for a Word document. Simply click the Word option under the Result Type heading to refine your results to include only Word documents.

It's important to understand how search has changed between MOSS 2007 and SharePoint 2010 and how these changes can be utilized to increase the search experience for the business.

Search Administration

It's also important to understand what options are available at the search administration level and how using these features can impact search and create a better search experience. In every environment, there is going to be content that is commonly searched for. This might be a PTO policy, expense report form, or W4 document from Human Resources. For content you know is going to be regularly searched, we recommend that you create a Best Bet. Best Bets can be created at the site collection level from Site Actions ➤ Site Collection Administration ➤ Search Keyword ➤ Add Keyword. The keyword phrase is the common search query for the desired content, with Synonyms being other common search queries. The Best Bet section allows for a URL and title, which could link outside of SharePoint, or directly to a document within SharePoint, as shown within Figure 10-12.

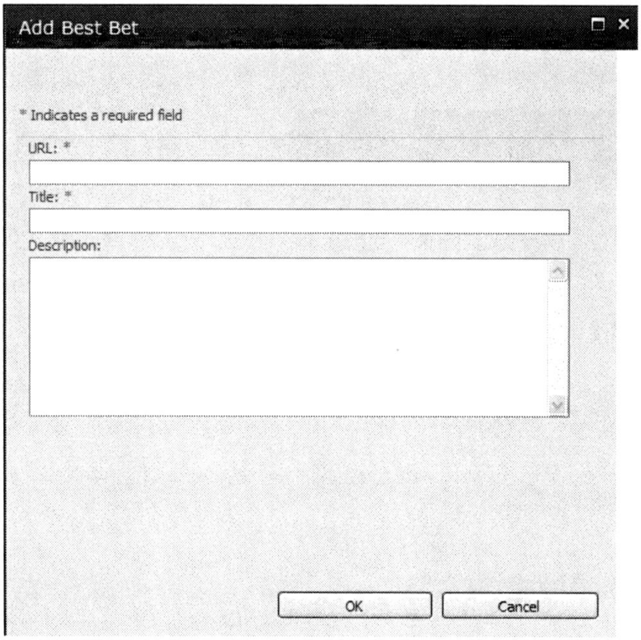

Figure 10-12. Configure Best Bet

You might be asking yourself, "Well, how do I know what people are searching for to create the Best Bet?" Good question, and if you aren't lucky enough to get this type of feedback from the business, SharePoint can fill you in. This will be discussed in the next section.

SharePoint search scopes provide the ability to narrow down the search result set even before performing a query. Typically, when a search query is executed, the entire index is used to return the applicable results. Using a scope with your search query greatly reduces the number of items in the index and therefore returns more targeted results by only looking for content that falls within that scope.

When setting up a scope, you first give it a name, and then apply the rules to define that scope. A scope can be source, or all content. For example, a Forms scope could be created, which would search all the forms contained within the HR site. Scopes are compiled or updated by a timer job every 15 minutes, so after a scope is created it may not return results immediately. Like Best Bets and search keywords, it's important to work with the business team and identify a set that will aid the business. However, keep in mind that sometimes too many scopes can be worse than none at all. While it's hard to provide a hard number here, feedback from the business team should dictate this number. Remember to utilize the SharePoint search reports to identify what users are searching for in order to help build better Best Bets and search scopes. These scopes should go through a committee to determine whether another similar scope exists, or if there truly is a business need to create this additional scope. It's common for each business unit or group to feel they need numerous scopes to better function within SharePoint Search. While this may be the case, it's important to work with them to truly understand their needs before creating every scope they think they need.

Search Reports

SharePoint 2010 search reports contain a plethora of information on how users are using search. Web analytics reports should be turned on from Day One of the farm, so user information on how search is being utilized should be available from Day One. The reports contain information such as total number of queries performed on the site, average number of queries on the site per day, and what queries gave users zero results. These reports also show a graphical representation of the number of queries shown over time.

Overall health and performance of search should also be of concern when managing SharePoint. Administration reports are available from the Monitoring section within Central Administration. These reports track the overall performance of search, including how long it's taking to crawl each content source, and how long it's taking for queries to return results. This should be the first stop if users are complaining about search responsiveness or if crawling a content source is taking longer than expected.

Search Web Parts

So now we've talked about all the nice updates in SharePoint 2010 and how the features can be used to provide a better search experience, let's look at some of the Web Parts used to deliver the search results. When a search query is executed in SharePoint, the default search page is the OSSSearchResults.aspx page. This page contains the Search Core Results Web Part, along with the refinements found on the left side of the page. While this page displays the results as expected, the page cannot be customized or have additional Search Web Parts added.

Typically an environment that utilizes Search will have one or more Search Centers defined within the site collection. The Search Center is an available site template that can be created within the site collection, and then the SharePoint search box results can be directed to this new Search Center. Directing the search results to this new site can be done by navigating to Site Settings ➤ Search Settings under the Site Collection Administration heading. Changing the Site Collection Search Results Page path to the new site and page will send all site collection search results to this new page. This new site will allow for the addition of new search-related Web Parts. We'll investigate a few and see how they can be used to deliver information to the user.

Search Core Results Web Part

The Search Core Results Web Part is essential to SharePoint Search as it is responsible for rendering the result set back to the user. This Web Part can be found on the OSSSearchResults.aspx page or it can be added to the page within the Search Center. It's common for this Web Part to be customized using XSLT to display search results in a manner that better fits the business needs. For a more in-depth look into customizing the Search Core Results Web Part, please visit the following MSDN article: http://technet.microsoft.com/en-us/library/gg549987.aspx. This Web Part can also be used to display predefined search results. This can be done by changing the Fixed Query setting to a property and the Cross-Web Part query ID to anything but User Query.

Advanced Search

Advanced Search is a Web Part that can be utilized within search to narrow down the results returned from search by adding additional information to the query. The biggest benefit comes from the ability to use one-to-many SharePoint properties in the search query as shown in Figure 10-13.

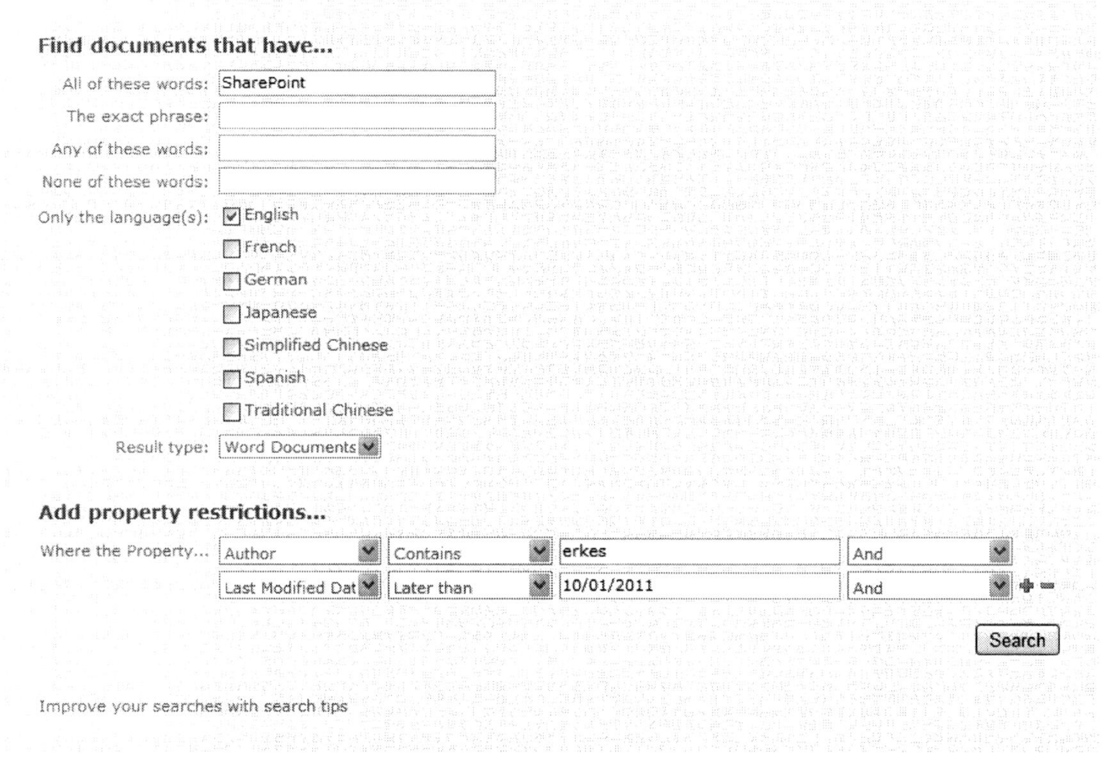

Find documents that have...

All of these words:	SharePoint
The exact phrase:	
Any of these words:	
None of these words:	
Only the language(s):	☑ English
	☐ French
	☐ German
	☐ Japanese
	☐ Simplified Chinese
	☐ Spanish
	☐ Traditional Chinese
Result type:	Word Documents ▼

Add property restrictions...

Where the Property...	Author ▼	Contains ▼	erkes	And ▼
	Last Modified Dat ▼	Later than ▼	10/01/2011	And ▼ ➕ ➖

Search

Improve your searches with search tips

Figure 10-13. Advanced Search Web Part

Federated Results

The Federated Results Web Part can be used to add results from different data sources that provide a single search experience within SharePoint. A common federation is to use the Microsoft search engine Bing. When a search query is entered into the SharePoint search box, the Federated Results Web Part performs a search on Bing and returns results from this source as well. The Web Part can be configured to limit the number of items to display. This functionality may not be applicable in all business settings, but can be a big win for those environments that can benefit from this additional result set.

The complete list of search-related SharePoint Web Parts can be found by navigating to a Web Part page within SharePoint, editing that page, and selecting Add a Web Part from a Web Part zone on that page. On the Page Tools tab, select Search under categories and a list of Search Web Parts will appear, as shown in Figure 10-14. A brief description of the Web Part can be found on the right side of the page under About the Web Part. Become familiar with these Web Parts and how they can be utilized within the environment to improve the search experience.

Figure 10-14. Search Web Parts

People Search

No discussion of SharePoint Search is complete without mention of the People Search functionality. This capability focuses on the concept of knowledge mining, centered on SharePoint tagging, which was covered earlier. People Search provides the ability to find individuals within the organization who might have knowledge or a skill set that is needed. For People Search to be very effective, the following requirements must be met:

- Everyone within SharePoint participates in tagging. This focuses content within SharePoint Search based on what is being searched.

- Within the Ask Me About property, users must indicate their areas of knowledge.

- Within the Interest property, users must indicate their interests. These are items where the user would like to acquire more knowledge.

The more accurately these properties can be filled out by the end user, the more accurate and beneficial the People Search results will be. For example, let's say you are responsible for implementing a new SharePoint 2010 intranet site that is going to heavily utilize InfoPath forms to replace old Excel forms. A simple People Search using InfoPath in the Persons Keywords search box would render all users that list that experience within the About Me property. This can save valuable time and is a great way to quickly find a much needed skill set within the organization. Encouraging users to populate the information within their profile can sometimes prove challenging, however; a great way to do this is to create a contest. The first 100 users to enter information into their profile gets their name entered into a drawing for a prize. This approach can be a win-win for the company, as it populates user profiles to enhance the People Search, but also encourages users to interact with SharePoint and experience its capabilities.

When viewing the People Search results, you immediately see how closely the results are tied to the knowledge mining concept. Figure 10-15 shows the People results page. The left side of the page contains the People Refinement Panel, which allows you to further filter the returned results.

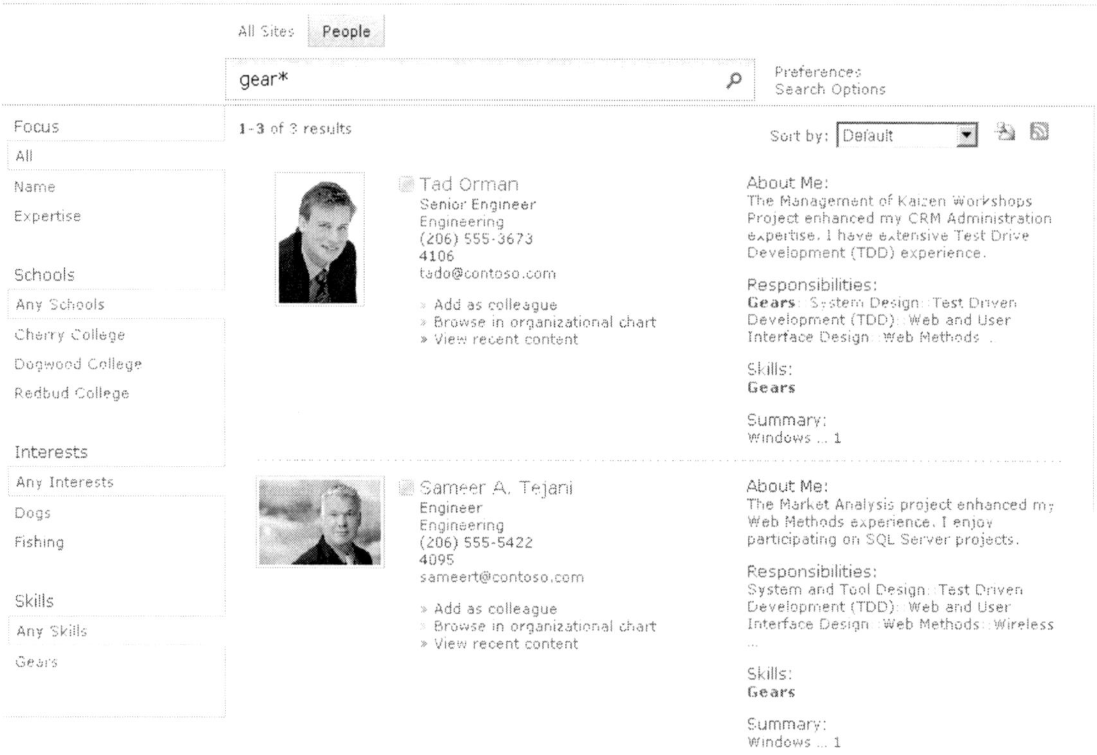

Figure 10-15. People Search results

After a search is performed, an abundance of information is available within each result. Clicking a person's name will direct you to that person's profile. Each result will provide the ability to "Add as colleague" if they are not already associated with the user performing the search. As you probably already guessed, selecting "Browse in organizational chart" will display that particular user in a very user-friendly Silverlight control. From this control, you are able to see individuals and their relative positions in the organizational hierarchy in relation to the user selected. Also, the "By person's name" shows a list of documents and pages that the person has recently worked on. Each result also shows the properties that have been completed by the user, such as About Me or Skills.

SharePoint also provides the ability to determine how people reached the currently logged-in user's profile. When the users searches for themselves, a section called "Help people find me" appears, which shows the number of searches that led to that profile, and what keywords were used. Links to sections that potentially need updating are also listed in this area. This method provides a great way to understand how people are reaching your page and what content might need to be updated to better satisfy these results.

People Search can be a very powerful tool within an organization. It's important to encourage users to fill out their profile properties so People Search results are accurate. Push managers and supervisors to encourage their employees to update their profiles regularly as new skills and areas of interest are acquired. Educate the business team about this functionality; the more it is used, the more incentive employees will have to update their profiles.

Summary

In this chapter you learned

- The types of information stored within SharePoint
- How content can get out of date and how to prevent it
- How to deliver information through audience targeting
- How the creation of wireframes for initial page layouts is beneficial
- How to deliver information using SharePoint Search and People Search

CHAPTER 11

Branding the User Interface

While it may not always be top of mind when deploying or administrating a SharePoint environment, branding and user interface design are key components. A brand is a powerful thing, and something most companies put a lot of time and effort into developing. Think of company logos, such as the swoosh for Nike, the golden arches for McDonald's, or the red bull's-eye for Target. These icons and company colors automatically get you thinking about the company and perhaps a product or service they provide. When working on a SharePoint user interface, keep in mind that the company brand needs to be displayed throughout this environment. Following company branding standards such as color palette, font type, and other general branding guidelines will help align the SharePoint environment with other company systems.

What Will You Learn in This Chapter?

- How to determine branding needs
- How to make use of branding components: themes, master pages, and Cascading Style Sheets (CSS)
- Branding pitfalls
- Navigation

Determining Branding Needs

Before attempting to start branding a new SharePoint environment, it's important to understand the needs of the business and its requirements around branding. Much as with any other project, requirement gathering and analysis is important, in which small discrete requirements should be developed and planned. It's important to involve stakeholders up front in the process, especially those who could potentially influence the project in the later stages. This will decrease the chance for those painful, costly changes late in the game that can cause larger issues.

Most companies have a brand standard. This typically consists of guidelines on the colors, fonts, and logos the company uses. Obtain these guidelines as early in the process as possible; not following them could require some rework down the road. A common approach to determining branding needs is to create a wireframe of the home page, and any supporting page within the environment that does not follow a typical SharePoint layout page (Web Part page). The goal of these exercises is to determine what level of SharePoint branding is needed. Determining these needs up front may save lots of unneeded customizations to master pages or Cascading Style Sheets (CSS) later on. We'll focus on this a little later in the chapter. Now, let's take a look at some of the more important aspects of branding planning.

SharePoint Multilingual Support

In today's global world, it may be a requirement for sites within your farm to support the local language at the farm's location. SharePoint 2010 utilizes language packs for both SharePoint Foundation 2010 and SharePoint Server 2010, available for download from `http://microsoft.com.downloads`. Every web front end in your farm will need to have the appropriate language packs installed. Installing language packs will allow for the creation of new sites in a local language as well as translate the existing site's interface based on the language the user chooses as the default. After the language packs have been installed, the Multilingual User Interface (MUI) will appear and a language settings option will appear in the site settings menu of each site.

If multilingual support is a requirement within the environment, it's important to plan for it accordingly. Ask the following questions:

- What languages need to be supported?

- What variations will you need?

- What elements will require language pack support?

  - Ribbon elements

  - Lists and site column headers

  - Site settings interface

  - Managed metadata

  - Search

Supporting multiple languages in SharePoint 2010 is not complicated, but proper planning and determining the level of language pack integration are necessary for successful implementation.

SharePoint Publishing and Branding

When you are considering the branding needs of the organization, it's important to know which version of SharePoint you are working with. SharePoint Server 2010 includes the Publishing feature, which proves to be a very nice feature for branding projects for the following reasons:

- Publishing provides the ability to create templates for page content known as page layouts. Page layouts are editable by content authors and designers.

- Publishing enables easier control over the navigational structures, especially if you wish to change them from the SharePoint user interface.

- Publishing allows for a master page to be easily changed by a site administrator.

- Publishing allows for more flexibility with themes, even allowing the theme to be applied to a site and all subsites at the same time.

Even if you do not wish to use the Publishing feature throughout the entire site, it's a good idea to create the top-level site collection using the publishing site template. This will allow for easier manipulation of the master page and supporting CSS.

Publishing also allows you to delegate work. For instance, if you have a SharePoint developer working on the master page while a UI developer works on the CSS, this work can be done independently and later pulled together and published through an approval workflow. The workflow could include key members from the marketing team and those necessary to ensure company brand standards are met.

Types of SharePoint Sites

SharePoint is typically deployed in one of three types of web sites: public-facing Internet sites, internal-facing intranet sites, or a combination of the two, which is an extranet. The use of each site varies, and therefore the branding of each type of site also differs.

- *Internet sites*: These sites are typically driven by marketing and tightly controlled, allowing very few users to publish content. Because they are public facing, they display a strong company brand and follow strict publishing guidelines. Administrators of these sites cannot control the type of browser or the screen resolution that will be used to visit the site.

- *Intranet sites*: These sites are typically geared towards internal employees to help them collaborate and work more efficiently. Intranet sites typically have less corporate branding, but more content publishers. Because these sites are internal, the company controls the browser and sometimes the screen resolution of the users accessing the site.

- *Extranet sites*: These sites are a hybrid of an Internet and intranet site. They typically have a separate area that an external user will need to authenticate into. Depending on the need, the extranet may be branded to cater to the company that your company is doing business with. However, these types of sites are typically used more for collaboration, so extensive branding may not be needed.

Types of Browsers

Another important decision you will need to make is to determine which browsers will be hitting your SharePoint site. While this might be easy if you are administering an intranet site, it is obviously more difficult for an Internet or extranet site. The most popular browsers as of September 2011, according to W3Counter.com, are shown in Table 11-1.

Table 11-1. Browsers Used

Browser	% Used
Internet Explorer 8	18.59%
Firefox 6	14.25%
Chrome 14	10.17%
Chrome 13	8.96%
Internet Explorer 7	7.29%
Internet Explorer 9	7.00%
Firefox 3.6	6.82%
Safari 5	5.24%
Internet Explorer 6	2.22%
Firefox 5	1.65%

Keep in mind that these numbers can change monthly, so before undertaking a branding effort, we recommend that you visit a site that publishes browser statistics, such as http://w3counter.com/globalstats.php, which is where the data in Table 11-1 was obtained. Older browsers, such as Internet Explorer 6, are not supported by SharePoint 2010. If you are supporting an internal SharePoint site and determine that users are still hitting your site with Internet Explorer 6, it might be helpful to display a message stating that their browser isn't supported and it's time to upgrade. Work with your internal infrastructure team to ensure that browsers that support SharePoint 2010 are standard, or will be available to those users that interact with SharePoint 2010. For a complete list of features supported within each version of Internet Explorer, visit the Microsoft article on Planning Browser Support at http://technet.microsoft.com/en-us/library/cc263526.aspx.

Branding Trends

While developing the brand and layout of a new site, it's important to be aware of some trends being utilized by other popular public-facing sites. While your brand may be unique, the layout and structure of the page should be familiar with users that visit other popular sites. These companies have spent the time to understand branding trends and research how the users view the different sections of a page when it first appears. Take Facebook.com or Bing.com: notice how the user sign-in information is in the upper-right corner? Notice how the logo appears in the upper-right corner? These are common trends across web sites, and your users will expect the same from internal sites as well. Review the sites you visit often and see if this holds true for those sites as well. To get a better idea of how some of the trends are being utilized in a SharePoint site, you can visit the following site, which has many examples of SharePoint 2010 public facing sites: http://www.wssdemo.com/livepivot/. You'll notice that this web site follows the common layout patterns as described above.

Branding Breakdown

Given the different elements involved in a SharePoint effort, it's important to understand all the options for creating a branded SharePoint site. Typically, SharePoint branding can be broken down into three major approaches, ranging from very simple to complex. As the branding scope increases, so do the skill sets needed to complete the branding effort. Let's take a look at the breakdown of the three branding approaches.

- *Low effort*: This approach uses out-of-the-box SharePoint master pages, CSS, and themes to create a simple SharePoint branded site. SharePoint 2010 provides 20 out-of-the-box themes and 2 master pages, v4.master and nightandday.master, to provide limited branding. This approach will not require any additional skill sets or resources outside of the SharePoint administrator to apply the theme or master page. This approach is typically used within intranet deployments where collaboration is the main focus and time doesn't need to be spent enhancing the look and feel.

- *Medium effort*: This approach utilizes the out-of-the-box SharePoint master pages, but also custom or alternative CSS files to provide a more customized brand. This effort might also include development of a custom theme which is much easier to create in SharePoint 2010 than it was in SharePoint 2007. This approach is common for intranet sites that require a more customized look and feel. For those larger deployments that focus on content publishing, this level of branding effort might be considered high. A person with web design experience, or at least experience with CSS, will be required to create the custom CSS files needed.

- *High effort*: This approach includes custom master pages, custom CSS, and potentially custom page layouts. This approach is common for public-facing sites or those internal sites that require a more polished and directed look and feel. This effort will require someone with traditional web design skills or knowledge of how master pages work in ASP.NET.

Now that we've talked about the different levels of effort depending on the branding need, we'll discuss each of these topics in more detail to get a better feel for the needed branding approach.

Branding Components

As previously discussed, branding elements are typically broken down into three main elements: themes, master pages, and CSS files. This section will provide insight into each element and how to utilize it to make your sites come alive.

Themes

SharePoint themes are by far the easiest option for creating light branding for a SharePoint site. Themes allow for 12 colors and 2 fonts to be applied to any SharePoint site. Microsoft completely revamped how themes work in SharePoint 2010, making the creation of a theme much easier than it was in MOSS 2007. Themes in MOSS 2007 involved creating a lot of CSS and images to be stored in a folder in the 12 folders (14 folders in SharePoint 2010). This also required a modification to the .INF file and an XML file. To make matters worse, this also required an IISRESET and the theme to be applied on every site. Needless to say, MOSS 2007 themes were difficult to create and manage. Unlike in SharePoint 2007, where theme-related CSS would be added after the core CSS, SharePoint 2010 actually looks for a special type of CSS comment and injects the CSS into the core CSS so that only the one file has to be loaded by the browser. SharePoint 2010 themes do not have the ability to define an image in contrast with SharePoint 2007 themes.

SharePoint 2010 simplified the theme creation process by allowing themes to be created directly within Microsoft Office, as shown in Figure 11-1 and Figure 11-2. A .THMX file can be created through Word 2007/2010 or PowerPoint 2007/2010. These applications provide the 12 colors and 2 fonts as well, which are then packaged up in the .THMX file, can be uploaded into SharePoint, and applied to any site.

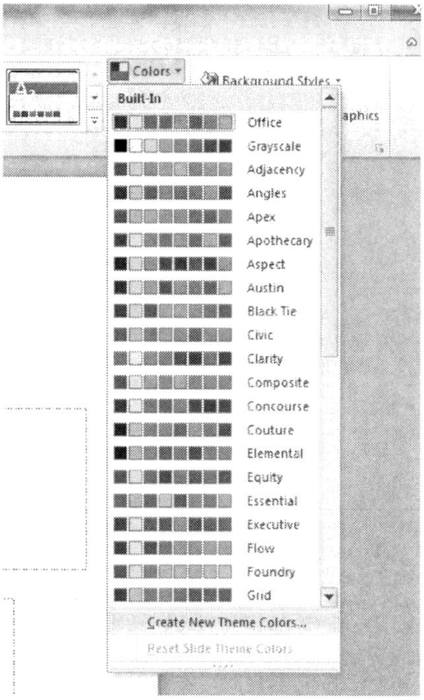

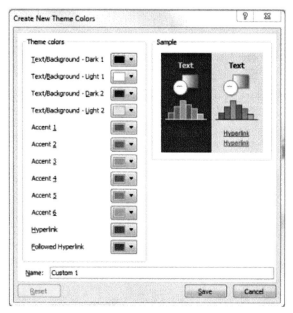

Figure 11-1. *PowerPoint theme creation*

Figure 11-2. *Theme color options*

After the theme has been created, simply navigate to the Theme Gallery at the site collection level and upload the newly created theme. After the theme is uploaded and saved, it will appear in the Site Theme menu as an available theme to be applied to the site.

SharePoint 2010 provides a number of themes out of the box, as shown in Figure 11-3. While you may find one that exactly fits your needs, it is more likely that one or more of these will come close, without being an exact fit. It is possible to take an existing theme and change any of the 12 colors or 2 fonts that are already defined.

■ **Note** If upgrading from MOSS 2007, old themes will still exist until the visual upgrade is performed. After the visual upgrade is performed, the new theme engine will not contain the old theme.

Figure 11-3. Customize available theme

Similar to the master pages, if the publishing template was used to create the site, the theme can be applied at the site level, but also made to reset all subsites with this new theme as well. Themes within SharePoint 2010 are self service, meaning someone with the appropriate permissions could apply a new theme or make changes to the current theme. While this may seem like a good idea, allowing users to modify themes can cause branding disconnects between sites and raise issues from not following a corporate standard. We'll describe these issues later in the chapter.

Master Pages

In the early days of web development, each page within a site was developed using HTML. This required each page within the site to have the same look and feel elements added as there was not a way to have all these pages use the same source. This made site changes and maintenance a nightmare. ASP.NET 2.0 introduced the concept of master pages, a separate page that controlled the layout components from one central location. Because SharePoint 2010 is based on ASP.NET, SharePoint also utilizes master pages to control the layout components.

When a page loads within SharePoint, that particular page finds the associated master page and places the content within the defined regions. These defined regions are known as content placeholders, or regions that load content from referring pages. SharePoint 2010 provides a handful of master pages available for use out of the box:

- *Default.master*: This is the master page used in SharePoint 2007, which can only be used when SharePoint 2010 is in a SharePoint 2007 Visual Upgrade mode. It is very similar to the default.master page that is available in SharePoint 2007.

- *V4.master*: This master page is the replacement for default.master in SharePoint 2007. An example of this new master page can be found in Figure 11-4, which shows the publishing template.

- *Minimal.master*: Not to be confused with the minimal.master page available in SharePoint 2007, this master page is available for those pages that need extra white space or custom navigation. This master page should not be used as a template to start the creation of a master page as it's missing numerous controls.

- *NightandDay.master*: This master page is available only if the Publishing feature is enabled. This master page is similar to the blueband.master page that was available in SharePoint 2007. However, like the V4.master page, it has been updated for SharePoint 2010.

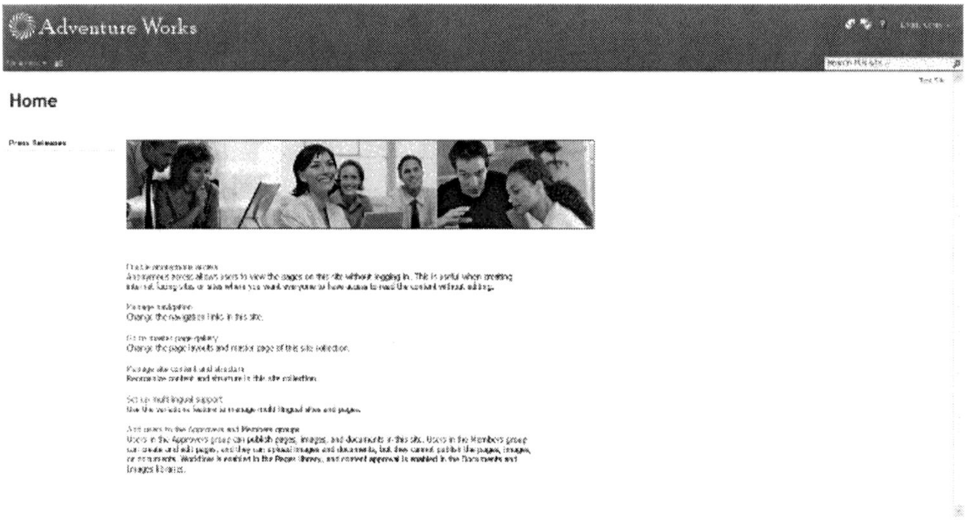

Figure 11-4. V4 master page

To see a list of all available master pages, navigate to Site Actions ➤ Site Settings ➤ Galleries ➤ Master pages and page layouts. The master pages can be quickly identified as they use the extension.master.

Minimal Master Page in SharePoint 2010

As described in the preceding section, Microsoft does not provide a minimal.master page that can be used as a base for starting to develop a custom master page. While you could use the V4.master page as a base, there may be more time spent removing unwanted content placeholders and controls than if you started from scratch. If you are looking for a good starter master page, there is a project on CodePlex that has three starter master pages: publishing, foundation, and meeting workspace. This is a well-respected project and should be utilized if heavy branding is going to be performed. This project can be found at http://startermasterpages.codeplex.com/.

Microsoft also provides guidance on updating SharePoint 2007 master pages to SharePoint 2010 in the following article: http://msdn.microsoft.com/en-us/library/ee539981%28office.14%29.aspx. This article focuses on adding the missing SharePoint 2010 content placeholders as well as the ribbon.

Master Pages and Publishing Feature

As discussed earlier, if the Publishing feature is enabled, an extra master page appears, the NightandDay.master. While this is a nice addition, the real benefit of the Publishing feature is the ability to version, kick off an approval workflow, and publish when advised. In larger deployments, it's common to have an individual or team work on the overall brand. This typically includes master pages and supporting CSS files. If the Publishing feature is enabled, it will create a style library for the CSS files and a Master page and page layouts document library. The teams can work within these libraries to update the files as needed, while not interrupting the current brand until the files are published. These same files can also be put through an approval process so that they remain visible only to the design team until someone with the privileges approves the files to be published and visible to users on the portal.

Master Pages and SharePoint 2007 Upgrade

To help ease the migration of SharePoint 2007 to SharePoint 2010, Microsoft provides the Visual Upgrade feature. The Visual Upgrade provides the ability to render content, master pages, and CSS from SharePoint 2007 in SharePoint 2010. This is handy as SharePoint 2007 master pages and CSS do not upgrade in SharePoint 2010. When migrating SharePoint 2007 to SharePoint 2010, the default is to keep the master page and supporting CSS in SharePoint 2007 mode until a visual upgrade is completed. After a migration, there are three options around the Visual Upgrade, which can be found by selecting Site Actions ➤ Visual Upgrade as shown in Figure 11-5:

- *Use the previous user interface*: This option allows you to continue to use the master page and CSS from SharePoint 2007.

- *Preview the updated user interface*: This option allows you to preview your site in SharePoint 2010 and enables you to revert back to a previous user interface if needed. The Visual Upgrade option still appears in the Site Actions if you want to switch back.

- *Update the user interface*: This option switches the user interface to SharePoint 2010. The Visual Upgrade option will disappear from the Site Actions menu. However, if you need to revert back to the previous user interface, this can be done through Windows PowerShell.

Figure 11-5. Visual Upgrade

Keep in mind that the Visual Upgrade is scoped at the web level, so each web page below the main site collection will need to have the Visual Upgrade performed. It's recommended to use a Windows PowerShell script to loop through all the webs and perform the Visual Upgrade. Be sure to visually inspect each site that has been upgraded because the visual upgrade process doesn't fix any potential branding issues automatically.

Master Pages and Application Pages

If you've done any branding in SharePoint 2007, you've probably come across the issue of trying to brand the application pages. These pages are often found in the Site Settings menu, or anything that has _layouts in the URL of the page. SharePoint 2007 applications utilized the application.master and would not inherit the master page referenced by the rest of the site. This resulted in a few pages that did not follow the rest of the brand. SharePoint 2010 provides the ability to brand the application pages as well. Within SharePoint 2010 Server, this option is under Site Actions ➤ Site Settings ➤ Look and Feel ➤ Master Page, as shown in Figure 11-6.

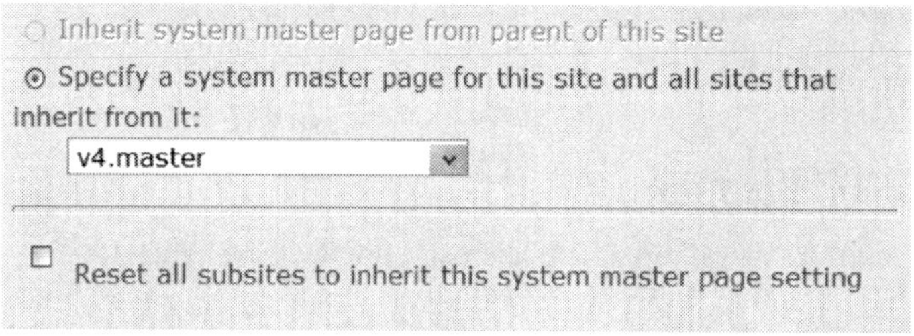

Figure 11-6. System master page

Page Layouts

Page layouts are available only when the Publishing feature is enabled, so these types of branding elements are not available with SharePoint 2010 Foundation or within Team Sites. Page layouts provide the ability to arrange content on a SharePoint page. The areas on the page that can be edited are known as field controls, while the areas on the page that have the capability to add a Web Part are called Web Part zones. The out-of-the-box page layouts can be found in the same library as the master pages, or by clicking Site Actions ➤ Site Settings ➤ Master page and page layouts under the Galleries heading. To create a new page layout, select Site Actions ➤ New Page. The available out-of-the-box page layouts are shown in Figure 11-7.

Type	Name	Modified	Modified By	Checked Out To	Compatible UI Version(s)	Approval Status	Contact	Hidden Page	Associated Content Type
	Editing Menu	10/27/2011 3:25 PM	System Account			Approved			
	en-us	10/27/2011 3:25 PM	System Account			Approved			
	Preview Images	10/27/2011 3:25 PM	System Account			Approved			
	ArticleLeft.aspx	10/27/2011 3:25 PM	System Account			Approved			Article Page
	ArticleLinks.aspx	10/27/2011 3:25 PM	System Account			Approved			Article Page
	ArticleRight.aspx	10/27/2011 3:25 PM	System Account			Approved			Article Page
	BlankWebPartPage.aspx	10/27/2011 3:25 PM	System Account			Approved			Welcome Page
	default.master	10/27/2011 3:25 PM	AD-ENT\cerkes		3	Approved			
	EnterpriseWiki.aspx	10/27/2011 3:25 PM	System Account			Approved			Enterprise Wiki Page
	minimal.master	10/27/2011 3:25 PM	AD-ENT\cerkes		4	Approved			
	nightandday.master	10/27/2011 3:25 PM	System Account		4	Approved			
	PageFromDocLayout.aspx	10/27/2011 3:25 PM	System Account			Approved			Article Page
	PageLayoutTemplate.aspx	10/27/2011 3:25 PM	System Account		4	Approved		Yes	
	ProjectPage.aspx	10/27/2011 3:25 PM	System Account			Approved			Project Page
	RedirectPageLayout.aspx	10/27/2011 3:25 PM	System Account			Approved			Redirect Page
	v4.master	10/28/2011 10:58 AM	System Account		4	Approved			
	VariationRootPageLayout.aspx	10/27/2011 3:25 PM	System Account		4	Approved		Yes	Redirect Page
	WelcomeLinks.aspx	10/27/2011 3:25 PM	System Account		4	Approved			Welcome Page
	WelcomeSplash.aspx	10/27/2011 3:25 PM	System Account			Approved			Welcome Page
	WelcomeTOC.aspx	10/27/2011 3:25 PM	System Account			Approved			Welcome Page

Figure 11-7. Page layouts gallery

It's important to remember that page layouts are based on a content type. This provides the ability to add metadata to newly created page content types. The pages are typically stored in a Pages document library within the site that is utilizing them. Custom page layouts can be created but need to be based on a base content type. The base content type is typically the Article Page, but this may vary depending on the use of the page. It's possible that when you attempt to create a new page, not all the page layouts are available to be created. These can easily be added by navigating to the page layouts and site templates menu by clicking Site Actions ➤ Site Settings ➤ Look and Feel ➤ Page layouts and site templates, as shown in Figure 11-8.

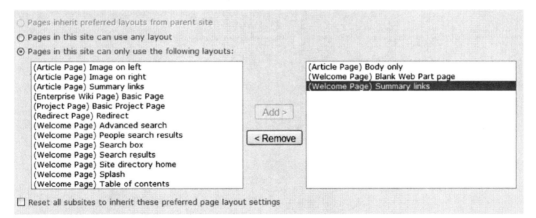

Figure 11-8. Page layouts

Custom page layouts can be created using SharePoint Designer 2010. This approach provides some flexibility over using the out-of-the-box page layouts. However, even when creating page layouts from within SharePoint Designer 2010, these pages still need to be based on a base content type.

Cascading Style Sheets

Cascading Style Sheets (CSS) enable you to change the look and feel of a site, by changing the color of an element, the size of a particular font, or the style of an entire control, for example. CSS is perhaps the most important concept when it comes to branding in SharePoint. SharePoint 2007 stored almost all the CSS in the core.css file. SharePoint 2010 stores almost all its CSS in a similar file called corev4.css. However, in SharePoint 2010, the page also loads additional CSS files depending on what content is contained within the page. When creating or modifying SharePoint CSS files, it's handy to have a reference to see which CSS tag refers to which content within SharePoint. If you're familiar with the SharePoint 2007 CSS reference chart provided by Heather Solomon, you'll be happy to know that she created one for SharePoint 2010 as well. This is an excellent resource and should be consulted often when working with CSS. That reference can be found at `http://sharepointexperience.com/csschart/csschart.html`.

Another great tool to use is Developer Tools, available in the most recent releases of Internet Explorer. This tool allows you to select an element on the page and view the supporting master page and CSS tags associated with it. If available, this tool can be accessed by hitting F12 on your keyboard while Internet Explorer is open, as shown in Figure 11-9. If Developer Tools is not available in your browser, it can be downloaded as an add-on to Internet Explorer.

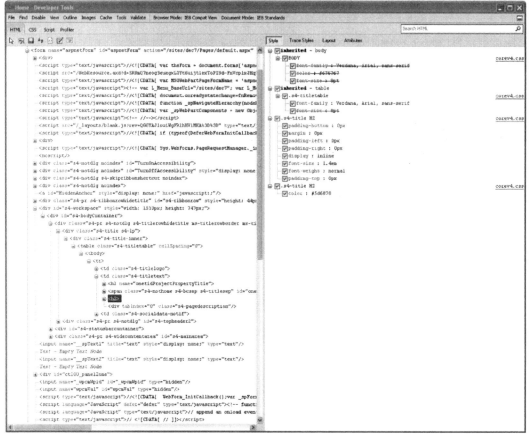

Figure 11-9. IE Developer Tools

Customization Pitfalls

One common concern when working on SharePoint branding is properly understanding the concept of customized files. Previous versions of SharePoint commonly referred to this as *ghosted*, but this term has been replaced with *customized* in SharePoint 2010. When a page within SharePoint is accessed by an end user, SharePoint references the content database to see if that page is based on a page that resides on the file system and then presents this page to the user. These types of files are considered *uncustomized*, as they can be displayed based on a file that resides on the server. However, if a page gets customized, this page gets stored in the content database. Since this file now resides in the content database and not on the file system, the file is now considered customized. While this may not cause issues immediately, these files typically cause issues during a migration.

While working on creating new branding components, it's perfectly acceptable to work on them in a development environment and make modifications to the files directly to speed up the development effort. However, when it's time to deploy these files (master page, CSS, etc.) to SharePoint, a SharePoint solution, or .WSP file, should be created to deploy these changes to the farm. A SharePoint solution can be created through Microsoft Visual Studio, as described in great detail in Chapter 13.

SharePoint Navigation

A chapter on the SharePoint user interface wouldn't be complete without talking about navigation. While the navigation isn't necessarily something that can be branded, it plays an important role in the overall user experience. SharePoint navigation is broken down into two main sections, global navigation and quick launch, also referred to as local navigation.

Global Navigation

Global navigation is the area at the top of most SharePoint sites in which the links appear. This top navigation often contains links to other webs within the same site. These links are security trimmed, so if a user does not have access to the site, it will not appear for them in the navigation. This navigation can be easily changed by selecting Site Actions ➤ Site Settings ➤ Navigation, as shown in Figure 11-10.

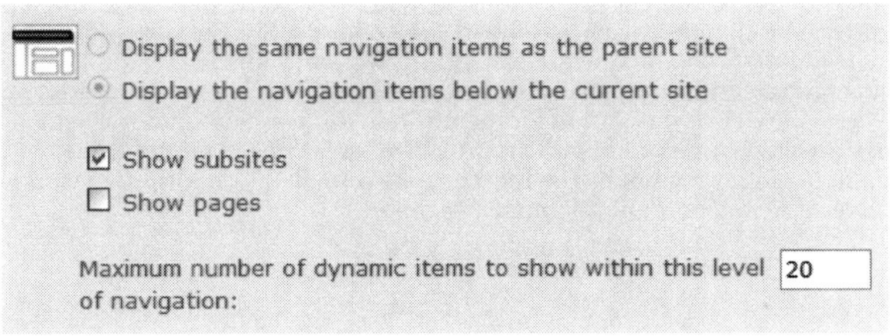

Figure 11-10. Global navigation

As discussed in Chapter 9, it's important to work with the business units and determine what this navigation structure needs to look like. It's not uncommon during these exercises for business units to ask for their sites to be located within the main level of navigation. Don't give into business units that feel they may be more important than others. Stick to the navigation that was driven by the business team during the taxonomy exercises.

The global navigation can be updated to include a flyout menu if desired. This can be done by modifying the following code and changing the MaximumDynamicDisplayLevels to something greater than two, as shown in Figure 11-11. For the flyouts to appear, each web below the main site needs to have those webs adjust their navigation to enable the appearance of subsites below the current site by selecting Show Subsites within the menu options.

```
<SharePoint:AspMenu
   ID="TopNavigationMenuV4"
   Runat="server"
   EnableViewState="false"
   DataSourceID="topSiteMap"
   AccessKey="<%$Resources:wss,navigation_accesskey%>"
   UseSimpleRendering="true"
   UseSeparateCss="false"
   Orientation="Horizontal"
   StaticDisplayLevels="2"
   MaximumDynamicDisplayLevels="2"   ←
   SkipLinkText=""
   CssClass="s4-tn"/>
```

Figure 11-11. Maximum number of display levels

The global navigation is typically based on the top-level site collection and all webs below. It's important to understand that the out-of-the-box global navigation cannot span multiple site collections. If this functionality is needed, a separate control will need to be added to the master page. There are a few custom controls and many third-party Web Parts that will aid in this area. It's important to use a control that will security trim the list of sites that the current user can access. If a site cannot be accessed by the individual logged in, it shouldn't appear in the navigation. This can lead to user satisfaction as well as put a strain on the administrator as users may try and request access to the site even if it's unwanted or unneeded.

Quick Launch

The SharePoint *quick launch* can be found on the left side of the screen in most SharePoint sites. Much like the global navigation, this too can be changed by navigating to Site Actions ➤ Site Settings ➤ Navigation. The quick launch links can be found under the Current Navigation section, shown in Figure 11-12. It's also important to note that the quick launch links can be security trimmed. This is a great way to target content to certain users, and provide a clear navigation for them within the site. Sometimes it can also be helpful to create headings within the quick launch. This provides a great way to group similar links. As with the global navigation, the following holds true for the quick launch: it's important to work with the owners of each site to determine the best quick launch navigation.

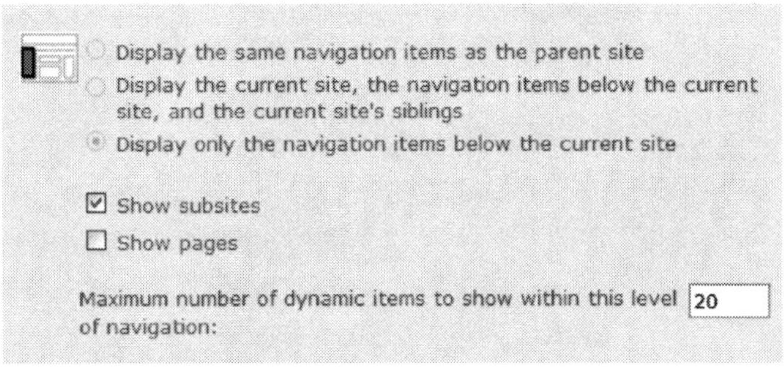

Figure 11-12. Quick launch navigation

Summary

In this chapter you learned

- How to determine branding for your SharePoint sites
- How to make effective use of the branding components
- What branding pitfalls to be aware of
- How to consistently position user interface navigation elements

CHAPTER 12

Customization and Tools

In this chapter, we will introduce application management. An application in this context refers to any custom functionality created for deployment to a SharePoint site. This could include creating a custom user experience using themes, page layouts, and navigation controls (sometimes called *skinning the site*). It could also involve writing new source code modules that are deployed to the farm to run alongside the SharePoint server application.

What Will You Learn in This Chapter?

- The tools used to customize the look and functionality of a SharePoint site

- Which tools are appropriate for which types of customization work

- How to control access to these tools to ensure proper enforcement of the site's customization policies

- The different techniques used to customize the user interface and content stored within SharePoint

- The various types of additional functionality that can be implemented in a SharePoint-based solution

- The types of tools available to the development team to ensure reliability, stability, and scalability when deploying application enhancements to SharePoint

Introduction to Application Management

Creating solutions for a SharePoint environment is similar in many respects to any other type of software development. It is important that you manage requirements, versions, and upgrades in a way that provides a predictable, repeatable process. This process is called Application Lifecycle Management (ALM) and is covered in more detail in Chapter 14. This chapter is devoted to exploring the types of components and modules you might typically create for a SharePoint application.

Any SharePoint solution can be broken down into two main categories of components: content and functionality. *Content* refers to the pages, lists, documents, and other items that are created by users and stored in SharePoint to be served to the visitors of the web site. *Functionality* refers to the logic that manages or processes that information. When customizing a SharePoint site it is sometimes difficult to distinguish between content and functionality.

Traditionally, end users create content and software developers and other IT staff create or deploy functionality. However, in the case of SharePoint, many items containing business process logic, such as workflows or InfoPath forms, can and should be created by business end-users instead of IT professionals.

Another way to distinguish content from logic would be to look at where they are stored. SharePoint stores its content as a series of *content databases*. Unfortunately, some items that must be managed as application components are stored in the content databases, so this is not ideal either.

For the purposes of SharePoint governance, we will define an *application* as a set of components that needs to be developed, deployed, and upgraded by a central development team. This may include user interface components, reusable content, software modules, workflow definitions, and so on. These components will be created, tested, and packaged by one group and deployed to the production farm for all to use.

Depending on the governance policies established for the site, it may also be acceptable for some of these types of components to be created by other groups within the organization. In that case, Share-Point contains controls that prevent independently-created applications from creating problems for the farm as a whole. These controls will be discussed later in this chapter and in the next.

Tools for Customization

The SharePoint platform supports a variety of tools for performing different types of customizations. In this section, we will explore these tools and their uses. We will also discuss the appropriate types of controls that can be applied to limit their use in a production environment.

SharePoint Designer

SharePoint Designer (SPD) is a Windows client application used to design rich, highly-customized SharePoint solutions. SPD 2010 is the latest version of the product previously known as FrontPage. It is available in both 32-bit and 64-bit versions, depending on the operating system on which it will be used and the version of Microsoft Office installed on the client computer.

SharePoint Designer is intended for use primarily by web site designers to enable detailed customization of pages, lists, libraries, and many other SharePoint artifacts. While there are features within SharePoint Designer that may be useful to developers and administrators, SPD is first and foremost a design tool. SharePoint Designer is ideal for creating business process workflows, integrating with line-of-business databases and creating custom presentations of business information on the SharePoint Server platform. Note that SharePoint Designer 2010 is only compatible with the SharePoint 2010 Foundation and Server products.

While SharePoint Designer and, previously, FrontPage were once offered as traditional commercial products, as of March 31, 2009, Microsoft is no longer selling SharePoint Designer but giving it away. It is available for free from the following Microsoft download sites:

- 32-bit: http://www.microsoft.com/downloads/en/details.aspx?displaylang= en&FamilyID=d88a1505-849b-4587-b854-a7054ee28d66

- 64-bit: http://www.microsoft.com/downloads/en/details.aspx?FamilyID= 566D3F55-77A5-4298-BB9C-F55F096B125D

SharePoint Designer 2010 can be a very powerful tool for creating SharePoint 2010 solutions. Like any powerful tool, it can be dangerous in the wrong hands. SharePoint Designer may not be appropriate to use in a production environment. As such, there are multiple configuration options within SharePoint Server 2010 that control which actions can be performed by SharePoint Designer users.

The first set of options can disable SharePoint Designer access or limit the changes it can make. These settings are configured using the SharePoint Central Administration web site, under General Application Settings. From the General Application Settings page, select Configure SharePoint Designer

Settings. This page, shown in Figure 12-1, displays the available options and their current settings. Note that you set these options on a per web application–basis. To set these options for a web application other than the default, select it using the drop-down control at the top of the form.

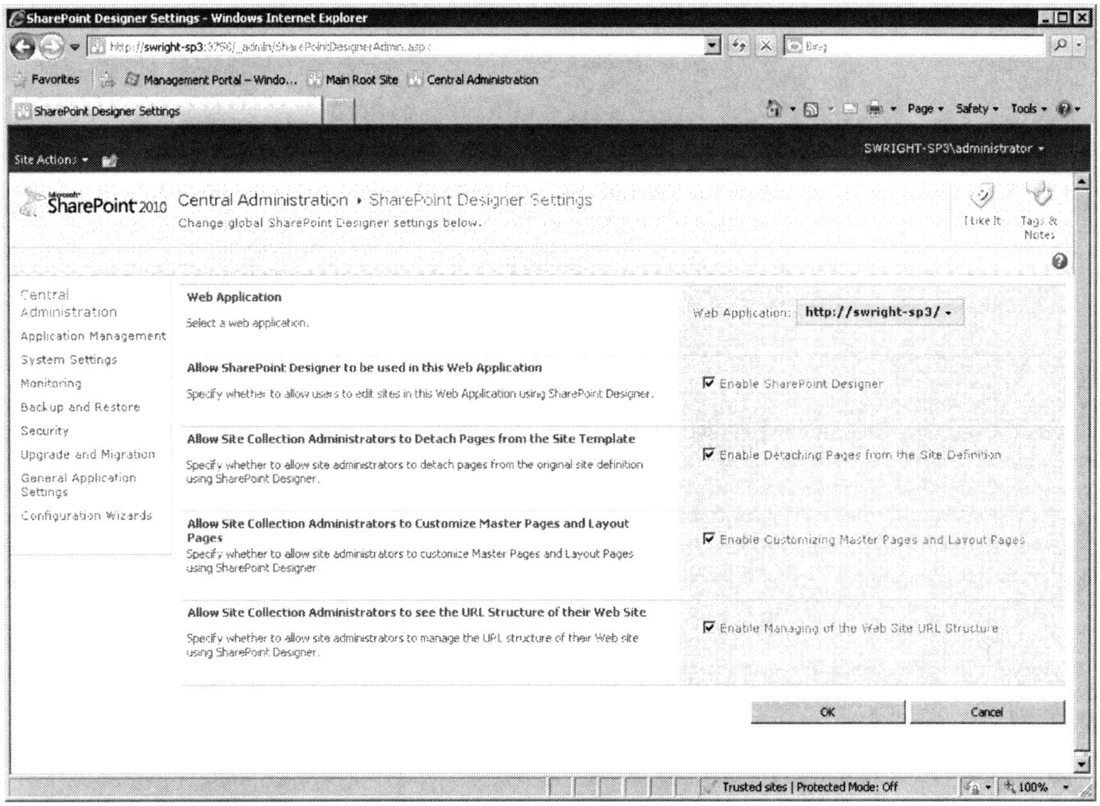

Figure 12-1. SharePoint Designer settings in Central Administration

■ **Tip**   If you need to control these settings at the site collection level instead of at the web application level, this can be done using the Site Settings page in the root site of the collection. Look for the SharePoint Designer Settings option under Site Collection Administration.

Table 12-1 provides descriptions of the various settings available on the Designer Settings page.

Table 12-1. Available SharePoint Designer Settings

Setting	Description
Allow SharePoint Designer to be Used in this Web Application	This setting controls the ability of SharePoint Designer to attach to the web application. If this option is unchecked, all of the other settings become irrelevant.
Allow Site Collection Administrators to Detach Pages from the Site Template	Enabling this option allows SharePoint Designer to run in *Advanced* mode instead of *Normal* mode. Advanced mode allows the user to *ghost* pages by modifying them from the content they originally had in the site definition stored on the server's hard drive. The customized version of the page is stored in the SharePoint content database. Any changes made to the site definition files are not reflected in pages that have been detached. This can create maintainability problems and should be used with care.
Allow Site Collection Administrators to Customize Master Pages and Layout Pages	Master and layout pages (along with themes) are the keys to branding sites within SharePoint. SharePoint Designer contains powerful tools for updating these files. Most organizations prefer to maintain tight control of their site branding. Disabling this option helps to lock down the site's appearance in a production environment.
Allow Site Collection Administrators to see the URL Structure of their Web Site	SharePoint Designer allows the user to examine and rearrange the pages and folders within a site. Since this can dramatically impact users of the site, this is a function that should be limited in many environments.

In addition to configuring SharePoint Designer access to a web application or site collection, the user connecting to the site must have the Use Remote Interfaces permission. This permission allows the user to use several types of remote interfaces including SharePoint Designer, web services and the WebDAV publishing interface. The Use Remote Interfaces permission is part of all of the default permission levels except Limited Access and Restricted Read. Any user that is assigned any of the other permission levels can connect to the web site with SharePoint Designer. However, SharePoint Designer still obeys all of the normal permissions enforced by SharePoint Server. If the user does not have permission to read or change an item in the SharePoint site, they will not be able to do so using SharePoint Designer.

For a more detailed look at using SharePoint Designer to create custom SharePoint solutions, see *Pro SharePoint Designer 2010* by Steve Wright and David Petersen (Apress, 2011).

Visual Studio

Another tool that is useful for creating SharePoint solutions is Microsoft Visual Studio 2010. This is Microsoft's environment for professional development. In Visual Studio, a developer can create new features, Web Parts, event receivers and other code components that run "under the covers" in SharePoint. Visual Studio is a very powerful tool but it is not intended for use by non-developers.

Visual Studio 2010 contains a large number of templates for creating all manner of SharePoint artifacts and packaging them for deployment to SharePoint. These artifacts are typically compiled into a solution package which is then deployed to the SharePoint server farm in either a "sandboxed" or "farm-level" deployment. A *solution package* is a single file that contains all of the executables and metadata necessary to install a working set of components into the server farm. We will discuss the packaging and deployment of Visual Studio–based solutions in the next chapter.

Visual Studio is the primary tool used for developing custom functionality on the SharePoint platform. Because of the potential for causing instability in the server farm, Visual Studio should only be used to directly interact with development SharePoint servers. This allows the solution to be debugged and updated as needed without affecting the production environment. Once development and testing are complete, the compiled solution package can be deployed to the production farm using the web interface, the STSADM command-line tool, or the PowerShell scripting language.

InfoPath Designer

InfoPath forms allow designers to create rich custom forms that can create and consume data from a variety of sources. InfoPath and SharePoint are designed to work well together and there are some interesting features that can best be leveraged using both technologies together.

InfoPath integrates with SharePoint in several different ways but the underlying technology supporting that integration is the InfoPath Forms Services subsystem. This component is only part of the Enterprise edition of SharePoint Server 2010. Forms Services is configured in SharePoint's Central Administration site. To configure Forms Services, select the General Application Settings link in the left-hand menu and look for the InfoPath Forms Services group.

In order to enable InfoPath Forms Services features within SharePoint a site collection, the "Share-Point Server Enterprise Site Collection features" feature, must be activated. This feature activates the Web Parts and menu actions necessary to host InfoPath forms within the site collection. Deactivating this feature is sufficient to prevent InfoPath forms from being used, but doing so may cause other desirable features to be disabled as well since they are a part of the same feature.

Types of Forms

Once Forms Services is configured and enabled in the site collection, there are a number of different ways in which InfoPath form templates can be used.

InfoPath forms are XML-based. This means that all of the data entered is encoded into an XML document that is then submitted to a data store of some kind. The most basic use of InfoPath forms in SharePoint is a SharePoint document library used as a repository for storing completed forms. SharePoint provides several useful features for working with completed form documents including versioning, access security, and workflow processing.

The next most common use for InfoPath within SharePoint is to create customized forms for workflows. SharePoint workflows allow users to perform controlled business processes managed by the Windows Workflow (WF) engine hosted within SharePoint. The WF engine can assign tasks, send e-mails, or perform a number of other activities to complete a business process. At each step in the process, user input may be required. The forms for entering this data are called *task forms*. InfoPath can be used to create highly-customized templates for these forms. Creating and deploying workflows will be discussed later in this chapter.

A new feature in InfoPath and SharePoint Server 2010 is the ability to create custom list forms in InfoPath. When a list or library is created in SharePoint, a set of default data entry forms is created. These forms create new items and edit or display existing items. A site designer can now customize these forms using InfoPath more easily than using the other methods available. The ability to create these forms is controlled by the security settings on the SharePoint list and the permissions granted to the user.

Form Security

Security is a complex topic when dealing with InfoPath forms because a form will often touch many resources outside the form. InfoPath forms can contain *data sources* which retrieve data from databases, web services, or other locations. Each of these interfaces may require its own authentication and authorization mechanism to function properly. Form templates may also contain managed .NET code that can access files on the user's system or perform other potentially dangerous actions.

To control the use of these features, InfoPath uses the concept of *form security levels.* Each security level places a different set of restrictions on what actions the form template can perform. The form-filling environment also affects what actions a form can take. Forms running in the InfoPath client application have greater freedom than those running in a web browser. A comprehensive discussion of the rules governing the restrictions placed on forms at different security levels is beyond the scope of this book, but policies regarding the use of these levels should be established.

The two security levels most often encountered in SharePoint sites are Domain and Full Trust. The third level, Restricted, is typically used only for e-mail-based forms.

The *Domain* security level is the most commonly used mode for InfoPath forms in SharePoint. Domain mode forms can access external data as long as that data is accessible according to the security zone for the domain as defined by Windows Internet Explorer.

■ **Note** It is important to recognize that InfoPath's use of the word *domain* is not the same as a domain in Active Directory or in Internet web addresses. For example, the Internet addresses `www.microsoft.com` and `office.microsoft.com` may or may not represent different security domains depending on the configuration of zones in Internet Explorer.

When a form is opened from a SharePoint list or library, the URL used to open the template is checked against the security zones defined on the user's desktop to determine if it is in the Internet or Local Intranet zone. In domain mode, external resources are restricted based on their zone relative to the zone of the form template.

The most permissive level of security for an InfoPath template is *Full Trust.* In Full Trust mode, a form can access any resources that the person filling out the form has access to. This may include databases, files on the local hard drive and registry settings. Obviously, Full Trust forms should be used only when absolutely necessary because of their potential for unintended impacts on the user's system.

The good news is that forms cannot get Full Trust just by asking for it. In fact, it can be quite difficult to get a form template installed in a way that allows Full Trust. In order to run a form in SharePoint using Full Trust, the form must be digitally signed using a trusted root certificate and installed by a farm administrator through SharePoint's Central Administration site. It can't be directly published by the designer.

Microsoft Visio

Microsoft Visio is a client application that allows the user to create intelligent diagrams using stencils. These stencils contain many shapes that can be connected and configured in various ways.

Visio Services is a new service within Microsoft SharePoint Server 2010 Enterprise Edition that allows Visio drawings to be displayed as part of a web page. The Visio Web Drawing file format allows the drawing to be displayed in any browser from a SharePoint site. The shapes within the drawing can also link to data within SharePoint or from other data sources such as relational databases. This data can be used to add labels to shapes or change their appearance. This creates a number of opportunities to create advanced visualizations. Like InfoPath Forms Services, Visio Services is enabled and configured using the Central Administration site and the Enterprise feature.

The Visio client application can publish web drawings directly to a document library in SharePoint. That diagram can then be viewed online directly or through a Web Part embedded into a web page.

Visio diagrams are also used in conjunction with PerformancePoint Services to generate interactive dashboards as shown in Figure 12-2. These diagrams are sometimes referred to as *Strategy Maps*.

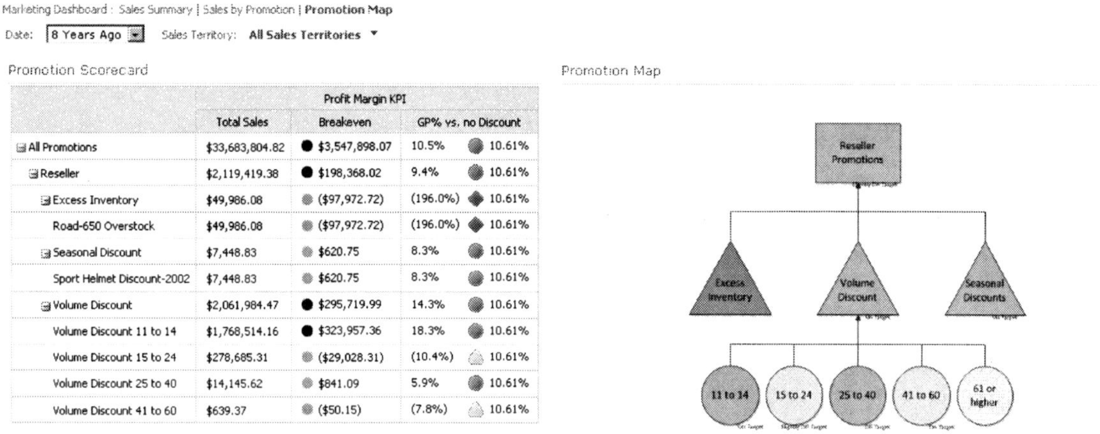

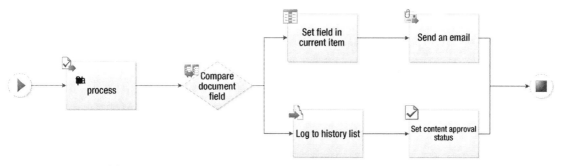

Marketing Dashboard : Sales Summary | Sales by Promotion | **Promotion Map**

Date: | 8 Years Ago ▼ | Sales Territory: **All Sales Territories** ▼

Promotion Scorecard   Promotion Map

	Total Sales	Profit Margin KPI		
		Breakeven	GP% vs. no Discount	
All Promotions	$33,683,804.82	● $3,547,898.07	10.5%	● 10.61%
Reseller	$2,119,419.38	● $198,368.02	9.4%	● 10.61%
Excess Inventory	$49,986.08	● ($97,972.72)	(196.0%)	● 10.61%
Road-650 Overstock	$49,986.08	● ($97,972.72)	(196.0%)	● 10.61%
Seasonal Discount	$7,448.83	● $620.75	8.3%	● 10.61%
Sport Helmet Discount-2002	$7,448.83	● $620.75	8.3%	● 10.61%
Volume Discount	$2,061,984.47	● $295,719.99	14.3%	● 10.61%
Volume Discount 11 to 14	$1,768,514.16	● $323,957.36	18.3%	● 10.61%
Volume Discount 15 to 24	$278,685.31	● ($29,028.31)	(10.4%)	● 10.61%
Volume Discount 25 to 40	$14,145.62	● $841.09	5.9%	● 10.61%
Volume Discount 41 to 60	$639.37	● ($50.15)	(7.8%)	● 10.61%

Figure 12-2. A Visio-based strategy map in PerformancePoint Services

Another use of Visio is in workflow development. Visio 2010 uses a set of stencil shapes to define the steps in a workflow, as shown in Figure 12-3. This allows a business user to design the workflow in Visio and then hand it off to a developer.

Figure 12-3. A Workflow design in Visio

Once the workflow is designed, the developer will add logic and data connections to complete the workflow using either SharePoint Designer or Visual Studio. In this case, the Visio client application is not interacting directly with SharePoint but is involved in developing a solution that will run in SharePoint.

SharePoint Workspace

SharePoint Workspace 2010 is a client application that allows users to take SharePoint content offline. Workspace is the latest version of the Microsoft Groove client available as part of Office 2007. The application also allows the creation of peer-to-peer collaboration without using a SharePoint server.

If you need to prevent SharePoint Workspace users from accessing a site's content, there is an option under Site Settings that can accomplish this. First, select "Search and offline availability" from the Site Administration group as shown in Figure 12-4.

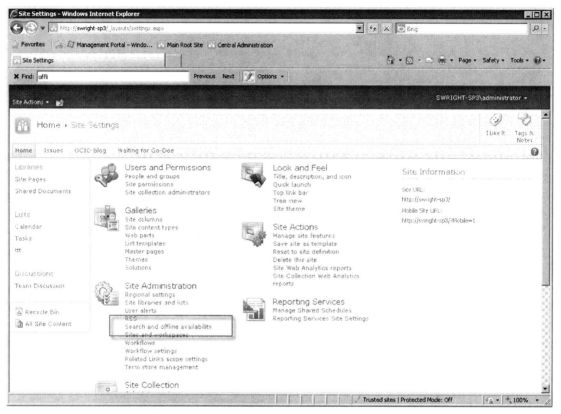

Figure 12-4. *Site Settings—offline availability*

The site administrator can block or allow access on the configuration page, as shown in Figure 12-5. Unfortunately, this is a site-level setting so it must be set to be blocked in each site. Access is allowed by default.

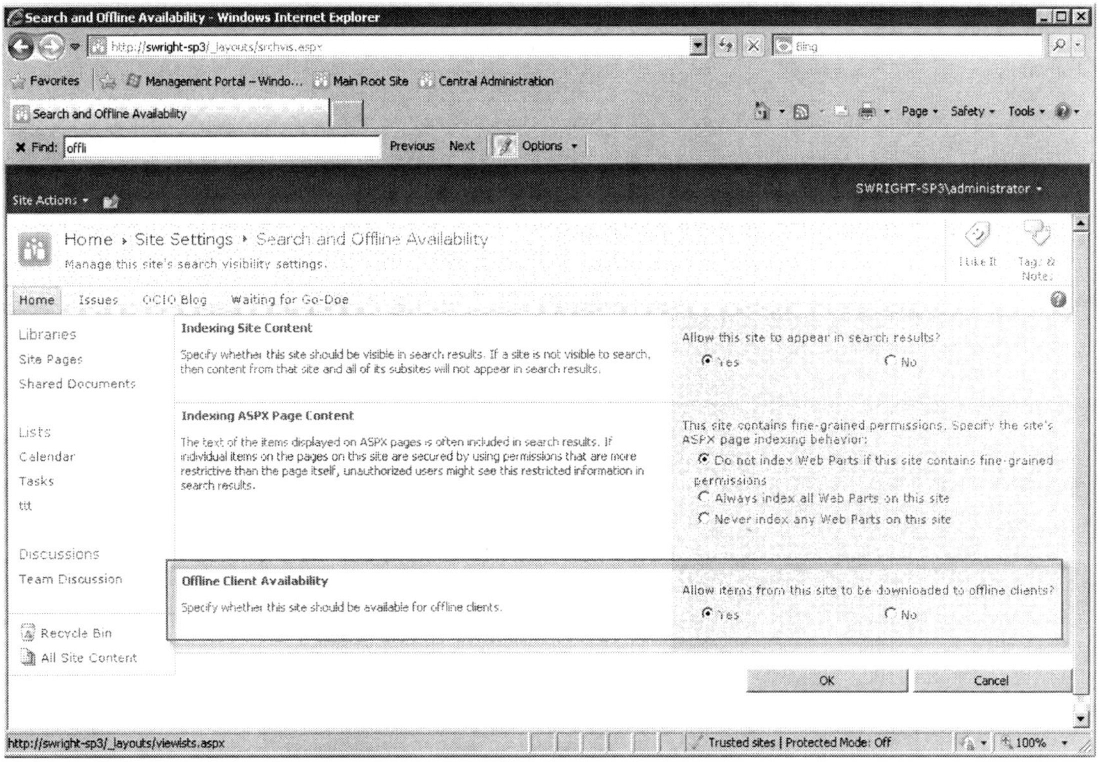

Figure 12-5. Search and Offline Availability page

SharePoint Workspace can synchronize documents and lists with the SharePoint site when a connection is made. This allows users who are not always connected to contribute content and collaborate with other users on a SharePoint site. SharePoint Server still enforces all of the usual content restrictions when sending content to or receiving updates from Workspace. While SharePoint Workspace can be used to access and collaborate, the user's ability to customize SharePoint through this tool is quite limited. The risk of allowing access to authorized users is therefore relatively low.

Customizing Content

Out of the box, SharePoint has a certain appearance. It has a set of colors, fonts, page layouts, and navigation features that are built into the default site templates provided. This look and feel is designed to work well for general purpose intranet sites, but it is somewhat bland and utilitarian looking. Fortunately, SharePoint supports dramatically customizing this appearance with a variety of tools. The process of changing the site-wide look and feel of a site is referred to as *branding* the site.

Applying your own brand to a SharePoint site is done in different ways, depending on the desired changes to be made. Changing the default colors and fonts used on the site is done using *themes*. Changing the overall page layout of the site is done using *master pages*. Changes to the site's navigation features are also typically done through master pages by embedding a set of custom SharePoint controls that render menus in the web browser.

In this section, we will describe the branding process at a high level as it relates to deploying application components that relate to branding. For a more detailed description of the branding process, see Chapter 11.

Master Pages

Master pages are a feature of ASP.NET that allows several pages to inherit their structure and other common elements from a shared source file. This enables the maintenance of these elements in a central location. A master page typically contains the HTML tags that define the layout of a page with "content areas" designated for page-specific content. Master pages can also include web controls that are common to all pages, like navigation menus, and often common CSS links as mentioned above.

Figure 12-6 shows a typical SharePoint page. The rectangles indicate where the customizable content areas might be. In this case, many of these areas have been provided with default content such as navigation menus. The author of a page using a tool such as Visual Studio or SharePoint Designer can replace this default content with content specific to the page.

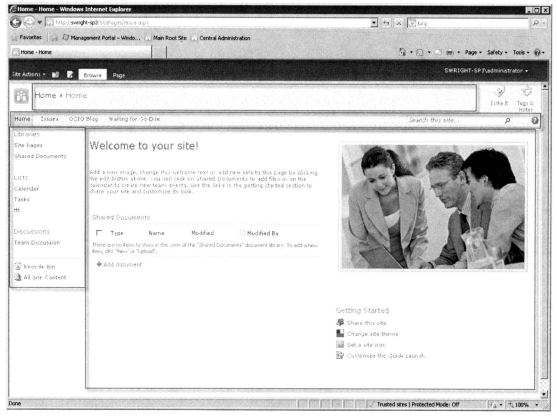

Figure 12-6. Structuring a page with master pages

SharePoint extends the functionality of ASP.NET master pages by managing the relationship between the master pages and the pages that use them. A SharePoint site can be associated with a new master page, thereby completely changing its layout and appearance.

Master page files are stored in a Master Page Gallery. The Master Page Gallery is created automatically in all SharePoint sites. It is a best practice to limit yourself to using only the root master page gallery unless you have good reason to do otherwise. Having custom master page files spread throughout a site collection can quickly become unmanageable.

It is also a good idea to limit the number of users that can create, edit, and apply master pages in the gallery. This is done by setting the permissions on the gallery itself and the permissions on the site. You should remove or restrict access to any master pages that are not standard in your environment. This will prevent them from being used by mistake.

Themes

To those familiar with themes from previous versions of SharePoint, the themes in SharePoint 2010 will seem entirely new. Microsoft Office 2010 contains a *theming engine* that has been incorporated into the various Office applications and into SharePoint.

Specifically, a theme is now a much more lightweight concept than it was in the past. Instead of referring to a collection of cascading style sheets (CSS) and images, in Office 2010 a theme is just a small set of font and color declarations as shown in Figure 12-7. These are typically stored in a file with a THMX extension. When a theme is applied to a SharePoint site, a set of standard CSS files is processed by the theming engine to create the actual CSS files sent to the user's web browser. Unlike in previous versions, these standard CSS files should not be tampered with. Instead, if additional CSS definitions are needed, they should be placed into separate files that are applied outside of the theming engine. This process is discussed in Chapter 11.

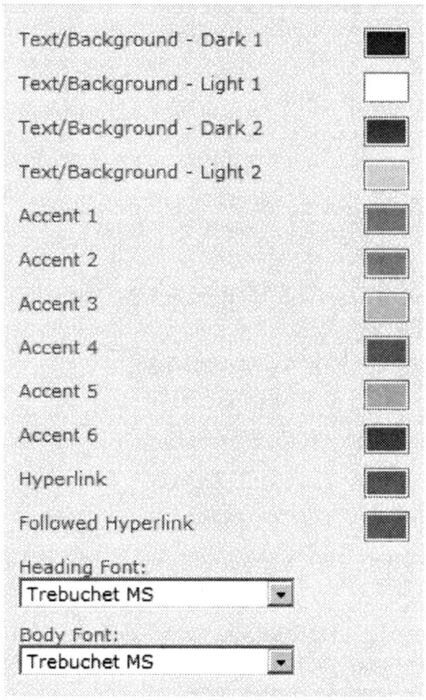

Figure 12-7. An Office 2010 theme definition

Theme files are stored in the *Theme Gallery*, which is a special library that exists in each SharePoint site collection. There is a default set of themes that appear by default in the Theme Gallery. An organization that intends to control its brand should start by removing or restricting access to the theme files in this gallery. A common technique would be to place one approved theme in the gallery that must be used by all sites. Additionally, the permissions to edit and create themes should be restricted to prevent users from creating their own themes. This will ensure that the organization's standards are maintained.

In some cases, more than one theme may need to be left in the Theme Gallery to allow for different brands or types of sites to be created. Different divisions within a company may have their own brands that need to be supported. Also, public-facing sites may use a rigidly-defined theme whereas internal-facing or extranet sites may have more flexibility. The key is to remember that the Theme Gallery exists at the site collection level. Areas of the site that require different sets of themes are probably good candidates for being in separate site collections.

An organization's themes are typically set by a design or marketing department. Themes can be created using an Office application like PowerPoint 2010 and exported to THMX files. Theme files can be uploaded to the gallery using the web browser or as part of a solution package created by a developer. The choice depends on how the themes will be managed and by whom. If the themes will be managed by a non-IT department, they will usually deploy it using the web browser. An application development team will generally use a solution package to deploy custom themes.

There are times when the standard CSS files provided by SharePoint need to be extended. In this case, there are several options for adding additional style information to a page. Style tags can be added to the master page or the content areas of the individual pages. However, this can result in a site that is difficult to maintain since all of the style information is not in one place.

A better solution is to create separate CSS files and deploy them to the site. SharePoint contains a control called CSSRegistration which is designed to add custom CSS files to the set of files provided by SharePoint. This control can place a given file reference before or after other style sheets in the page to create the desired precedence order for the styles contained within it. The CSS files themselves can be deployed using a solution package or they can be placed on the site as content files. The CSSRegistration control is typically embedded in the site's master page.

There are additional ways to provide styles to your site that only become available when using publishing sites.

Publishing

The SharePoint publishing feature is used to create a more controlled environment for managing important content. This type of feature is often referred to as *Web Content Management*. An authorized user can edit a publishing site's content and submit it for approval.

Publishing sites differ from non-publishing sites in the types of controls that are available. This can be very useful for governing the creation and approval of content.

- Content changes on a non-publishing site are made visible to all users as soon as they are saved. Publishing site changes are not visible until they are approved.

- Content on a publishing site can be scheduled to appear or disappear at an arbitrary time in the future.

- The approval process can be customized using SharePoint's workflow engine.

- Publishing sites have additional functionality supporting style sheets, navigation, and controlling the master pages applied to the site.

- Content changes can be staged in a separate environment and migrated to the production farm using *content deployment paths*. This prevents unauthorized or unreviewed changes from being inadvertently exposed on a public-facing web site. Complex topologies of authoring, staging, and production servers can be supported.

Publishing site pages contain an additional level of structure called a *page layout*. Layout pages are similar to master pages but they enable rich content–editing and publishing by non-technical users. Layout pages are stored in the master page gallery. As shown in Figure 12-8, the content is built up in layers with the page layout in the middle. In the case of a publishing site, the content applied to the page layout is handled more like data fields than like HTML or Web Parts.

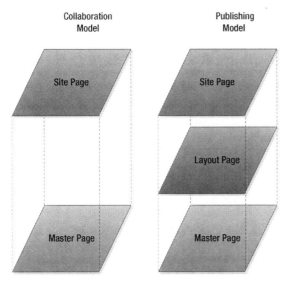

Figure 12-8. Publishing vs. collaboration page construction

Publishing sites are most often used for non-collaboration sites. The restrictions placed on the creation and approval of content makes them ideal for public-facing web sites and corporate- or division-level pages within a company's intranet. Non-publishing sites are best used for sites that manage projects and exchange information informally.

Site Templates

One of the best ways to encourage adherence to standards is to make it easy. That makes site templates a great place to start. When any user creates a new site, it will always be based on one of the available site templates. This will create a predefined set of lists, libraries, master pages, and even content that will be available to the users immediately. By creating a set of standard templates for your organization, you can help users create consistent sites.

A site template in SharePoint 2010 is a solution package file (.wsp) that contains the definition of the contents of a site when it is created. The easiest way to create a site template is to save an existing site as a template using the Save Site as a Template option on site settings. SharePoint packages all of the lists, libraries, forms, workflows, pages, and (optionally) content items into a single file in the Solution Gallery. As we will discuss in Chapter 13, the solution gallery is used to hold solution packages that have been deployed to the local site collection.

A site template can be customized using Visual Studio. The developer can download the template file and import it into a new Visual Studio project. This makes all of the artifacts that were packaged into the template available for editing. Once the customizations are completed, the project can be recompiled and redeployed into the solution gallery. In this way, the organization can create the precise site templates desired.

Site templates have some limitations, however. There are certain items within the original site that are not reflected in the template's solution file.

- Customized permissions within the site are not retained.

- Running workflow instances and any associated tasks are not stored as content in the template.

- Certain types of field values are not retained including people/group fields and managed metadata.

Site templates can also only be created when using certain types of sites. "My Sites" and publishing sites depend on items that cannot be stored to the template file and therefore these types of sites are not supported for saving as a template. Site templates for these sites can still be created but only using a development tool such as Visual Studio.

Because site templates are stored in the solution gallery, the ability to create and use them is controlled by the solution gallery as well. Once created in the solution gallery, a site template is available to all users that have the permissions necessary to create sites in the site collection. To hide a template from end users it is necessary to turn on the publishing feature in SharePoint Server. This adds an option on the Site Settings page called Page Layouts and Site Settings. Ironically, turning on publishing, even on a site based on a non-publishing template, will prevent the site itself from being saved as a template. Clearly, careful planning is important when determining the site templates that will be allowed in your environment.

▨ **Note** It is possible to hide SharePoint's built-in site templates without enabling the publishing feature. To do this, it is necessary to edit one of the files that are part of the SharePoint product. This file (WEBTEMP.xml) lists all of the site templates that are available by default within all site collections in the farm. Changes to this file affect the entire farm and should be made very carefully. It may also be necessary to restore any customizations to this file after a patch or upgrade is applied to SharePoint.

Creating Custom Functionality

This section deals with the creation of components for deployment to a SharePoint server farm. Most of these components contain some amount of software code and generally require development skills and tools to create. This discussion is intended to provide an understanding of the purpose of each of these components, not a detailed tutorial on creating them. The goal is to understand the issues that the governance team must consider when performing application management in the SharePoint environment.

Solutions and Features

When creating components for SharePoint, there are two ways of describing how they are grouped: solutions and features. While these terms may seem quite similar, they have very different meanings in SharePoint.

A *solution* in SharePoint is a file containing a set of artifacts and configurations that are deployed as a unit. The development team uses a tool such as Visual Studio to create a solution package file with a WSP extension. This file is then deployed to the farm and used by the end users. Solution packages can be deployed in one of two ways:

- *Farm Deployment*: A package deployed to the farm solution store is available to all site collections in the farm, if desired. Farm solutions can obtain full security trust and must be deployed by a farm administrator. The tools for installing and managing farm solution packages are only available to farm administrators.

- *Sandbox Deployment*: A package can also be deployed to the Solution Gallery in a specific site collection. This is called sandbox deployment because these solutions are limited to SharePoint's sandbox environment. This limits their security level and access to the farm's resources.

Farm and sandbox solutions are the same in structure but very different in the environment they run in. A package could be deployed as a sandbox solution for testing and then moved to a farm deployment once it is considered safe. Farm solutions have the ability to run in Full Trust mode but are not required to do so. Sandbox solutions can only access resources within their local site collection and cannot run in full-trust.

Whereas a solution package can be viewed as the *unit of deployment*, a feature is the *unit of functionality* within SharePoint. A feature is a conceptual grouping of items that work together to provide a set of functionality. For example, SharePoint's publishing features contain many list templates, content types, workflows, and so on to provide a cohesive web content management solution.

Features also have a scope but, unlike solutions, they are not limited to farm or site collection levels. A feature can have one of these scopes:

- *Farm*: Components are made available to the entire server farm.

- *Web Application*: Components are made available to all of the site collections hosted by the web application.

- *Site Collection*: Components are made available to all sites in the collection.

- *Site (Web)*: Components are made available only to the local site.

Each feature will have one declared scope depending on the nature of the functionality it provides. Some sets of functionality are split into separate features because they affect items in multiple scopes. For example, the SharePoint Publishing Infrastructure feature is a site collection scoped feature because it contains libraries and content types that need to be deployed at the site collection level. The SharePoint Publishing Site feature is a site scoped feature because it enables publishing functionality on a single SharePoint site.

■ **Note** Farm and web application scoped features should not be deployed to a site collection's Solution Gallery since their scope requires them to affect more than a single site collection. They will not function unless deployed to the farm solution store.

When developing custom functionality for SharePoint, the components are defined and packaged in layers. First, a set of components, such as forms, content types, assemblies, and Web Parts, is created in Visual Studio. These components are grouped together into features to control how they will be made active and available to users. A set of features and their supporting artifacts are then compiled into a solution package for deployment. A solution package can contain one or more features, but a feature can exist in only one solution. A feature can contain many components, but each component can only belong to one feature.

The process of creating and maintaining features and solution packages will be described in detail in Chapter 13.

Web Parts

Web Parts are familiar to anyone who has used SharePoint for any length of time. They are on-screen controls that can be added to a page, moved, and configured as needed. SharePoint comes with many built-in Web Parts but it is also possible to create custom Web Parts that perform new functions. Web Parts can be connected to one another to pass information and create interactive web pages.

Each SharePoint site collection contains a *Web Part gallery*. All of the Web Parts available to users must be deployed in the Web Part gallery. Unlike site templates, restricting access to built-in Web Parts does not require modifying any files on the server. The Web Part gallery functions more like a normal list or library. Each item in the gallery represents a type of Web Part. To remove a Web Part from the site collection, simply remove it from the Web Part gallery. Each Web Part also has its own set of permissions. To prevent certain users from using a Web Part, restrict access to the Web Part in the gallery. This will remove it from the user interface for those users.

Because the Web Part gallery exists within each site collection, features that contain Web Parts should generally be scoped at the site collection level. Custom Web Parts are actually contained in compiled .NET assemblies. Features that deploy Web Parts will contain the Web Part's assembly (.dll) and a Web Part description file (.webpart). The Web Part file is deployed to the Web Part gallery in order to make the Web Part available.

In non-publishing sites, SharePoint has the concept of a *personal view* of a page and its Web Parts. A user's personal view refers to a customized version of the page specifically for that user. Personal views allow a user to add or reconfigure Web Parts and even add content. When the page is saved, only the user making the change will see those changes. The initial view of the page is known as the *shared view*.

Personal views have been known to cause confusion for end users. Any changes made to the shared view after a personal view is created will not be reflected on the page when the user visits it unless they explicitly switch to the shared view. For example, if a user creates a personal view of the site's home page and later a news feed is added to that page by a site administrator, that user will never see that news feed unless they know to look for it. If the decision is made to disable personal views, this can be done using site-level permissions as shown in Figure 12-9.

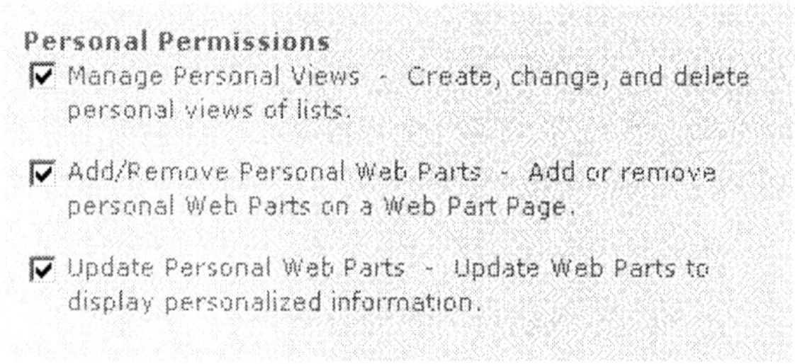

Personal Permissions

☑ Manage Personal Views - Create, change, and delete personal views of lists.

☑ Add/Remove Personal Web Parts - Add or remove personal Web Parts on a Web Part Page.

☑ Update Personal Web Parts - Update Web Parts to display personalized information.

Figure 12-9. Personal view permissions

These permissions appear at the bottom of the list of permissions in SharePoint and are easy to miss. By default, all members of the site will have personalization permissions. These can be turned off globally in a site collection by altering the built-in permission levels.

Publishing sites do not support personal and shared views because their content is managed by SharePoint's publishing features. The contents of the pages and Web Parts are versioned as part of the page and not for an individual user.

Events

Events in SharePoint are triggered when various actions are taken. These include things like creating a site, moving a page or deleting a Web Part. There are events that fire on most objects stored within Share-

Point including lists, libraries, sites, Web Parts, and features. A developer can create a .NET class that will be executed in response to an event. This allows for custom behaviors to be added to SharePoint.

The classes that receive these events are known as *event receivers*. Because they consist of .NET code, event receivers must be compiled and deployed in an assembly. This is normally done through the use of solution packages and features. Once the assembly is in place, the event receiver can be associated with the event using SharePoint API code or via declarations in the package.

Event receivers must obey the same rules as any other piece of code running in SharePoint. If they are deployed in a sandbox solution, then they have all of the normal restrictions associated with running in the sandbox. Because the common uses of event receivers, other than feature receivers, often involve manipulating data or structures outside of the local site, it is frequently necessary to deploy them within farm-based solutions.

Application Pages

Application pages are special types of pages that exist in every site on the server farm. They are called application pages because they are not part of any specific site, but belong to the server as a whole.

A commonly used application page is the All Site Content page shown in Figure 12-10. Application pages are deployed into a special directory on the server's file system called the LAYOUTS folder. This is why an application page always has _layouts in its URL. The *_layouts* folder is linked into every SharePoint site making these pages universally available.

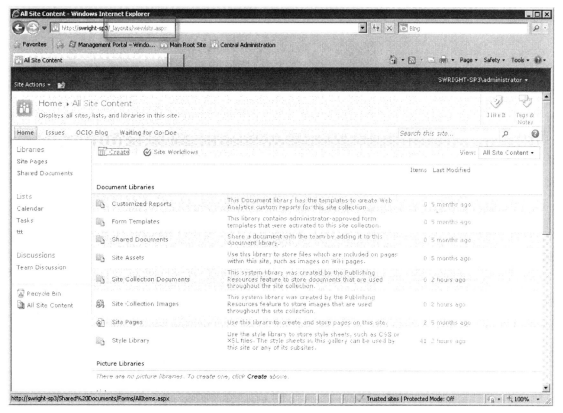

Figure 12-10. All Site Content application page

Developing and deploying application pages is different from creating Web Parts or site pages. These pages are more like normal ASP.NET pages than true SharePoint pages. Application pages always run outside of the sandbox because they require access to the LAYOUTS directory. As such, application pages cannot be deployed from a solution file in a site collection's Solution Gallery, only from a farm-level solution.

Because they operate outside the protected sandbox environment, application pages and their components should be tested thoroughly in a non-production farm before deployment. There are special security considerations to be accounted for when developing application pages to prevent their use by non-authorized users. For example, the Site Settings page is an application page that contains security trimming logic to hide options to which the current user must not be given access.

■ **Note** When *security trimming* is active, those elements of the user interface which the current user does not have permission to use will be automatically removed from the page. For example, documents within a document library list will only be shown if the user has the right to read the document. If not, the entry for the document is omitted from the page.

Timer Jobs

A *timer job* in SharePoint is a .NET class that can be scheduled to run periodically in the background on one or more of the farm's servers. Timer jobs are generally used for housekeeping tasks like cleaning up log files or replicating data. Creating custom timer jobs is a good way to create logic that runs on a schedule. Because they run in the background and not within a particular site collection, timer jobs cannot operate within the sandbox and can only be deployed in a farm-level package.

All of the usual warnings concerning non-sandboxed code apply to timer jobs. Timer jobs are always run by the SharePoint Timer Service. This is a Windows service that runs on each SharePoint server. The service account for this service determines the default permissions that a timer job will have. Timer jobs should generally be thought of as running with full trust within the context of the service account.

InfoPath Forms

InfoPath forms were introduced earlier in this chapter. These are data entry forms that can be used to gather information or edit list items within SharePoint. When an InfoPath form is created, it is saved as a template file with an XSN extension. Deploying an InfoPath template as part of a solution package makes the template available to content types, lists, and libraries within SharePoint.

InfoPath Forms Services is a SharePoint service application that can render certain InfoPath forms within a web browser page. If an InfoPath form is not web-enabled it can still be used like any other form in SharePoint except that the InfoPath client application will be launched when the form is used.

InfoPath form templates can include .NET code. InfoPath Forms Services will ensure that this code will always run within the sandbox when running as part of a web-based form. Forms that require non-sandboxed access to the system can still be deployed to SharePoint but they must be filled out using the InfoPath client application in Full Trust mode. This ensures that the .NET code within the form only runs on the user's local desktop, not on the SharePoint server.

Another governance consideration with respect to InfoPath forms is versioning. When a new version of a form template is deployed, it may be necessary to take into account any existing forms on the farm that were filled out using the old template. A complete discussion of versioning InfoPath forms is out of scope for this discussion but it should be considered when making updates to existing form templates.

Workflows

SharePoint Server 2010 contains a powerful workflow engine based on the .NET Framework's Workflow Foundation. Workflows allow SharePoint to manage complex business processes automatically.

Workflows are defined using a designer, typically either SharePoint Designer or Visual Studio. The workflow definition is then deployed to the SharePoint environment and associated with a list, a content type, or (new in SharePoint 2010) a site. An instance of the workflow may be started based on the creation of a document, a manual action, or the action of a program.

A workflow running in SharePoint has access to many of SharePoint's resources and can perform actions such as checking files in and out, creating or moving list items, setting item permissions, and so on. The most common actions taken by workflows are to send e-mail notifications and to assign tasks to users. SharePoint maintains the state of the workflows and provides the interface for managing instances. SharePoint also maintains a detailed log of all workflow actions and results.

The tools most commonly used to create workflows in SharePoint are SharePoint Designer and Visual Studio. SharePoint Designer places certain restrictions on the types of workflows that can be created. For example, SharePoint Designer does not support custom .NET code, looping constructs, or state machine workflows. Even so, most common business processes can be modeled very well with the workflow features that are available in SharePoint Designer. Those that cannot are generally complex enough that a developer should be engaged to create the best implementation possible. These highly-customized workflows should be created through a development tool like Visual Studio.

When a user starts a workflow instance, either intentionally or as a side effect to some other action, that instance will execute using that user's credentials. Even if the workflow continues to run long after the user has left the site, the workflow engine will still use those credentials. Any permissions associated with the initiating user, such as file or list item access rights, will be applied to the instance when it is running.

This security context has often proven too restrictive for some proposed workflow designs. For example, say a user creates a vacation request and saves it in a document library. As a result, an approval workflow is started. Once the request is approved, you want to move it into a protected archive for approved requests. Since the user that initiated the workflow doesn't have access to the protected archive, the workflow can't move the request into it.

One of the most important workflow improvements in SharePoint 2010 was created specifically to deal with this type of situation. A new type of workflow step, called an *Impersonation Step*, can be added to a workflow just like any other step. The difference is that the security context for the impersonation step is not that of the initiating user but of the workflow's author. The workflow's author is generally the user that last updated the workflow's definition. That user can be given the necessary permissions to perform the needed actions that the initiator may lack.

Essentially, a workflow has two potential security contexts. By default, it runs as the user that started the workflow. For certain steps, it may request elevated privileges. Be certain that any workflows running in the farm that use the Impersonation Step are thoroughly tested.

As with other aspects of SharePoint Server, workflow as a subject could easily fill its own book, or several of them. To get a more in-depth look at workflow development, see *Beginning WF: Windows Workflow in .NET 4.0* by Mark Collins (Apress, 2010) and *Pro WF: Windows Workflow in .NET 4.0* by Bruce Bukovics (Apress, 2010).

The Client Object Model

SharePoint 2010 contains a new set of features called the SharePoint Foundation 2010 client-side object model (CSOM), illustrated in Figure 12-11, or just the client object model. Note that we will use the abbreviation *CSOM* instead of *COM* to avoid confusing it with the old Component Object Model. The purpose of the CSOM is to provide a client-side subset of the SharePoint API that can be used from a variety of platforms. The object model is available for .NET Framework applications, Silverlight applications, and web sites using ECMAScript-compatible scripting languages such as Jscript and JavaScript.

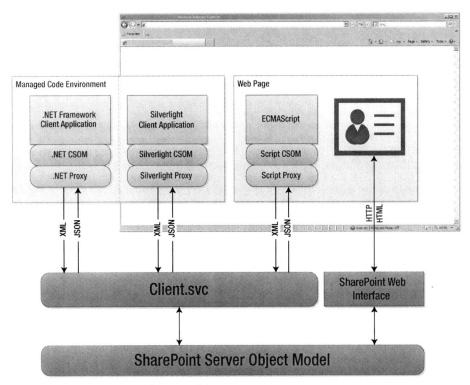

Figure 12-11. Client-side object model components

Each version of the client object model has a similar component structure. The specifics of each environment will be discussed in a later section. For now, we will look at the architecture that is common to them all.

On the SharePoint server, there is a new component called Client.svc. This service acts as a façade for the SharePoint server object model running on the server. The client service receives client requests in XML form, executes the request against the server API and returns objects to the caller in JavaScript Object Notation (JSON) format.

Each client object model implementation consists of two layers. The first layer is the client-side object model classes. These classes map directly in most cases to a corresponding SharePoint server object model class. For example, the SPSite server object is represented by the Site object in each client object model.

The second layer of the implementation consists of a proxy layer or runtime. The purpose of the proxy component is to streamline the passing of requests and responses to and from the server. A key difference between the server and client object models is the effect of the proxy layer. When a call is made to the client object model, that request is not immediately processed on the server. The proxy batches the requests until the client application explicitly tells it to contact the server. At that point, all of the outstanding requests are processed in order and the results are returned to the client. This makes writing good client-side SharePoint code very different from writing server-side code.

The ECMAScript client object model is used when writing JavaScript code within web pages. The method of delivering the script to the web page may vary. It could be included in a Content Editor Web Part or other standard control, as you will see in our example. It could also be emitted by a custom web control or embedded in a .js script file.

There are some limitations associated with the ECMAScript object model because of the environment in which it executes. Objects created with the model can only access the local site collection. In the server API or the other client object models, you can create a Site (or SPSite) object that points to any SharePoint site collection anywhere on the network. Because script objects exist within a certain web page, any attempt to access another site collection would be considered a cross-site scripting attack and is therefore prevented.

Using client-side scripting is an excellent way to improve the performance of the user experience in SharePoint. SharePoint automatically implements all of the same security checks for client-side data access that it does on the server. In most cases, there is no need to prevent the use of the client object models, but if the need arises, this can be done by blocking clients from accessing the '/_vti_bin/client.svc' web service, by using a firewall or IIS settings as needed.

Summary

In this chapter, we have:

- Examined the tools available to customize the look and feel of a SharePoint site.

- Described the tools used to create custom software modules for SharePoint.

- Explored the appropriate usage scenarios and controls for each tool used for customizing SharePoint.

- Reviewed the mechanisms within SharePoint for implementing a custom user experience using themes, layouts, and content publishing.

- Discussed the types of additional functionality that can be created for and deployed to a SharePoint portal.

- Described the governance policies and controls that need to be established to protect a production environment from issues created by non-standard customization tools and techniques.

CHAPTER 13

Packaging Solutions

Creating applications for deployment to a SharePoint environment is different from developing them for the desktop or a web site. This chapter will describe some of the technical details associated with creating, deploying, and maintaining solution packages in a production SharePoint environment. We will not attempt to provide all of the details a developer might need. This discussion is focused on the capabilities and limitations of solution packages in different environments. The goal is to provide the guidance needed to plan solutions and features so that they can be effectively managed.

What Will You Learn in This Chapter?

- The purpose and benefits of the SharePoint solution framework

- The structure of a solution file and the types of items stored within it

- How to compare farm-based vs. sandboxed solutions, including the tools for managing them in production

- The limitations imposed on sandboxed solutions relative to farm solutions

- How full-trust proxies can be used to escape the sandbox in a secure, controlled way

- How to define and manage resource points and quotas

- The common tools for creating and customizing solution package files

- The new SharePoint 2010 features for upgrading a solution in place instead of through removing and reinstalling

- Some best practices for planning and managing solutions in a production server farm

Solution Framework Overview

The SharePoint family of products, including SharePoint Foundation and Server, use the *solution framework* to install custom enhancements into a SharePoint environment. This replaces the other installer technologies used in the Windows environment such as MSI files and ClickOnce. The solution framework allows custom components to be deployed, activated, and updated in a controlled manner that is designed to keep the SharePoint server farm stable. Solution packages can also contain resource files for a consistent approach to localizing your custom components.

As we described briefly in Chapter 12, solution packages provide a means to bundle all of the components associated with a custom enhancement into a file with a WSP extension. These files can then be deployed to the farm so that all of the components are installed simultaneously on all of the servers in the farm. This removes the need to maintain web page files, templates, and executables separately on each server. The SharePoint 2010 solution framework also includes new features that make it possible to update solution packages in place without interfering with the operation of the farm. This is done by versioning each deployed feature and providing custom actions to be taken when upgrading from one version of a feature to another.

Solution Package Structure

A solution package file is a single file with a WSP file name extension. However, what appears to be one file is, in fact, several files archived into one. The WSP file format is actually nothing more than a standard Windows cabinet (CAB) file. To prove this, take any solution file and change the extension from WSP to CAB. Now open the file and you will see a file structure similar to the one shown in Figure 13-1.

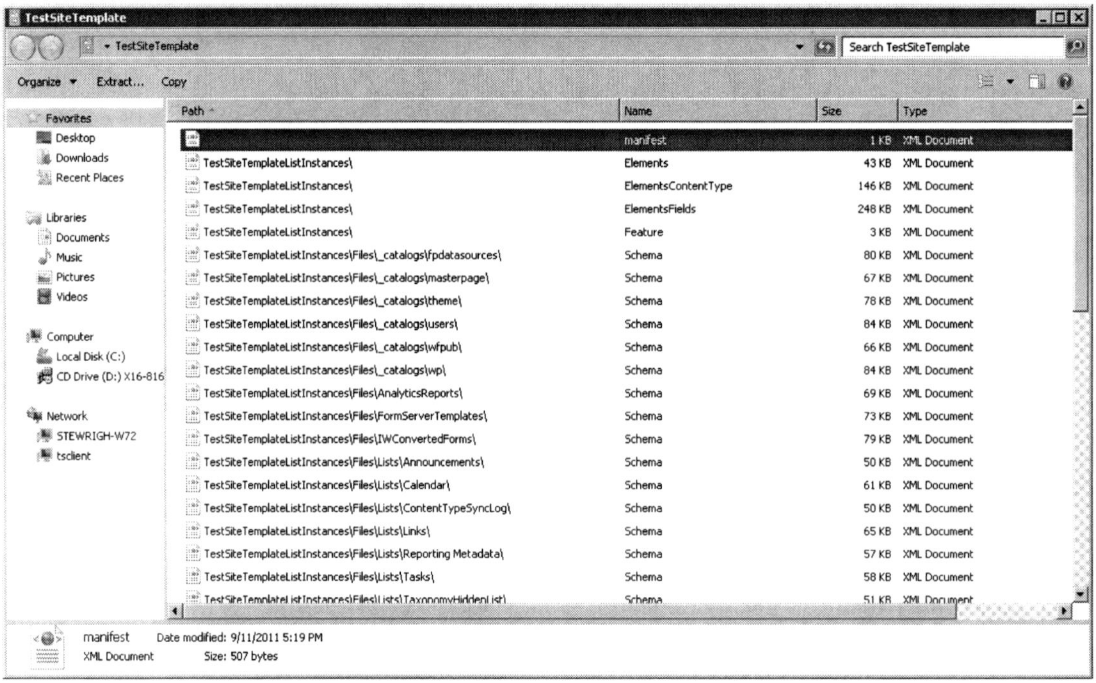

Figure 13-1. The contents of a solution package

We will describe the contents of these files in more detail later. For the moment, notice the overall structure of the files. There is a package manifest file in the root directory and then one or more subdirectories containing other components. Many of these components are XML files containing configuration information for lists, sites, content types, and so on.

The most common files found in a solution package (shown in Figure 13-2) are

- *Manifest.xml*: There is one manifest in a package. It contains a description of everything that is in the package, either directly or through references to other files.

- *Feature.xml*: These files describe the configuration and components associated with a feature that can be turned on or off in the SharePoint environment.

- *Elements.xml*: These files contain lists of individual components and their configuration information. The components can be things such as list instances, content files, site columns, content types, and event receivers.

- *Schema.xml*: These files contain the metadata specifications for an object such as a list template.

Many other types of files can appear in a solution package, but these are the most important because they control the configuration of the features and components being deployed. We will describe how to create and update these files later. First, you need to understand a little about the environment to which they will be deployed.

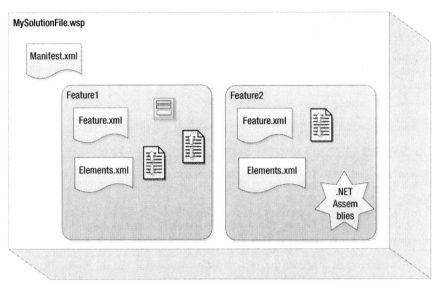

Figure 13-2. Solution package structure

Understanding Deployment Environments

When a solution package is deployed to a SharePoint server farm, it is deployed into one of two runtime environments. The first environment is the server farm itself. This gives the components in the solution the ability to access resources throughout the farm and beyond, within the limits of the access permissions on those items. The second environment, the sandbox, is far more limited. When a solution package is running in the sandbox, its ability to affect the farm as a whole is restricted. Understanding the difference between farm solutions and sandboxed solutions is critical to planning for the deployment of custom enhancements.

The first thing to consider is where the solution will be deployed. As shown in Figure 13-3, farm solutions are deployed to a centralized location within SharePoint called the Farm Solution Store, while sandboxed solution packages are stored in the Solution Gallery associated with a site collection. This is the key. Farm solutions are global to the server farm; sandboxed solutions are local to a specific site collection. A sandboxed solution that needs to be used by multiple site collections must be deployed to each one separately.

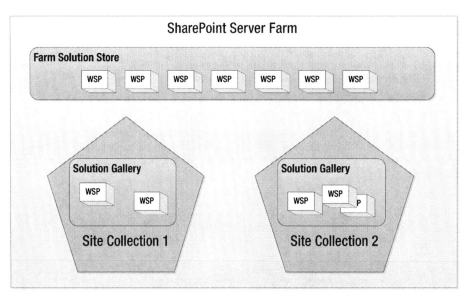

Figure 13-3. *Deployment locations (farm vs. site collection)*

The most important difference between farm and sandboxed solutions is security. Farm solutions generally run with full trust. Using .NET Code Access Security (CAS), it is possible to create farm solution components that run with less than full trust. This is a good idea from a security standpoint since it allows the code to run with the minimal set of privileges needed. Farm deployment should be reserved for code that is well tested and highly trusted.

Sandboxed solutions run in a very different security environment. Their access to resources is limited to the site collection to which they are deployed. There are also resource restrictions and quotas that can be applied to prevent rogue solution components from compromising system performance. Misbehaving sandboxed solutions can be disabled by a Farm Administrator and prevented from running entirely, if needed. Table 13-1 provides a high-level comparison of farm and sandboxed solutions. These differences will be described in more detail in the following sections.

Table 13-1. *Farm vs. Sandboxed Solutions*

	Farm Solutions	Sandboxed Solutions
Where is it deployed?	The Farm Solution Store	The Solution Gallery in a specific site collection.
Who can deploy it?	Farm Administrators only	Site Collection Administrators or certain privileged users.
What process do the components run in?	IIS worker process	A sandboxed worker process provides isolation.
What SharePoint resources can it access?	Anything in the farm	Only content within local site collection.

Managing Farm Solutions

Deploying a solution package to a SharePoint server farm consists of two distinct operations: *Add* and *Deploy*. The Add operation uploads the solution file into SharePoint's configuration database where it can be accessed by each server in the farm. Deploying a solution refers to installing the files contained in the solution into various file system directories on each server in the farm.

Adding a Solution to the Farm Store

Adding a solution to the farm solution store can be done only by a farm administrator. There is no page in Central Administration that allows a package to be uploaded. This step must be accomplished using a command-line tool. Solutions can also be added programmatically using the SharePoint API.

To use the STSADM tool to add the package, use a command such as the following:

```
stsadm -o addsolution -filename MySolution.wsp
```

To perform the same operation using Windows PowerShell, use a command such as the following:

```
Add-SPSolution -LiteralPath MySolution.wsp
```

Once the Add operation is complete, the package will appear on the Solution Management page of the Central Administration site as shown in Figure 13-4. The package file has now been uploaded, but its features are not yet ready to use. At this point, the solution files have not been installed on each Share-Point server.

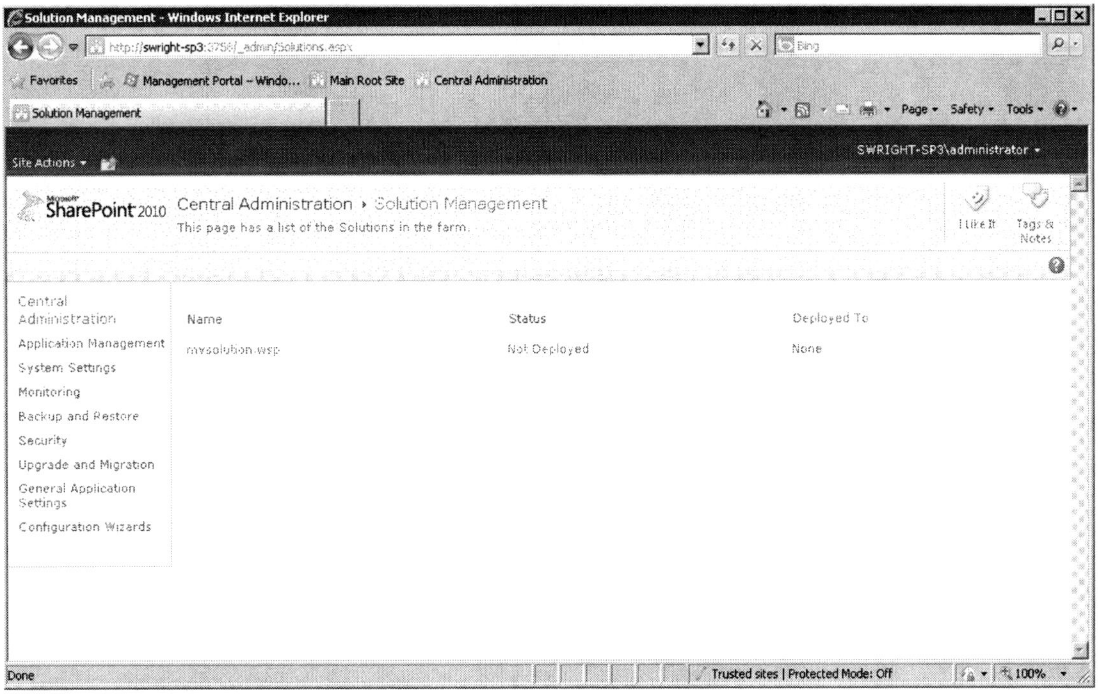

Figure 13-4. The farm solution store

Deploying a Solution to the Farm

Now that you have added the package to the farm solution store, you are ready to deploy it to the farm. There are two ways to deploy a package from the farm store: local deployment and via a timer job.

Performing a *local deployment* installs the solution files on one server in the farm. This type of deployment can only be done from the command line and only affects the server on which it is run. The solution will not be usable until it is deployed on all of the farm's servers. Therefore, it will be necessary to execute the command on each server.

The more common type of deployment uses the SharePoint Timer Service. This type of deployment can be performed using either the command line or the Central Administration web site. When the deployment is started, a *timer job* is created that will run on each server in the farm. This has the same effect, in one step, of performing local deployments on each server. (See Figure 13-5.)

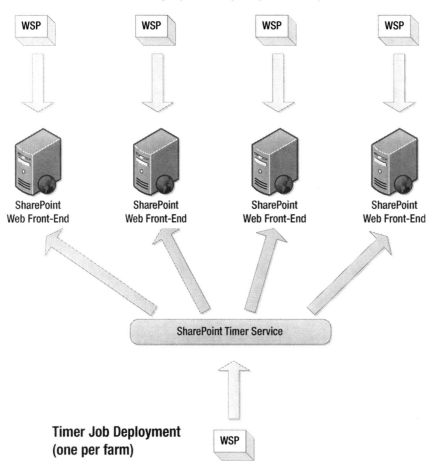

Figure 13-5. Local vs. timer job deployment

In addition to allowing deployment in a single step, timer job deployments also automate the process of restarting the IIS worker processes. This is necessary to enable the new solution's files to be recognized properly by SharePoint. There may be a brief outage experienced when the IIS worker process is restarted but it will be no more than a few seconds in most cases.

To perform a farm deployment from the command line, you can use either the -deploysolution option on the STSADM tool or the Install-SPSolution cmdlet in Windows PowerShell.

■ **Note** No, that is not a typo. The PowerShell cmdlet is called *Install-SPSolution*, not *Deploy-SPSolution*, for some unknown reason.

Both of these commands have a -local flag to perform a local deployment. To use a timer job that will run at a given time, you can use the -time option on either command. To use a timer job that executes immediately after the command is entered, use the -immediate option on STSADM or just leave the -local and -time options off of the Windows PowerShell command.

Several other options can be specified when deploying a farm solution. Here are a few of the most important:

- *Web Application*: Some solutions contain resources that need to be deployed within the IIS web application directory structure. When deploying a solution, you can select a set of web applications to target for these resources.

- *Global Assemblies*: If the solution package contains assemblies that need to be deployed to the Global Assembly Cache (GAC), an option is required to prevent the administrator from unknowingly deploying fully-trusted code.

- *Code Access Security*: CAS policies control the permissions granted to partially-trusted code running in the farm. If a solution package contains new CAS policies, a flag must be supplied to ensure that the administrator is aware of their presence.

You can also deploy a solution from the Central Administration web site. Select System Settings from the left menu. Then, select Manage Farm Solutions. A freshly added package will be displayed with a status of Not Deployed. Click the package name and the screen shown in Figure 13-6 will be displayed.

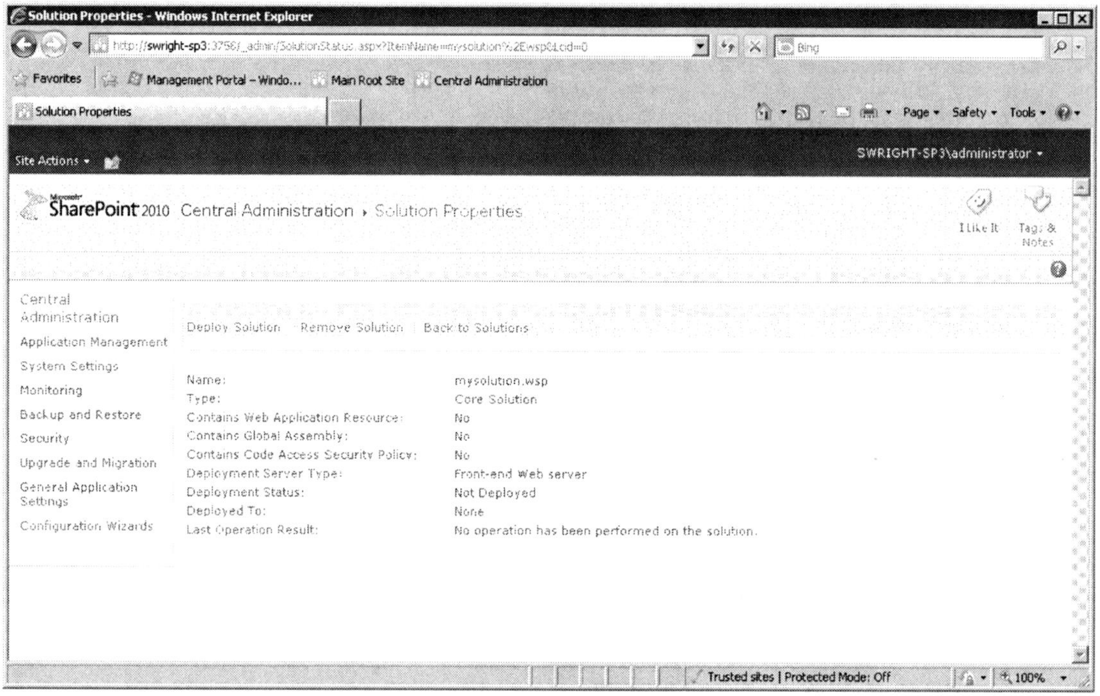

Figure 13-6. *Manage Farm Solutions (Central Administration)*

This page contains a lot of useful information about the package including whether it contains items that require special handling during deployment like fully-trusted assemblies or CAS policies. Clicking the Deploy Solution link will display a form that can be used to start a timer job for deployment (see Figure 13-7). Local deployments cannot be performed through the web interface.

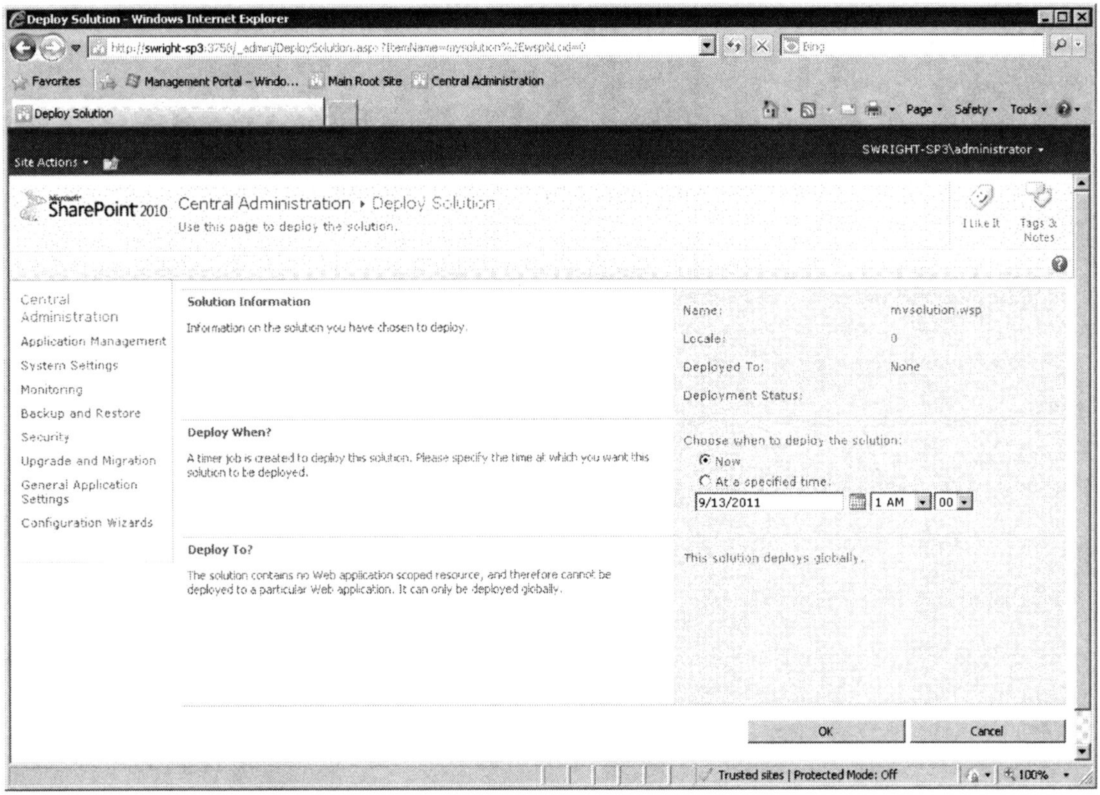

Figure 13-7. Deploy Solution (Central Administration)

Managing Sandboxed Solutions

Deploying a sandboxed solution to SharePoint is very different from deploying a farm solution. Instead of an Add followed by a Deploy, a sandboxed deployment consists of *Deploy* and *Activate* steps. Since these steps do not have to be performed by a farm administrator, we will not be using the administrator tools to manage these solutions.

Deploying a Solution to the Solution Gallery

The Deploy operation involves uploading the solution package into a site collection's Solution Gallery. This can be done by a site collection administrator or a user with Contribute rights for the root site of the collection. However, if the package contains any .NET assembly files, it can be deployed only by a site collection administrator.

To upload a new solution package, go to the root site of the collection and select Site Settings from the Site Actions menu. Under the Galleries heading, select the Solutions link. This displays the Solution Gallery for the collection. It can be difficult to find the Upload Solution option on this screen because it is not visible at first. Click the Solutions tab in the ribbon menu to display these options. Click the Upload Solution button, and select the WSP file to upload. (See Figure 13-8.)

233

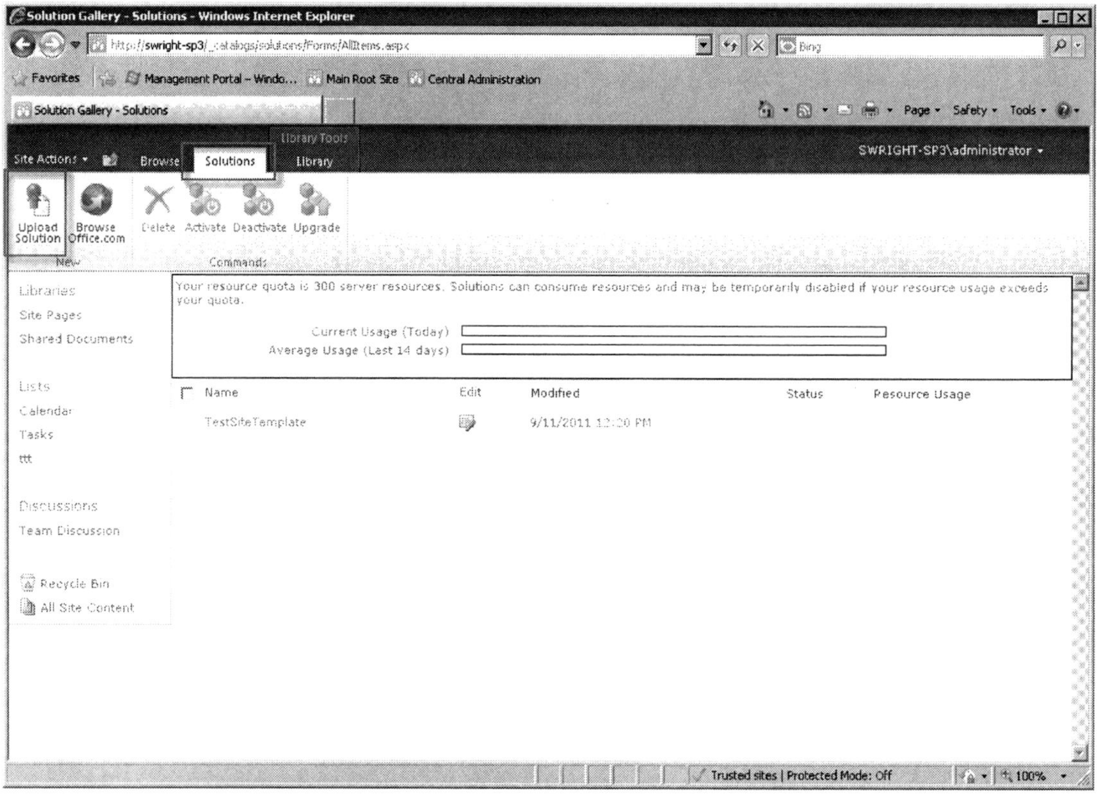

Figure 13-8. The Solution Gallery

Activating a Sandboxed Solution

Once the file is uploaded, it will appear in the Solution Gallery but it will not be activated. To activate the solution, select it in the gallery and click the Activate button. A dialog box will appear, as shown in Figure 13-9. You need to click Activate again on this dialog to complete the activation of the solution. Clicking Close will cancel the operation.

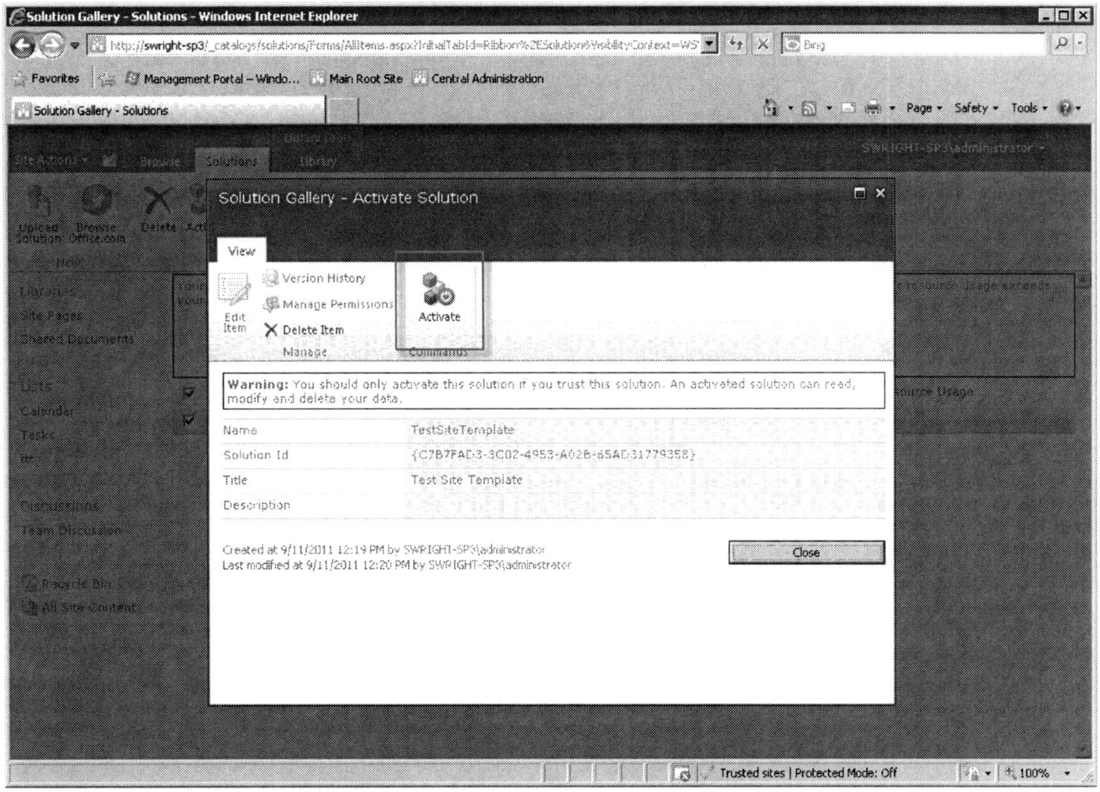

Figure 13-9. *Activate Solution*

SharePoint runs a validation against the package before activating it which ensures that no malicious code is contained in the file. If the solution passes this validation, it will be made active and available to users within the site collection. Any Web Parts, workflows, forms, or other components within the package will be made available to users within the site collection at this point.

The Solution Gallery can also be used by the site collection administrator to monitor the resources used by each solution. A solution that exceeds its quotas or becomes a problem may be disabled by the collection administrator or farm administrator, or automatically by SharePoint. We will describe the monitoring of resources and quotas later in this chapter.

The Solution Gallery page can also be used to deactivate and delete packages as necessary.

Understanding the SharePoint Sandbox

Running code in an isolated process, called the sandbox, is a new feature in SharePoint 2010. Code running in the sandbox is prevented from accessing resources outside the sandbox through a series of proxies that regulate what APIs can be called successfully. This feature is referred to as either the *SharePoint User Code Service* or the *SharePoint Sandboxed Code Service.* This section explores the architecture of this service and how it can be used to manage the operations of the farm.

Here are some of the restrictions placed on code running in the sandbox:

- Sandboxed code cannot access any SharePoint content outside of the site collection to which it is deployed. This includes resources on other SharePoint farms.

- Sandboxed code cannot access non-SharePoint resources on the SharePoint server such as the registry or the file system.

- Sandboxed code cannot connect to network resources such as file shares and TCP/IP ports.

- Sandboxed code cannot connect to databases such as SQL Server or Oracle.

- A sandboxed assembly is limited in its access to the .NET Framework and SharePoint API libraries. It also cannot alter its threading model or call unmanaged code.

While these restrictions may seem to limit the use of sandboxed solutions, the purpose is to allow SharePoint to support a multi-tenancy environment. In such an environment, multiple groups may deploy custom solutions which must not be allowed to interfere with one another or the SharePoint farm as a whole. Sandboxed solutions are ideal for providing business logic and components that are targeted to implementing a single business process. They are not appropriate for integration between different systems and data stores. For those scenarios, a farm solution is more appropriate.

The sandbox service is one of many service applications that run on SharePoint servers. Like other services, it can be started and stopped on the servers in the farm as needed. To start or stop the sandbox service, log on as a farm administrator and open the Central Administration web site. Select Application Management and then Manage Services on Server from the Service Application section. On the page that is displayed, you will select the server to configure and then look for the service called Microsoft SharePoint Foundation Sandboxed Code Service. As shown in Figure 13-10, the entry for this service will indicate whether or not the service is started. The link to the right can be used to start or stop the service.

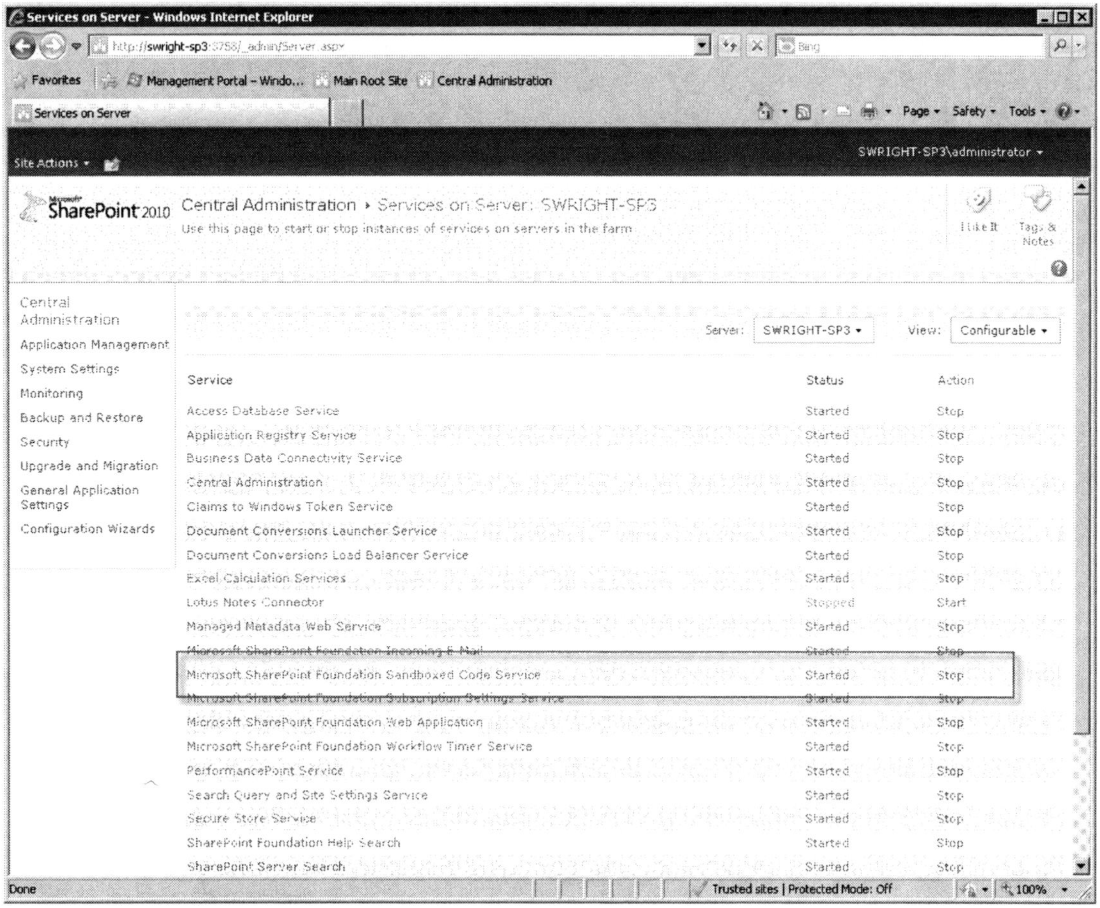

Figure 13-10. Enable or disable the Sandboxed Code Service

■ **Note** Turning off the sandbox service will prevent the processing of all sandboxed solutions on that server. Generally, the service should be left running unless there is a reason to ensure that no sandbox solutions can run on the server.

Another common administration task is to disable a problem solution package. This task is also accomplished using the Central Administration site. To manage blocked solutions, select System Settings and go to Manage User Solutions under the Farm Management heading. (See Figure 13-11.)

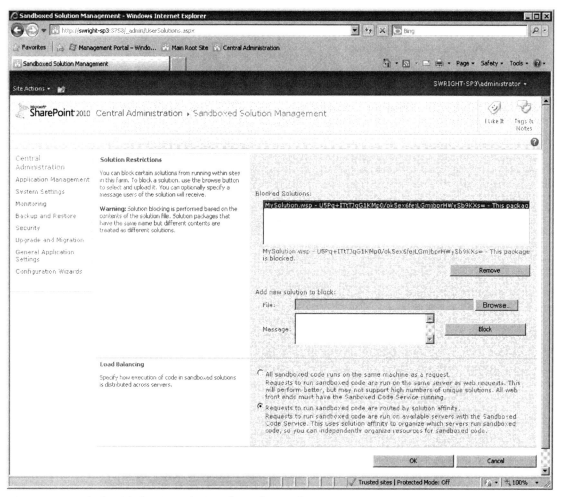

Figure 13-11. Block misbehaving solutions from the sandbox.

When you add a solution file to the list of blocked solutions, SharePoint reads the solution ID (GUID) from the package. That is the key used to identify the solution, not the file name. We will discuss the other option on this page when we discuss load balancing later in this chapter.

Sandbox Service Architecture

The Sandboxed Code Service manages the execution and isolation of sandboxed solutions. To do this, it creates a series of processes to execute the application code in separate .NET app domains.

As shown in Figure 13-12, sandboxed solutions are divided into tiers that can be configured to run applications in different ways. By default, all solutions run in a single tier. The farm administrator can create and configure multiple tiers to house solutions. Depending on the load created by each request to a solution, it can be placed into a specified tier. Poorly written or resource-intensive solutions can be automatically shifted into separate tiers to prevent them from interfering with other solutions on the farm.

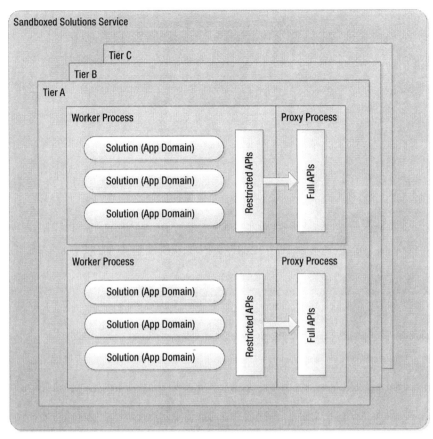

Figure 13-12. Sandboxed Solution Service Architecture

Within each tier are pairs of Windows processes. Each pair consists of a worker process and a proxy process. Each worker process runs up to ten .NET application domains in which a single solution's components execute. By default, each tier contains a single worker/proxy process pair. Again, a farm administrator can create additional worker processes to support additional scale and redundancy.

The worker process runs with low privileges. It monitors resource usage by each solution and shuts down any that cause a problem. The code running in the worker process can access a set of *shim* assemblies that represent the SharePoint API. These shims pass their calls through to the real SharePoint API assemblies which run in the proxy process. This process runs in full trust and prevents unwanted calls from passing into the SharePoint API.

When SharePoint is initially set up, there is only one tier and one worker process in that tier. Using Windows PowerShell, the farm administrator can create new tiers with different configurations for different kinds of solutions to run with. To view the tiers in the current farm, the farm administrator can run a Windows PowerShell script as shown in Figure 13-13.

```
Administrator: SharePoint 2010 Management Shell                    _ □ ×
PS C:\> $uc=[Microsoft.SharePoint.Administration.SPUserCodeService]::local
PS C:\> foreach($tier in $uc.Tiers)
>> {
>>      Write-Host "Tier Name: $($tier.Name)"
>>      Write-Host "Tier MaximumWorkerProcess: $($tier.MaximumWorkerProcesses)"
>>      Write-Host "Tier MaximumConnectionsPerProcess: $($tier.MaximumConnection
sPerProcess)"
>>      Write-Host "Tier MaximumAppDomainsPerProcess: $($tier.MaximumAppDomainsP
erProcess)"
>>      Write-Host "Tier PriorityPerProcess: $($tier.PriorityPerProcess)"
>>      Write-Host "Tier ResourceMaxValue: $($tier.ResourceMaxValue)"
>>
>>      Write-Host "*********************************************************"
>>
>> }
>>
Tier Name: Tier1
Tier MaximumWorkerProcess: 5
Tier MaximumConnectionsPerProcess: 10
Tier MaximumAppDomainsPerProcess: 10
Tier PriorityPerProcess:
Tier ResourceMaxValue: 0.1
*********************************************************
Tier Name: Tier2
Tier MaximumWorkerProcess: 5
Tier MaximumConnectionsPerProcess: 10
Tier MaximumAppDomainsPerProcess: 10
Tier PriorityPerProcess:
Tier ResourceMaxValue: 10
*********************************************************
PS C:\> _
```

Figure 13-13. Sandbox tier configurations (PowerShell)

In Figure 13-13, two tiers are defined. Each tier has several parameters that control the solutions in the tier.

- *ResourceMaxValue*: Defines the cutoff for solutions that run in the tier. This value must be greater than zero or the tier is ignored. Once a solution uses more than the tier permits, it is promoted to another tier, if possible.

- *MaximumWorkerProcesses*: The number of worker processes to run in the tier. Default=1.

- *MaximumAppDomainsPerProcess*: The number of .NET application domains that can run in a worker process. Each sandboxed solution runs in its own app domain. Default=10.

- *MaximumConnectionsPerProcess*: This is the maximum number of connections supported by each worker process. Default=1.

- *PriorityPerProcess*: Controls the operating system priority to be assigned to the tier's worker processes. Common options are Above Normal, Normal, and Below Normal. Default=Normal.

Resource Monitoring and Quotas

Sandboxed solutions are monitored closely to ensure that they do not negatively affect other solutions in the farm. To do this, the worker process tracks the solution's usage of system resources.

Among the resources monitored are CPU time, I/O byte counts, and threads used. The process also tracks events like exceptions and crashes of the solution's code. There are a total of 15 such *resource measures* that are tracked for each site collection. For each of these measures, a number of *resource points* is calculated.

For example, if a solution uses 20 million bytes of I/O and the *resources per point* value is set to 10 million, the site collection is charged 2 points. If all of the solutions in the site collection consume enough resource points to exhaust their daily quota, the site collection is disabled and taken offline until after the nightly resource point processing is completed. In that case, the site collection may need a higher quota or a solution may need to be updated or blocked.

The complete list of resource measures is as follows:

- Abnormal Process Termination Count

- CPU Execution Time

- Critical Exception Count

- Idle Percent Processor Time

- Invocation Count

- Percent Processor Time

- Process CPU Cycles

- Process Handle Count

- Process I/O Bytes

- Process Thread Count

- Process Virtual Bytes

- SharePoint Database Query Count

- SharePoint Database Query Time

- Unhandled Exception Count

- Unresponsive Process Count

Aside from the resources per point configuration described above, each resource measure also has an *absolute limit* configuration. This limit is used to stop a request that is consuming too many resources. If a single request reaches the absolute limit for a resource, the entire worker process is recycled to clear the problem. This may cause several solutions, in addition to the problem solution, to be recycled. If this happens often, it may be necessary to block the solution, change the limit or move solutions into multiple tiers.

The number of resource units that go into each point and the absolute limit can be adjusted by the farm administrator, but the defaults should be used in most cases. These values can only be viewed (see Figure 13-14) and altered in Windows PowerShell or through the SharePoint API. They are not accessible through the Central Administration web site.

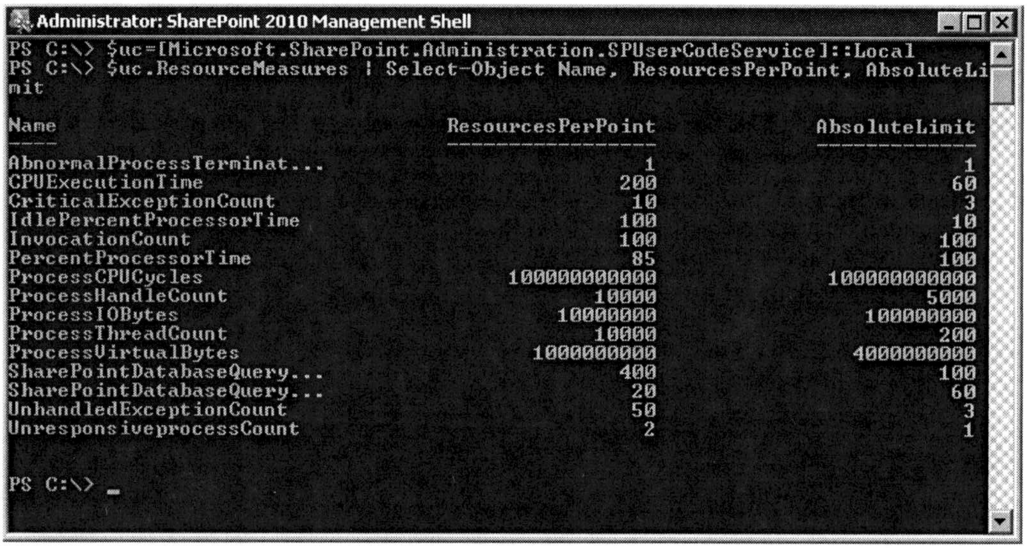

Figure 13-14. Resource measure configurations (PowerShell)

Daily quotas are assigned to each site collection in the farm. These quotas determine the resources the site collection can consume before it is automatically disabled and becomes unusable. The resource points are reset when the Solution Daily Resource Usage Update timer job runs. This timer job runs each night by default.

To assign quotas in a consistent way, a quota template should be created for each category of site collection to be managed on the farm (see Figure 13-15). To create a quota, log on as a farm administrator and open the Central Administration web site. Select Application Management from the menu. Then, select Specify Quota Templates from the Site Collections section.

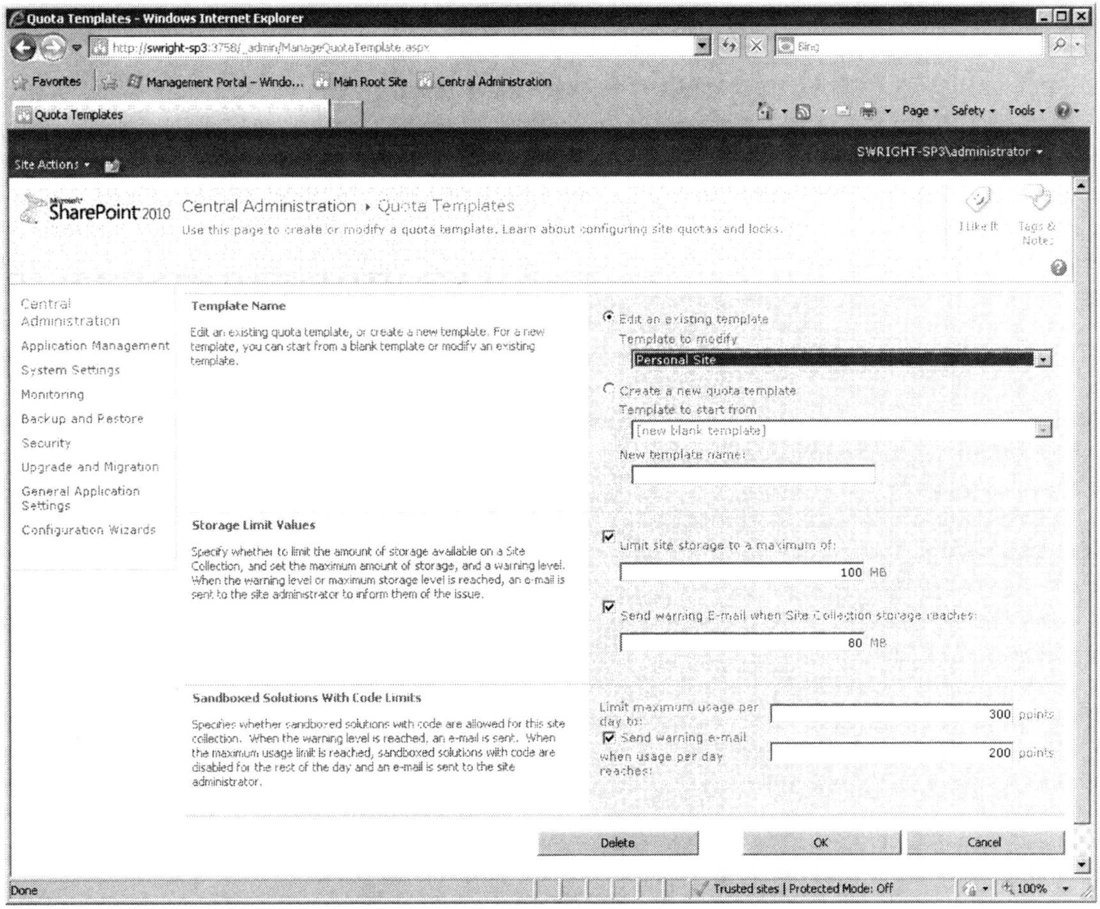

Figure 13-15. Define a quota template

Using this page, the farm administrator can define a quota template that limits both the storage size and resource points used by a site collection that is assigned to use the template. In both cases, a warning message can be sent when the storage or resource points approach a critical level. This e-mail is sent to the site collection administrator to let them know that a potential problem is in the offing.

To configure the quotas for a particular site collection, select Configure Quotas and Locks from the Application Management page. This page (Figure 13-16) allows the farm administrator to select a site collection and either assign unique quotas to it or assign a quota template.

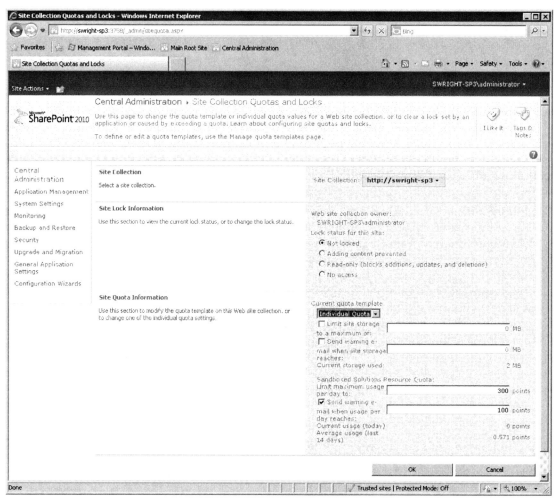

Figure 13-16. *Set a site collection's quotas*

Full-Trust Proxies

Obviously, the restrictions placed on sandboxed code are not always workable. How do you break out of the sandbox when needed without creating security holes that can be exploited by malicious sandboxed code? SharePoint has two primary methods for doing this without redeploying the solution as a farm solution.

First, the solution developer can imbed client-side JavaScript code that makes calls into SharePoint using the SharePoint Client Object Model. This allows access to some additional functionality but this solution is still quite limited. Browser-based client-side code can still access only content within the site collection. It can access network resources, such as web services, but these connections come from the browser, not the SharePoint server, and may not be able to access resources behind a firewall.

A better solution is to create a *full-trust proxy* operation. This is a component that is deployed as part of a separate farm-based solution. Because it is in a farm solution, it can run in full trust inside the proxy process as shown in Figure 13-17.

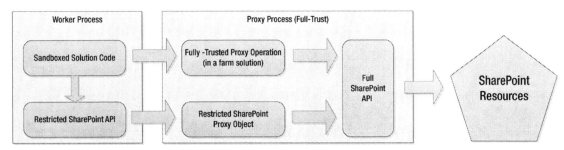

Figure 13-17. Full-trust proxy architecture

Because it is part of a farm solution, the proxy operation component must be deployed by a farm administrator. This prevents malicious proxy code from being given full trust unintentionally. This also means that full-trust proxies cannot be used in situations where farm deployment is not possible, such as hosted or multi-tenancy environments. Only the hosting entity would be able to deploy a farm-based solution, and it would be made available to all site collections in the farm.

To create a proxy operation, the (farm solution) developer will create a class that derives from the SPProxyOperation class. To call the operation, the (sandboxed solution) developer will then make a call to the ExecuteRegisteredProxyOperation method. This will pass the call from the worker process to the proxy process that is hosting the corresponding proxy object.

In addition to allowing access to SharePoint resources outside the site collection, a full-trust proxy operation can access network resources and databases and do anything else that fully-trusted code can do. As such, a common use of proxy operations is to provide a toolkit of trusted operations to a farm's sandboxed solutions. For example, a central customer database used by many departments might be exposed using a set of proxy operations. This would allow any sandboxed solution created by a non-IT department to use these operations without the need to deploy their solutions at the farm level.

Load Balancing

A page request received by a SharePoint front-end web server is processed by IIS on that server. For sandboxed components, calls are made to the sandbox service for processing. Which server processes the sandboxed component for a request depends on the load-balancing configuration for the sandbox service. The service supports two forms of load balancing: local and remote.

In *local* load balancing, any sandboxed calls are handled by the Sandbox Service instance on the same server that received the original request. Essentially, whatever load balancing is being used to balance incoming requests will also control the load balancing of sandboxed solutions.

When this is not optimal, remote load balancing comes into play. *Remote* load-balancing allows the sandbox service to forward requests to an appropriate server rather than process it locally. There are cases where a solution should run only on certain servers in the farm. This is called *solution affinity*. Because not all requests take the same time and resources to process, local load balancing can also cause the load on the servers to become unbalanced. Solution affinity and remote load balancing can be used to move solutions onto the servers that are best able to support them.

Under remote load balancing, the Sandbox Service on each server will forward requests to the appropriate server for processing instead of processing it locally. The farm administrator configures the load-balancing scheme and solution affinity within the farm. See Figure 13-18.

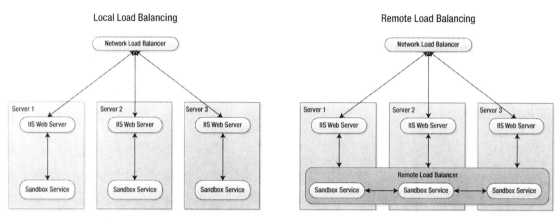

Figure 13-18. *Local vs. remote load balancing*

Creating Solution Packages

Creating a solution package for deployment to SharePoint can be a complicated process. A package contains many XML files, folders, pages, and executables that have to be configured and compiled in a certain way.

The easiest way to create a solution package is to save an existing SharePoint site as a site template. This packages everything needed by the site into a WSP file and installs it in the site collection's Solution Gallery as a sandboxed solution. This file can then be copied to other site collections or farms as needed. The problem with this type of solution is that you have very little control of its contents. SharePoint decides what to include and how.

Another, much harder, way to create a solution file is to use the MAKECAB utility. As noted earlier, a WSP file is really just a CAB file that has been renamed. To create a solution file using MAKECAB, you have to perform all of these steps manually:

1. Create each artifact (page, Web Part, executable, configuration file, etc.) for the solution by hand.

2. Copy these files into a directory structure that mimics the layout of the solution packages.

3. Create a CAB definition file (DDL). This is a text file that describes the exact contents and layout of the cabinet file to be created.

4. Download and install the MAKECAB utility from Microsoft (http://go.microsoft.com/fwlink/?LinkId=107292).

5. Use MAKECAB to create the cabinet file and rename it to have a WSP extension.

In the early days of SharePoint development, MAKECAB was the only tool available for packaging SharePoint solutions. This was a tedious, error-prone, and time-consuming process. Fortunately, Microsoft eventually published SharePoint Tools for Visual Studio. This was an add-on to the Visual Studio application development tool that allows it to produce solution files much more easily. This toolkit has improved greatly over time. In Visual Studio 2010, the SharePoint toolkit is now included with all editions of Visual Studio. It is no longer downloaded and installed as an add-on.

Visual Studio simplifies the creation of solutions by providing visual editors and templates for most SharePoint artifacts. This makes it unnecessary to edit XML configurations, manifests, and element files, by hand in most cases. Visual Studio supports deploying and debugging solutions on a development SharePoint server. The solution file (WSP) can then be built and deployed to test and production environments. Using Visual Studio, the developer can compile and add custom deployment code, event receivers and other .NET assemblies to the solution. Through its integration with Team Foundation Server (TFS), Visual Studio supports source code control and versioning of all of the components within a solution as well as the solution definition itself.

Creating a Simple Solution

Let's take a look at how you can use Visual Studio 2010 to create a solution file. The solution you are going to create will contain a new, highly impressive Web Part that will change the world forever. You will create your Web Part in C# and then deploy it to your development server as a sandboxed solution.

1. Open Visual Studio 2010.

2. Select File ➤ New ➤ Project…

3. Select the Empty SharePoint Project template (see Figure 13-19).

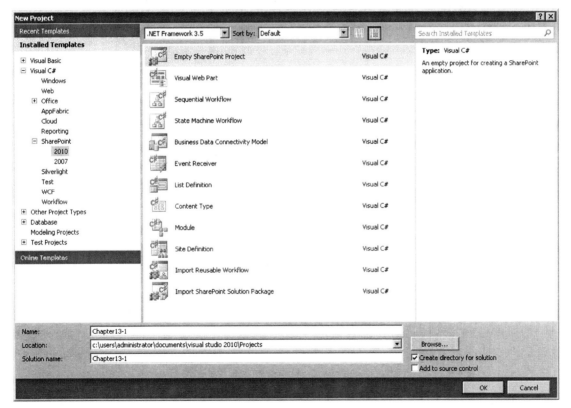

Figure 13-19. Create an Empty SharePoint Project

4. Enter **Chapter13-1** for the name.

5. Click OK.

6. Enter the destination site collection URL (see Figure 13-20).

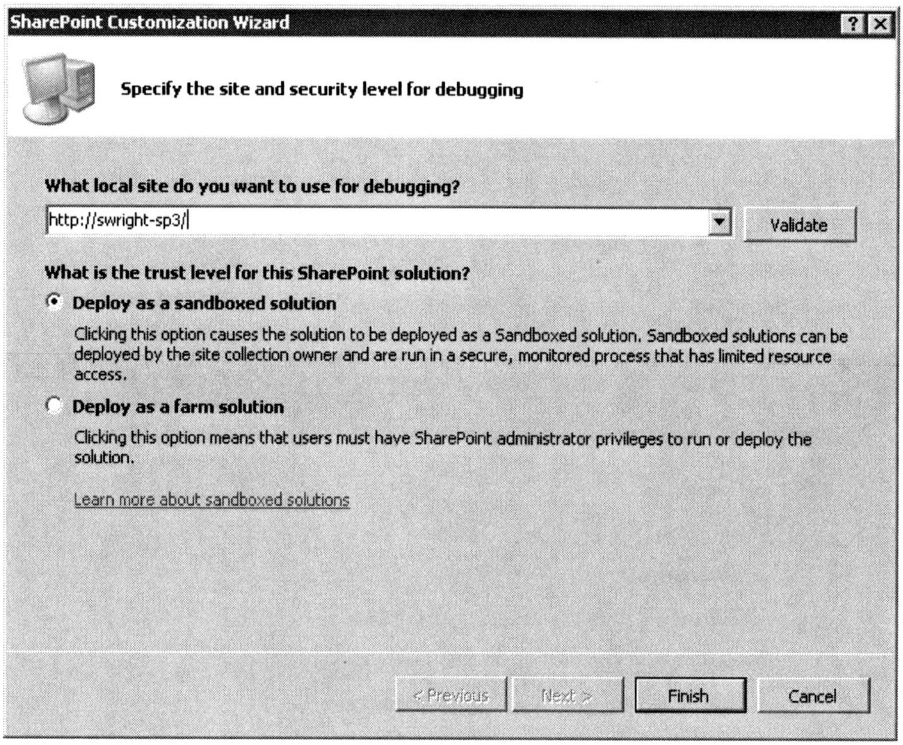

Figure 13-20. Configure the debugging environment

7. Select "Deploy as a sandboxed solution."

8. Click Finish. The project created contains the items necessary to create a new, empty solution file.

9. Right-click the project in Solution Explorer and select Add ➤ New Item.

10. Select the Web Part item template (see Figure 13-21).

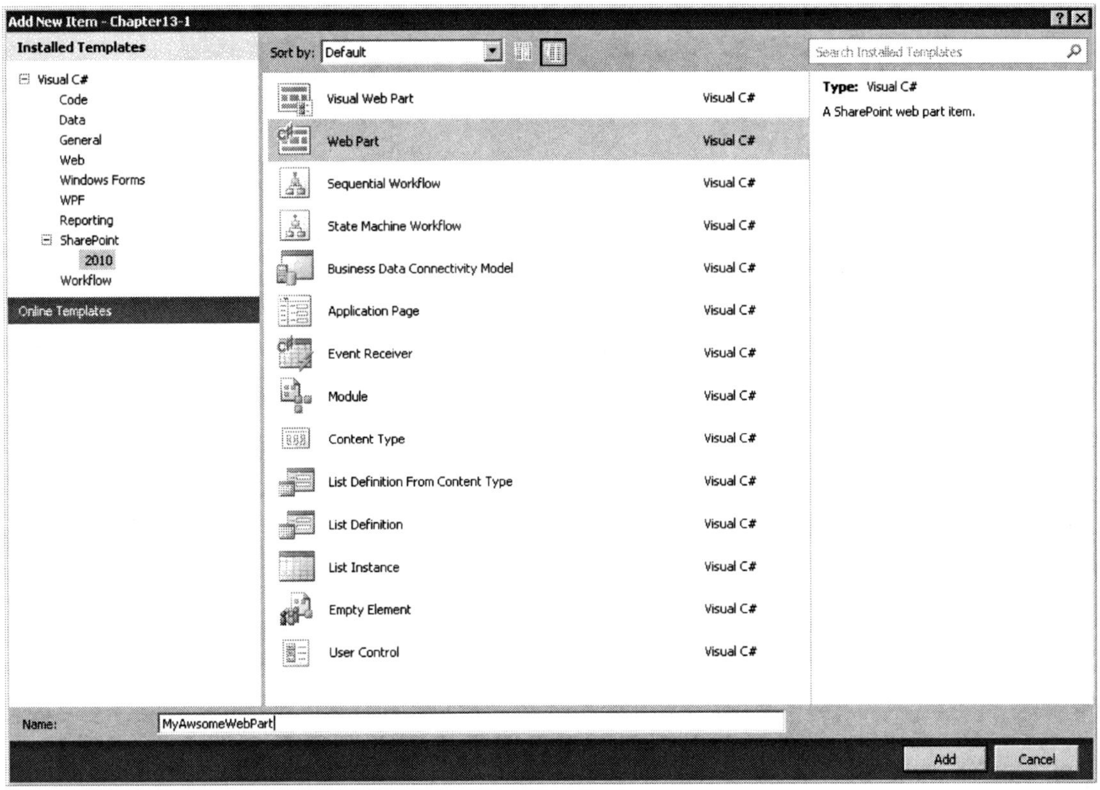

Figure 13-21. Create a New Web Part

11. Enter **MyAwesomeWebPart** for the name.

12. Click Add.

Your solution project now contains a folder called MyAwesomeWebPart. Inside that folder are three files:

- *Elements.xml*: This file will be included in the solution package to control deploying the Web Part.

- *MyAwesomeWebPart.cs*: This is the C# source file for the Web Part.

- *MyAwesomeWebPart.webpart*: This is an XML file that describes the Web Part and the executable class that supports it. This file will be included in the solution package. It will eventually be deployed to the Web Part Gallery. (See Figure 13-22.)

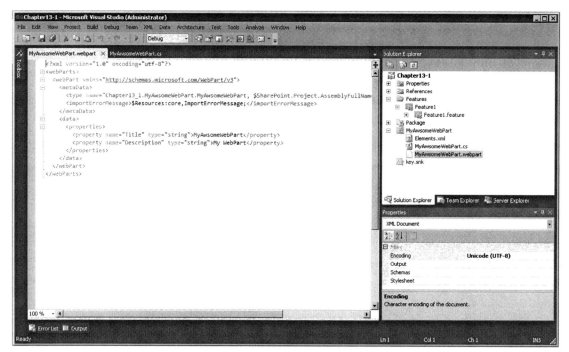

Figure 13-22. Web Part configuration file

13. Update the MyAwesomeWebPart.cs file to contain the code in Figure 13-23.

```
[ToolboxItemAttribute(false)]
public class MyAwsomeWebPart : WebPart
{
    public string MyMessage = "This web part is useless!";

    protected override void CreateChildControls()
    {
        this.Controls.Add(new LiteralControl(this.MyMessage));
    }
}
```

Figure 13-23. Web Part source code

14. Open the MyAwesomeWebPart.webpart file.

15. Update the Title and Description properties as shown in Figure 13-24.

```
<?xml version="1.0" encoding="utf-8"?>
<webParts>
  <webPart xmlns="http://schemas.microsoft.com/WebPart/v3">
    <metaData>
      <type name="Chapter13_1.MyAwesomeWebPart.MyAwesomeWebPart, $SharePoint.Project.AssemblyFullName$" />
      <importErrorMessage>$Resources:core,ImportErrorMessage;</importErrorMessage>
    </metaData>
    <data>
      <properties>
        <property name="Title" type="string">My Awesome Web Part</property>
        <property name="Description" type="string">This web part will revolutionize the IT industry.</property>
      </properties>
    </data>
  </webPart>
</webParts>
```

Figure 13-24. Web Part description

16. Double-click the Feature1 node in Solution Explorer.

17. Enter **Chapter 13 Test Feature** for the feature name.

18. Double-click the Package node in Solution Explorer.

19. Enter **Chapter 13 Test Solution** for the package name. (See Figure 13-25.)

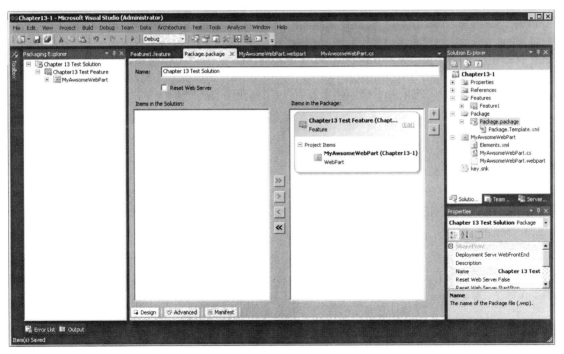

Figure 13-25. Solution package editor

20. Save all your changes.

21. Select Deploy Chapter13-1 from the Build menu.

Visual Studio will now build the solution package file (WSP) and deploy it to the Solution Gallery in the site collection whose URL you provided earlier. This package will be uploaded and activated automatically.

22. Open the web site to which the package was deployed in a browser.

23. Click the Page tab in the ribbon menu.

24. Click Edit Page on the ribbon.

25. Click Add a Web Part in any Web Part zone.

26. In the Categories pane, select Custom (see Figure 13-26).

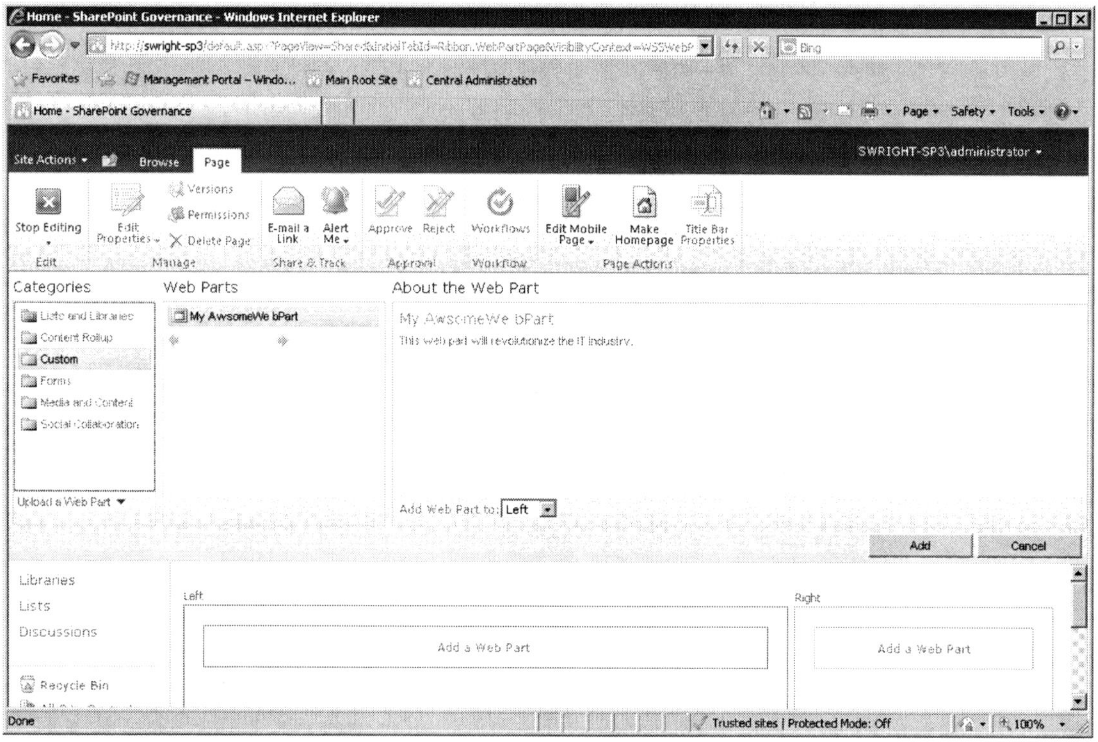

Figure 13-26. *Add a Web Part to a page*

27. Select My Awesome Web Part.

28. Click Add.

29. Click Stop Editing in the ribbon.

The updated page is shown in Figure 13-27.

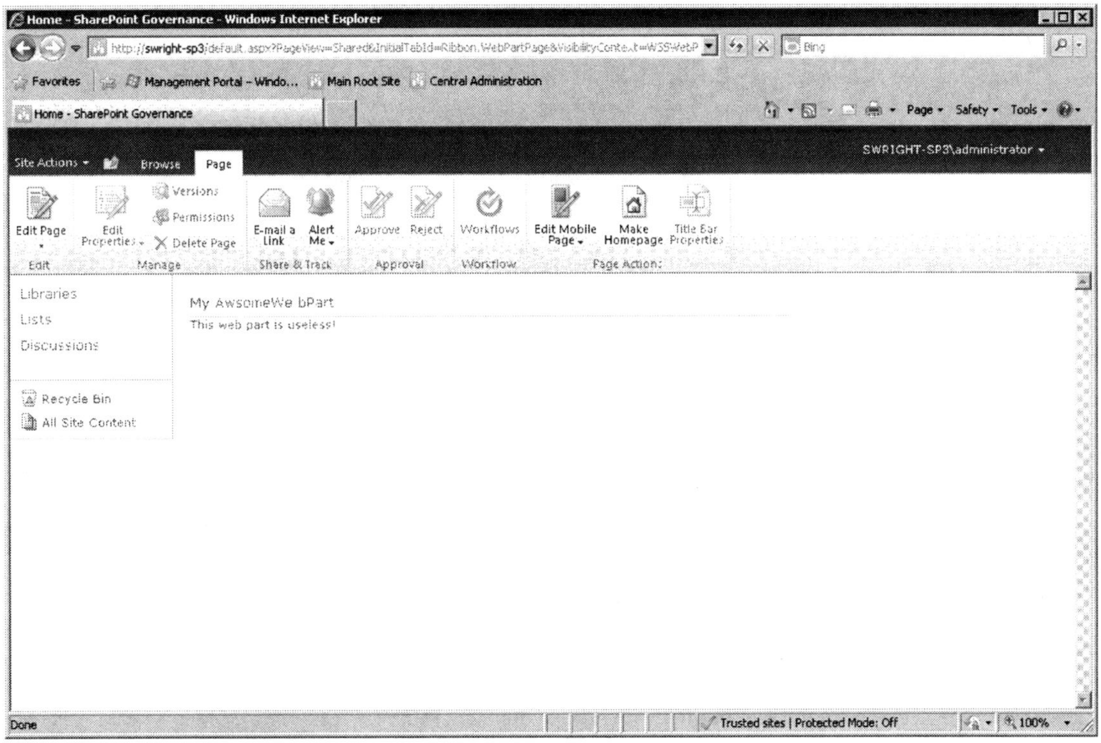

Figure 13-27. Updated page

Using Visual Studio's SharePoint templates you have created a full-function solution in just a few steps. Now let's take a look at customizing an existing solution package.

Customizing a Solution Package

In the previous exercise, you learned how to create a solution file from scratch. What if you have a solution file and need to customize it in some way? Obviously, the easiest thing to do would be to open the original Visual Studio project and change it there. However, in some cases that may not be possible because you do not have the original project or the solution was not created in Visual Studio. What do you do in that case?

Visual Studio has a project template that can generate a project from an existing WSP file by importing its components into a new project. The most common reason for doing this is because you want to customize a site template file that was created by SharePoint. Some other reasons for customizing an existing solution file include the following:

- You may need to add additional components to the package such as pages, images, etc.

- If a solution file contains a feature that has the same name as one already deployed on the farm, the folders used to store their files may conflict. You can modify the package to deploy the files to a folder with a different name.

- If the environment requires sites in multiple languages, you can add resource files to handle the translation of text on the site. This is called *localizing* the site.

- You may need to add event receivers to the features in the package to handle situations that are unique to your environment.

- .NET assemblies that are intended for the Global Assembly Cache may need to be diverted to a partially-trusted folder. You may also need to add Code Access Security policies to go along with the change.

All of these changes can be made to a solution using the techniques you are going to demonstrate in the following exercise. You are going to import the solution file you created in the previous exercise into a new project. You will add a new list instance to the package and replace the version you created before. Note that you are not updating the original Visual Studio project but updating the solution file directly using Visual Studio.

1. Open the web site to which the solution is deployed.

2. Select Site Settings from the Site Actions menu.

3. Select Solutions from the Gallery group (see Figure 13-28).

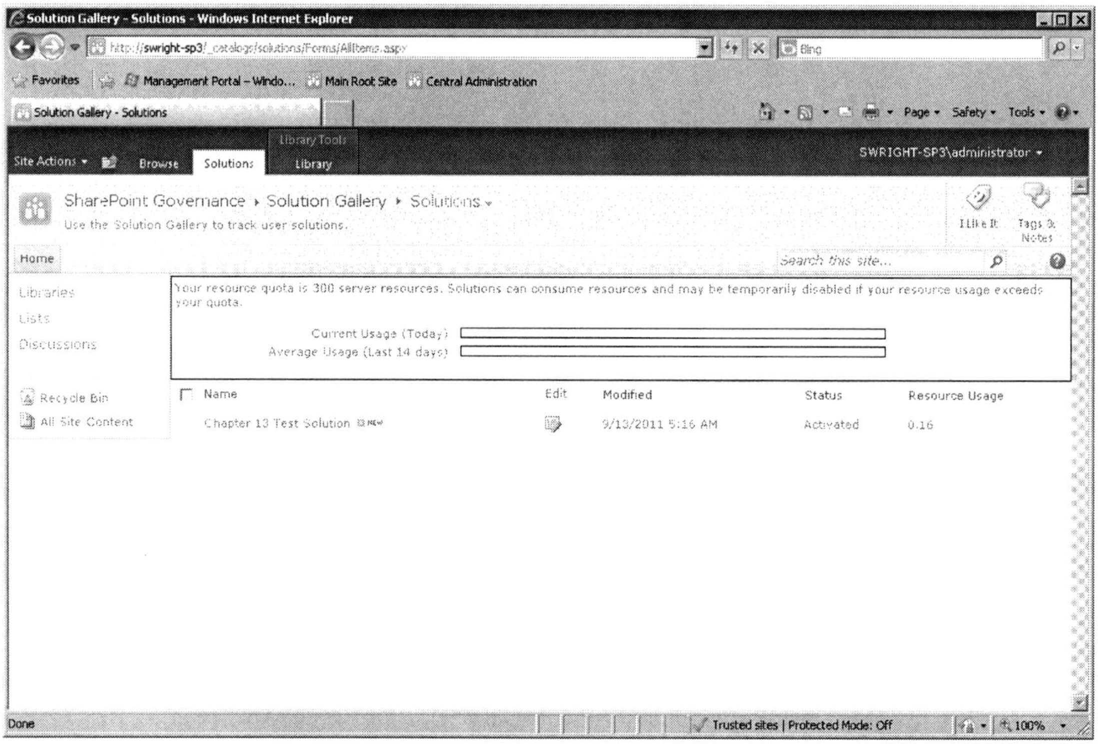

Figure 13-28. Solution Gallery

4. Click the Chapter 13 Test Solution link.

5. Download the WSP file to your desktop.

6. Open Visual Studio 2010.

7. Select File ➤ New ➤ Project…

8. Select the Import SharePoint Solution Package template.

9. Enter **Chapter13-2** for the name.

10. Click OK.

11. Enter the destination site collection URL.

12. Select "Deploy as a sandboxed solution."

13. Click Next.

14. Enter the path to the solution file that was downloaded from SharePoint (see Figure 13-29).

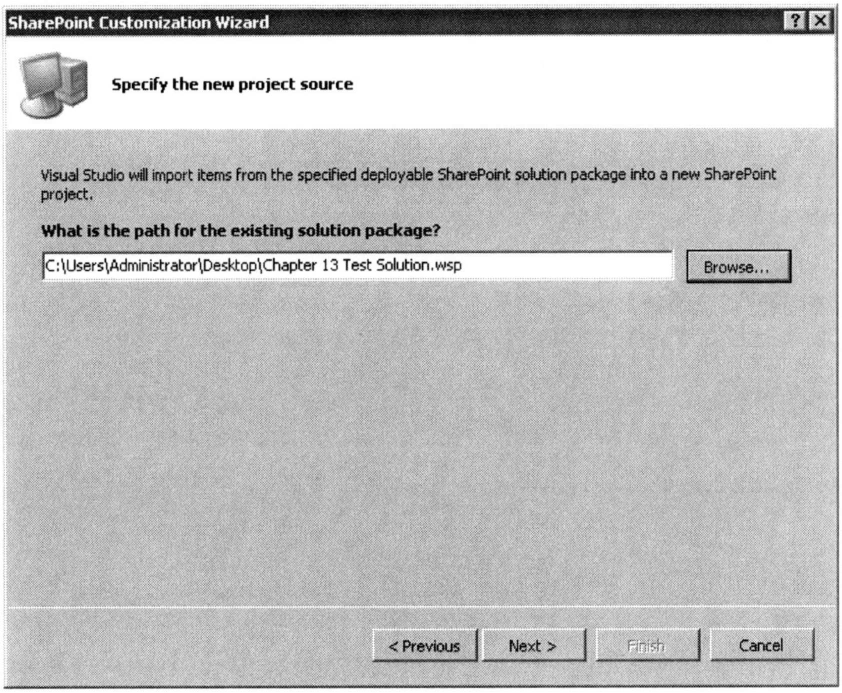

Figure 13-29. Import the solution file.

15. Click Next.

16. Select all of the items shown in the Select Items to Import wizard page (Figure 13-30).

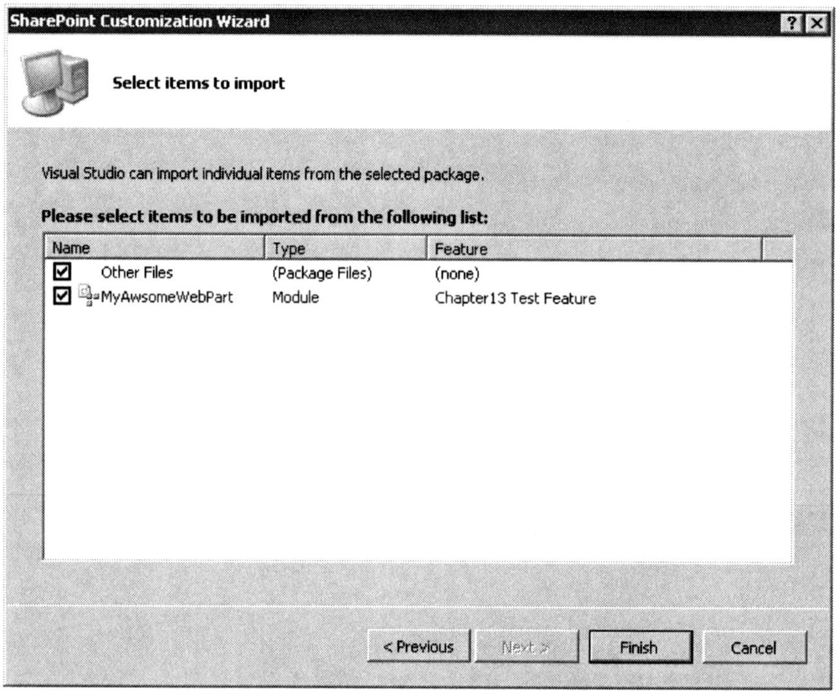

SharePoint Customization Wizard ? X

Select items to import

Visual Studio can import individual items from the selected package.

Please select items to be imported from the following list:

Name	Type	Feature	
☑ Other Files	(Package Files)	(none)	
☑ MyAwsomeWebPart	Module	Chapter13 Test Feature	

< Previous   Next >   Finish   Cancel

Figure 13-30. Select the items to import.

17. Click Finish. The project you created contains the items imported from the solution file (Figure 13-31).

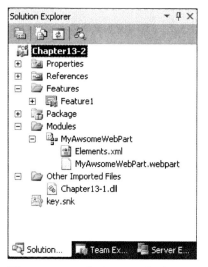

Figure 13-31. The imported solution project

At first blush, this project looks just like the one you used to create the file, with two important differences: the Web Part's source file is missing and there is a new folder called Other Imported Files which contains the compiled DLL containing the Web Part. The import process was able to extract all of the solution and feature information, but the Web Part's source code was not in the solution file, so you do not have it in your imported project. This is not a problem. It simply means that you will not be able to make code changes to the Web Part or recompile the DLL.

18. Right-click the project node in Solution Explorer and select Add ➤ New Item…

19. Select the List Instance template.

20. Enter My Awesome Docs for the name.

21. Click Add.

22. Select Document Library from the list of list definitions.

23. Set the name and relative URL as you wish (see Figure 13-32).

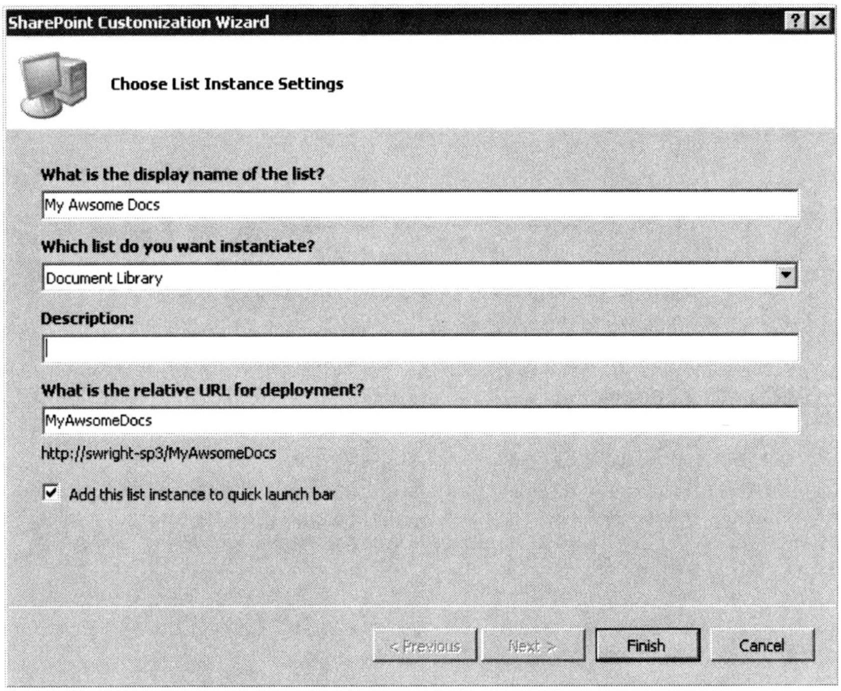

SharePoint Customization Wizard

Choose List Instance Settings

What is the display name of the list?

My Awsome Docs

Which list do you want instantiate?

Document Library

Description:

What is the relative URL for deployment?

MyAwsomeDocs

http://swright-sp3/MyAwsomeDocs

☑ Add this list instance to quick launch bar

< Previous   Next >   Finish   Cancel

Figure 13-32. List Instance Customization Wizard

24. Click Finish.

25. Select Deploy Chapter 13-2 from the Build menu.

Visual Studio will recognize that a previous version of this solution is already deployed to the Solution Gallery. It will retract that solution and replace it with the one you have customized. If you return to the Solution Gallery page you will notice that the file name for the solution has changed and the new document library has been created. (See Figure 13-33.)

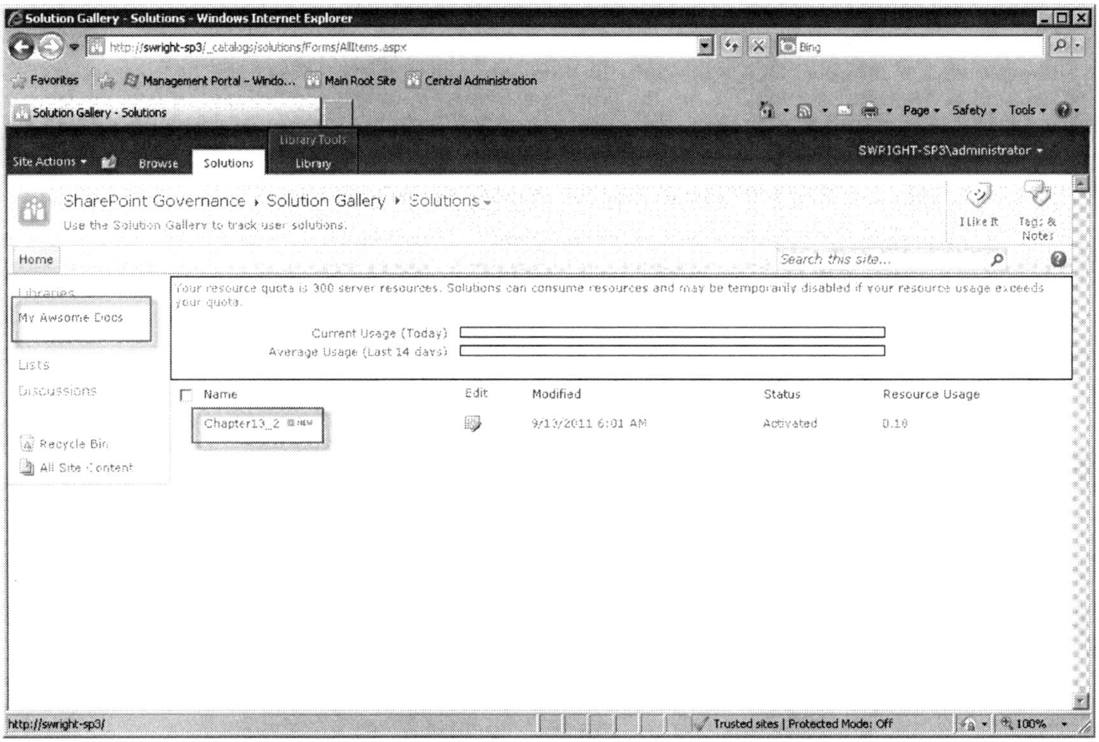

Figure 13-33. Solution Gallery after redeploying the solution

Upgrading a Deployed Solution

One of the problems SharePoint developers encountered in past versions of the product is that it was difficult to update solutions once they had been deployed to the farm. If a feature deploys elements like content types or list instances when it is activated, how do these get updated if they are altered in a later version? In 2010, SharePoint introduced a new set of configuration options designed to make these upgrades, if not exactly easy, at least manageable.

Feature Versioning

The key to upgrading a solution package successfully is a new technique called *feature versioning*. Each feature in a solution file has an associated feature.xml file. This file identifies all of the parameters and components of the feature. New markup options in SharePoint 2010 allow the feature to be given a version number and have a set of upgrade actions defined. When the solution is upgraded, this information is used to perform any actions needed to upgrade existing content that was created based on a previous version of the solution.

When performing an upgrade, the new solution package must be deployed into the same environment (farm or sandbox) as the original version. Here are some of the options that can be specified in the feature.xml file:

- The <UpgradeActions> tag is used to specify an event receiver for handling upgrade events. This is a custom .NET class that can perform whatever actions are needed during the upgrade that are not covered by the other automated options listed below.

- The <VersionRange> tag is used to group upgrade actions that apply to certain version number ranges. One range could handle upgrades from version 1.0.0.0 to version 2.0.0.0 while another handles moving from version 2.0.0.0 to version 2.5.0.0. SharePoint will manage performing the necessary actions in the correct order.

- The <AddContentTypeField> tag is used to add a data field to a previously deployed content type.

- The <ApplyElementManifests> tag allows new elements like files and pages to be added by a subsequent version of the feature.

- The <CustomUpgradeAction> tag defines the name and parameters for the actions to be performed during the upgrade. These are passed as parameters to the event receiver named in the <UpgradeActions> tag.

- The <MapFile> tag can be used to rename previously deployed files.

Performing the Upgrade

The process for carrying out the upgrade of a solution can take one of two forms. The original means of updating a solution file is still valid, which is to retract the solution and deploy a new file in its place.

In SharePoint 2010, it is also possible in some cases to upgrade a solution without retracting the original version first. In this case, SharePoint manages the updating of files and assemblies from the old version to the new. In order to upgrade a solution in place, the changes from version to version must obey some restrictions. If any of these rules are violated, it will be necessary to retract and replace the solution.

- The set of features in the new solution must be exactly the same as those in the original solution. Features cannot be added or removed.

- The following properties of each feature must remain the same as in the previous version:

  - Feature ID: A GUID that uniquely identifies the feature.

  - Scope: Defines the parts of the farm affected by the feature.

  - Event Receiver: Custom .NET code used to handle feature installation and activation events.

  - Properties: These are name/value pairs configured for the feature.

- The element.xml files included in the solution must remain unchanged. The <ApplyElementManifests> element in a feature should be used to update the manifest for a feature.

Upgrading solution packages without the need to retract the previous version is an important addition to SharePoint in the 2010 version. This allows upgrades to be performed in a more controlled manner with less downtime and fewer errors due to incorrect updates to existing sites.

Best Practices

In this section, we are going to discuss some guidance around governing the use of solutions in a production SharePoint farm. These practices will be broken into two categories: when to use solution packages and when to use sandboxed solutions instead of farm solutions.

When and Why to Use Solutions

Here are some things to consider when planning customizations to SharePoint:

- Any customizations to SharePoint that may affect more than one piece of content should be deployed using a solution package. This allows the customizations to be managed and versioned properly.

- Do not allow changes directly to the files on the individual SharePoint servers. In the past, it was common to place or edit files in the "hive" directories where SharePoint stores its content on the server. This practice should be discouraged. These updates should be handled by SharePoint during the deployment of a solution.

- Solution packages, and the features they contain, should be versioned and upgraded in a controlled manner. Specifically, this allows changes to be made to the content and functionality sites that have already been created based on a previous version of the solution.

- Solutions should be planned with versioning in mind. Always try to allow an in-place upgrade of the solution instead of requiring a retract-and-replace type of deployment. This allows upgrades to be deployed with minimal impact to end users.

- When a user saves a site template in SharePoint, a WSP file is created and stored in the local site collection's Solution Gallery. These files can be downloaded and shared with other site collections and server farms.

- Farm solutions can contain elements that affect the server farm's stability and performance. These packages should always be tested in a non-production environment before being deployed to production.

When and Why to Play in Your Own Sandbox

When deciding between deploying a solution as a farm or a sandboxed solution, here are some important considerations.

- A solution that needs to run in the production farm without going through a rigorous testing phase should always be run in the sandbox. If it runs successfully for a period of time, the organization may decide to redeploy it as a farm solution. This is often the case with solutions developed by business units outside of the central IT department. This allows other departments to create and use solutions tailored to their own needs without impacting the rest of the server farm.

- In a hosted or multi-tenancy environment, such as Office 365 or SharePoint Online, only sandboxed solutions should be permitted. This allows each tenant to create workflows, forms, and site templates to support their own needs without interfering with other customers. If the hosting organization develops a solution for use by all its customers, that solution can be deployed as a farm solution. Creating a full-trust proxy component can allow customers to access components from such a solution within their custom sandboxed solutions.

- Sandboxed solutions are deployed and managed by site collection administrators. This allows farm administrators to delegate these tasks out of the central IT department without losing configuration control over the servers.

- Sandboxed solutions run within the sandbox service process which can be relegated to certain servers within the server farm. This can be used to move processing off of heavily loaded servers. Farm-based solutions do not have these options. They always run locally.

- Sandboxed solutions can be assigned resource quotas and load balanced using the sandbox service configuration. This allows the farm administrator to monitor and regulate the use of system resources by these components.

- When running solutions in the sandbox in production, we recommend that remote load balancing be used instead of local. This prevents overall performance from getting out of balance when front-end web requests become unbalanced. This can sometimes happen because of the use of *sticky* sessions (where all requests from a browser session are routed to the same server in the farm) and some requests take longer to process than others.

For more guidance and technical details on the use of the sandbox, see the TechNet article at `http://technet.microsoft.com/en-us/library/ee721992.aspx`.

Summary

In this chapter, we have:

- Described the purpose and benefits of the SharePoint solution framework

- Examined the structure of a solution file

- Described the essential differences between a farm-based and sandboxed solution

- Learned the procedures for deploying farm-based or sandboxed solutions in SharePoint

- Explored the limitations imposed on sandboxed solutions relative to farm solutions

- Looked at the value of using full-trust proxies to allow non-trusted sandboxed solutions to a make use of trusted solution components

- Defined resource points and quotas and how they are used to control sandboxed solutions

- Described the most common tools for creating, customizing, and upgrading solution packages

- Reviewed some best practices with regard to planning and managing solutions

CHAPTER 14

Application Lifecycle Management

Chapter 12 explored the components of a SharePoint application including Web Parts, workflows, master pages, and themes. In Chapter 13, you learned how to compile these disparate components into Share-Point features and solution packages that could be deployed to a server farm in a controlled, updatable way. In this chapter, we will look at the processes that need to be in place to manage the teams that create and maintain SharePoint solutions. These processes, taken as a whole, are known as Application Lifecycle Management (ALM).

What Will You Learn in This Chapter?

- The terminology and concepts surrounding Application Lifecycle Management (ALM)

- Why ALM, and project management in general, is so vital to deploying a solid SharePoint solution

- The phases and sub-processes that make up an application's lifecycle

- Which development tools are most appropriate for developing different types of application components

- How to set up a development environment that will be productive and effective

- Strategies for structuring development teams creating interrelated solutions for a single SharePoint environment

- Testing strategies for testing applications prior to production deployment

- Server farm topologies used to create a smooth testing and deployment sequence for solution updates

Designing an ALM Process

Application management processes are as unique as the application being managed. However, there are certain features that a complete ALM process should have. Specifically, decisions governing requirements, versioning, testing, and change management need to be documented and communicated to the organization. The roles and responsibilities associated with each phase of the process will vary based on the size and culture of the organization.

In this section, we will describe general ALM steps and discuss the pros and cons of different approaches to designing a process that fits an organization and its applications.

Establishing Standards

Prior to beginning development, it is important to establish a set of expectations for each part of the organization involved. A common way to do this is to create a flowchart for the development process. Figure 14-1 shows an example of how such a process might be structured.

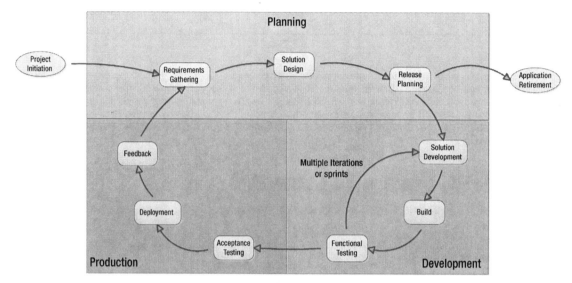

Figure 14-1. Sample ALM process flow

We will describe each of these steps in more detail in the next section. For now, notice that the steps in the application lifecycle form a cycle. This is a common property of any realistic ALM process. It is not reasonable to expect that an application can be created and deployed and never need to be updated in the future. Even if an application could be created that contained no bugs and satisfied its requirements perfectly, the business would eventually undergo changes that would require it to be updated.

The design of an effective ALM process will depend on the habits and needs of the organization, but there are some common types of processes that have been used widely over time.

▨ **Note** These concepts and processes often have many names in the industry. We will try to be consistent in our use of these terms, but you should expect to encounter the same concepts used under very different names.

The *waterfall* approach is the oldest of the processes and dates back to the 1960s or even earlier. In a waterfall process, a software development project is divided into phases such as Requirements, Design, Coding, Testing, and Deployment. The entire application is created and perfected in a single initial delivery. For this reason, the waterfall is often referred to as the "Big Bang" approach. This approach works well for very small applications but it does not scale well. Generally, larger applications cannot have complete requirements prior to the beginning of design. The application's design may need to adjust based on information gained during the coding phase. In general, the problem with the waterfall approach is that it does not allow for the flexibility needed to learn and adapt as a project progresses.

To overcome the shortcomings of the waterfall approach, the iterative waterfall was invented. The *iterative waterfall* uses the same phases as the waterfall approach but the project is planned as a series of incremental releases instead of one giant Big Bang. For example, when building a multi-tiered application, it may make sense to build one tier of the application in each iteration. Alternatively, it may be more appropriate to design the iterations as to complete a set of distinct use cases with each iteration. Once all of the iterations are complete, the application is fully implemented. The advantage of this approach is to allow lessons learned in one iteration to be applied to later iterations.

The most recent type of ALM methodology to be introduced is the *Agile* philosophy. The Agile movement was started in 2001 and is based on a set of principles that can be found at `http://www.agilemanifesto.org`. The idea of Agile development is to make the development of software more responsive to the end user by creating more opportunities to interact with and get feedback from the customer. There are many other concepts and terms that have been created around Agile projects, such as backlogs, stories, sprints, burn-down charts, pair-programming, and "extreme" programming. You can find several good books and tools available for use with Agile projects. For example, for guidance relevant to .NET development, take a look at *Pro Agile .NET Development with SCRUM* (Apress, 2011) by Jerrel Blankenship.

The most important difference in these approaches is the frequency of their development cycles and the amount of feedback that the different phases and cycles can get from each other. Whereas a waterfall project might consist of a single cycle lasting 2–3 years, an iterative waterfall plan for the same project could consist of several cycles lasting 2–3 months each. With Agile projects, cycles (known as *sprints*) are often as short as 2–3 weeks.

Phases of the ALM Process

Regardless of the style of ALM process adopted by the organization, there are certain steps that will always need to occur. In order to establish effective governance, these steps, and the deliverables from each, should be well defined and understood by everyone involved.

A project's deliverables will generally include more than just deliverable executables. They will include requirements and design documentation, work items, release and testing plans, along with the project's source code. Refer to Figure 14-1 as we define the steps of a typical ALM process.

Planning Phase

In the planning phase, the governance team will be directly involved in defining what is to be built and what the application needs to do.

Project Initiation

Project initiation is the step where the organization decides that a new solution is required. This step often involves creating a business case to justify the expense of creating and maintaining such a solution. Once the business has signed off on the project, a team must be established to begin creating the plan for development.

Requirements Gathering

Requirements are gathered from the business team or end users to determine what features are needed in the application. This may include business processes, data definitions, simple user interface prototypes, and so on. These requirements are usually captured in a set of documents that are reviewed and approved by the project's sponsor.

One approach to managing requirements is to enter each requirement into a tool such as Microsoft's Team Foundation Server (TFS). A requirement then becomes a distinct data element that can be associated with other items such as source code, bug reports and development work items. This allows each requirement to be connected to the entire set of related activities in the project. This is known as *requirement traceability* and can significantly enhance a project's manageability.

Solution Design

Also known as *solution architecture,* the design phase translates the requirements into a set of application components that need to be built or modified. The components should be assigned to features and solution packages in SharePoint. Each of the development tasks should be broken out and given estimates. These tasks form a Work Breakdown Structure (WBS) for the functionality to be implemented.

Release Planning

Once the solution has been designed and the WBS is complete, the tasks can be broken down into releases. A release represents a piece of functionality that will be released to the end users. The release plan defines the order and contents of each release.

Development Phase

The development phase occurs primarily within the IT development groups. In this phase the application is created or updated in a series of iterations, or sprints. Once the release is ready it is delivered to the production phase.

Solution Development

The application development teams examine the release plan and the development tasks and create a plan for organizing the functionality into one or more iterations of internal deliverables. As application components are completed, they are checked in to the source control system for testing.

Application Builds

Building an application refers to the process of compiling the source code and other project components into a deployable set of files. In a SharePoint environment, this usually involves compiling source code into a set of executable DLLs and packaging them with other artifacts into a set of solution package (WSP) files.

Performing application builds consistently is critical to ensuring that the process is error-free and repeatable. Modern development systems, such as TFS, often contain features that allow for automated builds and deployments to occur on a regular basis. For example, each night at a certain time, the source control system can be accessed to retrieve the most current versions of each source file. The automated process will then compile and package these components into WSP files. These packages can then be automatically deployed to a central SharePoint farm within the development group for testing.

Functional Testing

Functional testing is performed to ensure that the application is performing as expected by the developers. There are two levels of functional testing that should be addressed within the development group: unit testing and integration testing.

Unit testing is a process where a developer creates both the code to be tested and a set of code designed to exercise that code. This testing is done at the component level and is intended to ensure that the component works as expected. By creating one set of code to test another, these tests can easily be rerun whenever the code changes. If a test that used to work fails, the developer knows that they need to examine the situation being tested for errors. Either the code changes are incorrect or the unit test needs to be updated. Rerunning unit tests each time the system is built is another good use for automation. A developer who checks in a set of code changes one day could find an e-mail waiting for them the next morning detailing a set of unit tests that have failed due to their changes.

One popular technique for unit testing is called *Test-Driven Development* (*TDD*). Advocates of TDD suggest that the unit test code for a component should be written *before* the component itself. This essentially gives the developer an executable set of requirements to write against. There are a number of good tools and resources available on test-driven development including *Test-Driven Development by Example* (Addison-Wesley, 2003) by Kent Beck.

Once component-level testing is complete, the development team should perform integration testing. *Integration testing* involves loading the completed solution onto a central SharePoint server farm to ensure that all of the components work together. These tests can sometimes be automated but some may need to be run by hand.

Production Phase

The *production phase* is where the rubber meets the road (or the application meets the end users, anyway): the application goes through its final testing and deployment to production. This phase provides the feedback needed to guide and plan the future releases of the product.

Acceptance Testing

Acceptance testing is where the solution packages delivered from development are tested independently to ensure that they meet requirements. This testing is often performed by a separate Quality Assurance (QA) department. Acceptance testing should include a well-documented plan for what is to be tested and by whom. Regression testing should also be performed to ensure that no functionality has been lost from previous releases unintentionally.

See "Testing Environments" later in this chapter for a discussion of common SharePoint farm configurations used for acceptance testing.

Deployment

After acceptance testing is completed, the application changes are deployed to production. This process can be quite complex if updates are being deployed for an existing application.

The deployment procedure is just as important as any other part of the application and needs to be designed, tested, and documented just as carefully. A failed SharePoint deployment has the potential to corrupt data within the SharePoint farm. Therefore, the first step in any deployment plan should read "Back up all configuration and content databases in the server farm!"

Feedback

Perhaps the most important step in providing maximum value from an application in SharePoint is the collection of feedback from end users. This provides the governance team with the information needed to prioritize changes and plan future releases. Here are some common techniques for obtaining feedback from end users:

- Help Desk tickets

- Bug reports

- Feature requests

- System outage reports

Some additional ideas for collecting feedback take advantage of SharePoint's collaboration functionality:

- Add a "Send Us Your Feedback" link to the master page for your site, making it available on all pages.

- Turn on SharePoint's content rating feature and enable content rating for lists and libraries on your site.

- Use SharePoint's social features such as Social Tagging to collect information about how users access and organize information.

- Use features like Wikis and Discussion Groups to exchange ideas and tips with end users.

Managing Development

Creating applications for a complex multi-server environment like SharePoint requires many tools and processes. These tools enable developers to create and debug their applications in a productive way. This section will provide suggestions for the types of tools and standards that may be needed when developing for SharePoint.

Remember that these are only suggestions. A good governance plan should give the development team as much flexibility in their work processes as possible. This will allow them to create and innovate when creating new functionality.

Component Development Tools

A SharePoint application is composed of many different types of components. Therefore, it is not surprising that no single tool is the best choice for all situations. Table 14-1 lists the commonly used SharePoint development tools. The first column describes what that tool is best at. The second describes those components that should be developed elsewhere in most cases.

Table 14-1. Preferred Tools for Development

Tool	Good For	Not So Good For
Visual Studio	Writing source code Creating complex workflows Creating detailed form logic Packaging features and solutions Source control Component versioning	Master and layout page editing Simple workflows Creating branding elements Site templates
SharePoint Designer	Creating sites, lists and libraries Creating content types Customizing lists Master pages and layouts Branding sites Simple to moderate workflows Creating site templates	Packaging solutions Source control Component versioning Complex workflows
InfoPath Designer	Creating data entry forms Creating customized list forms Creating workflow forms Creating document information panels	Complex form logic
Microsoft Visio	Designing high-level workflows Creating data visualizations	Complex development operations
Web Browser Interface	Adding content Configuring Web Parts Assigning permissions	Custom business logic Detailed UI (HTML) customization

One of the strengths of SharePoint is the way in which it stores content. Most items that are created as content, either using the web interface or SharePoint Designer, can be downloaded or extracted as a file. These files can then be moved into another tool for further development or packaging. Here are some common examples of this concept in practice:

- A SharePoint site can be saved as a site template in either the web interface or SharePoint Designer. That template is stored as a solution file that can be imported into Visual Studio for customization and source control.

- A workflow can be designed in Visio and saved to a file. That file can then be used in SharePoint Designer or Visual Studio to add functionality.

- A workflow created in SharePoint Designer can be saved to a file and imported into a Visual Studio solution.

- An InfoPath form can be deployed as part of a solution package in Visual Studio.

- A list or library customized in SharePoint Designer (and possibly InfoPath) can be saved to a template that can be imported into a Visual Studio solution.

The list could go on indefinitely. The best practice is to create the component in the best tool for that type of component. If it is to be part of an application, it should eventually be brought into a Visual Studio project for versioning, packaging, and source control.

Team Development Environment

In a large development project, there will always be a need to manage many types of information created and used by the development team (see Figure 14-2). It is preferable to have a central repository for this information that integrates with the other tools used by the team.

There are several team development products available to help software development teams collaborate and communicate. As mentioned earlier in this chapter, Microsoft's product for this space is called Team Foundation Server (TFS). As a Microsoft product, TFS has advantages when used for Share-Point development. It is tightly integrated with both Visual Studio and SharePoint. If an organization does not already have such a tool and will primarily be developing applications for the Microsoft Windows environment, TFS should be considered for this role.

Regardless of the product chosen, there are some features that such a platform should have including the following:

- *Source Code Control*: Maintains a record of each change to each source file in the solution. Note that SharePoint library versioning is *not* appropriate for this purpose. A true source control system supports many features beyond tracking a single sequence of file changes.

- *Requirement Management*: Traces each bug, source file, and work item back to the requirements that they are related to.

- *Work Item Tracking*: Logs the bug reports, help desk tickets, feature requests, releases, and tasks associated with the project.

- *Build Automation*: Compiles the source files into deployable solution files.

- *Test Management*: Records automated and manual test cases, automates regression and unit testing, manages deployment to test server farms, and performs load testing.

Not all team development products will support all of the features listed here. Source code control is the one function that is absolutely necessary to maintain a stable application base. The other functions may be more or less important to a particular organization. It may be acceptable to use separate, non-integrated tools for some of them as well.

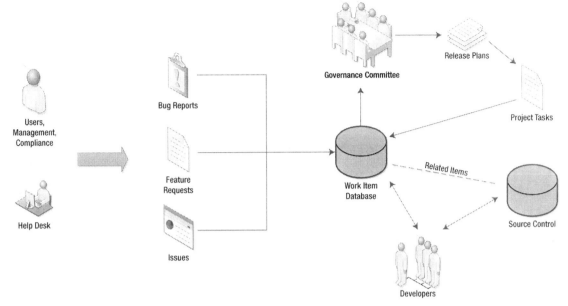

Figure 14-2. Work item management and source control

Structuring Development Teams

There are many differing opinions on how large a development team should be. Agile proponents prefer smaller teams because regular one-on-one communication is considered essential. For large development projects, a single small team may not provide enough capacity to satisfy the need for new functionality. In this case, creating multiple small teams is usually more effective than creating a single ever-larger team. Creating a division of labor between multiple teams becomes essential. In this section we will look at three possible ways of structuring multiple development teams to create a single application:

- Parallel team structure
- Linear team structure
- Component-based team structure

Remember that in SharePoint, a solution package is the unit of deployment. While it is possible to create a single massive solution package for a large application, it is usually preferable to break it up into several related packages that can be tested and versioned separately.

Parallel Team Structure

The first team structure we will look at is one in which different teams work in *parallel* to create a set of solution packages that make up the final release. Figure 14-3 illustrates this type of strategy. Each team is responsible for one or more solution packages. Features within these packages may depend on one another but, ideally, should not depend on packages produced by another team.

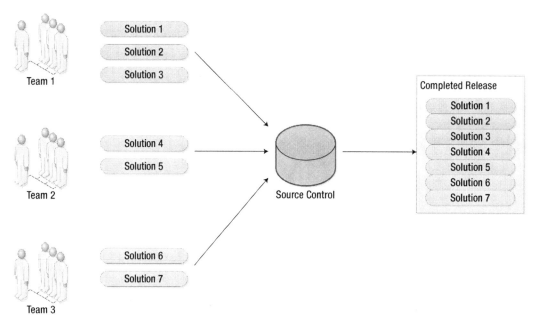

Figure 14-3. A parallel team structure

A parallel structure works best when the application's functionality can be broken into more or less independent sub-applications. Each team creates and unit tests their own components and checks them into source control. The automated build process then combines the packages from various teams into a single release. This enables teams to work independently of one another most of the time with a minimum of coordination required between teams during development.

Linear Team Structure

The next structure to consider is a *linear*, or layered, team structure. In this case, each team is responsible for developing functionality at one layer of the application. The example in Figure 14-4 shows three teams developing solution packages that are layered together. Team 1 creates the bottom framework layer and checks it into source control. Team 2 retrieves the solutions from Team 1 and uses them as a framework or toolkit for building the next layer up the stack. Team 2 then passes the second layer of components to Team 3.

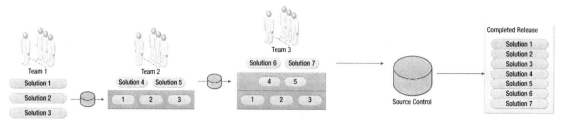

Figure 14-4. A linear team structure

A linear structure as shown here is best suited to situations where an application is built in layers of abstraction or frameworks. SharePoint itself is a good example of this type of design. The features that make up the SharePoint Foundation create a layer of tools that can be used by other SharePoint-based applications. One example of an application built using this toolkit is SharePoint Server 2010. The server product is really just a set of components built on top of the foundation provided by SharePoint Foundation. Other examples include Microsoft Project Server and Microsoft CRM.

When developing solutions in layers, each layer will usually be dependent on the features provided at lower levels in the stack. These dependencies can be declared in the solutions and features that are developed to ensure that all prerequisites are met when activating a feature in a SharePoint site.

Component-Based Team Structure

Whereas the parallel and linear approaches separate development by assigning solution packages to different teams, there are cases where this is not possible. In this case, a *component-based* approach may be necessary. As shown in Figure 14-5, this type of structure assigns components such as Web Parts, forms, workflows, and the like to various teams. These are tested separately and checked into source control. Only then are these components packaged for delivery.

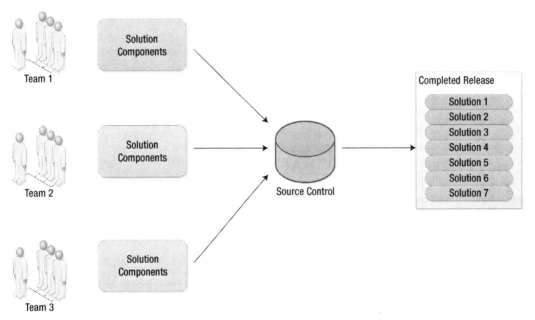

Figure 14-5. A component-based team structure

This type of structure is very flexible because components can be moved from one team to another as needed without affecting the packaging of the application. Unfortunately, this makes the various teams very interdependent. Teams working in the same solution packages need to be sure that any changes that may affect components developed by other teams are clearly communicated. Integration testing based on running the final packages is critical in this type of environment, since the most likely source of bugs in any system are at the boundaries between components developed by different teams.

Team Development Strategy

There are several other considerations to keep in mind when developing a team development strategy:

- Will each team have a separate automated build schedule?

- Will each team have a separate integration test farm or will they all share one?

- How will releases be planned to allow each component to be completed in the order needed by other teams that depend on it?

- How much communication is required within and between teams?

- Will all teams be in the same physical location?

- Who is responsible for integration testing the final release prior to delivery for acceptance testing?

Of course, as applications become larger and more complex, it is likely that no single team structure will be appropriate. A hybrid approach using a combination of parallel, linear, and component-based teams becomes the norm in large organizations. The governance team should ensure that all teams understand their assigned responsibilities and that rigorous testing is always performed.

Developer Environments

One of the more challenging aspects of SharePoint development is setting up a productive development environment. This refers to the area where an individual developer can work to create and debug their assign components or updates. Because SharePoint is a server-side technology, components designed to run on a SharePoint server generally have to be developed on one as well.

A common mistake is to attempt to have one "development server" that is used by all of the developers on a team. Unless team members are working on totally unrelated components and never need to do common things like restart Internet Information Services (IIS) or attach a debugger to an IIS process, this type of development generally does not work well. Developers need to have complete control over the server to effectively debug issues. Isolating developers from one another is the best way to keep everyone productive.

Another misconception is that you can develop on a client system running Visual Studio and debug on a remote server running SharePoint. While it is possible to debug a SharePoint solution running on another server, SharePoint still must be installed on the system compiling SharePoint server-side code. The libraries used by server-side code are available only on a SharePoint server. They cannot be installed separately on a client computer to allow code to be compiled.

■ **Note** If you are developing client applications using *only* the new Client Object Models (COM) introduced with SharePoint 2010, you can compile them on a system that does not have SharePoint installed.

A minimal SharePoint development environment should include the following:

- A 64-bit Windows operating system compatible with SharePoint 2010 (Windows 2008, Windows Vista SP1, or Windows 7)

- Visual Studio 2010

- SQL Server Express Edition
- SharePoint Foundation or Server components as needed

The following tools are often useful and should be included whenever possible:

- Microsoft Office applications
- SQL Server Developer Edition
- Microsoft Visio
- InfoPath Designer
- SharePoint Designer (free download)

In addition to which tools to install, there are also several options to consider regarding where to install them. Figure 14-6 illustrates the most common configurations used when developing for SharePoint.

The first, and simplest, option is to load all of the tools and SharePoint directly on the developer's desktop computer. This requires a 64-bit OS that is compatible with SharePoint. This configuration is easy to use since all of the necessary tools are readily available. Unfortunately, this configuration is limited by the power of the desktop computer, the storage of the hard drive, and the fact that only one SharePoint configuration can be used. A developer who moves between projects frequently may find this type of configuration difficult to manage.

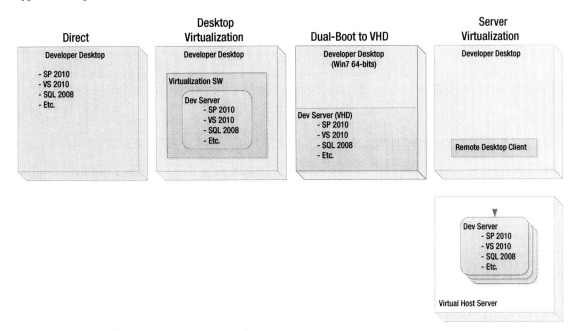

Figure 14-6. Development environment options

The next option is to use a desktop virtualization product such as Oracle's VirtualBox or VMWare Workstation. Again, be certain that whatever virtualization tool you use can support a 64-bit guest OS. This configuration has many of the same limitations as directly installing the environment on the desktop. Performance is not typically very good and large disk files are required to support desktop virtualization. The advantage of this type of environment is that it allows multiple SharePoint configurations to be hosted in separate virtual machines (VMs) on the same desktop. Typically, memory and performance requirements do not allow more than one VM to be running at a time, however.

Introduced in Windows 7, the next option shown in Figure 14-6 uses a new feature. The developer can create a virtual hard drive (VHD) file and run it directly on the system without going through a desktop virtualization product. This is similar to the old "dual-boot" setup for a system, except that instead of using a separate partition for the second OS, a VHD file is used within the existing OS's file system. This configuration has the advantage of utilizing all of the system's hardware without requiring a second operating system to be running to host the development server. The only disadvantage is that any applications loaded on the desktop's client OS are not available while running the development environment. This is quickly becoming the most popular configuration for SharePoint developers since it provides the flexibility of desktop virtualization without incurring the performance costs.

▨ **Note** For more information on running multiple operating systems using Windows 7's new boot configuration, see Keith Comb's blog article at `http://blogs.technet.com/b/keithcombs/archive/2009/05/22/dual-boot-from-vhd-using-windows-7-and-windows-server-2008-r2.aspx`.

The final configuration we will consider uses server virtualization. This could be Microsoft's Hyper-V, VMWare, or any other server virtualization product. For an enterprise with a good virtualization infrastructure this is an excellent option. A virtual machine is provisioned on a VM host server and that server is used to house the entire development environment. Using a remote desktop (RDP) client, the developer has access to a complete environment without making any changes or installations on their local environment. The only disadvantage with this configuration is that you must be able to connect to the VM server in order to do development. You cannot "take it with you."

Testing Environments

Once development is complete, the application should be put through a rigorous, well-defined testing regimen. This requires that the application be loaded into one or more non-production environments prior to deployment to production. These environments go by many names including integration, test, stage, user acceptance test (UAT), pre-production, and so on. For this discussion, we will use the terms integration, pre-production, staging, and production to describe our server farms.

Figure 14-7 shows a typical arrangement of testing farms. The integration farm is used by the development group to test all of the compiled components in an environment that does not contain any development tools. The presence of Visual Studio or other development tools on a system can sometimes mask errors that only occur when those tools are not available.

Once the release is tested, it is delivered to the quality assurance (QA) group, or whatever department is responsible for User Acceptance Testing (UAT). The release will then be loaded to the pre-production farm. This farm should be as similar to the production farm as possible to enable the testing group to assess the release's readiness for production. For example, if the production farm has multiple front-end web servers, so should the pre-production farm. Virtual servers are often substituted for physical servers to make the testing environments more cost effective.

Finally, once UAT is complete, the application can be deployed to the final production server farm.

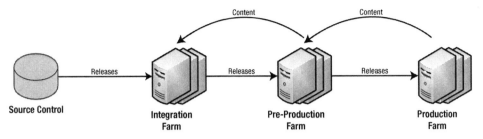

Figure 14-7. *Test environment with one production farm*

Note the arrows in Figure 14-7 labeled Content. These arrows represent the movement of content data. When testing a new release, it is important to use content that is as similar to the content in production as possible. For example, if a user has customized some item in a site in the production farm that interferes with a change made to the application, it may not be noticed if the change is only tested against "phony" test data. An excellent source of realistic content data for testing is the production server farm. The content databases in production can be backed up and restored in the test environments very easily in most cases.

■ **Tip** Code moves *forward* from development to test and then to production; content moves *backward* from production to test and then to development.

Another common configuration for testing and deploying SharePoint applications is to use a staging server farm as shown in Figure 14-8. With this technique there are two complete server farms running at all times. One is being used by the end users and the other is standing by to receive a new release. Once the release is deployed to the staging farm, the network is reconfigured to route incoming traffic to the staging farm. Thus, the stage servers become production and the production servers switch to staging.

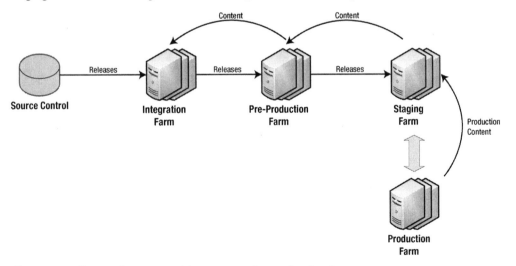

Figure 14-8. *Test environment with a stage and a production farm*

This is a very useful technique for public-facing sites that cannot allow downtime. The time required to swap out the server farms is only as long as it takes to reroute the network traffic. Obviously, it is vital that all content updates that have occurred in production are moved to the staging farm prior to deploying the new release. To prevent updates after the content starts being copied, SharePoint allows content databases to be locked temporarily.

When this technique is used, the staging environment can also serve as a hot stand-by for the production farm. If production suffers a catastrophic failure, the staging server can be brought up quickly to restore service. If this is part of the system's disaster recovery plan, production content should be copied to the staging farm regularly, even when new releases are not being deployed. It may also be useful to have the staging and production farms hosted in separate physical locations to provide location redundancy as well.

Summary

In this chapter, we have

- Defined Application Lifecycle Management (ALM) and discussed its importance in a SharePoint environment

- Described the steps to be taken in creating and maintaining a SharePoint-based application

- Examined the standards to be established with regards to documentation and development tools

- Described different ways in which a SharePoint development environment can be created

- Explored the different types of team structures that have been found useful for developing large SharePoint applications

- Considered the types of testing that should be done before deploying new or updated applications to production

- Examined the pros and cons of different strategies for structuring test, staging, pre-production, and production server farms

- Described some best practices around application deployment and management

APPENDIX A

Online Resources

Before starting work on a governance plan, or any related governance content, it's worthwhile to determine what resources are available from Microsoft and other companies. You'll be happy to find that Microsoft has developed more governance content than was available in previous versions of SharePoint.

Governance Overview

Before working on developing a governance plan for your environment, it's important to understand what needs to be governed and how it needs to be governed. You will also need to understand what policies must be created and determine who will monitor these policies. Microsoft provides great insight into the governance overview. As discussed early on in this book, governance is for the people, by the people, and should not be a hindrance.

Governance Overview:

http://technet.microsoft.com/en-us/library/cc263356.aspx

Governance Model for SharePoint 2010

http://www.microsoft.com/download/en/details.aspx?displaylang=en&id=13594

Planning

Governance Planning

http://www.microsoft.com/download/en/details.aspx?displayLang=en&id=401

Implementing Governance in SharePoint 2010

http://go.microsoft.com/fwlink/?LinkId=201194

Operations Framework and Checklists

http://go.microsoft.com/fwlink/?LinkId=203289

User Adoption and Training

SharePoint Server 2010 Adoption Best Practices White Paper

http://www.microsoft.com/download/en/details.aspx?id=1288

SharePoint Adoption Kit

http://sharepoint.microsoft.com/iusesharepoint/Pages/get-the-kit.aspx

The Productivity Hub 2010

http://www.microsoft.com/download/en/details.aspx?displaylang=en&id=7122

Microsoft Learning Center for SharePoint

http://www.microsoft.com/learning/en/us/training/sharepoint.aspx

Channel 9 SharePoint Videos

http://channel9.msdn.com/Tags/sharepoint

SharePoint Shepherd's Guide by Robert Bogue

http://www.sharepointshepherd.com

IT Governance

The links below will help define the roles and responsibilities usually assigned to the Information Technology department when governing a SharePoint environment. The IT department can utilize the resources below to determine what and how to monitor services and content within SharePoint.

Implementing Governance in SharePoint 2010

http://go.microsoft.com/fwlink/?LinkId=201195

SharePoint 2010 Administration Toolkit

http://technet.microsoft.com/en-us/library/cc508851.aspx

Site Provisioning and Management

Site Creation and Maintenance Worksheet

http://go.microsoft.com/fwlink/?LinkId=193521&clcid=0x409

Manage Unused Web Sites

http://technet.microsoft.com/en-us/library/cc262420.aspx

Planning Process for Creating Sites

http://technet.microsoft.com/en-us/library/cc263483.aspx

Planning Site Maintenance and Management

http://technet.microsoft.com/en-us/library/cc262509.aspx

Quotas and Resources

Planning Quota Management

http://technet.microsoft.com/en-us/library/cc891489.aspx

Monitoring

Reporting and Usage Analysis Overview

http://technet.microsoft.com/en-us/library/gg266383.aspx

Data Backup and Recovery

SharePoint 2010 Products Backup and Recovery Planning Workbook

http://www.microsoft.com/download/en/details.aspx?displaylang=en&id=10895

Restore a Service Application

http://technet.microsoft.com/en-us/library/ee428305.aspx

Planning for Backup and Recovery

http://technet.microsoft.com/en-us/library/cc261687.aspx

Information Management

Information management is a critical stage in any governance plan as almost all SharePoint implementations will contain content in one form or another. Utilizing planning worksheets and relying on guidance from Microsoft will lead to a better overall use of the information management features in SharePoint 2010.

Implementing and Governing Information Architecture

http://technet.microsoft.com/en-us/library/cc262900.aspx

Site Structure

Planning Sites and Site Collections

http://technet.microsoft.com/en-us/library/cc263267.aspx

Working with Site Templates and Definitions

http://go.microsoft.com/fwlink/p/?LinkID=119099&clcid=0x409

Identify Users and Analyze Document Usage

http://technet.microsoft.com/en-us/library/cc261954.aspx

Document Library Planning

http://technet.microsoft.com/en-us/library/cc262215.aspx

Enterprise Content Storage Planning

http://technet.microsoft.com/en-us/library/cc263028.aspx

User Interface Design

Heather Solomon on SharePoint Branding

SP 2010: http://blog.sharepointexperience.com

MOSS 2007: http://www.heathersolomon.com/blog

Planning Site Navigation

http://technet.microsoft.com/en-us/library/cc262951.aspx

Metadata

Planning Managed Metadata

http://technet.microsoft.com/en-us/library/ee530389.aspx

Content Type and Workflow Planning

http://technet.microsoft.com/en-us/library/cc262735.aspx

Content Management

Document Management planning

http://technet.microsoft.com/library/cc263266(office.14).aspx

Web Content Management Planning

http://technet.microsoft.com/library/ee476993(office.14).aspx

Information Management Policy planning

http://technet.microsoft.com/en-us/library/cc262490.aspx

Records Management Planning

http://technet.microsoft.com/library/ff363731(office.14).aspx

Information Management Policies

http://technet.microsoft.com/en-us/library/cc262490.aspx

Versioning, Content Approval, and Check-Out Planning

http://technet.microsoft.com/en-us/library/cc262378.aspx

Planning Content Approval and Scheduling

http://technet.microsoft.com/en-us/library/cc263156.aspx

Digital Asset Management Planning

http://technet.microsoft.com/library/ee428298(office.14).aspx

Planning Content Deployment

http://technet.microsoft.com/en-us/library/cc263428.aspx

Planning Workflows

http://technet.microsoft.com/en-us/library/cc263134.aspx

Social Computing

Planning for Social Computing and Collaboration

http://technet.microsoft.com/en-us/library/ee662531.aspx

Privacy and Security Implications of Social Tagging

http://technet.microsoft.com/en-us/library/ff608006.aspx

Application Management

Application management allows the organization to control the way potentially harmful functionality is tested and deployed without threatening the stability of the system. These resources will help with managing application development and customizations performed to the environment.

ALM Resource Center

http://msdn.microsoft.com/en-us/sharepoint/dd552992.aspx

SharePoint Developer Center

http://msdn.microsoft.com/en-us/sharepoint

CodePlex Open Source Community (Sponsored by Microsoft)

http://www.codeplex.com

SourceForge Open Source Community

http://www.sourceforge.net

Development Tools

Team-Based Development in SharePoint 2010

http://msdn.microsoft.com/en-us/library/gg512102.aspx

ASP.NET and SharePoint: How Development Differs

http://msdn.microsoft.com/en-us/library/ee536974.aspx

Setting Up a Development Environment for SharePoint 2010 on Windows Vista, Windows 7, and Windows Server 2008

http://msdn.microsoft.com/en-us/library/ee554869.aspx

Using Visual Studio for SharePoint Development

http://msdn.microsoft.com/en-us/library/ee539321.aspx

Site Design

Using SharePoint Designer for SharePoint Development

http://msdn.microsoft.com/en-us/library/ff458496.aspx

Localizing Columns, Content Types, and Lists

http://msdn.microsoft.com/en-us/library/ff955226.aspx

Localizing a Web Part

http://msdn.microsoft.com/en-us/library/gg491702.aspx

Solution Packaging

Solutions Framework Overview

http://msdn.microsoft.com/en-us/library/aa543214.aspx

Deploy Solution Packages

http://technet.microsoft.com/en-us/library/cc262995.aspx

Solution XML Files

http://msdn.microsoft.com/en-us/library/ms442108.aspx

Farm Solutions in SharePoint 2010

http://msdn.microsoft.com/en-us/library/gg575564.aspx

Upgrading a Farm Solution in SharePoint 2010

http://msdn.microsoft.com/en-us/library/aa543659.aspx

Full-Trust Proxies

http://msdn.microsoft.com/library/gg622616.aspx

Working with Language Pack Farm Solutions

http://msdn.microsoft.com/en-us/library/gg576899.aspx

Localizing Farm Solutions in SharePoint 2010

http://msdn.microsoft.com/en-us/library/aa544282.aspx

Sandboxed Solutions

Sandboxed Solutions in SharePoint 2010

http://msdn.microsoft.com/en-us/library/ee536577.aspx

SharePoint Team Blog: Managing Upgrades to Sandboxed Solutions

http://blogs.msdn.com/b/sharepoint/archive/2010/06/23/managing-upgrades-on-sandbox-solutions.aspx

Logging Events

Debugging and Logging Capabilities in SharePoint 2010

http://msdn.microsoft.com/en-us/library/gg512103.aspx

MSDN Sample – Debugging and Logging in SharePoint 2010

http://code.msdn.microsoft.com/msdnsp2010logdebug

Business Connectivity Services

Business Connectivity Services in SharePoint Foundation

http://msdn.microsoft.com/en-us/library/ee538728.aspx

Governance Case Studies

While it's nice to talk about governance and its benefits, it's even nicer to have case studies that show the direct impact a governance policy can have on a SharePoint implementation. Microsoft provides two case studies where they've applied SharePoint governance to internal SharePoint portals to help reduce cost, improve performance, ensure information security standards, and increase search relevance.

Implementing SharePoint 2010 Site Governance and Lifecycle Management

http://technet.microsoft.com/en-us/library/hh305231.aspx

IT Showcase On: Microsoft SharePoint

http://technet.microsoft.com/en-us/library/hh219235.aspx

Community Resources

While the majority of the online governance content comes directly from Microsoft, there are a few other resources in the SharePoint community that are worth checking out.

Microsoft SharePoint Team Blog

http://sharepoint.microsoft.com/blog/Pages/default.aspx

Microsoft Enterprise Content Management Team Blog

http://blogs.msdn.com/ecm/default.aspx

Microsoft Enterprise Search Team Blog

http://blogs.msdn.com/enterprisesearch/

Microsoft SharePoint Developer Team Blog

http://blogs.msdn.com/b/sharepointdev/

Channel 9

http://channel9.msdn.com/

Mark Schneider's SharePoint Taxonomy and Governance Blog

http://www.sharepointplan.com/mark_schneiders_sharepoin/taxonomy/

SharePoint Governance and Manageability

http://www.sharepointplan.com/

Avoid Newbie Mistakes: 10 Steps to Successful SharePoint Deployments

http://sharepointmagazine.net/articles/avoid-newbie-mistakes-10-steps-to-successful-sharepoint-deployments

Earley & Associates Blog (Information Architecture, Taxonomy, and Governance Focus)

http://www.earley.com/blog

The Governance Plan

The hardest part of creating a governance plan is determining where to begin. The following comprehensive governance plan template is a good starting point. You will want to customize your plan, as needed, to fit the business and situation.

In this appendix, we will present outlines for a number of different documents that create a complete set of governance documents. Whether your organization chooses to publish these as a set of separate documents or as one large document is up to you. We will present them in the way that has worked best for us.

The Main Governance Plan

This document, as described in Chapter 3, details the overall vision and responsibilities associated with the governance effort:

- Governance Overview
  - Vision and mission
  - Scope
  - Key objectives
  - Guiding principles
- Roles and Responsibilities
  - Role Definitions
    - Define role
    - Define purpose
    - Define governance board
  - Role Assignments
    - Define duties
    - Responsibility (RACI) matrices
- Content Policies and Standards
  - Site structure
    - Sites vs. site collections

- Available site templates
- Site hierarchy
- Storage quotas
- Site creation process
- Site deletion process
- Security policies
  - Permissions management
- User interface standards
  - Navigation
  - Language support
  - Themes use
  - Branding rules
- Metadata management
  - Enterprise content storage plan
  - Taxonomy
  - Folksonomy
- Content Management
  - Document Content Management
  - Web Content Management
  - Records Content Management
  - Digital Asset Management
- Information management
  - Versioning, content approval, and scheduling
  - Workflow management
  - Social computing and collaboration
- Technical policies and standards
  - Monitoring requirements
    - Management of services
    - Site cleanup
  - Uptime and performance goals
    - Define Service Level Agreements

- Outage planning procedures
    - Intended downtime procedure
    - Unintended downtime procedure
- Support requirements and schedules
- Customization policies and standards
    - Site provisioning
    - Themes
    - Content management and IRM
    - Sandboxed solutions
- General Procedures
    - How to . . .
    - How to . . .
    - How to . . .

User Communication Plan

The user communication plan (see Chapter 5) contains the plan for communicating effectively between the governance team and the end users.

- Vision and Scope
- Goals
    - To monitor the communication events completed.
    - To gain feedback on communication events.
    - To improve communication processes.
- Guiding Principles
    - These are the high-level framing decisions that describe the communication strategy to be used.
- Communication Strategies and Methods
    - Details the general responsibilities for carrying out the communication plan.
    - Describes the role of the governance team in crafting the messages to be delivered.
    - Describes the preferred communication channels to be used for delivering the message.
- Communication Stakeholders
    - Identifies each stakeholder by name, department, and role.
    - Describes the information needs of each stakeholder.

- Identifies each stakeholder's preferred method of communication.
- Implementation Plan
  - Includes a high-level schedule of milestones to be achieved in implementing the plan.
  - Details the budget, material, and personnel resources available for carrying out the communication plan.
  - Describes the various tools used to create and deliver the messages to be conveyed.
- Communication Events (Action Plan)
  - Identifies each type of communication that needs to occur.
  - Details a specific set of goals and techniques to be used.
  - See "Communication Events" below.
- Evaluation Criteria
  - Describes measurable criteria used to determine the progress and effectiveness of the plan after implementation.

User Training Plan

The user training plan (see Chapter 5) lays out the strategies to be used to provide training to end users before, during, and after deploying new portal services.

- Vision and Scope
- Goals
- Training Strategies
  - Details the general responsibilities for carrying out the training plan.
  - Describes the preferred methods of training delivery.
  - Describes how training will be coordinated between the governance team and the users.
- Audiences
  - Identifies each audience that needs to receive training by the role use user plays in the portal.
  - Describes the skills needed by each audience.
  - Identifies each audience's common tasks.
- Levels of Training
  - Identifies each unit of training that needs to be delivered.
  - Describes the goals to be achieved through the training.
  - Describes the methods and materials to be used.

- Delivery Strategies
  - Describes the techniques that will be used to engage users.
  - Describes the timing and coordination of the training.
  - Describes other techniques that will be used to drive adoption through building end-user skills.
- Evaluation Criteria
  - Describes measurable criteria used to determine the progress and effectiveness of the plan after implementation.

Operations Plan

The operations plan (see Chapter 8) lays out the strategies to be used to support and manage a SharePoint farm effectively.

- Capacity and Availability
  - Capacity
    - Determines desired system response time
    - Determines storage capacity per site
    - Plans for growth in needed capacity
  - Availability
    - Defines Service Level Agreement (SLA) for uptime
    - Plans for disaster recovery
      - Item level
      - Site level
      - Farm level
      - Server level
    - Plans SharePoint Operations monitoring
    - Plans SharePoint Operations reporting
- Change Management
  - Defines involvement of team
    - Server team
    - Network team
    - SharePoint administrators
    - Testers
  - Defines process for change, including major, minor, and standard changes
  - Defines process for change request

- Defines documentation needed and level of detail
- Configuration Management
  - Determines process to track hardware changes
  - Determines process to track software configuration
  - Identifies patching process
- Ongoing Tasks
  - Defines daily operational tasks
  - Defines weekly operational tasks
  - Defines monthly operational tasks
- Evaluation Criteria
  - Describe measurable criteria used to determine the progress and effectiveness of the plan after implementation

Governance Checklists

This appendix contains a set of checklists that Information Technology (IT) and business professionals can use to ensure that each of the concepts discussed in this book is addressed in the final implementation plan. These checklists are organized following the same conceptual framework used to structure the book: Establishing Governance, IT Governance, Information Management, and Application Management.

Establishing Governance

The items in the following checklist will help you establish governance for SharePoint 2010 within your environment and get the buy-in and support necessary to make it successful. The supporting detail behind this checklist can be found in the first section, or the first five chapters, of this book.

☐ Getting started

    ☐ Identify the executive sponsor

    ☐ Create a governance vision statement

    ☐ Create a mission statement

    ☐ Establish the scope of the site and its governance

☐ Start communicating

    ☐ Ask for nominations for the governance team

    ☐ Ask for content and feature proposals

    ☐ Collect ideas and requirements for the site and governance

☐ Establish a governance board

    ☐ Identify stakeholders

    ☐ Define key objectives

- ☐ Define roles and responsibilities
- ☐ Organize regular meetings
- ☐ Identify governance documents
- ☐ Assign document drafting teams

☐ Establish key governance processes

- ☐ Service Planning
  - ☐ Identifying mandatory services
  - ☐ Identifying optional services
  - ☐ Implementation planning
  - ☐ Monitoring services
  - ☐ Maintaining and updating services
  - ☐ Preparing for service decommissioning
- ☐ Adoption plan
  - ☐ Determine portal rollout strategy
  - ☐ Plan for data migration
  - ☐ Plan initial training for end users, help desk, and administrators
- ☐ Communication plan
  - ☐ Identify general communications strategies
  - ☐ Determine preferred communications methods
  - ☐ Identify communication stakeholders
  - ☐ Plan communication event schedules
- ☐ Training plan
  - ☐ Identify general training strategies
  - ☐ Determine preferred training channels

- ☐ Identify training audiences
- ☐ Lay out the levels of training required
- ☐ Create detailed training delivery plan
- ☐ Acquire training materials
- ☐ Schedule training delivery to correspond with first use of skills

☐ User support plan

- ☐ Establish and train the help desk
- ☐ Identify automated feedback mechanisms (monitoring)
- ☐ Identify explicit feedback mechanisms (surveys, contact info, etc.)

IT Governance

The following checklist will help define items usually assigned to the Information Technology department when governing a SharePoint environment. The IT department can utilize the resources below to determine what services to monitor and how to monitor services and content within SharePoint. Supporting details around IT governance can be found in Chapters 6, 7, and 8.

☐ Define Service Level Agreements (SLAs)

☐ Plan for managing content

☐ Plan site maintenance and management

- ☐ Identify types of sites to deploy (intranet, extranet, Internet)
- ☐ Plan for creating site collections
- ☐ Plan for creating subsites
- ☐ Define process for removing unused sites
- ☐ Plan for site access request processing
- ☐ Plan for site ownership roles and responsibilities
- ☐ Create content crawling schedules for search

- ☐ Plan content controls
    - ☐ Create quota templates for each type of site
    - ☐ Define usage reporting and analysis needs
    - ☐ Determine use of My Sites and User Profiles
    - ☐ Create site templates
    - ☐ Enable publishing in portal sites
    - ☐ Monitor content database size
    - ☐ Block unwanted file types
    - ☐ Plan content auditing requirements
    - ☐ Create workflow policies and template workflows
    - ☐ Determine SharePoint Designer usage policies
    - ☐ Create Information Management policy templates
- ☐ Plan for managing the SharePoint farm
    - ☐ Design the server topology
        - ☐ Establish the server roles to be deployed
        - ☐ Determine the number of servers to deploy in each role
        - ☐ Establish guidelines for deploying additional servers in a role
    - ☐ Plan for backup and recovery
        - ☐ Define item level recovery plan
        - ☐ Define site level recovery plan
        - ☐ Define web level recovery plan
        - ☐ Define farm level recovery plan
        - ☐ Define server level recovery plan
        - ☐ Define process for restoring service applications

☐ Establish security policies

    ☐ Define managed service accounts

    ☐ Implement user profiles

    ☐ Define permission policies

    ☐ Define permission levels

    ☐ Define process for creating SharePoint groups

    ☐ Define process for requesting membership in a group

    ☐ Plan authentication providers

    ☐ Plan for anonymous access

    ☐ Plan application pools

☐ Plan for server upgrades and maintenance

    ☐ Create server and software patching plan

    ☐ Define downtime schedule

    ☐ Define response procedures to unplanned outages

    ☐ Perform disaster recovery test at each level of the farm

☐ Create monitoring plan

    ☐ Configure resource throttling

    ☐ Configure the Sandbox Service

    ☐ Create performance monitoring profile

    ☐ Create baseline for capacity planning

    ☐ Establish automated alerts for performance issues

☐ Plan for collecting log and trace data

    ☐ Deploy ULS logs to a non-system drive

    ☐ Set trace levels and file schedules

    ☐   Enable event log flood protection

    ☐   Deploy the SharePoint logging database

    ☐   Configure usage data collection and processing

    ☐   Configure customized health analyzer rules

    ☐   Assign responsibilities for health analyzer alerts

    ☐   Set automated health alerts

Information Management

Information management is a critical stage in any governance plan because almost all SharePoint implementations will contain content in one form or another. Utilizing planning worksheets, such as the following checklist, and relying on guidance from Microsoft will lead to a better overall use of the information management features in SharePoint 2010. Supporting details for this section can be found in Chapters 9, 10, and 11.

☐   Establish information architecture

    ☐   Plan for sites and site collections

        ☐   Determine available site templates

        ☐   Plan for web content management

        ☐   Plan for content deployment

    ☐   Plan information metadata and topology

        ☐   Plan for document management

        ☐   Determine use of audiences

        ☐   Plan for versioning, content approval, and check-out

        ☐   Plan managed metadata

        ☐   Plan content types and workflows

    ☐   Plan for information processes and structure

        ☐   Plan for workflows

- ☐ Plan for social computing

- ☐ Plan for digital asset management

- ☐ Plan for information management policies

- ☐ Plan for use of content type hub

☐ Plan for search

- ☐ Define search strategy

- ☐ Define content sources

- ☐ Determine use of search center and associated web parts

- ☐ Define best bets and keywords

- ☐ Determine crawl schedule

- ☐ Integrate taxonomy with search planning

- ☐ Define people search user profile properties

- ☐ Define process for enhancing search based on search results analysis

☐ Define user interface standards

- ☐ Navigation

  - ☐ Define top level site navigation

  - ☐ Define lower level site navigation

  - ☐ Determine use of breadcrumbs

- ☐ Branding

  - ☐ Build wireframes of most popular pages (portal landing page, team site landing page, search center, etc.)

  - ☐ Follow company-defined branding standards

  - ☐ Define what part of each template can and cannot be changed by site owner

  - ☐ Create and manage solution to deploy master page and supporting cascading style sheets within environment

□   Determine use of themes

□   Determine needed language packs

□   Define use of acceptable tools (SharePoint Designer 2010, etc.)

Application Management

Application management allows the organization to control the way potentially harmful functionality is tested and deployed without threatening the stability of the system. These resources will help with managing application development and customizations performed to the environment. The supporting details for the following checklist can be found in Chapters 12, 13, and 14.

□   Set customization policies and standards

    □   Establish preferred/allowed tools

        □   Enable/disable SharePoint designer access

        □   Limit Visual Studio access to non-production servers

        □   Create policies for workflow and form development

    □   Content customization policies

        □   Create a set of approved master pages

        □   Remove non-approved master pages from the system

        □   Create a set of approved themes

        □   Remove non-approved themes from the system

        □   Create a set of approved site templates

        □   Remove non-approved site templates from the system

        □   Establish a set of approved page layouts for publishing

        □   Establish standard approval workflows for publishing

    □   Custom functionality standards

        □   Establish policies for sandboxed solution usage

- ☐ Establish policies governing farm-level solutions
- ☐ Create guidelines for creating application pages
- ☐ Create guidelines for event handlers
- ☐ Create guidelines for Web Parts
- ☐ Create guidelines for Client Object Model (COM) code
- ☐ Create guidelines for full-trust proxies

☐ Manage solution packages

   ☐ Farm solutions

- ☐ Limit farm administrators to a few individuals
- ☐ Establish testing requirements for solutions
- ☐ Create standards for handling upgradeable features

   ☐ Sandboxed solutions

- ☐ Configure sandbox load balancing
- ☐ Configure resource and quota limits
- ☐ Plan for monitoring of sandboxed resource usage
- ☐ Training site collection administrators to manage local solutions

☐ Plan for Application Lifecycle Management (ALM)

   ☐ Planning Phase

- ☐ Define governance board's role in project planning and approval
- ☐ Define project initiation process
- ☐ Define requirements documentation format
- ☐ Establish a release plan
- ☐ Establish a sprint/iteration plan
- ☐ Create a project management plan

☐   Development Phase

    ☐   Establish source control environment

    ☐   Create requirement database

    ☐   Establish work item tracking database

    ☐   Establish build procedures and automation

    ☐   Determine team structures relative to components and packages

    ☐   Set standards for which assemblies may be installed in Global Assembly (GAC) cache and which may not

    ☐   Define solution packaging guidelines

    ☐   Determine use of SharePoint services like Business Connectivity services and Excel services

    ☐   Standardize design and implementation documentation

    ☐   Establish standard developer environment ,including tools

    ☐   Create standards for unit testing or test-driven development

    ☐   Create automated regression tests

☐   Production phase

    ☐   Define the testing environments to be used

    ☐   Establish processes for user acceptance testing

    ☐   Establish policies for solution updates and installation scripts

    ☐   Create a process for periodically repopulating production data into stage and development environments

    ☐   Plan feedback and communication mechanisms around rollouts

Index

I, J, K, L

M

CPSIA information can be obtained at www.ICGtesting.com
Printed in the USA
LVOW130307170212

269121LV00006B/1/P